Interest Group Politics

Second Edition

edited by

Allan J. Cigler
Burdett A. Loomis
University of Kansas

CQ
PRESS

A division of Congressional Quarterly Inc.
1414 22nd Street N.W., Washington, D.C. 20037

JK
1118
.I565
1986

Library of Congress Cataloging in Publication Data

Interest group politics.

    1. Pressure groups—United States. I. Cigler,
Allan J., 1943-   . II. Loomis, Burdett A.,
1945-   .
JK 1118.I565   1986   322.4'3'0973   86-16528
ISBN 0-87187-372-9

Contents

Preface   vii

1. Introduction: The Changing Nature of Interest Group Politics
   Burdett A. Loomis and Allan J. Cigler   1

2. Direct Action and the Abortion Issue:
   The Political Participation of Single-issue Groups
   Marjorie Randon Hershey   27

3. From Protest Group to Interest Group:
   The Making of American Agriculture Movement, Inc.
   Allan J. Cigler   46

4. PACs and Congressional Elections in the 1980s
   M. Margaret Conway   70

5. Big Bucks and Petty Cash:
   Party and Interest Group Activists in American Politics
   John C. Green and James L. Guth   91

6. PAC Contributions and Roll-call Voting:
   Conditional Power
   Diana M. Evans   114

7. The New Group Universe
   Michael T. Hayes   133

8. Washington Lobbyists: A Collective Portrait
   Robert H. Salisbury   146

9. Interest Group Responses to Partisan Change:
   The Impact of the Reagan Administration upon the
   National Interest Group System
   Mark A. Peterson and Jack L. Walker   162

10. Policy and Interests: Instability and
    Change in a Classic Issue Subsystem
    William B. Browne   183

11. Reagan and the Intergovernmental Lobby:
    Iron Triangles, Cozy Subsystems, and Political Conflict
    Charles H. Levine and James A. Thurber   202

12. American Business and Politics
    Graham Wilson   221

13. One Nation, Many Voices:
    Interest Groups in Foreign Policy Making
    Eric M. Uslaner   236

14. Coalitions of Interests:
    Building Bridges in the Balkanized State
    Burdett A. Loomis   258

15. Interest Groups in the Courts:
    Do Groups Fare Better?
    Lee Epstein and C. K. Rowland   275

16. Groups without Government:
    The Politics of Mediation
    Andrew S. McFarland   289

17. Moving On: Interests, Power, and Politics in the 1980s
    Allan J. Cigler and Burdett A. Loomis   303

    Contributors   317

Preface

In the years since the first edition of *Interest Group Politics,* several changes have taken place in both American politics and the scholarship that keeps it under constant surveillance. In the past we had noted a near sense of panic about the dangers of special interests, which many thought would overwhelm the political system. Now we see a closer integration of interest groups into the political process, and, with some exceptions, less stridency and less reliance on confrontational methods. From a professional point of view, we are especially pleased to see that more political scientists are doing more good work on interest groups.

The second edition of *Interest Group Politics* reflects the growing emphasis on the role of interest groups within the policy-making process. Although we continue to focus our attention on questions of participation (Chapters 2, 3, and 7) and elections (Chapters 4, 5, and 6), more than half of the chapters deal with the policy-making roles of interests and groups.

That proportion seems correct in light of the historical link between groups and policy making. Contemporary political scientists continue to draw insights and inspiration from E. E. Schattschneider's *The Semi-Sovereign People,* first published in 1960. In addition, events and scholarship have combined to encourage us to move beyond the study of interest groups in the political process to the more systematic examination of the role of interests, whether organized as a traditional group or not. To the extent that we study the representation of interests, as opposed to interest groups, we are more likely to look at the policy-making process and less likely to examine the internal working of organized groups.

Our view, expressed in the first edition, remains that "the major challenge to the American political system . . . is its ability to respond to a demanding electorate in a political environment that supports numerous diverse interests—often passionately expressed—yet has few means to aggregate them." At the same time, we acknowledge that the political system has adapted to such a challenge, both through strengthened party organizations and innovative interest group tactics, such as coalition building and increasingly sophisticated Washington representation.

Although it is heartening to see the increasing quantity and quality of research on interest groups, we are aware that this research does not have the impact it deserves. The popular press still places heavy, often simplistic, emphasis on the roles of PACs and would-be Washington influence peddlers. Without question, the rise of PACs and new forms of top-level interest representation are important developments, but the PAC phenomenon and the emergence of a new generation of high-priced lobbyists, such as ex-Reagan aide Michael Deaver, must be considered within the contexts of long-term trends and the current research on groups and interests. Both historical perspectives and ongoing work offer well-informed, relatively objective means for assessing the value of interests' money and lobbyists' powers to persuade. We hope that this volume contributes substance and direction to the study of interest group politics.

Once again, our contributors have been cooperative, insightful, and good-humored throughout the process. We thank them one and all. Our editors at CQ Press, Joanne Daniels and Carolyn Goldinger, have been supportive, tough-minded, and extremely helpful. We also acknowledge Susan Joseph's fine copyediting work. To the extent that putting together a reader can ever be considered a pleasure, they have made it so.

After two go-rounds, we continue to learn from each other. Neither of us has yet concluded that the other is truly beyond help, although on occasion the thought does come to mind.

Finally, we dedicate this volume to our own "special interests"—Beth and Kirsten Cigler and Michel and Dakota Loomis.

1. Introduction: The Changing Nature of Interest Group Politics

Burdett A. Loomis and Allan J. Cigler

From James Madison to Madison Avenue, political interests have played a central role in American politics. That is a great continuity in our political experience, as is the ambivalence with which citizens, politicians, and scholars have approached interest groups. James Madison's warnings on the dangers of faction echo in the rhetoric of reformers ranging from Populists and Progressives near the turn of the century to contemporary "public interest" advocates.

If organized special interests are nothing new in American politics, can today's group politics be seen as changing in fundamental ways from the past? Acknowledging that many important, continuing trends do exist, we seek to place in perspective a broad series of changes in the modern nature of interest group politics.

Among the most substantial of these changes are:

(1) a great proliferation of interest groups since the early 1960s;

(2) a centralization of group headquarters in Washington, D.C., rather than New York City or elsewhere;

(3) major technological developments in information processing that promote more sophisticated, timely, and specialized grass-roots lobbying;

(4) the rise of single-issue groups;

(5) changes in campaign finance laws (1971, 1974) and the ensuing growth of political action committees (PACs);

(6) the increased formal penetration of political and economic interests into the bureaucracy (advisory committees), the presidency (White House group representatives), and the Congress (caucuses of members);

(7) the continuing decline of political parties' abilities to perform key electoral and policy-related activities;

(8) the increased number, activity, and visibility of so-called "public interest" groups, such as Common Cause, and the Ralph Nader-inspired public interest research organizations; and

(9) the growth of activity and impact by institutions, including corporations, universities, state and local governments, and foreign interests.

All these developments have their antecedents in previous eras of American political life; there is little genuinely new under the interest group sun. Political action committees replace (or complement) other forms of special interest campaign financing. Group-generated mail directed at Congress has existed as a tactic since at least the early 1900s.[1] Many organizations have long been centered in Washington, members of Congress have traditionally represented local interests, and so on.

At the same time, the level of group activity, coupled with growing numbers of organized interests, leads us to see contemporary group politics as distinct from the politics of earlier eras. Current trends of group involvement lend credence to the fears of scholars such as political scientist Theodore Lowi and economist Mancur Olson, who view interest-based politics as contributing to governmental stalemate and reduced accountability.[2] If accurate, these analyses point to a fundamentally different role for interest groups than those suggested by Madison and later group theorists.

In addition, several contemporary studies, such as those by Olson and political scientists Robert Salisbury and Terry Moe, illustrate the weakness of much interest group analysis that does not adequately account for the reasons groups form and persist.[3] Only during the last twenty years, in the wake of Olson's path-breaking research, have scholars begun to examine realistically why people join and become active in groups. It is by no means self-evident that citizens should naturally become group members—quite the contrary, in most instances. We are faced, then, with the paradoxical and complex question of why groups have proliferated, as they certainly have, when it is usually economically unwise for individuals to join them.

Interest Groups in American Politics

Practical politicians and scholars alike generally have concurred that interest groups (also known as factions, pressure groups, and special interests) are natural phenomena in a democratic regime. That is, individuals will band together to protect their interests.[4] If it is thus agreed that, in Madison's words, "the causes of faction . . . are sown in the nature of man," controversy continues as to whether groups and group politics are benign or malignant forces in American politics. "By a faction," Madison wrote,

> I understand a number of citizens, whether amounting to a majority or minority of the whole, who are united and actuated by some common impulse of passion, or of interest, adverse to the rights of other citizens, or to the permanent and aggregate interests of the community.[5]

Although Madison rejected the remedy of direct controls over factions as "worse than the disease," he saw the need to limit their negative effects by promoting competition among them and by devising an elaborate system of procedural "checks and balances" to reduce the potential power of any single, strong group, whether representing a majority or minority position (see Chapter 14).

Hostility toward interest groups became more virulent in an industrialized America, where the great concentrations of power that developed far outstripped anything Madison might have imagined. After the turn of the century, many Progressives railed at various monopolistic "trusts" and intimate connections between interests and corrupt politicians. Later, in 1935, Hugo L. Black, then a senator (and later a Supreme Court justice), painted a grim picture of group malevolence:

> Contrary to tradition, against the public morals, and hostile to good government, the lobby has reached such a position of power that it threatens government itself. Its size, its power, its capacity for evil, its greed, trickery, deception and fraud condemn it to the death it deserves.[6]

Similar sentiments remain intact today. Many citizens, journalists, and reformers view interest groups with great suspicion, especially in light of PAC contributions to escalating campaign expenditures. In the 1983-1984 election cycle, PAC spending in federal elections grew 29 percent since the 1981-1982 cycle, and the proportions of candidates' expenditures from PAC funds continued to climb. Nevertheless, as of the 1984 elections, the rate of increase in PAC spending and revenues has slowed considerably. PACs may be entering a new phase as mature participants in the political process (see Chapter 4). Even so, PACs remain the target of many reformers, both in and out of government. One typical expression of dismay came from Common Cause, the self-styled public interest lobby:

> The Special Interest State is a system in which interest groups dominate the making of government policy. These interests legitimately concentrate on pursuing their own immediate—usually economic—agendas, but in so doing they pay little attention to the impact of their agendas on the nation as a whole.[7]

Despite the considerable popular distrust of interest group politics, political scientists and other observers have often viewed groups in a much more positive light. This perspective also draws upon Madison's *Federalist* writings, but it is more tied to the growth of the modern state. Political science scholars such as Arthur Bentley, circa 1910, and David Truman, forty years later, place groups at the heart of politics and policy making in a complex, large, and increasingly specialized governmental system. The interest group becomes an element of continuity in a changing political world. Truman notes the "multiplicity of co-ordinate or nearly co-ordinate points of access to governmental decisions," and concludes that

> The significance of these many points of access and of the complicated texture of relationships among them is great. This diversity assures various ways for interest groups to participate in the formation of policy, and this variety is a flexible, stabilizing element.[8]

Derived from Truman's work, and that of other group-oriented scholars, is the notion of the pluralist state in which competition among interests, in and out of government, will produce policies roughly responsive to public desires, and no single set of interests will dominate. As one student of group politics summarizes,

> Pluralist theory assumes that within the public arena there will be countervailing centers of power within governmental institutions and among outsiders. Competition is implicit in the notion that groups, as surrogates for individuals, will produce products representing the diversity of opinions that might have been possible in the individual decision days of democratic Athens.[9]

In many ways the pluralist vision of American politics corresponds to the basic realities of policy making and the distribution of policy outcomes, but a host of scholars, politicians, and other observers have roundly criticized this perspective. Two broad (although sometimes contradictory) critiques have special merit.

In the first place, some interests systematically lose in the policy process, while others habitually win. Without making any elite-theory contentions that a small number of interests and individuals conspire together to dominate societal policies, one can make a strong case that those interests with more re-sources (money, access, information, etc.) usually will obtain better results than those who possess fewer assets and employ them less effectively. The numerically small, cohesive, well-heeled tobacco industry does well, year in, year out, in the policy-making process; marginal farmers and the urban poor produce a much less successful track record. Based on the continuing inequalities of results, critics of the pluralist model argue that interests are still represented unevenly and unfairly.

A second important line of criticism generally agrees that inequality of results remains an important aspect of group politics. But this perspective, most forcefully set out by Theodore Lowi, sees interests as generally succeeding in their goals of influencing government—to the point that the government itself, in one form or another, provides a measure of protection to almost all societal interests. Everyone thus retains some vested interest in the ongoing structure of government and array of public policies. This does not mean that all interests obtain just what they desire from governmental policies; rather, all interests get at least some rewards. From this point of view, the tobacco industry surely wishes to see its crop subsidies maintained, but the small farmer and the urban poor also have pet programs, such as guaranteed loans and food stamps, which they seek to protect.

Lowi labels the proliferation of groups and their growing access to government "interest-group liberalism," and he sees this phenomenon as pathological for a democratic government:

> Interest-group liberal solutions to the problem of power [who will exercise it] provide the system with stability by spreading a *sense* of representation at the expense of genuine flexibility, at the expense of democratic forms, and ultimately at the expense of legitimacy.[10]

Interest-group liberalism is pluralism, but it is *sponsored* pluralism, and the government is the chief sponsor.

On the surface, it appears that the "unequal results" and "interest-group liberalism" critiques of pluralism are at odds. But reconciliation is relatively straightforward. Lowi does not suggest that all interests are effectively represented. Rather, there exists, in many instances, only the appearance of representation. Political scientist Murray Edelman pointed out that a single set of policies can provide two related types of rewards—tangible benefits for the few and symbolic reassurances for the many.[11] Such a combination encourages groups to form, become active, and claim success.

A Climate for Group Proliferation

Substantial cleavages among a society's citizens are essential for interest group development. American culture and the constitutional arrangements of the U.S. government actively encourage the emergence of multiple political interests. In the pre-Revolutionary period, sharp conflicts existed between commercial and landed interests, debtor and creditor classes, coastal residents and those in the hinterlands, and citizens with either Tory or Whig political preferences. As the new nation developed, its vastness, characterized by geographical regions varying in climate, economic potential, culture, and tradition, contributed to a great heterogeneity. Open immigration policies further led to a diverse cultural mix with a wide variety of racial, ethnic, and religious backgrounds represented among the populace. Symbolically, the notion of the United States as a "melting pot," emphasizing group assimilation, has received much attention, but a more appropriate image may be the "tossed salad." [12]

The Constitution also contributes to a favorable environment for group development. Guarantees of free speech, association, and the right to petition the government for redress of grievances are basic to group formation. Because political organization often parallels government structure, federalism and the separation of powers principles embodied in the Constitution greatly influence the existence of large numbers of interest groups in the United States.

The decentralized political power structure in the United States allows important decisions to be made at the national, state, or local levels. Even within governmental levels, there are various points of access. For example, business-related policies such as taxes are acted upon at each level, and interest groups may affect these policies in the legislative, executive, or judicial arenas. Because several organizations, like the U.S. Chamber of Commerce, are federations, their state and local affiliates often act independently of the national organization. Numerous business organizations thus focus upon the multiple channels for access.

In addition, decentralized American political parties are less unified and disciplined than parties in many other nations. The resulting power vacuum in the decision-making process offers great potential for alternative political organizations such as interest groups to influence policy.

Finally, American cultural values may well encourage group development. As Alexis de Tocqueville observed 150 years ago, values such as individuality and the need for personal achievement underlie the propensity of citizens to join groups. And the number of access points, especially local ones, probably contributes to Americans' strong sense of political efficacy when compared with that expressed by citizens of other nations.[13] Not only are Americans joiners, but they tend to belong to more political groups than do people of other countries.[14]

Theories of Group Development

A climate favorable to group proliferation does little to explain how interests are organized. Whatever interests are latent in society and however favorable the context for group development may be, groups do not arise spontaneously as a result. Farmers and a landed interest existed long before farm organizations first appeared; laborers and craftsmen were on the job prior to the formation of unions. In a simple society, even though distinct interests exist, there is little need for interest group formation. Farmers have no political or economic reason to organize when they work only for their families. In the early history of the country before the industrial revolution, workers were craftsmen, often laboring in small family enterprises. Broad-based political organizations were not needed, although local guilds often existed to train apprentices and to protect jobs.

David Truman has suggested that increasing societal complexity is fundamental to group proliferation, characterized by economic specialization and social differentiation.[15] In addition, technological changes and the increasing interdependence of economic sectors often create new interests and redefine old ones. Salisbury's discussion of American farming is instructive:

> [T]he full scale commercialization of agriculture, beginning largely with the Civil War, led to the differentiation of farmers into specialized interests, each increasingly different from the next. . . . The interdependence which accompanied the specialization process meant potential conflicts of interests or values both across the bargaining encounter and among the competing farmers themselves as each struggled to secure his own position.[16]

Many political scientists assume that an expansion of the interest group universe is a natural consequence of growing societal complexity. Group formation, however, "tends to occur in waves," and is greater in some periods than in others.[17] Groups organize politically when the existing order is disturbed, and certain interests are, in turn, helped or hurt.

Not surprisingly, economic interests develop both to improve their position and to protect existing advantages. For example, the National Association of Manufacturers (NAM) was originally created to further the expansion of business opportunities in foreign trade, but it became a more powerful organization largely in response to the rise of organized labor.[18] Mobilization of business interests in the 1960s and 1970s often resulted from threats posed by consumer advocates and environmentalists.

Disturbances that act to trigger group formation need not be strictly economic or technological. Wars, for example, place extreme burdens on draft-age men; organized resistance to U.S. defense policy arose during the Vietnam era. Likewise, broad societal changes may disturb the status quo; the Ku Klux Klan's origin lies in the fear that increased numbers of ethnic and racial minorities threatened white, Christian America.

Truman's theory of group proliferation suggests that the interest group universe is inherently unstable. Groups formed from an imbalance of interests in one area induce a subsequent disequilibrium, which acts as a catalyst for individuals to form groups as counterweights to the new perceptions of inequity. Group politics thus is characterized by successive waves of mobilization and countermobilization. The liberalism of one era may prompt the resurgence of conservative groups in the next. Similarly, periods of business domination are often followed by eras of reform group ascendancy.

Personal Motivations and Group Formation

Central to theories of group proliferation are the pluralist notions that elements of society possess common needs and share a group identity or consciousness, and that these are sufficient conditions for the formation of effective political organizations. While the perception of common needs may be necessary for political organization, whether it is sufficient for group formation and effectiveness is open to question. Historical evidence documents many instances in which groups do not spontaneously emerge even when circumstances such as poverty or discrimination would seem to require it.

Mancur Olson effectively challenged many pluralist tenets in *The Logic of Collective Action,* published in 1965. Using a "rational economic man" model as the basis of his analysis, Olson posited that even individuals who have common interests are not inclined to join organizations that attempt to address their concerns. The major barrier to group participation is the "free-rider" problem: "rational" individuals choose not to bear the participation costs (time, membership) because they can enjoy the group benefits (such as favorable legislation) whether or not they join. Groups that pursue "collective" benefits, which accrue to all members of a class or segment of society regardless of membership status, will have great difficulty forming and surviving. According to Olson, it would be economically irrational for individual farmers to join a group seeking higher farm prices when benefits from price increases would be enjoyed by all farmers, even those who contribute nothing to the group. Similarly, it would be irrational for an individual consumer to become part of organized attempts to lower consumer prices, when all consumers, members or not, would reap the benefits. The free-rider problem is especially serious for large groups because the larger the group the less likely an individual will perceive his or her contribution as having any impact on group success.

For Olson, a key to group formation—and especially group survival—is the provision of "selective" benefits. These rewards, such as travel discounts, informative publications, and the like, go only to members. Organizations in the best positions to offer such benefits are those initially formed for some nonpolitical purpose and that ordinarily provide material benefits to their clientele. In the case of unions, for example, membership may be a condition of employment. For farmers, the American Farm Bureau Federation offers inexpensive insurance, which induces individuals to join, even if they disagree with AFBF goals. In professional societies, membership may be a prerequisite for occupational advancement and opportunity.

Olson's notions have sparked several extensions of the rational man model, and a reasonably coherent body of "incentive theory" literature now exists.[19] Incentive theorists view individuals as rational decision makers, interested in making the most of their time and money by choosing to participate in those groups that offer benefits greater than or equal to the costs they incur by participation.

Three types of benefits are available. As an economist, Olson was most concerned with *material* benefits—tangible rewards of participation, such as income or services that have monetary value. *Solidary* incentives, the socially derived, intangible rewards created by the act of association, such as fun, camaraderie, status, or prestige, are also significant. Finally, *expressive* (also known as *purposive*) rewards, derived from advancing a particular cause or ideology, clearly are important in explaining individual actions.[20] Groups formed on both sides of issues such as abortion or the Equal Rights Amendment (ERA) illustrate the strength such of expressive incentives.

The examination of group members' motivations, and in particular the focus upon nonmaterial incentives, allows for some reconciliation between the traditional group theorists' expectations of group development and the recent "rational actor" studies, which emphasize the barriers to group formation. It is the nonmaterial incentives, such as fellowship and self-satisfaction, that may encourage the proliferation of highly politicized groups:

> [Nonmaterial incentives] have the potential for producing a *more dynamic group context in which politics, political preferences, and group goals are more centrally determining factors* than in material associations, linking political considerations more directly to associational size, structure, and internal processes.[21]

Indeed, pure political benefits may attract potential members as well, and even collective benefits can prove decisive in inducing individuals to join large groups. Like elected officials, groups may find it possible to "take credit" for widely approved government actions, such as higher farm prices or stronger environmental regulations.[22]

Contemporary Interest Group Politics

Several notable developments mark the modern age of interest group politics. Of primary importance is the large and growing number of active groups and other interests. The data here are sketchy, but one major study found that most current groups came into existence after World War II, and that group formation has accelerated substantially since the early 1960s.[23] Groups increasingly direct their attention toward the centers of power in Washington, D.C., as the scope of federal policy making has grown. Interest groups seeking influence "hunt where the ducks are," and there has been a steady movement of groups to the nation's capital since 1960. As a result, the 1960s and 1970s marked a veritable explosion in the number of groups lobbying in Washington.

A second key change is evident in the composition of the interest group universe. Beginning in the late 1950s, political participation patterns have undergone some significant transformations. Conventional activities such as voting have declined, and political parties, the traditional aggregators and articulators of mass interests, have become weaker. Yet at all levels of government, evidence of citizen involvement is apparent, often in the form of new or revived groups. Particularly impressive has been the growth of citizens' groups—those organized around an idea or cause (at times a single issue) and having no occupational basis for membership. Fully 30 percent of such groups have formed since 1975, and in 1980 they comprised more than one-fifth of all groups represented in Washington.[24]

A "participation revolution" is occurring in the country as large numbers of citizens are becoming active in an ever-increasing number of protest groups, citizens' organizations, and special interest groups. These groups often are composed of issue-oriented activists or individuals who seek collective material benefits. The free-rider problem has proven not to be an insurmountable barrier to group formation, and many new interest groups do not use selective material benefits to gain support.

Third, government itself has had a profound effect on the growth and activity of interest groups (see Chapter 9). Early in this century, workers found organizing difficult because business and industry used government-backed injunctions to prevent strikes. By the 1930s, however, with the prohibition of injunctions in private labor disputes and the rights of collective bargaining established, most governmental actions directly promoted labor union growth. In recent years, changes in the campaign finance laws have led to an explosion in the number of political action committees, especially among business, industry, and issue-oriented groups. Laws facilitating group formation certainly have contributed to group proliferation, but government policy in a broader sense is at least equally responsible.

Fourth, not only has the number of membership groups grown in recent decades, but also a similar expansion has occurred in the political activity of many other interests, particularly individual corporations and institutions such as universities.[25] Historically, most of these interests have been satisfied with representation by trade or professional associations. Since the mid-1960s, however, many of these institutions have chosen to employ their own Washington representatives (see Chapter 12). The chief beneficiaries of this trend are Washington-based lawyers, lobbyists, and public relations firms (see Chapter 17). The number of attorneys in the nation's capital, taken as a rough indicator of lobbyist strength, tripled between 1973 and 1983, and the growth of public relations firms was dramatic. The lobbying community of the 1980s is large, increasingly diverse, and part of the expansion of policy domain participation, whether in agriculture, the environment, or industrial development (see Chapters 8, 10, and 14).

Governmental Growth

Since the 1930s, the federal government has become an increasingly active and important spur to group formation. A major aim of the New Deal was to use government as an agent in balancing the relationship between contending forces in society, particularly industry and labor. One goal was to create greater equality of opportunity, including the "guarantee of identical liberties to all individuals, especially with regard to their pursuit of economic success." [26] For example, the Wagner Act, which established collective bargaining rights, attempted to equalize workers' rights with those of their employers. Some New Deal programs did have real redistributive qualities, but most, even Social Security, sought only to ensure minimum standards of citizen welfare. Workers were clearly better off, but "the kind of redistribution that took priority in the public philosophy of the New Deal was not of wealth, but a redistribution of power." [27]

The expansion of federal programs has accelerated since 1960. In what political scientist Hugh Heclo termed an "Age of Improvement," [28] the federal budget has grown rapidly (from nearly $100 billion in 1961 to almost a trillion in 1986) and has widened the sweep of federal regulations. Lyndon Johnson's Great Society—a multitude of federal initiatives in education, welfare, health care, civil rights, housing, and urban affairs—created a new array of federal responsibilities and program beneficiaries. The growth of many of these programs has continued, although markedly slowed by the Reagan administration. In the 1970s the federal government further expanded its activities in the areas of consumer affairs, environmental protection, and energy regulation, as well as redefining some policies such as affirmative action to seek greater equality of results.

Many of the government policies adopted early in the Age of Improvement did not result from interest group activity by potential beneficiaries. Several targeted groups, such as the poor, were not effectively organized in the period of policy development. Initiatives typically came from elected officials responding to a variety of private and public sources, such as task forces composed of academics and policy professionals.[29]

The proliferation of government activities led to a mushrooming of groups around the affected policy areas. Newly enacted programs provided benefit packages that served to encourage interest group formation. Consider group activity in the field of policy toward the aging. The radical Townsend Movement, based on age grievances, received much attention during the 1930s, but organized political activity focused on age-based concerns had virtually no influence in national politics. Social Security legislation won approval without the involvement of age-based interest groups. Four decades later, by 1978, roughly $112 billion (approximately 24 percent of total federal expenditures) went to the elderly; and it is projected that in fifty years the outlay will be 40 percent of the total budget.[30] The development of such massive benefits has spawned a variety of special interest groups and has encouraged others (often those formed for nonpolitical reasons) to redirect their attention to the politics of the aging.

Across policy areas, two types of groups develop in response to governmental policy initiatives: *recipients* and *service deliverers*. In the elderly policy sector, recipient groups are mass-based organizations concerned with protecting—and if possible expanding—old-age benefits. The largest of these groups, and one of the largest voluntary associations represented in Washington, is the American Association of Retired Persons (AARP). Originally formed to provide the elderly with adequate insurance, the AARP has become an active political group that opposes mandatory retirement and seeks, among other things, to protect Social Security. The National Council of Senior Citizens (NCSC), another important recipient group, was organized by the labor movement for an explicit political purpose—the passage of Medicare legislation. Since its inception the NCSC has broadened its concerns to include many more aging issues, and like the AARP, this group offers its members a host of selective material benefits.

Federal program growth also has generated numerous organizations among service delivery groups. In the aging policy area there are several trade associations, one professional association, and a confederation of social welfare agencies concerned with problems of the elderly.

Federal government policy toward the aging is probably typical of the tendency to "greatly increase the incentives for groups to form around the differential effects of these policies, each refusing to allow any other group to speak in its name."[31] The complexity of government decision making increases under such conditions, and priorities are hard to set. Particularly troublesome for decision makers concerned with national policy is the role played by service delivery groups. In the area of the aging, some groups are largely "organizational middlemen" concerned with their status as vendors for the elderly. The trade associations, for example, are most interested in the conditions surrounding the payment of funds to the elderly. The major concern of the Gerontological Society, an organization of professionals, is to obtain funds for research on problems of the aged. Middleman organizations do not usually evaluate programs according to the criteria used by recipient groups; rather, what is important to them is the relationship between the program and the well-being of the organization. Because many service delivery groups offer their members vitally important selective material incentives (financial advantages and job opportunities), they are usually far better organized than most recipient groups. As a result, they sometimes speak for the recipients. This is particularly true when recipient groups represent disadvantaged people, such as the poor or the mentally ill.

Middleman groups have accounted for a large share of total group growth since 1960, and many of them are state and local government organizations. Since the late 1950s, the federal government has grown in expenditures and regulations, not in personnel and bureaucracy. Employment in the federal government has risen only 20 percent since 1955, while that of states and localities has climbed more than 250 percent. Contemporary federal activism largely involves overseeing and regulating state and local governmental units, which seek funding for a wide range of purposes. The intergovernmental lobby, composed of groups such as the National League of Cities, the International City Manager Association, the National Association of Counties, the National Governors' Association, and the U.S. Conference of Mayors, has grown to become one of the most important in Washington. In addition, many local officials such as transportation or public works directors are represented by groups, and even single cities and state boards of regents have established Washington offices (see Chapter 11).

Not only do public policies contribute to group proliferation, but government often directly intervenes in group creation. This is not an entirely new activity. In the early twentieth century, both the American Farm Bureau Federation and the U.S. Chamber of Commerce were encouraged to form by relevant governmental officials in the Agriculture and Commerce Departments, respectively. Since the 1960s, the federal government has been especially active in providing start-up funds and sponsoring groups. One study found that government agencies have concentrated on sponsoring organizations of public service professions.

> Federal agencies have an interest in encouraging coordination among the elements of these complex service delivery systems and in improving the diffusion of new ideas and techniques. Groups like the American Public Transit Association or the American Council on Education ... serve as centers of professional development and informal channels for administrative coordination in an otherwise unwieldy governmental system.[32]

Government sponsorship also helps to explain the recent rise of citizens' groups. Most federal domestic legislation has included provisions requiring some citizen participation, which have spurred the development of various "citizen action groups," including grass-roots neighborhood associations, environmental action councils, legal defense coalitions, health care organizations, and senior citizens' groups. Such group sponsorship evolved for two reasons:

> First, there is the ever-present danger that administrative agencies may exceed or abuse their discretionary power. In this sense, the regulators need regulating. Although legislatures have responsibility for doing this ... the administrative bureaucracy has grown too large for them to monitor. Therefore, citizen participation has developed as an alternative means of monitoring government agencies. Second, government agencies are not entirely comfortable with their discretionary power. ... [T]o reduce the potential of unpopular or questionable decisions, agencies frequently use citizen participation as a means for improving, justifying, and developing support for their decisions.[33]

Citizen participation thus has two often inconsistent missions: to act as a watchdog over an agency, and as an advocate for its programs.

Government funding of citizens' groups takes numerous forms. Several federal agencies, including the Federal Trade Commission (FTC), the Food and Drug Administration (FDA), and the Environmental Protection Agency (EPA), have reimbursed groups for participation in agency proceedings.[34] At other times the government makes available "seed" money or outright grants. Interest group scholar Jack Walker found that nine citizens' groups in ten (89 percent) received outside funding in their initial stages of development.[35] Not all the money was from federal sources, but much did come from government grants and/or contracts. Government can take away as well as give, and the Reagan administration has made a major effort to "defund" interests on the political Left, especially citizens' groups (see Chapter 9). Once established, however, groups have strong instincts for survival. Indeed, the Reagan administration has provided an attractive target for many citizens' groups in their recruiting efforts.

Citizens' groups, numbering in the thousands, continually must confront the free-rider problem, since they are largely concerned with collective goods and rarely can offer the selective material incentives so important for expanding and maintaining membership. With government funding, however, the development of a stable group membership is not crucial. Increasingly, groups have appeared that are essentially "staff" organizations with little or no membership base (see Chapter 7).

Government policies contribute to group formation in many *unintended* ways as well. Policy failures can lead to group formation, as happened with the rise of the American Agriculture Movement in the wake of the Nixon administration's grain export policies (see Chapter 3). An important factor in the development of Moral Majority was the perceived harassment of church-run schools by government officials, and the 1973 Supreme Court decision on abortion played a major role in right-to-life group mobilization (see Chapter 2).

Finally, the expansion of government activity itself often *inadvertently* contributes to group development and the resulting complexity of politics. A rather obscure example may prove most instructive. Consider the development of the Bass Anglers Sportsman Society (yes, the acronym is BASS).

It all began with the Army Corps of Engineers, which dammed enough southern and midwestern streams to create a host of lakes. These lakes provided a most inviting habitat for largemouth bass. Anglers arrived in droves to catch their limits, and the fishing industry responded by creating expensive boats filled with specialized and esoteric equipment from which the fishermen could cast upon the waters. The number and affluence of bass aficionados did not escape the attention of Ray Scott, an enterprising soul who began BASS in 1967. In 1982, with more than 400,000 members, BASS remained privately organized, offering its members selective benefits such as a slick magazine filled with tips to help anglers catch their favorite fish, packages of lures and line in return for joining or renewing their memberships, instant information about fishing "hot spots," and many discounts on equipment. BASS also provided a number of solidary benefits, such as the camaraderie of fishing with fellow members in specially sanctioned fishing tournaments and the vicarious excitement of fishing with "BASS pros," whose financial livelihood revolved around competitive tournament fishing. The organization is an excellent example of Robert Salisbury's exchange theory approach to interest groups, as it provides benefits to both members and organizers in a "mutually satisfactory exchange." [36]

Like most groups, BASS did not begin as a political organization, and, for the most part, it remains a sportsman's group. But BASS has entered politics. Its monthly publication, *Bassmaster,* has published political commentary ranging from an endorsement of Republican George Bush for president to statements dealing with U.S. restrictions on travel to Cuba, where potential world-record bass may lurk. In recent years the organization has supported various environmental causes, funded research at public institutions, and helped influence state agencies in setting policies. Some state and local BASS chapters have vigorously sought the appointment of their members to state fish and game commissions.

Regardless of the entrepreneurial skills of Ray Scott, however, there would probably be no BASS if it were not for the federal government and the Army Corps of Engineers. (Indeed, there would be far fewer largemouth bass.) The Corps' fifty years of dam building has altered the nature of fish populations. Damming rivers and streams has reduced the quality of fishing for coldwater species like trout or pike and has enhanced the habitat for largemouth bass, a game fish that can tolerate the warmer waters and mud bottoms of man-made lakes. Finally, because many of these lakes are located close to cities, the government has made bass fishing accessible to a large number of anglers.

From angling to air traffic control, the federal government has affected, and sometimes dominated, group formation. Governmental activity does not, however, exist in a vacuum, and many other forces have contributed to group proliferation, often in concert with increased public-sector involvement.

The Decline of Political Parties

In a diverse political culture characterized by divided power, political parties emerged early in our history as instruments to structure conflict and facilitate mass participation. Parties function as intermediaries between the public and formal government institutions, as they reduce and combine citizen demands into a manageable number of issues, thus enabling the system to focus upon the society's most important problems.

The party performs its mediating function primarily through coalition building—"the process of constructing majorities from the broad sentiments and interests that can be found to bridge the narrower needs and hopes of separate individuals and communities." [37] The New Deal coalition, forged in the 1930s, illustrates how this works. Generally speaking, socioeconomic divisions dominated politics. Less affluent citizens tended to support government provisions for social and economic security and the regulation of private enterprise. Those better off economically usually took the opposite position. The Democratic coalition, by and large, represented disadvantaged urban workers, Catholics, Jews, Italians, eastern Europeans, and blacks. On a variety of issues, southerners joined the coalition along with smatterings of academics and urban liberals. The Republicans were concentrated in the rural and suburban areas outside the South; the party was made up of established ethnic groups, businessmen, and farmers, and was largely Protestant. Party organizations dominated electoral politics through the New Deal period, and interest group influence was felt primarily through the party apparatus.

Patterns of partisan conflict are never permanent, however, and since the 1940s, various social forces have contributed to the creation of new interests and the redefinition of older ones. This has had the effect of destroying the New Deal coalition without putting a new partisan structure in its place and has provided opportunities for the creation of large numbers of political groups—many that are narrowly focused and opposed to the bargaining and compromise patterns of coalition politics (see Chapter 5).

Taken as a whole, the changes of recent decades reflect the societal transformation that scholars have labeled "postindustrial society," centering on

> Several interrelated developments: affluence, advanced technological development, the central importance of knowledge, national communication processes, the growing prominence and independence of the culture, new occupational structures, and with them new life styles and expectations, which is to say new social classes and new centers of power.[38]

At base is the role of affluence. Between 1947 and 1972, median family income doubled, even after controlling for the effects of inflation. During that same period, the percentage of families earning $10,000 and more, in constant dollars, grew from 15 percent to 60 percent of the population.[39] A large proportion of the population thus enjoys substantial discretionary income and has moved beyond subsistence concerns.

The consequences of spreading abundance did not reduce conflict, as some observers had predicted.[40] Instead, conflict heightened, as affluence increased dissatisfaction by contributing to a "mentality of demand, a vastly expanded set of expectations concerning what is one's due, a diminished tolerance of conditions less than ideal."[41] By the 1960s the democratizing impact of affluence became apparent, as an extraordinary number of people enrolled in institutions of higher education. Not surprisingly, the government was under tremendous pressure to satisfy expectations, and it too contributed to increasing demands both in rhetoric and through many of its own Age of Improvement initiatives.

With the rise in individual expectations, class divisions and conflicts did not disappear, but they were drastically transformed. Political parties scholar

Walter Dean Burnham noted that the New Deal's class structure changed
and that by the late 1960s the industrial class pattern of upper, middle, and
working class had been "supplanted by one which is relevant to a system
dominated by advanced postindustrial technology." [42] At the top of the new
class structure was a "professional-managerial-technical elite . . . closely
connected with the university and research centers and significant parts of it
have been drawn—both out of ideology and interest—to the federal government's social activism." [43] This growing group tended to be cosmopolitan and
more socially permissive than the rest of society. The spread of affluence in
postindustrial society was uneven, however, and certain groups were disadvantaged by the changes. At the bottom of the new class structure were the
victims of changes, those "whose economic functions had been undermined or
terminated by the technical revolution of the past generation . . . people, black
and white, who tend to be in hard core poverty areas." [44] The focus of the
War on Poverty was to be upon this class.

The traditional political party system found it difficult to deal effectively
with citizens' high expectations and a changing class structure. The economic,
ethnic, and ideological positions that had developed during the New Deal
became less relevant to parties, elections, and voter preferences. The strains
were particularly evident among working-class Democrats. New Deal policies
had been particularly beneficial to the white working class, enabling that
group to earn incomes and adopt life styles that resembled those of the middle
class. Age of Improvement policies initiated by Democratic politicians often
benefited minorities; many white workers viewed these policies as attempts to
aid lower-class blacks at whites' expense. By the late 1960s, the white
working class had taken on trappings of the middle class and conservatism,
both economically and culturally.

At the same time, New Deal divisions like ethnicity also had lost their
cutting edge due to social and geographic mobility. One analyst observed in
1973 that

> It does not seem inaccurate to portray the current situation as one in which
> the basic coalitions and many of the political symbols and relationships,
> which were developed around one set of political issues and problems, are
> confronted with new issues and new cleavages for which these traditional
> relationships and associations are not particularly relevant. Given these
> conditions, the widespread confusion, frustration, and mistrust are not
> surprising.[45]

Various conditions lead to the party system's inability to adapt to the
changing societal divisions by "realigning"—building coalitions of groups to
address new concerns. For instance, consider the difficulty of coalition
building around the kinds of issues that have emerged over the past fifteen or
twenty years.

"Valence" issues—general evaluations of the "goodness" or "badness" of
the times—have become important, especially when related to the cost of
living. Yet most such issues do not divide the country politically. Everyone is
against inflation and crime. A second set of increasingly important issues are

those of a highly emotional/cultural/moral character, such as abortion, ERA ratification, the death penalty, marijuana laws, and a nuclear freeze; these divide the electorate, but elicit intense feelings from only a few citizens. Opinion on such issues often is unrelated to traditional group identifications. Moreover, public opinion is generally disorganized or "in disarray"—that is, opinions are often unrelated or weakly related to one another on major issues, further retarding efforts to build coalitions.

There is some question whether parties retain the capacity to shape political debate even on issues that lend themselves to coalition building. Although the decline of parties began well before the 1960s, the weakening of the party organization has accelerated in the postindustrial age. The emergence of a highly educated electorate, less dependent upon party as an electoral cue, has produced a body of citizens that seeks out independent sources of information. Technological developments, such as television, computer-based direct mail, and political polling, have enabled candidates to virtually bypass political parties in their quest for public office. The rise of political consultants has reduced even further the need for party expertise in running for office. The recruitment function of parties also has been largely lost to the mass media, as journalists now "act out the part of talent scouts, conveying the judgment that some contenders are promising, while dismissing others as of no real talent." [46]

Evidence does suggest that parties are finally starting to adapt to this new political environment, but party organizations no longer dominate the electoral process. The weakness of political parties has helped to create a vacuum in electoral politics since 1960, and in recent years interest groups have aggressively moved to fill it (e.g., PACs, see Chapter 5).

The Growth of Interest Groups

While it is still premature to formulate a theory that accounts for spurts of growth, we can identify several factors fundamental to group proliferation in contemporary politics. Rapid social and economic changes, powerful catalysts for group formation, have produced both the development of new interests (e.g., the recreation industry) and the redefinition of traditional interests (e.g., higher education). The spread of affluence and education, coupled with advanced communication technologies, further contribute to the translation of interests into formal group organizations. Postindustrial changes have generated a large number of new interests, particularly among occupational and professional groups in the scientific and technological arenas. For instance, genetic engineering associations have sprung up in the wake of recent DNA discoveries.

Perhaps more important, postindustrial changes altered the pattern of conflict in society and created an intensely emotional setting composed of several groups ascending or descending in status. Ascending groups, like members of the new professional-managerial-technical elite, have both benefited from and supported government activism; they represent the new cultural liberalism, politically cosmopolitan and socially permissive. At the same time, "rising expectations" and feelings of "entitlement" increased pressures on government from aspiring groups and the disadvantaged. The 1960s and early 1970s witnessed wave after wave of group mobilization based on causes ranging from civil rights to women's issues to the environment to consumer protection.

Abrupt changes and alterations in status, however, threaten many citizens. "Middle America," perceiving itself as downwardly mobile, grew alienated from the social, economic, and cultural dominance of the postindustrial elites on one hand, and resentful toward government attempts to aid minorities and other aspiring groups on the other. The conditions of a modern, technologically based culture also are disturbing to more traditional elements in society. Industrialization and urbanization can uproot people, cutting them loose from familiar life patterns and values, while simultaneously depriving them of meaningful personal associations. Fundamentalist elements feel threatened by various technological "advancements" (such as test-tube babies) as well as the more general secular liberalism and moral permissiveness of contemporary life. And the growth of bureaucracy, in and out of government, antagonizes everyone at one time or another.

Postindustrial threats can be felt by elites as well. The nuclear arms race and its potential for mass destruction underlie the revived peace movement of the 1980s and its goal of a freeze on nuclear weapons. In addition, the excesses and errors of technology, such as oil spills and toxic waste disposal, have led to group formation among some of the most advantaged and ascending elements of society.

Illustrating the possibilities here is the mid-1980s' growth of the animal rights movement. Although traditional animal protection organizations, like the Humane Society, have existed for decades, the last ten years have "spawned a colorful menagerie of pro-animal offspring" such as People for Ethical Treatment of Animals (PETA), Progressive Animal Welfare Society (PAWS), Committee to Abolish Sport Hunting (CASH), and the Animal Rights Network (ARN). Reminiscent of the 1960s, there is even the Animal Liberation Front, an extremist group.[47]

One major goal of these groups is to stop or greatly retard scientific experimentation upon animals. Using a mix of protest, lobbying, and litigation, the movement has contributed to the closing of several animal labs, including the Defense Department's Wound Laboratory and a facility at the University of Pennsylvania involved in research on head injuries. The National Institutes of Health canceled a number of grants at least in partial response to the movement's activities. Membership in the animal rights movement may approach one million; PETA, in existence since 1980, claims eighty thousand members.[48]

While postindustrial conflicts generate the issues for group development, the massive spread of affluence also systematically contributes to group formation and maintenance. Affluence creates a large potential for "checkbook" membership. Issue-based groups have done especially well. Membership in groups such as PETA and Common Cause might once have been considered a luxury, but the growth in discretionary income has placed the cost of modest dues within most citizens' reach. For a $15 to $25 membership fee, people could make an "expressive" statement without incurring other organizational obligations. Increasing education was also a factor in that "organizations become more numerous as ideas become more important." [49]

Reform groups and citizens' groups depend heavily upon the educated, white middle class for their membership and financial base. A 1982 Common Cause poll, for example, found that members' mean family income was $17,000 above the national mean and that 43 percent of the members had an advanced degree.[50] Other expressive groups, including those on the political Right, also were aided by the increased wealth of constituents and the community activism that result from education and occupational advancement.

Groups also can overcome the free-rider problem by finding a sponsor who will support the organization and reduce its reliance upon membership contributions. During the 1960s and 1970s private sources (often foundations) backed various groups. Jeffrey Berry's 1977 study of eighty-three public interest organizations found that at least one-third received more than half of their funds from private foundations, while one in ten received more than 90 percent of its operating expenses from such sources.[51] Jack Walker's 1981 study of Washington-based interest groups confirmed many of Berry's earlier findings, indicating that foundation support and individual grants provide 30 percent of all citizens' group funding.[52] Such patterns produce many "staff" organizations with no members, raising major questions about the representativeness of the new interest group universe (see Chapter 7). Groups themselves can sponsor other groups. The National Council of Senior Citizens was originally started by the AFL-CIO, which helped recruit members from the ranks of organized labor and still pays part of NCSC's expenses.

Postindustrial affluence and the spread of education also have contributed to group formation and maintenance through the development of a large pool of potential group organizers. This group tends to be young, well educated, and from the middle class, caught up in a movement for change and inspired by ideas or doctrine. The 1960s was a period of opportunity for entrepreneurs, as college enrollments skyrocketed and powerful forces such as civil rights and the antiwar movement contributed to an "idea-orientation" in both education and politics. Communications-based professions, from religion to law to university teaching, attracted social activists, many of whom became involved in the formation of groups. The government itself became a major source of what James Q. Wilson called "organizing cadres." Government employees of the local Community Action Agencies of the War on Poverty and numerous VISTA volunteers were active in the formation of voluntary associations, some created to oppose government actions.[53]

Compounding the effects of the growing number of increasingly active groups are changes in what organizations can do, largely as a result of contemporary technology. On a grand scale, technological change produces new interests, like cable television or the silicon chip industry, which organize to protect themselves as interests historically have done. Beyond this, communications breakthroughs make group politics much more visible than in the past. Civil rights activists in the South understood this, as did many protesters against the Vietnam War. Of equal importance, however, is the fact that much of what contemporary interest groups do derives directly from developments in information-related technology. Many group activities, whether fund raising or grass-roots lobbying or sampling members' opinions, rely heavily on computer-based operations that can target and send messages and process the responses.

Although satellite television links and survey research are important tools, the technology of direct mail has had by far the greatest impact on interest group politics. With a minimum initial investment and a reasonably good list of potential contributors, any individual can become a group entrepreneur. These activists literally create organizations, often based on emotion-laden appeals about specific issues, from "Save the Whales" to "Ban the Books." To the extent that an entrepreneur can attract members and continue to pay the costs of direct mail, he or she can claim—with substantial legitimacy—to articulate the organization's positions on the issues, positions probably defined initially by the entrepreneur.

Aside from helping entrepreneurs develop organizations that require few (if any) active members, information technology also allows many organizations to exert considerable pressure on elected officials. The Washington-based interests increasingly turn to grass-roots techniques to influence legislators. Indeed, by the mid-1980s these tactics have become the norm in many lobbying efforts.

Information-processing technology is widely available, but expensive. Although the Chamber of Commerce can afford its costly investment in extensive television facilities, many groups simply cannot pay the cost of much technology, at least beyond their continuing efforts to stay afloat with direct mail solicitations. Money remains the mother's milk of politics. Indeed, one of the major impacts of technology may be to inflate the costs of political action, especially given group support for candidates engaged in increasingly expensive election campaigns.

Group Impact on Policy and Process

Assessing the policy impact of interest group actions has never been an easy task. We may, however, gain some insights by looking at two different levels: a broad, societal overview and a middle-range search for relatively specific patterns of influence (for example, the role of direct mail or PAC funding). Considering impact on the level of individual lobbying efforts is also possible, but even the best work relies heavily on nuance and individualistic explanations.

Patterns of Influence

Although the public at large often views lobbying and special interest campaigning with distrust, political scientists have not produced much evidence to support this perspective. Academic studies of interest groups have demonstrated few conclusive links between campaign or lobbying efforts and actual patterns of influence. This does not mean, we emphasize, that such patterns or individual instances do not exist. Rather, we see the question of determining impact as exceedingly difficult to answer. The difficulty is, in fact, compounded by groups' claims of impact and decision makers' equally vociferous claims of freedom from any outside influence.

The major studies of lobbying in the 1960s generated a most benign view of this activity. Lester Milbrath, in his portrait of Washington lobbyists, paints a Boy-Scout-like picture, depicting them as patient contributors to the policy-making process.[54] Rarely stepping over the limits of propriety, the lobbyists' impact is marginal at best. Similarly, Raymond Bauer, Ithiel de Sola Pool, and Lewis Dexter's lengthy analysis of foreign trade policy, published in 1963, finds the business community to be largely incapable of influencing Congress in its lobbying attempts[55] (but see Chapters 6 and 12). Given many internal divisions within the private sector over trade matters, this was not an ideal issue to illustrate business cooperation, but the research stood as the central work on lobbying for more than a decade—ironically, in the very period when groups proliferated and became more sophisticated in their tactics. Lewis Dexter, in his 1969 treatment of Washington representatives as an emerging professional group, suggested that lobbyists will play an increasingly important role in complex policy making, but he provided few details.[56]

The picture of benevolent lobbyists who seek to engender trust and convey information, while accurate in a limited way, does not provide a complete account of the options open to any interest group that seeks to exert influence. Lyndon Johnson's long-term relationship with the Texas-based construction firm of Brown & Root illustrates the depth of some ties between private interests and public officeholders. The Washington representative for Brown & Root claimed that he never went to Capitol Hill for any legislative help, because "people would resent political influence." [57] But Johnson, first as a representative and later a senator, systematically dealt directly with the top management (the Brown family) and aided the firm by passing along crucial information and watching over key government-sponsored construction projects.

> [The Johnson-Brown & Root link] was, indeed, a partnership, the campaign contributions, the congressional look-out, the contracts, the appropriations, the telegrams, the investment advice, the gifts and the hunts and the free airplane rides—it was an alliance of mutual reinforcement between a politician and a corporation. If Lyndon was Brown & Root's kept politician, Brown & Root was Lyndon's kept corporation. Whether he concluded that they were public-spirited partners or corrupt ones, "political

allies" or cooperating predators, in its dimensions and its implications for the structure of society, their arrangement was a new phenomenon on its way to becoming the new pattern for American society.[58]

Subsequent events, such as the Abscam investigation, demonstrate that legislators can be easily approached with illegal propositions; such access is one price of an open system. More broadly, the growth of interest representation in the 1980s has raised long-term questions about the ethics of ex-government officials acting as lobbyists.

Contemporary Practices

Modern lobbying emphasizes information—often on complex and difficult subjects. Determining actual influence is, as one lobbyist notes, "like finding a black cat in the coal bin at midnight," [59] but we can make some assessments about the overall impact of group proliferation and increased activity.

First, more groups are engaged in more forms of lobbying than ever before, both in "classic" forms, such as offering legislative testimony, and newer forms, such as mounting computer-based direct mail campaigns to stir up grass-roots support.[60] As the number of new groups rises and existing groups become more active, the pressure on decision makers—especially legislators—mounts at a corresponding rate. Thus, a second general point can be made: congressional reforms that opened up the legislative process during the 1970s have provided a much larger number of access points for lobbyists. Most committee (and subcommittee) sessions, including the markups or writing of legislation remain open to the public, as do many conference committee meetings. More roll-call votes are taken, and congressional floor action is televised. In short, interests can monitor the performance of individual members of Congress as never before. This does nothing to facilitate disinterested decision making or foster statesmanlike compromises on most issues.

The government itself has encouraged many interests to organize and articulate their demands. The rise of group activity thus leads us to another level of analysis, encompassing the impact of contemporary interest group politics upon society. Harking back to Lowi's description of interest-group liberalism, we see as the eventual result an immobilized society, trapped by its willingness to allow interests to help fashion self-serving policies that embody no firm criteria of success or failure. Even in the midst of financial crisis, the government continues to offer guarantees to various sectors, based not on future promise but on past bargains and continuing pressures.

The notion advanced by Olson that some such group-related stagnation affects all stable democracies makes the prognosis all the more serious. In summary form, Olson argued, "The longer societies are politically stable, the more interest groups they develop; the more interest groups they develop, the worse they work economically." [61] The United Auto Workers' protectionist leanings, the American Medical Association's fight against FTC intervention into physicians' business affairs, and the insurance industry's successful prevention of FTC investigations all illustrate the possible linkage between self-centered group action and poor economic performance; that is, higher automobile prices, doctors' fees, and insurance premiums for no better product or service.

Conclusions

The ultimate consequences of the expanding number of groups, the increasing federal focus, and the growth of citizens' groups remain unclear. From one perspective, such changes have made politics more representative than ever before. While most occupation-based groups have traditionally been well organized in American politics, many other interests have not. Population groupings such as blacks, Hispanics, and women have mobilized since the 1950s and 1960s; even animals and the unborn are represented in the interest group arena, as is the broader "public interest," however defined.

Broadening the base of interest group participation may have truly opened up the political process, thus curbing the influence of special interests. For example, agricultural policy making in the postwar era was almost exclusively the prerogative of a tight "iron triangle" composed of congressional committee and subcommittee members from farm states, government officials representing the agriculture bureaucracy, and major agriculture groups like the American Farm Bureau. Activity in the 1970s by consumer and environmental interest groups has changed agricultural politics, making it more visible and lengthening the agenda to consider questions such as how farm subsidies affect consumer purchasing power and the effects of various fertilizers, herbicides, and pesticides on public health. Broadening the scope of agriculture politics may encourage enlightened decision making, in that more information and interests are included in the policy process (see Chapter 10).

From another perspective, however, more interest groups and more openness do not necessarily mean better policies or ones that genuinely represent the national interest. "Sunshine" and more participants may generate greater complexity and too many demands for decision makers to process effectively. Moreover, the content of demands may be ambiguous and priorities difficult to set. And finally, the elected leadership may find it practically impossible to build the kinds of political coalitions necessary to govern effectively.

This second perspective suggests that the American constitutional system is extraordinarily susceptible to the excesses of minority faction—in an ironic way a potential victim of the Madisonian solution of dealing with the tyranny of the majority. Decentralized government, especially one that wields considerable power, provides no adequate controls over the excessive demands of special interest politics. Decision makers feel obliged to respond to many of these demands, and "the cumulative effect of this pressure has been the relentless and extraordinary rise of government spending and inflationary deficits, as well as the frustration of efforts to enact effective national policies on most major issues." [62]

In sum, the "problem" of contemporary interest group politics is one of representation. For particular interests, especially those that are well defined and adequately funded, the government is responsive on the issues of their greatest concern. But representation is not just a matter of responding to specific interests or citizens; the government also must respond to the collective needs of a society, and here the success of individual interests may foreclose the possibility of overall responsiveness. The very vibrancy and success of contemporary groups help contribute to a society that finds it increasingly difficult to formulate solutions to complex policy questions.

Notes

1. Kay Lehman Schlozman and John T. Tierney, "More of the Same: Washington Pressure Group Activity in a Decade of Change," *Journal of Politics* 45 (May 1983): 351-377.
2. Theodore J. Lowi, *The End of Liberalism,* 2d ed. (New York: W. W. Norton, 1979); Mancur Olson, *The Rise and Decline of Nations* (New Haven, Conn.: Yale University Press, 1982).
3. Mancur Olson, *The Logic of Collective Action* (Cambridge, Mass.: Harvard University Press, 1971); Robert Salisbury, "An Exchange Theory of Interest Groups," *Midwest Journal of Political Science* 13 (February 1969): 1-32; Terry M. Moe, *The Organization of Interests* (Chicago: University of Chicago Press, 1980).
4. David Truman's widely used definition of interest groups is "any group that, on the basis of one or more shared attitudes, makes certain claims upon other groups in the society for the establishment, maintenance or enhancement of forms of behavior that are implied by the shared attitudes." Truman, *The Governmental Process,* 2d ed. (New York: Alfred A. Knopf, 1971).
5. James Madison, "Federalist 10," in *The Federalist Papers,* 2d ed., ed. Roy P. Fairfield (Baltimore: Johns Hopkins University Press, 1981), 16.
6. L. Harmon Ziegler and Wayne Peak, *Interest Groups in American Society,* 2d ed. (Englewood Cliffs, N.J.: Prentice-Hall, 1972), 35.
7. Common Cause, *The Government Subsidy Squeeze* (Washington, D.C.: Common Cause, 1980), 11.
8. Truman, *The Governmental Process,* 519.
9. Carole Greenwald, *Group Power* (New York: Praeger, 1977), 305.
10. Lowi, *The End of Liberalism,* 63.
11. Murray Edelman, *The Politics of Symbolic Action* (Chicago: Markham Press, 1971).
12. Theodore J. Lowi, *Incomplete Conquest: Governing America* (New York: Holt, Rinehart & Winston, 1976), 47.
13. Gabriel Almond and Sidney Verba, *The Civic Culture* (Boston: Little, Brown, 1963), chaps. 8 and 10.
14. Ibid., 246-247.

15. Truman, *The Governmental Process,* 57.
16. Salisbury, "An Exchange Theory of Interest Groups," 3-4.
17. Truman, *The Governmental Process,* 59.
18. James Q. Wilson, *Political Organizations* (New York: Basic Books, 1973), 154.
19. Major works include the following: Olson, *The Logic of Collective Action;* Peter Clark and James Q. Wilson, "Incentive Systems: A Theory of Organizations," *Administrative Science Quarterly* 6 (September 1961): 126-166; Wilson, *Political Organizations;* Moe, *The Organization of Interests;* and "A Calculus of Group Membership," *American Journal of Political Science* 24 (November 1980): 593-632. The notion of group organizers as political entrepreneurs is best represented by Salisbury, "An Exchange Theory of Interest Groups," 1-15.
20. See Clark and Wilson, "Incentive Systems: A Theory of Organizations," 129-166; and Wilson, *Political Organizations,* 30-51. In recent years researchers have preferred the term "expressive" to "purposive," since, as Salisbury notes, the term purposive includes what we call collective material benefits. Material, solidary, and expressive would seem to be mutually exclusive conceptual categories. See Salisbury, "An Exchange Theory of Interest Groups," 16-17.
21. Moe, *The Organization of Interests,* 144.
22. John Mark Hansen, "The Political Economy of Group Membership," *American Political Science Review* 79 (March 1985): 79-96.
23. Jack L. Walker, "The Origins and Maintenance of Interest Groups in America," *American Political Science Review* 77 (June 1983). 390-406; for a conservative critique of this trend, see James T. Bennett and Thomas Di Lorenzo, *Destroying Democracy* (Washington, D.C.: Cato, 1986).
24. Walker, "The Origins and Maintenance of Interest Groups," 16; and data presented in this volume, chap. 9, Table 9-1.
25. Robert H. Salisbury, "Interest Representation and the Dominance of Institutions," *American Political Science Review* 78 (March 1984): 64-77.
26. Samuel H. Beer, "In Search of a New Public Philosophy," in *The New American Political System,* ed. Anthony King (Washington, D.C.: American Enterprise Institute, 1978), 12.
27. Ibid., 10.
28. Hugh Heclo, "Issue Networks and the Executive Establishment," in *The New American Political System,* 89.
29. Beer, "In Search of a New Public Philosophy," 16.
30. Allan J. Cigler and Cheryl Swanson, "Politics and Older Americans," in *The Dynamics of Aging,* ed. Forrest J. Berghorn, Donna E. Schafer, and Associates (Boulder, Colo.: Westview Press, 1981), 171.
31. Heclo, "Issue Networks and the Executive Establishment," 96.
32. Walker, "The Origins and Maintenance of Interest Groups," 401.
33. Stuart Langton, "Citizen Participation in America: Current Reflections on the State of the Art," in *Citizen Participation in America,* ed. Stuart Langton (Lexington, Mass.: Lexington Books, 1978), 7.
34. Ibid., 4.
35. Walker, "The Origins and Maintenance of Interest Groups," 398.
36. Salisbury, "An Exchange Theory of Interest Groups," 25.
37. David S. Broder, "Introduction," in *Emerging Coalitions in American Politics,* ed. Seymour Martin Lipset (San Francisco: Institute for Contemporary Studies, 1978), 3.
38. Everett Carll Ladd, Jr., with Charles D. Hadley, *Transformations of the*

American Party System, 2d ed. (New York: W. W. Norton, 1978), 182.
39. Ibid., 196.
40. See, for example, Daniel Bell, *The End of Ideology* (New York: The Free Press, 1960).
41. Ladd and Hadley, *Transformations of the American Party System,* 203.
42. Walter Dean Burnham, *Critical Elections and the Mainsprings of American Politics* (New York: W. W. Norton, 1970), 139.
43. Ibid.
44. Ibid.
45. Richard E. Dawson, *Public Opinion and Contemporary Disarray* (New York: Harper & Row, 1973), 194.
46. Everett Carll Ladd, *Where Have All the Voters Gone?* 2d ed. (New York: W. W. Norton, 1982), 56.
47. Kevin Kasowski, "Showdown on the Hunting Ground," *Outdoor America* 51, Winter 1986, 9.
48. Ibid.
49. Wilson, *Political Organizations,* 201.
50. Andrew S. McFarland, *Common Cause* (Chatham, N.J.: Chatham House, 1984), 48-49.
51. Jeffrey M. Berry, *Lobbying for the People* (Princeton, N.J.: Princeton University Press, 1977), 72.
52. Walker, "The Origins and Maintenance of Interest Groups in America," 400.
53. Wilson, *Political Organizations,* 203.
54. Lester Milbrath, *The Washington Lobbyists* (Chicago: Rand-McNally, 1963).
55. Raymond Bauer, Ithiel de Sola Pool, and Lewis Dexter, *American Business and Public Policy* (New York: Atherton Press, 1963).
56. Lewis A. Dexter, *How Organizations Are Represented in Washington* (Indianapolis: Bobbs-Merrill, 1969), chap. 9.
57. See Ronnie Dugger, *The Politician* (New York: W. W. Norton, 1982), 273; and Robert A. Caro, *The Years of Lyndon Johnson: The Path to Power* (New York: Alfred A. Knopf, 1973).
58. Dugger, *The Politician,* 286.
59. Quoted in "A New Era: Groups and the Grass Roots," by Burdett A. Loomis, in *Interest Group Politics,* ed. Allan J. Cigler and Burdett A. Loomis (Washington, D.C.: CQ Press, 1983), 184.
60. Schlozman and Tierney, "Washington Pressure Group Activity," 18.
61. Robert J. Samuelson's description in *National Journal,* Sept. 25, 1982, 1642.
62. Everett Carll Ladd, "How to Tame the Special Interest Groups," *Fortune,* October 1980, 6.

2. Direct Action and the Abortion Issue: The Political Participation of Single-issue Groups

Marjorie Randon Hershey

During the 1970s, single-issue groups became a powerful force in American politics. Although many interests, ranging from feminists to environmentalists to the evangelical Right, adopted this emotional, highly focused approach, opponents to abortion represent the archetype of the single-issue style. During the late 1970s, through the elections of 1980, prolife forces helped a number of favored candidates win election to Congress. These victories did not, however, lead to any major alterations in abortion policies. Nor did the election of prolife ally Ronald Reagan bring about any substantive changes. The 1980s thus brought policy frustrations and organizational stress to the antiabortion movement.

In this chapter Marjorie Hershey discusses the nature and development of single-issue groups. Moving beyond her consideration of prolife electoral politics in the first edition of this book, she explores the problems confronted by groups that emphasize expressive issues, especially when policy victories do not follow initial successes at the polls. Hershey details adoption of "direct action" tactics and the problems of determining how to proceed both within and on the fringes of the political process. The problems are not unique to prolifers; farm groups, antiapartheid activists, and the women's movement, among others, continue to face similar questions of tactical decisions and organizational survival.

When newspaper columnists write about "single-issue" politics, the words *zealot, fanatic, extremist,* and *demagogue* are often sprinkled liberally about the pages. In such a context, it is easy to underestimate the persistent and important role that single-issue politics has played in American political history. Groups regarded as single-issue have been responsible for some of the most significant agenda setting in the nation's past: the abolitionists working to end black slavery, the suffragists seeking to establish women's right to vote, the civil rights activists of the 1960s working against racial discrimination, and the protesters trying to end American involvement in the Vietnam War.

But the single-minded approach to politics seems to have grown more common in recent years, as if single-issue groups have taken root and flowered in the fertile soil of the 1970s and 1980s. Groups demanding a ban on all abortions, those insisting that abortion remain legal, groups formed to ban handguns, those determined to protect gun owners' rights, groups organized to oppose sex education in the schools, the use of animals in laboratory experiments, drunk drivers, child abuse—all have become frequent contributors to political campaigns, congressional hearings, and the nation's mailboxes.

Despite the ready availability of opinion and commentary about single-issue politics, knowledge of these groups and their impact remains in short supply. Are political groups formed to promote a single issue really different from other types of interest groups? Are their activities distinctive, and, if so, in what ways? Does their single-issue character necessarily lead them to take positions that threaten the existence of "politics-as-usual"?

This chapter begins by examining the nature of single-issue politics and the reasons for its recent expansion. Then it explores the frustrating and fascinating question that has become the classic single issue of the 1980s—abortion and the movement committed to making abortions illegal again. A look at that movement's origins and political activities can shed light on the distinctive character of the single-issue approach to political action.

The Distinctive Character of Single-issue Politics

The term sounds straightforward and descriptive: *single*-issue politics, suggesting a type of political activity focused on one issue alone. But how wide are the boundaries of "one" issue? The answer varies from observer to observer. For example, environmental activists often have been described as single-issue by people who disagree with their goals. Yet environmental groups take stands on a number of policy questions, such as clean air, endangered species, energy, and the dumping of hazardous chemicals.

Single-issue politics, then, is not always a label to be taken literally. Most often, it is used to describe a *style* of political activism. To some analysts, the defining feature of that style is fanaticism, a level of zeal or intensity not usually seen in American politics. To others, the central quality of single-issue politics is its nearsightedness, its apparent obsession with one area of policy to the exclusion of concern about other important public matters.

A more comprehensive way to understand single-issue politics, however, is to begin with its symbolic dimensions. Any issue can be defined or symbolized in different ways. As Lance Bennett put it, "Issues are not preordained problems that have to emerge in the political arena in particular forms and at particular times." [1] The nature of any issue, and the meanings it takes on, reflect the nature of the groups or individuals who succeeded in placing it on the public agenda.

For present purposes, it is useful to distinguish between two types of symbolization: referential and condensational. [2] An issue can be defined *referentially* by its proponents—in other words, in a specific and concrete way, focusing on its objective elements so as to limit the scope of meaning and the depth of emotion it will invoke. A speaker at a convention of handgun dealers, for example, might discuss gun laws in terms of the different types of paperwork needed to administer them. The tone of the discussion is matter-of-fact, bureaucratic, full of detail. The speaker's definition of the issue does not invite the expression of strong emotions or the recollection of deeply personal experiences. This approach often is used to contain a potential conflict, to quiet a rebellious voice.

Another political actor might define the same issue in a *condensational* manner, with very different effects on the audience. Condensational symbols refer to things in a more emotionally provocative way. They expand the issue's scope to a level of abstraction that encourages listeners to respond intensely, emotionally, and very personally. This speaker, for instance, might refer to handgun laws as a sinister conspiracy to deprive Americans of their God-given right to defend their homes and families, as a drive to emasculate law-abiding citizens while hardened criminals do as they please. Each of these types of symbolization can influence a listener's political involvement and the fate of the issue in question.

Typically, the issues that drive single-issue politics are symbolized in the condensational mode. Issues defined in this manner emphasize beliefs and values that touch nerves in many people and reach into their deepest feelings. They have the power to create intense attachments. By their very nature, then, they tend to be emotionally arousing, and, where there is any difference of opinion, very divisive in politics.

Condensationally defined issues are divisive because they do not fit easily within the framework of politics-as-usual. To their advocates, these issues cry out for priority. Such issues differ fundamentally, their partisans say, from the more mundane concerns that politicians negotiate day after day. They are so vital, it is often claimed, that negotiation would be a kind of moral betrayal, a compromise of basic rights or freedoms. The issue is defined as so compelling that it must be treated as a kind of moral litmus test—no hedging, no compromises, no allowances for a political leader's other commitments or qualities, no alliances with groups concerned about other matters.

Single-issue politics insists that all other issues take a back seat, at least temporarily, until that compelling question is resolved. So single issues assume special importance because they do not readily lend themselves to the familiar process of incremental decision making and mutual accommodation. They resist the formation of coalitions that allow other policies to be made; they are the wrenches thrown in the machine of the political "establishment."

This core set of orientations to politics—the use of condensational definitions, an intense and emotional concentration on a policy area, an insistence on the issue's primacy, and a refusal to accept tentative or partial support or to accommodate other goals or interests—distinguishes single-issue politics from the bargain and compromise pattern with which Americans are so familiar.

The Increasing Use of Single-issue Politics

There are several reasons for the recent rise of single-issue politics, and they act in combination. First, the reach of government now extends further into people's lives than it did a generation ago. Legislation and regulation have touched many concerns that are close to people's hearts—religious broadcasting, church-run schools, the treatment of severely handicapped newborns. Public awareness of these value conflicts has grown as well, thanks to the media, which bring them to us every evening. At the same time, political institutions have become more complex, more intrusive, and, to many, more bewildering. Television shows us this, too.

Moreover, the political party, the institution that was long assumed to provide people with a means of interpreting and penetrating this complexity, has been steadily losing its hold on voters' behavior and affections. In the words of one analyst, the parties "are considered less relevant in solving the most important domestic and foreign policy issues of the day." [3]

Given these developments, it is not surprising that some people turn away from a complicated and apparently unreachable goal. They direct their attention instead to some focal point, an issue about which they feel strongly. That issue, on which individuals feel they can master the relevant information, take action, and make some difference, comes to symbolize their broader fears and hopes. A Senate press secretary tried to explain it:

> I think people feel impotent politically in the face of the problems that we face. . . . People seem frustrated by what they regard as overburdensome levels of taxation. Foreign policy seems so far away that it cannot be touched. I'm not saying this is *true;* I'm just saying that the complexity of it is such that people feel left out of the process. And so I think you find that people tend to look for things that they can have impact on politically. . . . "I can't get my hands on inflation and I'm against abortion; I know that if I get involved in the anti-abortion fight, for example, I might be able to do something that has tangible results." [4]

In addition, sophisticated new technologies have been created to help groups identify and mobilize a constituency—techniques that are especially well suited to the nature of single-issue appeals. Prominent among these is computerized direct mail, in which large numbers of mailing lists (of group members, petition-signers, or contributors to campaigns) can be gathered and then culled to develop a "house list" of people who share the group's concerns. In this way, groups can create a long-distance constituency of like-minded people, just as the urban political machines used to create a geographical constituency through personal contact in the precincts. The group's mailings can be designed to activate its readers and to raise money for the cause. If the appeal is effective enough, a group might build the kind of war chest that would make many party organizations envious. The types of appeals regarded as particularly effective in direct mail, those with emotional and dramatic fervor, flow naturally from the single-issue political style.

Direct mail also has the advantage of privacy; groups can reach their supporters without having to depend on the mass media to transmit messages fairly and accurately, and without alerting the opposition to their plans. In the memorable phrase of one of its developers, New Right mass mailer Richard Viguerie, direct mail is "like using a water moccasin for a watchdog—it's very quiet." [5]

Changes in the rules by which Congress is organized have given single-issue and other interest groups more points of access to congressional decisions. In particular, decentralization of the congressional committee system results in more centers of power for groups to try to influence.[6] At the same time, Congress members have come to depend more and more on organized groups as sources of campaign funds. The costs of campaigning are ever increasing, and reforms of the campaign finance laws during the 1970s sharply cut back on the opportunities for "fat cats," or individual donors of large sums. Groups' political action committees (PACs), whose formation was greatly stimulated by the reforms, have stepped into the breach, offering money to candidates who support their cause.[7]

Finally, single-issue politics is on the rise because, as at other times in American history, it seems to get results. The single-issue style is not an aberration, but rather a way of defining an issue and a style of activism adopted by many groups at various times. Several of these groups recently have been credited, rightly or wrongly, with great clout on particular policy decisions. That gives the single-issue style an aura of effectiveness and also prompts these groups' natural adversaries to get organized. Jeffrey Berry wrote about interest groups in general, "Successful groups set the example for others. Washington is really a town of few secrets, and what works for one group is quickly copied by others." [8]

All these factors have encouraged single-issue groups to form and to affect public policy. Let us examine these processes in the case of a particularly intriguing issue—abortion.

Abortion as a Political Issue

Abortion is not *necessarily* a political matter; there are questions of deep personal concern that never reach the agendas of political groups or government. But at several points in American history, and most recently by the hand of government itself, abortion crossed that threshold.[9]

In English common law, the foundation of the American legal system, an abortion was considered at worst a misdemeanor until the midpoint of pregnancy, the time called "quickening," when a pregnant woman could begin to feel movement in her womb. After quickening, abortion was treated as a more serious criminal act, although the penalties were not nearly as severe as those for murder. This common law standard also prevailed in the United States until the late 1800s.

By 1900, however, every American state had passed laws making it a felony to perform an abortion at *any* time during the pregnancy unless the mother's life was in danger. Kristin Luker makes a convincing case that physicians were the prime movers behind these more restrictive laws, in an effort to upgrade the moral and technical status of their profession.[10] Contributing to the change may have been an increasing concern about the dangers of surgery (before the days of antibiotics), an interest in using the law to define "appropriate" sexual conduct, and a greater value placed on population growth during the period when the West was being settled.

After this first right-to-life movement achieved its goals, the question of abortion slipped into the political background for a time. By the middle of this century, however, physicians were again in the vanguard of a movement to change abortion laws, but this time in the direction of liberalization. Some of these reformers were motivated by distress over the number of deaths and injuries caused by illegal abortions. As women's roles in the work force expanded, some women saw legalized abortion as a vital means of controlling their futures. The reformers pressed their case in a number of state legislatures during the 1960s. Colorado became the first, in 1967, to liberalize its abortion law, with North Carolina and California close on its heels.[11] By the beginning of 1973, about one-third of the states had passed abortion reform bills.

Then the political landscape shook. While this rush of state legislative action was making headlines, challenges to restrictive abortion laws had been moving through the courts almost unnoticed. On January 22, 1973, two of those cases exploded onto the national agenda. In *Roe v. Wade* and *Doe v. Bolton*, the Supreme Court struck down all state abortion laws. A pregnant woman, said the Court, has a right to privacy in choosing whether to bear her child.[12] This right could be limited by the state only for certain reasons: to protect the mother's health by regulating how second-trimester abortions can be performed and to restrict abortions during the last three months of pregnancy in the interest of protecting the "potential life" of the fetus or unborn child. Even in the last trimester, the Court ruled, states could not ban abortions that were considered necessary to preserve the mother's life or health.

The decision exceeded the reformers' wildest hopes. In doing so, it put abortion law well beyond the range of policy that most state legislatures had found acceptable. Recall that at the time the Court acted, two-thirds of the states still prohibited abortion throughout pregnancy except to save the mother's life. So *Roe v. Wade*, regarded by some observers as an unusually abrupt and sweeping move by the Court,[13] kept even the most conservative states from enforcing antiabortion laws, about which many church groups and state legislators felt very strongly.

The decision threatened the beliefs of many people whose opposition to abortion previously had been private, and it propelled them into political action. Literally within days, groups formed and multiplied with the purpose of returning abortion policy to its earlier status. A state prolife leader recalls, "I had eight chapters [in her state prolife organization] the day the [*Roe*] decision came down, and within a week I had eleven, you know; I mean, it was the reaction to the decision and the injustice of it."

Abortion as a Single Issue

The abortion issue can be defined referentially—as a low-key question of medical practice, for example. That was the dominant definition from the time the first right-to-life movement succeeded in the late 1800s until the issue reemerged in the early 1960s.[14] But the groups that objected to the Court's decision, and soon put the abortion issue on the public agenda, said it was much more than a medical matter. The canon law of the Catholic church and the doctrine of several Protestant denominations (especially the fundamentalist churches) and of other religious groups (Mormons, for instance) hold that when conception occurs, a new human life is present. They further agree that the ending of that life through abortion at any time after conception must be seen as the killing of a human being—not a "potential life," but a baby. The prolife movement was formed by people who accepted this view and assumed it to be widely shared.

Many of those who had already become prolife activists before 1973 traced their concern about abortion to their work in a health-related job.[15] Listen to one prolifer, now the head of a state prolife PAC, recall the experience that prompted her involvement:

> I was a student nurse at the time. These abortions were coming in scheduled as D & Cs. I was simply asked if I would like to scrub in on one. As I was standing there, [I saw the abortion of] about a ten-week-old baby, perfectly, perfectly formed; I could see fingers and details—the whole works. And you know, after seeing something like that, you come to the conclusion that it does not take a whole lot of education or conscience, it does not take any particular religious background [to see that] it is so very clearly a human being, you know? Just a perfectly formed human being.

After *Roe v. Wade,* a movement that had consisted largely of medical, legal, and public health professionals expanded greatly among the lay public. Many of these new activists were women raising families, new to politics, for whom religion was a vital, guiding force in their lives. Of their activism and that of men driven into the movement by the Court's decision, Luker wrote, "From a quiet, restricted technical debate among concerned professionals, abortion has become a debate that seems at times capable of tearing the fabric of American life apart."[16] Consider the views of these prolife leaders:

> The abortion battle is a battle to the death, because it is a battle between life and death.[17]

> Every day that passes more babies are murdered within their mothers' wombs. These babies suffer agonizing deaths, and their mothers are scarred psychologically, spiritually, and often physically for the rest of their lives. The abortion business is a soul-destroying evil paralleled only in the darkest moments of history.[18]

The important issue is the holocaust of 1.5 million babies, and doctors getting rich off it. . . . Women's bodies are being torn apart. Hostility is being put between the mother and her child. It is a straight due process question, when a group of people are defined as less than human and preyed upon by somebody else. Anyone, any group that has as the objective the killing of innocent preborn children is not a legitimate group, period.[19]

The symbols in these comments are emotionally powerful: agonizing deaths, babies murdered, holocaust, mothers scarred. They call forth our deepest fears and feelings about life itself. They show that to prolife partisans, the issue of abortion is no less than the protection of human life against those who would destroy it. As one national prolife leader put it, "The right to choose is the right to kill." [20] Thus the issue of abortion, as defined by the current prolife movement, is condensational to its core.

Also consistent with this chapter's definition of single-issue politics, the movement's leaders feel that the abortion issue takes priority over all other public policy matters. One state prolife group leader explained,

I'm concerned about a lot more issues than abortion, but this is the primary one, because I think so many issues hinge on this type of thing; anybody who would go for taking the life of little ones is not going to look out for my interests in anything else either, you know.

For that reason, and because it helps prolife groups maintain their internal unity, they have usually limited their political activities to the abortion issue alone.

Further, they regard the abortion issue as nonnegotiable. Compromise, they feel, is out of the question on a matter of life and death. "Our issue is totally and absolutely different than any other issue," a national prolife organizer argued.

You can't compromise with human life. . . . Compromise is the name of the game for many issues because, unfortunately, it's the only way to get things done. If I compromise with someone over the size of the budget, I'm not bothering anyone. But if I compromise on abortion, the compromise harms human life. And life is sacred.

Clearly, the prolife movement sees abortion as a single issue. Many prochoice groups respond in equally condensational terms. The issue is connected with people's beliefs about the value of motherhood and personhood, the importance of the family, the proper roles of women and men, the scope of state power, and the authority of God.

And that raises the intriguing dilemma of single-issue politics. How can a group that defines its sole focus, its passionate concern, in a condensational manner submit its aims to the slow, bargain and compromise workings of the American political system? How can a movement that sees abortion as the murder of human beings accept the need for working in campaigns and sitting in congressional hearings while an estimated four thousand to forty-five hundred abortions take place every day? Do prolifers in fact find a place for themselves in the activities of politics-as-usual, or, like the abolitionists fighting against slavery, do they cry out for direct action, civil disobedience, and even violence to halt the enemy's work?

The Use of Electoral Politics

Even before *Roe v. Wade* changed the political landscape, prolife groups were involved in legislative politics. Prolife organizations began forming during the late 1960s in states such as Minnesota, Ohio, Virginia, and Iowa. These groups concentrated on lobbying their state legislators to defeat bills that would have expanded the scope of legal abortions in that state. By 1970 some of these state activists had formed a loose-knit association known as the National Right to Life Committee (NRLC) for the purpose of sharing information about the legislative battles in their states and communities.

Once the Supreme Court wiped away state abortion laws with its *Roe* decision, however, the focus of activity changed. The federal government was now a major actor in the abortion issue. Without some change in the new federal policy, states would not be able to make or enforce laws that conflicted with the Court's decision permitting abortion virtually on demand. Within months, the NRLC had incorporated and developed a more formal structure. During the rest of the decade its mission involved developing educational programs and lobbying members of the U.S. House of Representatives and Senate to end federal funding of abortions, with the ultimate goal of passing a human life amendment to the Constitution to overturn *Roe v. Wade*.

Although the NRLC remained by far the largest of the national prolife organizations, it was soon joined by other groups concerned with lobbying and education on abortion—the National Committee for a Human Life Amendment (NCHLA), the American Life Lobby, March for Life, and the Christian Action Council, among others. But lobbying had its frustrations. A prolife organizer recalled,

> After a period [of time], everyone began to realize that we could educate and lobby till doomsday, but if people representing us in Congress didn't feel the same way we did, then we would never achieve a human life amendment. And that's when we began to turn to [electoral] political action.

Some state prolife groups had been active in campaigns earlier. But the first real glimmers of electoral success came in 1978. In Minnesota, which had one of the most highly developed state prolife groups, Rep. Donald Fraser, a prochoice leader favored to win the Democratic Senate nomination, was defeated in the 1978 primary. The following November the state elected two prolife senators and a prolife governor. In neighboring Iowa, the senior senator and a front-running candidate for statewide office, both prochoice Democrats, were unexpectedly defeated after a prolife group campaigned against them. Three other prochoice senators also lost their seats. It is not at all clear that the abortion issue was responsible for their defeats. But it was widely *perceived* that state prolife groups had made a difference in these races.[21]

Heartened by these apparent successes, several national prolife organizations began making plans for more extensive involvement in the 1980 elections. Some had already formed PACs—the Life Amendment PAC, National Pro-Life PAC, and Life-PAC—so they could become directly involved in and contribute to House and Senate races. In 1980 NRLC established its own PAC. And in the elections that November, the electoral efforts of the prolife movement bore some impressive fruit. Several leading Senate liberals, who had been stalwart prochoice votes and who had been targeted for defeat by national prolife PACs, lost their races in the Reagan tide; among them were George McGovern, a former Democratic presidential candidate, and Birch Bayh, who had headed the Senate subcommittee through which a human life amendment would have to pass.

The prolife movement was jubilant. It had been "victorious on all fronts," according to David O'Steen, currently executive director of the NRLC, and Darla St. Martin of Minnesota Citizens Concerned for Life:

> In the U.S. Senate, the prime target, eleven seats had switched from the pro-abortion to the pro-life column. In every one of those cases, pro-life citizens and political action committees were deeply involved in the successful efforts. In six of the races, the evidence strongly indicates that the net increment provided by pro-life political efforts was more than the margin of victory.[22]

The net prolife gain in the Senate in 1980 was nine seats, O'Steen reports, more than the margin by which Republicans gained control of the Senate for the first time since 1952. Prolifers also claimed a net increase of twenty House seats. And, of course, there was now a prolifer in the White House, with Ronald Reagan's victory over Jimmy Carter.

In the wake of these election results in 1980, it seemed that electoral action ultimately could lead to victory for the prolife cause. A major reason was that prolife citizens are more likely to be single-issue voters, to regard the abortion issue as the determining factor when they vote on candidates, than are prochoice citizens.[23] With this intense support, prolife leaders feel that in a number of states and congressional districts they can deliver an increment of 3 percent to 7 percent for antiabortion candidates.[24] Three percent may sound small, but it can be the difference between winning or losing in a close race; in fact, in 1980 eleven Senate races were won by margins of 3 percent or less, and, in both 1980 and 1984, twenty-one House seats were won by similar margins. O'Steen argued further that "in some congressional districts the prolife movement can put more volunteers out for a candidate than either party can."

But the aura of election success was soon diminished by what prolifers regard as seriously biased media accounts. In contrast to 1978, when a number of reporters drew attention to the abortion issue by featuring prolifers' campaign activities, by 1980 the movement's leaders felt that their real accomplishments were being systematically played down. Sandra Faucher, director of NRL PAC, wrote:

Not since 1974 . . . has a single issue so transformed the political landscape as did abortion in 1980. . . . But by and large, the successes of the movement, like that of Ronald Reagan, were explained away. Each candidate won, we were told, not on the strength of what he or she stood for, but on the weaknesses of their opposition. . . . The media elite, who exert such an incredible power in shaping the political conversation of this country, would not accept that the values *they* found appalling might well be the values the American people found congenial.[25]

That perception was heightened in 1982. The electoral environment was not nearly as open to prolife gains in that year as it had been in 1980. A deepening recession, undermining public support for the Republican administration, helped to improve the reelection chances of prochoice Democrats in Congress. NRLC claimed that even so, prolife forces in the Senate increased by two, although the gains made in the House in the previous election were wiped out. But media accounts portrayed the prolife movement as losing. Again in 1984, prolife leaders claimed a gain of about twelve House seats and the loss of only one seat in the Senate, but contended that reporters were ignoring their progress. O'Steen regarded this as part of a double standard in media coverage of the abortion issue:

When the movement wins big, its considerable successes are explained away, trivialized, or ignored as much as possible. Meanwhile, the failure to unseat pro-abortion senators who are virtually invulnerable is offered as proof that the movement lacks political clout. . . . Perhaps no cause in this century has been forced to win so often on the campaign battlefield with so little acknowledgment of its successes.[26]

It can be easily argued that the prolife movement's progress in elections and lobbying has been substantial. One national prolife leader points out that the number of senators willing to vote for a constitutional amendment to overturn *Roe v. Wade* had jumped from about twenty-seven in 1974-1975 to forty-nine in 1983. That remains far short of the two-thirds needed to pass such an amendment, but within reach of a simple majority to pass other bills. Since 1976 the House and Senate have annually passed various funding restrictions (called Hyde amendments after one of their original sponsors, Illinois Republican Henry J. Hyde) that limit the use of federal funds to pay for abortions. The result has been a dramatic decline in the number of federally funded abortions.

Prolifers have succeeded in cutting federal aid to American population programs overseas that perform or encourage abortions. Most states have followed Washington's lead in refusing to pay for abortions with tax money. A number of states have passed legislation requiring that when a woman who is legally underage wants an abortion, her parents must be notified before the abortion takes place. Abortion has become a major issue in presidential as well as congressional campaigns, as the extensive debate over the issue in the 1984 presidential race shows.[27] Some activists even see the influence of the prolife movement in the 1980 Supreme Court decision upholding the constitutionality of the Hyde amendments. One state prolife leader said immediately after that decision, "I don't think we would have seen that Supreme Court decision yesterday except that they know how to read the election results, too."

But the prolife movement has suffered major losses as well. The Reagan administration, while vocally supportive of the antiabortion cause, did not translate its sentiments into active lobbying in Congress on behalf of prolife bills. Sandra Day O'Connor, Reagan's appointee to the Supreme Court, was confirmed unanimously by the Senate despite intense prolife opposition, which was based on her earlier record as a state legislator. In 1983 the Supreme Court reaffirmed *Roe v. Wade* by overturning several city and state laws restricting abortions. And two weeks later, the Senate handily defeated the first prolife constitutional amendment it had ever voted on—the Hatch-Eagleton amendment, which states, "A right to abortion is not secured by the Constitution."

Nevertheless, leaders of the NRLC and the NCHLA believe that electoral action and lobbying have resulted in important steps toward the goal of protecting life before birth. Their commitment to electoral and legislative politics is a long-term one. Faucher said, "We know that this is going to be a very long range thing that we're involved in; it may be a lifetime effort. We know that the Constitution has not been amended very many times in history and that it takes years to amend it." The frustration of piecemeal change is evident, but as one national prolife leader put it, a commitment to the political process is necessary "because there's no other way to do it."

The Alternative of Direct Action

Another branch of the prolife movement sees these legislative and electoral accomplishments, while valuable, as too little, too slow, and even morally incomplete. The alternative, these prolifers feel, is nonviolent direct action—forcing abortion clinics to close or slow down, convincing doctors and other medical personnel to stop doing abortions, and persuading women entering a clinic to change their minds and continue their pregnancies. Forms of direct action were used by some prolifers even before *Roe v. Wade,* but their use has become especially widespread since the early 1980s.

Perhaps the most prominent proponent of this direct action approach is Joseph M. Scheidler, director of the Chicago-based Pro-Life Action League. To Scheidler, the abortion issue is a battle against evil, in which no good person should remain neutral:

> People are getting the message that they have to do something about injustice. And one of the greatest injustices they see, if they really look carefully, is the execution of defenseless children at the rate of 4,500 a day. That should turn any good person to a white hot rage. And compassion.

Those who believe in direct action do not deprecate more conventional political activity; they often engage in it. "We need the candidates," Scheidler said, "because we need to change the law; we need to stop the killing. But that is a long-range program, while the abortion clinics operate every day. And you can save lives today, right now, by going to the abortuaries."

Direct action in the prolife movement takes several forms. One of the more visible is "sidewalk counseling"—maintaining a prolife presence at abortion clinics and talking with the pregnant women entering them "to intercede for the baby's life . . . to stand between the killers and the victims," Scheidler wrote. "If someone came into your living room and grabbed your three-year old and rushed out of the house, threw the child into an automobile and drove off," he argued by analogy, "what would you do? Would you write a letter to the editor? Would you complain to your congressman?" No, he reasoned, you would chase the kidnapper and enter any building where the child was being held. "No one could keep you out. . . . You would try to save him. That is what we do when we go to an abortion clinic." [28]

As his words suggest, Scheidler also recommends going beyond a sidewalk vigil to actually enter abortion clinics and talk women out of having abortions. Here, "truth teams" of prolifers, claiming to be someone seeking an abortion and her companion or parent, make an appointment at a clinic. Once inside, the pair use their time in the waiting room to pretend that they are having second thoughts about their abortion. They talk out their "stress" within hearing of the clinic's real patients:

> Should we be having this abortion? Should we be here considering this at all? And you'll find people in the room there, as a rule, who are very ambivalent about the abortion. They've come this far, but they still have not set their mind in concrete about having the abortion. And these truth teams can get a discussion going. What you can do then is get up and say, "We can't go through with this. It's taking a human life; we don't know if we're able to cope with that," and walk out. And frequently, a couple, or two or three couples, will walk out with the truth team.[29]

Sit-ins also have been used to try to slow the rate at which clinics can perform abortions. Unlike sidewalk counseling, sit-ins give the prolifers a more extended time to talk with the clinic's patients. These events are also more likely to attract media coverage, which helps disseminate the activists' views about abortion. Sit-ins are especially valuable to Scheidler, moreover, because they expose the activist to the possibility of arrest.

> I think it's very important for every pro-lifer, at some time or other, to be arrested and locked up, because then you begin to realize what it's like to not have any choice over an important matter—to be helpless, to identify with the child in the womb that's being taken in to a place to be killed. When I'm sitting in a paddy wagon or a squad car, handcuffed, being taken to jail, the people who become extremely important to me are the ones who rescue me. And that's the same position as the pro-life activist: the people really important to that [unborn] child are the ones who rescue him, who go to the clinics.

Another form of direct action involves picketing the homes of physicians who perform abortions. The assumption is that these physicians are not proud of their abortion-related activities and try to hide them from neighbors and friends. The intention of the picketers is to make those activities known so that neighbors and friends might be distressed enough to pressure the physician into leaving the abortion business.

In some areas, activist groups have tried to disrupt clinic operations by persuading sanitation workers not to haul garbage from abortion clinics, informing them that the clinic's refuse contains dead bodies. Demonstrations at abortion facilities—for example, carrying a set of children's coffins draped in velvet, or a trash can filled with the broken bodies of dolls, often splotched with red paint to simulate blood—have become increasingly frequent. In 1984 more than a hundred groups committed to direct action came together to form a national Pro-life Action Network, to coordinate activities such as a national day of protest, during which prolifers planned to block the entrances of any abortion clinics that refused to close.

Some of these activities, such as blocking entrances to clinics, can be judged illegal, but Scheidler believes that they are nevertheless justified by the common law principle of the Defense of Necessity; that is, an illegal act is defensible if it must be taken to prevent a greater evil from taking place.[30] Blocking entrance to an abortion clinic, then, is defended on the ground that it saved the lives of the unborn children who would otherwise have been aborted during that time.

Other prolife writings make the point that when the law and government are committed to a policy permitting homicide, prolife citizens ought to obey the laws of God first and resist such policies, even to the extent of breaking the civil law.[31] As Scheidler put it when his group was accused of defacing abortion clinics' ads at train stations, "It is difficult to picture God punishing someone for removing an abortion ad. Jesus himself pushed over tables in the temple and drove out money changers, and Scripture does not record that He paid damages or even apologized for what he did. We should not be afraid to be led by a zeal for God's law." [32]

If abortion is so great an evil as to justify breaking the law to stop abortions, then wouldn't the destruction of abortion clinics also be justifiable? In fact, there have been a number of bombings and arson incidents at abortion facilities, more than two dozen since 1983. Most of these have been traced to individuals not connected with organized prolife activities.[33] Heads of the major prolife groups have repeatedly deplored the bombings. But some activists, while criticizing the use of violence, empathize with the feelings of those who are driven to commit it. Some compare the bombings to the violence by which abolitionists called attention to the injustice of slavery before the Civil War. While stating that he does not condone clinic bombings, Scheidler "refuses to condemn the destruction of real estate 'until the abortionists condemn the destruction of human life. I'm not going to be a hypocrite and grieve over the closing of a building which is nothing more or less than a death camp.' " [34] Perhaps the feeling is best expressed by a picketer's sign in Chicago, turning a phrase often used by prochoice advocates: "I'm personally opposed to the bombing of abortion clinics. But ... should I impose my morality on others?" [35]

Even with bombings ruled out, these activists regard nonviolent direct action as the movement's most effective tool. A day of sidewalk counseling at an abortion clinic, Scheidler said, will typically turn away one or two women from having abortions. Multiplied by the more than one thousand clinics across the nation, "even though we never come quite up to [saving] the 4500 they kill every day, that's still a significant dent in abortion." He expects that the combination of controversy and a loss of business will eventually shut the clinics down. Twenty-five clinics closed during 1984 and the first half of 1985, he stated, presumably in response to prolife activism. Calling those who shy away from direct action "wimps for life," [36] he argued, "It would in fact be criminal to remain a moderate in the face of such a crisis as abortion." [37]

Prolifers committed to the electoral process often define the situation differently. One leader explained, recalling the words of the president of England's right-to-life movement, "Trying to talk to somebody about having an abortion as they're going into a clinic makes about as much sense as trying to mop up the water of an overflowing bathtub without bothering to turn off the spigot. Trying to deal with the individuals who are having the abortions while abortions remain legal is a never-ending task that inevitably will not end abortion."

He continued:

> Illegal action is not going to change this country. It didn't change it in other areas. It was the slow process of working through the legislative system that ended slavery, that ended segregation. Yes, the situation in Selma, Alabama, [where police used brutal methods against demonstrating blacks] brought some attention to the cause, but it was by and large the legislative system and the people who worked behind the scenes who ground out the legislative changes that were enduring.

Scheidler did not agree. "No social movement in the history of this country has ever succeeded without taking to the streets," he said. In fact, he also chose the case of civil rights to prove his point, arguing that without the demonstrations led by Martin Luther King, Jr., the emancipation of blacks a century earlier would have remained a legal fiction. "It's not just changing laws; it's changing minds. It's not just telling a congressman, 'You ought to vote this way and we'll re-elect you.' It's telling a congressman, 'We're going to picket your home. We're going to stir up the whole country to dislike people who support abortion.' "

Single-issue Groups and American Politics

This chapter began by asking about the distinctiveness of single-issue politics: Do single-issue groups act differently from other types of interest groups? Does single-issue politics threaten the system by which political decisions are usually made?

At heart, the answer to both questions is yes. Many interest groups would like to take the position that the goals they seek are fundamental to the survival of American society, and, therefore, their demands must be nonnegotiable. But few groups dare to argue for such a position. Most come to accept, as a working premise, the idea that they will need to seek widely acceptable compromises to get bills passed, that they will have to give up some of what they want to get higher priority benefits. These are not the premises on which prolife groups have built their political participation. People who define their issue by saying, "the sin we are fighting is mortal and damnable in the sight of God," [38] are unlikely to be prone to compromise and accommodation. The way in which prolife citizens define the abortion issue sets them apart from other types of interest groups and gives rise to the kinds of activities, ranging from single-issue voting to direct action, that this chapter has examined. The chapter argues further that this condensational way of defining an issue is characteristic of single-issue groups generally; it is the hallmark of their political style.

But how can people who hold a condensational definition of the abortion issue, who believe that abortion is the murder of babies and that thousands of these murders are taking place every day, sustain a long-term commitment to "standard" political activities? How can they work in election after election when electoral change is slow, when the abortion clinics will continue to operate long after the polls have closed? How can they keep coming back to lobby Congress when the mores of that institution warn lobbyists to accept half a loaf or to risk getting nothing at all?

The answer, traditionally, has been that there is no alternative. To get abortions banned requires action by Congress or the Supreme Court. Congress will act, this view posits, only in response to effective lobbying or to a change in its membership produced by prolife electoral action. In the case of the Supreme Court, electoral action and lobbying must be directed at the presidency to obtain a prolife majority through appointments of new justices.

Increasingly, however, prolifers are seeking a new answer. One local right-to-life leader said, "We're not going to win our struggle by sitting behind our desks and making phone calls to Congress." [39] Those who agree are turning to protests and demonstrations, to other media-aimed activities such as mock trials of abortionists, and to sidewalk counseling of the clients of abortion clinics. Some of these forms of direct action are not very far removed from the traditional avenues of elections and lobbying. One purpose of protests and demonstrations, for example, is to attract media coverage, which in turn may convince elected officials that the issue will be important in the next election.

Other forms of direct action turn their adherents away from the electoral world altogether. In sidewalk counseling, individual prolifers try to convince individual abortion clinic patients to change their definitions of the meaning and morality of an abortion. These efforts have also taken a more institutional form: about fourteen hundred privately financed organizations, one-third of them run by the volunteer group Birthright, have been formed to counsel individuals against abortion and to offer advice and help to women with problem pregnancies.[40]

Activities such as these have political implications, of course. But at least in part, they reflect a rejection of the utility of standard political approaches and perhaps even a rejection of the idea that the dilemma of abortion has a political solution. It is a rejection born of frustration—frustration that is inevitable, given the way that prolife groups define their issue. It is a case in which a single-issue stance has led not only to the rejection of politics-as-usual, but, for some activists, to a privatization of their efforts on abortion.

Observing the annual antiabortion March for Life on the anniversary of *Roe v. Wade,* writer Michael Harrington said in 1979 that prolifers represented "one of the few genuine social movements of the 1970s." [41] In the 1980s that movement has become even more complex. Kristin Luker pointed out, "If there is one thing that the history of the abortion debate shows clearly, it is that the social meaning of abortion is not static but is continually being redefined, by individuals and by the society as a whole." [42]

Notes

1. W. Lance Bennett, *Public Opinion in American Politics* (New York: Harcourt Brace Jovanovich, 1980), 249.
2. See Edward Sapir, "Symbolism," *Encyclopedia of the Social Sciences* (New York: Macmillan, 1934), 492-495; and Murray Edelman, *The Symbolic Uses of Politics* (Urbana: University of Illinois Press, 1964), 6-7.
3. Martin P. Wattenberg, "The Decline of Political Partisanship in the United States: Negativity or Neutrality?" *American Political Science Review* 75 (December 1981): 941-950.
4. Unless otherwise noted, this and other quotations in the chapter come from telephone interviews by the author and political scientist Darrell West with state and national prolife leaders and Senate staff members. Some of the interviews were conducted with the stipulation that the interviewee would not be quoted by name.
5. McGovern Campaign Committee, Background memo, July 1980, 3.
6. See Leroy N. Rieselbach, *Congressional Reform* (Washington, D.C.: CQ Press, 1986).
7. See Michael J. Malbin, ed., *Money and Politics in the United States* (Chatham, N.J.: Chatham House, 1984).
8. Jeffrey M. Berry, *The Interest Group Society* (Boston: Little, Brown, & Co., 1984), 44.
9. See Kristin Luker, *Abortion and the Politics of Motherhood* (Berkeley: University of California Press, 1984).
10. Luker, *Abortion,* especially chap. 2.
11. Colorado's law and most of the other state reform bills were based on a sample statute drawn up by the American Law Institute in 1959, which would permit abortions when the pregnancy had resulted from rape or incest, was likely to produce serious physical or mental health damage to the mother, and when there was "substantial risk" that the baby would have grave physical or mental defects.

12. *Roe v. Wade,* 410 U.S. 113 (1973), and *Doe v. Bolton,* 410 U.S. 179 (1973). In this context, "privacy" refers to an individual's right to be free from unwarranted government intrusion. It was also the basis for earlier Court decisions overturning state laws against the sale and use of birth control devices.

13. See, for example, Richard Gregory Morgan, "*Roe v. Wade* and the Lesson of the Pre-*Roe* Case Law," in *The Law and Politics of Abortion,* ed. Carl E. Schneider and Maris A. Vinovskis (Lexington, Mass.: Lexington Books, 1980), 158-182.

14. Luker, *Abortion,* 40.

15. A prominent prolifer, Dr. Bernard N. Nathanson, confirmed that "Curiously, abortion appeared sometimes to have had a more profound effect on the people who were doing them than on those on whom they were being done." Nathanson with Richard Ostling, *Aborting America* (Toronto: Life Cycle Books, 1979), 141.

16. Luker, *Abortion,* 192.

17. Joseph M. Scheidler, "Three Days in Hell," *A.L.L. About Issues,* September 1984, 11.

18. Franky Schaeffer, "Foreword," in *Closed: 99 Ways to Stop Abortion* by Joseph M. Scheidler (Toronto: Life Cycle Books, 1985), 13.

19. Nellie Gray, head of March for Life, quoted in "Abortion Prompts Emotional Lobbying," *Congressional Quarterly Weekly Report,* Feb. 28, 1981, 384.

20. This explains why prolife groups cannot accept the argument that opposition to abortion is personal, so prolifers should not try to impose their views on others. According to one prolife writer, people who make that argument "are saying, exactly: 'I think Charles is a human being, but since you don't necessarily agree with me, I think it should be legal for you to kill Charles.' Either they are not very confident of Charles' humanity . . . or they do not believe in a rule of law." Grover Rees III, "The True Confession of One One-Issue Voter," *National Review,* May 25, 1979, 672.

21. See Marjorie Randon Hershey, *Running for Office* (Chatham, N.J.: Chatham House, 1984), chaps. 6 and 7.

22. David O'Steen and Darla St. Martin, "Single Issue Politics and the Double Standard: The Case of the Pro-Life Movement," in *To Rescue the Future,* ed. Dave Andrusko (Toronto: Life Cycle Books, 1983), 74.

23. For example, see Pamela Johnston Conover and Virginia Gray, *Feminism and the New Right* (New York: Praeger, 1983), 155-158.

24. O'Steen and St. Martin, "Single Issue Politics," 74.

25. Sandra Faucher, "The Best Kept Secret," in *To Rescue the Future,* 60.

26. O'Steen and St. Martin, "Single Issue Politics," 80, 96.

27. See, for example, Sam Roberts, "Cuomo to Challenge Archbishop Over Criticism of Abortion Stand," *New York Times,* Aug. 3, 1984, 1.

28. Scheidler, *Closed,* 19-20.

29. Scheidler, interviewed on National Public Radio's "All Things Considered," June 21, 1985.

30. Scheidler, *Closed,* 132.

31. See, for example, Randall J. Hekman, *Justice for the Unborn* (Ann Arbor, Mich.: Servant Books, 1984).

32. Scheidler, *Closed,* 305.

33. "Florida: More Abortion Bombings," *Newsweek,* Jan. 7, 1985, 17. See also Jon Nordheimer, "Bombing Case Offers a Stark Look at Abortion Conflicts," *New York Times,* Jan. 18, 1985, 7.

34. Hanke Gratteau and Linda Sarrio, "Abortion Clinics Tighten Security," *Chicago*

Tribune, Jan. 20, 1985, Sec. 2, 3.
35. Ibid., 1.
36. Jerry Adler with John McCormick, "Chicago's Unsilent Scream," *Newsweek,* Jan. 14, 1985, 25.
37. Scheidler, *Closed,* 240.
38. Ibid., 250.
39. Quoted in "America's Abortion Dilemma," by Melinda Beck et al., *Newsweek,* Jan. 14, 1985, 23.
40. Nadine Cohodas, "1,400 Private Groups Counsel Birth, Not Abortion," *Congressional Quarterly Weekly Report,* Nov. 17, 1984, 2953.
41. Quoted in "Old Labels Don't Stick to Pro-Lifers," by Colman McCarthy, *Detroit Free Press,* Jan 30, 1985, 9A.
42. Luker, *Abortion,* 239.

3. From Protest Group to Interest Group: The Making of American Agriculture Movement, Inc.

Allan J. Cigler

Increasing numbers of groups have come to grace the political landscape in recent decades. The universe of interest groups is highly unstable, however, and survival is often precarious. This is particularly true for groups that mobilize large numbers of citizens, rather than forming around narrow occupational or economic interests.

In this chapter, Allan Cigler uses incentive theory to investigate the organizational evolution of the American Agricultural Movement. The AAM was formed in 1977 as an ad hoc, system-challenging protest group. More recently it has attempted to become a permanent Washington-based lobby, complete with a political action committee. This transition has not been accomplished without disruption. The group has had to face the classic dilemma of issue-oriented, expressive groups. That is, how to retain the support of the intense, programmatic activists, who strongly value the group's protest tradition, and of those in the organization who view the group's long-term political effectiveness as tied to participation in mainstream legislative and electoral politics. The case study illustrates the pitfalls inherent in forming an interest group from a protest movement and the important impact that professional consultants may have upon an organization's evolution.

The postwar era has witnessed a proliferation of interest groups. While extensive growth has taken place in quarters not previously organized, established economic sectors such as agriculture also have contributed to the expanding group universe. The growth in the number of agriculture groups has been due largely to ever-increasing specialization, and most of the newer agriculture groups are relatively narrow in scope, representing commodity, supplier, processing, and marketing interests.

A notable exception to the narrow, specialized group trend is the American Agriculture Movement. The AAM is in the process of evolving from an ad hoc, grass-roots protest movement into an interest group, and it aspires to become the fifth general farm organization with a permanent presence in Washington.[1] Begun in 1977 as a farm strike group, in recent years the AAM has attempted to stabilize its membership and financial base, develop an organizational infrastructure, and become involved in a variety of electoral and legislative activities characteristic of "mainstream" interest groups. But the road to becoming an interest group has been filled with obstacles.[2]

An Incentive Theory of Political Group Development

The development of a political interest group can be viewed in terms of two interrelated phases. The first, mobilization, involves the identification of a problem common to a number of individuals and agreement among them of the need for collective action. Crucial to mobilization is the development of a cadre of leaders who are able to secure control over the resources necessary for collective action, to develop strategies for accomplishing collective goals, and to move the group rank-and-file to support and/or engage in actions directed toward achieving group goals.

The second phase, institutionalization and group maintenance, occurs after the group has developed an identity as a political collectivity to its adherents, its opponents, and other relevant political actors. The group becomes concerned with its permanence and turns its attention to matters such as organizational stability, leadership recruitment and continuity, the development of reliable membership and resource bases, and an enduring role in the political influence process.

"Incentive theory" provides a useful framework for studying stages of group development.[3] Incentive theory's central proposition is that individuals are rational decision makers interested in participating in those groups that offer benefits greater than the costs they incur. Three basic types of benefits are available: (1) material benefits, the tangible rewards of participation such as income or services that usually have monetary value; (2) solidary benefits, the socially derived, intangible rewards created by the act of association, such as fun, camaraderie, status, or prestige; and (3) purposive or expressive rewards, those derived from advocating a particular cause or ideological orientation.

From this perspective, the development of a political group is an exchange process involving leaders offering incentives to members in return for support. Group leaders develop a package of incentives for group involvement and offer them to potential participants with distinct wants, needs, and preferences. In the mobilization stage, leaders are able to launch their recruiting efforts when conditions or events make particularly salient the incentives they offer and when potential members have the capacity and willingness to bear costs.[4]

Group institutionalization and maintenance necessitate a different kind of test for the leadership. Because the demand for benefits and the willingness to bear costs among group populations may change in response to varying conditions and circumstances, a group's survival may depend upon the skill with which its leaders tailor and adapt group incentives to the changing context.[5]

Indeed, groups that are successful in the mobilization stage may fail to become stable, permanent political groups. This is particularly true of protest groups. Such groups most often seek to provide collective benefits—those that cannot be made available to members without also making them available to nonmembers. If a farm protest group succeeds in winning higher support prices, for example, its members receive those benefits, but so do all other farmers. Rational individuals will choose not to bear the participation costs (time, dues, etc.) because they can enjoy the group benefits without joining. While skillful group entrepreneurs often are able to mobilize people in the short run by collective material and expressive appeals (through the use of symbolism, emotionalism, and rhetoric), the "free-rider" problem is still significant. This is especially true in large groups, where an individual's contribution to group success is negligible.

For the bulk of political groups, the process of institutionalization and maintenance involves replacing incentives that fall into the category of collective benefits with those that are more selective or tangible, such as discount life insurance. Unlike collective benefits, selective benefits are provided exclusively to those who actually join the group. While collective benefits are often enhanced by special circumstances (like a period of low farm prices) the attraction of selective benefits is more constant, and provides an organization with a more stable incentive base.

Group leaders often offer selective benefits in competition with other groups and with private suppliers of tangible benefits. But adjustment in the incentive package is frequently disruptive because the leadership must cope with both internal and external threats to the group's existence. For example, because there is no completely successful incentive mix in a changing environment, group organizers and leaders may disagree among themselves as to what incentives to provide. While the leadership is often united during mobilization—because there is usually widespread agreement about collective material incentive (like higher farm prices) and expressive ones (to protect the integrity of the family farm)—any change in the incentive package is upsetting, as leaders risk losing those already satisfied. The danger is particularly acute in protest groups and social movements in which leaders may be faced with choosing among incompatible incentive packages. Leaders can satisfy the more radical expressive members who believe that to moderate demands and rely on selective benefits would compromise the group's original "protest character," or they can satisfy those in the organization who believe the group should develop incentives to broaden the financial and resource base by attracting new members.[6]

In short, the process of becoming a stable interest group is precarious and complex, involving the leadership's strategic packaging of incentives to appeal to potential group members. And often it must be done under changing contextual circumstances over which the leadership may have virtually no control.

AAM: Mobilization Stage

The rise of AAM parallels the rise of past farm movements.[7] Although today's farmers are more educated and integrated into the national community, they are still alienated from the economic and political centers of power. They view themselves as unappreciated and misundertood by commercial, labor, and consumer interests, and as vulnerable to economic conditions, government policies, financial institutions, and the vagaries of weather and competition. Thus, the possibility for frustration and anger is high, and, under unfavorable economic circumstances, farmers comprise a pool of potential radical activists. The 1970s provided just such a context, as well as the added tension of expectations suddenly raised and just as suddenly lowered.

After two decades of stability, agriculture prices fluctuated wildly in the early and mid-1970s. In 1971 the price of wheat averaged $1.74 per bushel. Foreign crop failures and declining yields increased demand for U.S. produce; wheat prices peaked at $5.52 in February 1974, due primarily to Soviet purchases of some 400 million bushels of grain.

Farmers responded to high grain prices with enthusiasm, encouraged by government actions that shifted farm policy from supply management to maximum production for export. Acreage limitations were lifted, and Secretary of Agriculture Earl Butz urged farmers to plant "fencerow-to-fencerow." Farmland prices skyrocketed, formerly idle acres were planted in grains, more young farmers entered the business, and many established farmers expanded their operations, often on credit.

Boom times were short lived, however, as world food supplies increased along with U.S. grain production. American farmers found themselves in a classic cost-price squeeze. As grain prices dropped, agricultural production costs increased substantially due to escalating interest rates and the delayed effect of the 1973 Arab oil embargo. Farm debt doubled between 1974 and 1977, and net farm income fell drastically. Among those hardest hit were farmers in the southwestern plains states who had entered the business or expanded during boom times.

Government aid was not forthcoming, as Washington turned its attention to battling escalating consumer prices. In 1975 President Gerald Ford vetoed an emergency farm aid package as too inflationary and blocked proposed exports to Poland and the USSR. The Carter administration appeared just as unresponsive, appointing a consumer advocate as assistant secretary of agriculture and opposing a version of the farm bill supported by agriculture interests. Many farmers felt the government had abandoned them.

In this context of worsening economic conditions, coupled with perceived government unresponsiveness, the American Agriculture Movement was born. Although the group gave the appearance of being a spontaneous uprising against the economic plight of farmers, "AAM's catalyst was its entrepreneurial leadership, not simply the momentum of opinion."[8] The key to understanding the rise of AAM lies in comprehending the ability of skillful organizers and spokesmen to induce broad-based participation by developing incentives to appeal to previously uninvolved farmers.

The group was the direct outgrowth of coffee shop discussions among five southeast Colorado farmers in the late summer of 1977. With a minimum of tangible resources, this small cadre of entrepreneurs was quickly able to mobilize a large number of farmers in an attempt to organize a strike to shut down farm production. The key elements were skillful use of solidary incentives in recruitment and organizational formation, along with an emotional message stressing collective and expressive goals.

The organization was constructed in pyramid fashion through an expanding number of meetings, rallies, and protests. Personal contacts to encourage the participation of friends and neighbors were crucial, and in places the group was accused of subtle and not so subtle coercion to get farmers to meetings. The rallies and meetings increased the group's resources by adding supporters, broadening the financial base, expanding media coverage, and contributing to the legitimacy of the founding Coloradans as representatives of a huge number of angry farmers.[9]

The leaders recognized quickly that they had few tangible selective benefits to offer participants and concentrated on political messages of a collective and expressive nature. The emphasis was on the need for "100 percent of parity," the importance of "protecting the family farm," and the necessity of direct protest.[10] Flamboyant orators themselves, the leadership also relied on outside speakers and organizations convinced of conspiratorial theories of money center banks, multinational firms, and world government, to "employ an ideology of anti-corporate neo-populism as the generalized myth of cheated farmers and their potential for power."[11]

The organizational set-up was grass roots in form, highly democratic, with loose central coordination. The leaders flew around the country setting up local organizations, the most active of which were then asked to create a statewide organization to coordinate local activity. An office in Springfield, Colorado, near the farms of the founders, was the base for national coordination. There were no membership arrangements in AAM, and those who came to meetings and rallies and who registered in attendance were considered "participants." The group claimed no leaders, only "spokesmen."

The group grew quickly in size and visibility. The first meeting in Colorado in September attracted forty farmers. Two weeks later, after an energetic national publicity campaign, more than two thousand farmers attended the nation's first "tractorcade," greeting Secretary of Agriculture Bob Bergland as he spoke in Pueblo, and threatening to destroy their crops and cease production if their demands were not met. Aided by media coverage of this and similar events, strike organizers from southeast Colorado, southwest Kansas, and Texas fanned out into other farming regions. By December, AAM "claimed" more than eleven hundred local chapters, forty state organizations, and the backing of large numbers of farmers, concentrated in the Great Plains and the South.[12]

Although a December 14 strike deadline passed rather quietly, AAM organizers planned a massive tractorcade to the nation's capital to coincide with the reconvening of Congress on January 18, 1978. More than three thousand farmers, many on tractors, journeyed to Washington that winter to explain their plight to representatives, bureaucrats, journalists, and anyone else who would listen. One result was that farm subsidies were raised 11 percent. But prices still fell short of parity, and farmers remained angry.

A second tractorcade in 1979 was a public relations disaster. After numerous confrontations, police confined the tractors to the Mall, where frustrated farmers caused an estimated $1.2 million in well-publicized property damage.[13] In the aftermath of this fiasco, participation in the group dropped drastically, and many strike offices and local chapters ceased to exist. But the group did not die. It changed.

AAM at the Organizational Crossroads

AAM faced substantial obstacles to its survival. In the mobilization phase it had capitalized on incentives that were either intangible or collective and whose value had been enhanced by special economic circumstances. Much of the appeal was expressive, conveyed by skillful, often inspiring speakers. The expressive appeal was enhanced by a decentralized and very personal organizational structure that fused expressive and solidary incentives. The decentralized, democratic, grass-roots style of organization itself had an almost ideological attraction—it stood in stark contrast to the "real" enemies—bureaucratic and undemocratic organizations like the Farm Bureau, the Department of Agriculture, agribusiness corporations, and, to some, the Trilateral Commission.[14]

Incentive Dilemmas

The collective material appeal of the AAM (parity and higher prices) made it highly vulnerable to the free-rider problem and exposed it additionally to the danger of being "vulnerable to both the granting of demands . . . and to the denial of them." [15] For example, when AAM aided in raising support prices in 1979, a number of moderates dropped out. With short-term goals accomplished, there was little left to bind anyone except ideologues to the group. In addition, as farm prices continued to drop, farmers in need of assistance would not have the resources necessary for group participation. The most economically vulnerable, for whom AAM was especially attractive, were leaving farming.

Incentive theory would suggest that if AAM were to survive it would have to develop a more stable incentive base. But in adjusting its incentive base, the group could be expected to face two large, interrelated problems. First, it was competing in an occupational sector already well organized, in which broad-gauged groups had well-developed, yet distinct, incentive packages (e.g., the Farm Bureau emphasizing insurance, the National Farmers

Organization with marketing experience). Moreover, sector organizations (e.g., the National Association of Wheat Growers) had a claim on the primary loyalty of many farmers interested in prices. But more important, AAM faced the classic dilemma of issue-based, expressive groups—how to retain the support of the intense, programmatic activists, while simultaneously offering membership incentives to attract and retain additional members.

Expressive organizations are prone to disputes over changes in incentive packages and organizational focus. Since AAM's mix of benefits was unique among farm groups, the large block of members could be expected to oppose a change in the types of benefits the group offered. The agrarian discontent of the 1970s was channeled into the AAM precisely because none of the established farm groups was responsive to farmers' expressive needs.

To many farmers, for example, the Farm Bureau and the Farmers Union were "just insurance companies," with little interest in representing farmers' political views. Any attempt by AAM to develop tangible selective benefits would be viewed by some participants as moving the group away from its political purpose and jeopardizing the group's responsiveness to farmers' expressive needs. But the development of selective material inducements would shift the focus of AAM recruiting appeals from controversial politics to uncontroversial services, thereby lowering AAM's high expressive costs to nonparticipants who agreed with AAM's goals, but not with its radical protest style.[16] Expressive benefits for some, in short, represent expressive costs for others. The problem of AAM leadership was to try to reconcile both elements in a new incentive mix.

The Seeds of Transition

Immediately after the 1979 tractorcade, the loosely knit leadership discussed strategy and organization. Although factionalism had been minimal in the mobilization phase due to widespread agreement concerning collective material goals and the efficacy of protest as a political tool, the tractorcade failure heightened the division between moderates and more radical elements over future strategy. Even those who believed in confrontation tactics felt that the intensity of a protest strategy could not be sustained and that organizational change was inevitable. One of the founding Coloradans remarked:

> The movement was a spontaneous reaction by farmers to a bad situation. They became directly involved in an organization which took hundreds of hours of their own time. It had to wind down from that, and it did and rather than see it die they saw a new organization grow out of it. . . . I know it won't be the same, because you won't have the same kind of personal involvement. But it couldn't have. You cannot continue intense involvement forever.[17]

The development of the "new" organization came slowly and with little planning. The group kept a low profile the year following the second tractorcade, as the leadership appeared to be evolving into two camps. One element, made up largely of southeastern Colorado and western Kansas farmers, continued to press for direct action political strategies. They represented some of the most financially troubled farmers in the AAM and had special interests in wheat prices. Many were victims of farm foreclosures in the early 1980s. The second camp, based largely in parts of Texas and Oklahoma, seemed increasingly convinced that the answer to farmers' problems lay with stepped up involvement in electoral and legislative politics. Many of the latter group had emerged during the tractorcades as AAM spokesmen in dealing with the press and elected officials. Some had been previously active in farm cooperatives, a few had had actual experience in government, and others had been involved in a variety of other farm interest groups.

The soul-searching in 1979 and early 1980 eventually led to a commitment to broaden the group's political strategy to "light the way to parity" and to "get more members." [18] Marvin Meek, AAM national chairman, conceded, "We know that there is no single answer for farmers, therefore we must attack in every direction." [19] One result was AAM's LAMP program—legislation, alcohol fuels, marketing, and politics. The program was broad enough to satisfy the moderates, while yet recognizing the potential political uses of protest. Although a recognition of the need for multiple political strategies had taken place, the harder question of how to pursue multiple strategies remained open.

For example, while the national delegate convention adopted a legislative program, lobbying efforts were ad hoc. An office in Washington remained open after the tractorcade (it had been used as a base of operation to coordinate tractorcade activities). State organizations were asked to support the effort with funds and volunteers to staff the office. Much of the testimony on Capitol Hill was done by the national chairman and others chosen by him. State delegations were invited to send members to Washington for lobbying purposes as the need arose. The Texas AAM provided most of the financial support for the national chairman's legislative efforts.

More organized were the group's efforts on behalf of alcohol fuels. Use of such fuels had the potential both to reduce the farmer's energy costs and to improve prices by absorbing surplus grain. The American Agriculture Foundation was set up as a nonprofit affiliated organization and was effective in disseminating information about alcohol products. In early February 1980, five small motorcades of alcohol-fueled vehicles left their home states for Washington, giving demonstrations along the way of how alcohol distillation works. When they reached Washington, four small stills were set up on Capitol Hill for demonstrations, an event that got relatively favorable press coverage for AAM.

Regardless of these activities, the group was still in disarray. Membership continued to decline and many state and local offices were closed. But a poll of seventy-eight congressional staffers revealed that 72 percent of those surveyed viewed the group as either "very influential" or "somewhat influential" on farm legislation. Only 23 percent saw the group as having no influence.[20] To some in AAM these results meant that efforts to strengthen the Washington operation should be given high priority.

The Growth of the National Office

In refocusing its activities in a more conventional direction, AAM faced problems similar to those faced by other social movements.[21] The kind of organizational transformation essential to create an effective lobbying and political operation posed a threat to the nonhierarchical, grass-roots organization so strongly valued by expressively oriented participants. These individuals tend to be suspicious of mainstream political activity. The willingness to pursue conventional political activity acknowledges the legitimacy of such activities and denigrates, in the eyes of some, what political scientist Theodore Lowi calls "disorderly" politics.[22] In the case of AAM, a high proportion of participants were not only distrustful of changing policy by traditional means, but also distrustful of political institutions themselves (the most radical element believing that farm prices and economic policies were set by the Trilateralists).

Another complication was that a move to sponsor effective lobbying and electoral activity would likely mean formalizing the organization, with dues, memberships, and a national governing body able to act for the group. Any movement in such a direction would threaten the autonomy of state groups as well as individuals and potentially create the feared organizational bureaucracy.

The evolution toward a more centralized, national political organization did not immediately challenge the group's decentralized structure. The lobbying effort in Washington and the increasing attention of Meek to national political activity (he was spending more time in Washington than at his Plainview, Texas, home and AAM's "official" headquarters) convinced a number of the leadership of the need for a permanent presence in Washington. In the spring of 1980 the executive committee of the national delegate body asked David Senter to become "national coordinator," a role combining chief lobbyist with responsibility to coordinate state delegate activity.

The decision was not controversial, largely because Senter had credentials that satisfied both the moderate and more radical elements of the leadership. He had an excellent grass-roots background, was an original state delegate from Texas, and had been active in a number of demonstrations and both Washington tractorcades. His mainstream credentials were impressive as well. He had been a staff member of an agriculture committee in the Texas legislature, had been involved in the legislative efforts of the dairy lobby, and was Gov. William Clements's agriculture coordinator for the State of Texas, a position that involved Washington activity.

Funding for the Washington office was to come from the interest generated by the 100% Parity Fund, made up largely of $1,000 contributions by various AAM participants. Such contributions were not the official property of AAM, and contributors had the option to request that their money be returned. State organizations were also to send money voluntarily to help run the national office. Senter was to be the AAM's only full-time paid employee.

The Washington office quickly became an important and visible element of AAM's operation. A hotline was set up to inform farmers about pending legislation of interest, and the office increasingly took on the role of a coordinating center for farmers who were forced to sell their operations by the Farmers Home Administration (FmHA). Senter spoke to state and local groups (they were asked to pay his travel expenses and provide lodging); he would also help with their recruiting efforts.

The legislative program of the group was broadened. In addition to 100 percent parity, AAM pushed for the establishment of a producers board within USDA, a tariff on all agricultural imports at 110 percent of parity, embargo protection for U.S. producers, as well as for a moratorium of federal farm loans. But the group made no real sustained effort to develop a package of selective material benefits.

There was some AAM activity during the 1980 elections, but it tended to involve individuals rather than the group. A variety of AAM members participated in the Reagan campaign. Alvin Jenkins, one of the group's founders, was a Republican party delegate and served on the agriculture platform committee. National chairman Meek was a Democratic convention delegate; he strongly opposed President Jimmy Carter and endorsed Reagan in the general election.

Grass-roots protest activity took place as well, but AAM was careful not to officially sponsor or sanction such behavior. For example, in February 1981, Wayne Cryts, a member of the AAM national delegate executive committee, attempted to remove his soybeans from a bankrupt grain elevator in Missouri in violation of a federal court order. The event and the subsequent trial and imprisonment of Cryts received much national media attention. Although AAM denied sponsorship, pictures in the newspapers and on television showed protesting farmers wearing AAM caps.

AAM was still a protest group, although it was becoming increasingly involved in mainstream political activity. In the final analysis, the series of events that moved the AAM rapidly toward mainstream political activity and a change in its incentive package was initiated by an outside force.

Enter the Political Consultant

While incentive theory posits that group success is often a function of group entrepreneurs developing successful incentive packages, in the contemporary political world it is often clever selective benefit providers selling their products to group leaders that initiate changes in a group's incentive mix. So it was in the case of the AAM.

In the summer of 1981 representatives of the Martin Haley Companies came to the national leadership of AAM with a proposal for a "comprehensive public affairs program," which was quickly embraced by chairman Meek and national coordinator Senter. Martin Haley touted itself as the "oldest, largest and most comprehensive private government relations service in the world." [23]

The firm had more than 170 clients ranging from the Associated Milk Producers to Labatts Beer and a reputation as an effective lobbyist for agriculture interests. A number of its staffers were influential on agriculture and related committees in both houses of Congress. The firm's president, Joe Johnson, had farmed in Texas, knew many of the AAM leaders there personally, and was credited with putting together the highly successful Associated Milk Producers' PAC.

The proposal was presented to the national delegate meeting in September. Believing that AAM "may well have more potential strength than any organization, dormant or active, in the United States," the consulting firm suggested that AAM must address two issues if it was serious about becoming a political force:

> The first is the lack of organization. In carefully maintaining the American Agriculture Movement as a movement, rather than an associa-tion, the American Agriculture Movement has sacrificed financial support and discipline. Membership in the Movement appears at present to be largely a state of mind. There is no number which can be stated as the American Agriculture membership. Thousands who wear the caps and believe in the goals of the American Agriculture Movement do not pay dues nor even subscribe to the newspaper. They are like professed Christians who don't belong to a church. They've got the spirit, but the spirit doesn't pay the rent. All those who support the American Agriculture Movement's goals in spirit must be convinced to support the Movement with their checks.
>
> The second point which must be addressed is the Movement's willingness and ability to employ extreme tactics. The heritage of the American Agriculture Movement is in the tractorcades, and it is a proud heritage. It should never be forgotten and should never be denied. But if the Movement is successful in achieving financial and organization support, and if a well-conceived program for achieving farm profit is developed and carried out, then there should never again be a need to have the tractors on city streets. The place for the tractors is just over the horizon, and they should remain there forever in a mythological staging ground. [24]

The firm proposed that it be hired to implement a three-stage program designed to make AAM self-sufficient. First, the company would solicit corporate sponsors for a one-time contribution to underwrite a membership drive that would make AAM financially independent. Using such funds as seed money, a second membership drive would then raise funds to operate a national office, pay Martin Haley a consulting fee, and develop a political ac-tion committee.

Second, AAM dues and memberships would be revised and formalized. Martin Haley recommended a $150 annual membership—$100 for dues and $50 for the PAC. Also to be created was a "Dollar-an-Acre Club" for farmers willing to contribute at that level, a new sustaining membership at a higher fee, and the development of a system for enhanced decision-making and policy-making roles for these members. State and local affiliates of the national AAM would have dues and membership arrangements unrelated to the new national requirements.

Third, the major political weapon for AAM would be its PAC.

> The growth of PACs raises the specter of a truly vicious money cycle, particularly with the "independent expenditure" with those unwilling to participate left outside the political pale, unable to influence legislation which can mean life or death.

> In this respect, agriculture, with the exception of the dairy coopera-tives, has been left "sucking hind teat," far behind business and labor in the political market place. And with the decline of political parties as fund-raisers or even as influence-wielders in the election process, those who wish to affect their future must accept the "new rules" of the political game and get into the ballgame.[25]

The proposal signified an abrupt shift in AAM's incentive package. Although collective material goals would remain the same (emphasizing parity), the switch to PAC strategies and to a centrally organized body would threaten the original "movement" members and their expressive and solidary benefits.

Selective material benefits were not part of the package. The feeling was that AAM simply could not compete with other groups on items like insurance, and any attempt to turn seriously to marketing strategies had to await a much larger financial base. The emphasis was to be upon political benefits and the personal satisfaction that comes with being associated with a successful political group. AAM's PAC was to be a "distinctive" benefit that would identify the group in the same way farmers associate the Farm Bureau with insurance. AAM would be the only general farm organization with a PAC.

It seemed that the group had little to lose because it was stipulated that no front money be provided for Martin Haley's fund-raising efforts (the company would collect later). The company would be limited in collecting no more than $50 for each group member. But there were some in AAM who thought they had a great deal to lose.

Coping with Internal Factionalism: Who Really Is AAM?

The proposal quickly became the basis of a major controversy within the AAM, begun initially by the forceful and rather tactless manner in which Martin Haley representatives presented their case at the September delegate meeting. One delegate ventured the opinion that AAMers wanted more protest and that farmers had to be active outside of Washington to en-hance political influence. Johnson, speaking for Martin Haley, immediately remarked,

We don't want to be part of that because it won't work. The first baseball cap that comes across the 14th St. Bridge [in Washington] that we didn't send for, we're going to hit 'em in the head wih a baseball bat.[26]

Johnson's remark drew little initial comment, but reports incensed many members who strongly valued AAM's protest tradition. The consultants felt that protest activity would create an "unsavory image" that would hurt the farmers' cause. To some AAM participants, however, Martin Haley was dictating the organization's political strategy and was insensitive to activists' priorities.

The controversy came to a head at the national grass-roots convention in January 1982 and at a national delegate meeting in early February. On both occasions, the AAM leadership and the Martin Haley representatives were grilled by delegates and participants as to the details of the company's proposal and the relationship between the two groups.

The scope of the conflict would probably have remained narrow and manageable by the leadership had it not been for the role played by the movement's "officially endorsed" newspaper. Over a period of time, the *American Agriculture News* took a position opposite to the leadership's and became the organ of factional forces opposed to moving AAM in a more mainstream direction.

The *American Agriculture News* (complete with the AAM logo as a masthead) was a privately owned and operated independent newspaper. The publishers, Alden and Micki Nellis of Irdell, Texas, originally had approached the founding AAM leaders early in 1978 about reporting the group's activities. Their offer was enthusiastically accepted by the leadership, which recognized that the group possessed few resources to communicate on its own. The *News* rapidly became the principal communication medium of the movement; reporting weekly (later biweekly) news from state organizations; printing material sent out by the leadership, including reports of various AAM committees; and presenting news of general interest to farmers and AAM participants. Presenting material in a lively manner, the *News* was widely viewed as an important element in AAM's early success.

As individuals, the publishers were strongly committed to the goals of AAM and were close friends of the founders. They not only published the *News*, but also printed the Washington newsletter that the group sent to sustaining members, as well as a variety of AAM mementos of important protest activities. Their interest in AAM was ideological as well as commercial, and the evidence suggests that publication of the *News* was done at a loss.[27]

In the controversy over the role of Martin Haley Companies, however, the publishers behaved as independent journalists. They printed detailed reports of the grass-roots and delegate meetings, including heated exchanges, directly quoting chairman Meek and representatives of the consulting firm in response to questions concerning the role of protest and the operation of the proposed PAC. But reporting tended to put both the AAM leadership and the consultants in a negative light, as responses to complex and loaded questions appeared defensive and vague. The impression was that Martin Haley was dictating political strategy to a passive AAM leadership. One Martin Haley representative observed

> What we're going to ask is that all our efforts be coordinated so we speak with a single voice. . . . We're the coach, he [Meek] is the captain, David's [Senter] the quarterback, and you guys are the team.[28]

The *News* made it clear that the PAC was to be the group's dominant political vehicle, and efforts to increase membership were to be delayed. Raising money for the new AAM-PAC took precedence. Meek strongly supported the consultants, but when it was reported that he claimed that more than 90 percent of his time was spent on PAC business, the publishers wondered aloud who then was running AAM. Meek also asserted at a delegate meeting that individuals who had not contributed to the PAC should have no say in its affairs. This raised the immediate objection that those people who have worked hard for AAM for years "not only have the right but the responsibility to see that it's used right. Just because someone hasn't been able to give $200 or $1,000 doesn't mean they shouldn't have a say." [29] While the firm claimed to have raised a substantial amount of the promised "seed money," it refused to reveal the contributors.

The controversy consumed AAM during the spring and summer of 1982. The battle was publicized on the pages of the *News,* as relations between the national leadership and the publishers and their allies became increasingly strained. The leaders felt that the "officially endorsed" group organ had an obligation to support leadership initiatives and pressured the publishers not to air "dirty laundry" and to give editorial support to AAM-PAC. The publishers argued that they were journalists first and had an obligation to air controversy and present truth as they saw it. Advertisements to raise money for AAM-PAC ran in the paper, but AAM was billed at regular rates.

The bulk of the letters printed by the paper were either pleas for reconciliation or negative toward the shift to a PAC-based political strategy. Often the grounds were moral.

> To take funds in hand and go looking around for some politicians to buy is an open confession of weakness. That very thing is what got us into this damn mess.[30]

But the main concern was with who was running the organization, AAMers or the consultants.

> Down the road a few years, I can see the Martin Haley Corporation [sic] being "the" voice of agriculture for maybe the 50,000 farmers left, and they will really be raking in the money, for right now, many good farmers are helping them get started, bleeding us of money and promising nothing in return for "possibly" 3 years. They are smart enough to know that there is a lot of money to be made off agriculture and they intend to get their share. They know we are struggling to stay alive. What does surprise me is how

gullible the people have been, willing to fall for anything. We now have a national chairman spending 90% of his time working for PAC. In the meantime, who is working for AAM? Very few of us.[31]

The paper removed the AAM logo from its masthead in April, declaring it intended to broaden its coverage of rural politics, though it would continue to cover AAM activity. AAM's national leadership removed its "official endorsement" of the paper and warned the publishers that they could no longer use the AAM logo. The operations of the national AAM (now referred to by the *News* as AAM, Inc.) were now almost totally centered in Washington (the Texas office of the national chairman was closed). A delegate meeting decided that only members who had paid dues could attend the grass-roots convention. The AAM leadership continued to expand its PAC fund-raising efforts in anticipation of the 1982 elections.

In August the *News* responded editorially to AAM, Inc., actions by charging that the movement had been taken over by twenty people. The leadership was accused of falsely reporting PAC activities, of siphoning off money from state chapters for PAC travel, and condemned for trying to control the paper. Calling itself the only "officially unendorsed newspaper," the *News* printed detailed accounts of how 100% Parity Fund money was spent by the national office (highlighting the salaries and expense accounts of the leadership).[32]

Grass-roots political activity continued independent of AAM, Inc. As farm foreclosures increased, so did local protests at sheriffs' sales. Some ex-participants became more involved in militant political activities. Keith Shive, a farmer from Holstead, Kansas, founded the Farmers Liberation Army, which threatened to destroy livestock and crops of farmers who did not support FLA goals.[33] Jerry Wright, one of the original five founders of AAM, was reported to have attended a Posse Comitatus survivalist training session.

The split between AAM, Inc., and grass-roots elements came to a head in September when the original founders from Colorado met in Dallas to resurrect the "real" AAM. On October 26 the *News,* again dressed in a masthead using the AAM logo, published a special edition announcing the revival of grass-roots AAM. It reported that Alvin Jenkins, AAM's original spokesman, would again become spokesman if elected by a ballot, which appeared in the paper. Funding to support the spokesman's efforts would come from interest generated by a new Farm Crisis Trust (similar to the 100% Parity Fund of AAM, Inc., discussed earlier). The intent was to make AAM again an organization with no leaders, dues, or members, and anyone who "supported" AAM was encouraged to vote. Jenkins was "elected" by 93 percent of the votes (the number of ballots cast was nowhere noted).[34]

There were now two AAMs: AAM, Inc., and Grass Roots AAM. Both groups were operating separately and were not in formal communication, although some individuals participated in and were active in both. But grass-roots members intended to be at AAM, Inc.'s, national convention in Nashville scheduled for early January 1983.

Could Two AAMs Coexist?

It soon became apparent that two groups sharing the same organizational logo and public identity was untenable from AAM, Inc.'s, perspective. The obvious dilemma was that the direct protest activity of Grass Roots AAM would tarnish the carefully cultivated political image that AAM, Inc., viewed as essential in its lobbying and electoral activities. In incentive theory terms, as Grass Roots AAM pursued activities that resulted in expressive benefits for its adherents, many of those oriented toward AAM, Inc., would incur expressive costs and possibly reduced political benefits, especially because the media and the public did not distinguish between the two groups.

By early 1983 a number of Grass Roots AAM activities had become embarrassing to AAM, Inc. A confrontation with authorities had turned violent at a Colorado sheriff's sale, and a number of Grass Roots AAM leaders were arrested. Two weeks later a front-page story in the *Rocky Mountain News* alleged that AAM members were boycotting local merchants and threatening utility and public employees with physical harm.[35] AAM, Inc., condemned the Colorado group and attempted to disassociate itself from any such activities.

At the national convention of AAM, Inc., a few weeks later, tension between supporters of the two groups ran high. AAM, Inc., officials, flanked by armed guards, stood at the door to enforce the $25 registration fee. Tension was eased somewhat when Grass Roots spokesman Jenkins announced that he did not desire to lead AAM, Inc., and that he was comfortable with coexistence between the groups. The key issue was whether Grass Roots AAM would be allowed to exert pressure in the country without being condemned by AAM, Inc. Coexistence was agreed upon, and the convention passed a policy statement: "Be it resolved that AAM, Inc., stands united and supports all AAM farmers and ranchers. We support the grass-roots effort in the country to build support for the solution to obtain parity."[36]

The truce had been in effect for less than a month when the *Denver Post* printed a feature story entitled "Farmers Turning Militant: Movement Teaches Combat, Bomb-Making."[37] The article detailed how AAM members were taught to make crude pipe bombs out of homemade black powder at a "community seminar" organized by AAM leaders at Campo, Colorado, home of Grass Roots AAM. The paper said the schools were taught by Eugene Schroder, one of the original AAM founders, who was pictured on the front page standing in front of a large AAM logo. The story linked the group to a variety of right-wing causes and groups such as the John Birch Society and the Ku Klux Klan and observed that material in the group's headquarters was "filled with the language of the militant right and complaints of the Rockefellers, the Trilateral Commission, the Council on Foreign Relations, the Federal Reserve System and vague conspiracies involving Jewish bankers." The story indicated that AAM was under investigation by the FBI and the Kansas Bureau of Investigation. No real effort was made to distinguish between AAM, Inc., and Grass Roots AAM.

AAM, Inc., was quick to disassociate the group from the negative publicity generated by the *Denver Post* story in a press release that emphasized the group's opposition to violence.

> The AAM does not advocate the use of violence nor unlawful acts. It has not sponsored, endorsed, encouraged, or participated in any seminars, meetings, or other activities which had as its purpose, avowed or secret, the use of violence, unlawful conduct or illegal acts. No officers or other person authorized to speak on behalf of AAM has engaged in or been associated with such activity.[38]

Clearly, any coexistence with Grass Roots AAM was now impossible.

AAM, Inc., Since the Split

The experience with Grass Roots AAM in late 1982 and early 1983 convinced AAM, Inc.'s, leadership that the militants represented only a small element of potential supporters and the factional problems should be left behind.[39] The difficulty they faced was in attempting to build a new organization in the midst of the worst farm depression since the 1930s.

Formalizing the Organization

Late in the spring of 1983 AAM, Inc., moved to create an organization that could control disruptive grass-roots elements. A new set of bylaws effectively centralized decision making in the hands of the national delegate body and the national officers.

Membership in AAM, Inc., was to be strictly on an individual basis. Voting members were to pay $50 a year to the national office. State AAMs could affiliate with AAM, Inc., but the constitution stated that "the National Delegate Body may terminate affiliation of any organization at any time and for any reason it shall deem sufficient by two-thirds majority." [40] Further, the executive committee of the delegate body was empowered to act for the whole delegate body, and the annual grass-roots convention was limited to making "advisory" recommendations to the delegates. The elected "president" would appoint all committees except the executive committee (composed of the five elected officers and six members selected by the delegate body). Clearly, AAM, Inc., had made the transition from a nonhierarchical grass-roots movement to an organization with strong internal control at the top.

Adjusting Incentives and Activities

By the summer of 1983 it was difficult to estimate the participant base of AAM, Inc. The group claimed to "represent" 150,000 farmers and to have organizations in thirty states, but representatives from fewer than ten states appeared at the quarterly delegate meetings.

AAM leaders initially hoped that members would be attracted by the group's distinctive political benefit—a PAC that was the largest of any general farm group. Indeed, in 1982 AAM-PAC had assets of more than $220,000 and donated up to $1,000 to ninety-five Democrats and twenty-five Republicans for national office, second only to the dairy lobby among all farm groups. However, AAM-PAC raised less than $21,000 in 1983-1984. The reduction probably stemmed from the factional battle, the impatience of many members with the lack of immediate political results, and the general decline of member incomes. AAM-PAC remains part of AAM's political strategy, and member contributions are slowly increasing. Ties with Martin Haley Companies were severed after the death of the firm's president in 1983, and AAM-PAC is run internally.

Group leaders also have attempted to attract farmers by adjusting the incentive package in another way—by reducing the solidary and expressive costs of AAM participation. Because the group's "radical" image was a barrier both to recruitment and policy effectiveness, a strategy was devised that takes advantage of the group's expressive attractiveness (in terms of the content of goals) without alienating both farmers and decision makers offended by confrontation tactics. Recognizing the AAM protest tradition as its most distinctive characteristic, leaders have attempted to draw upon the tradition in a carefully controlled and symbolic manner.

For example, tractorcades appeared at the Democratic agriculture platform meetings in Springfield, Illinois, in 1984 and at the Republican and Democratic national conventions. But only five tractors, symbolizing the five original AAM states, took part in the "demonstrations," and great effort was made not to antagonize law-enforcement authorities and to give the impression that farmers were law-abiding citizens.

The increasing plight of family farmers in early 1985 caused an increase in AAM protest activity and a revision of the low profile strategy it had followed since the factional split. Led by Cryts, an officer in AAM, Inc., and president of the Missouri chapter, activists organized rallies in the Midwest, the most noteworthy at the Chicago Board of Trade to protest manipulation of grain prices. In March the group organized a "March on Washington," bringing together more than one thousand farmers to call attention to the farm problem. Most of their time was spent not marching, but lobbying representatives on the farm credit issue.

Such activities, while calling attention to the farm problem, did little to strengthen AAM membership. The financial problems of farmers and the emphasis on cooperation among all farm groups have constrained attempts to recruit members. But AAM has earned the goodwill of many in the farm crisis organizations that have arisen in the Midwest for its activities in behalf of farmers and its willingness to advise and counsel the newer groups, factors that may eventually help AAM membership rolls.

The group currently has more than two thousand members located in thirty-one states, but concentrated in the Midwest, especially in Missouri, Illinois, and Arkansas. Most live on the land they farm, and produce cash crops, particularly wheat, soybeans, corn, rice, and milo.[41]

As of 1986, major membership efforts are on hold. The AAM consensus is that, if the group can demonstrate its political effectiveness in Washington, long-term membership concerns will be solved.

AAM in the Legislative Process

AAM's original rhetoric abounded with reference to saving the family farm, fighting conspiratorial forces in the market, and reversing the moral and economic decay of the nation. Current AAMers still hold strongly to such views, and the major attraction of the group still revolves around expressive and collective material goals. The group appears to be quite successful in designing a parity-based farm program consistent with its ideology.

At the same time, group leaders have actively pursued coalition strategies with a variety of other farm groups (especially the National Farmers Organization and the various farm crisis groups).[42] But their limited resources (only one paid lobbyist, who coordinates the efforts of an irregular number of volunteers) have forced the group to work closely with a small number of key legislators on the House and Senate agriculture committees, rather than become involved in converting large numbers of legislators.[43] The group has routinized the process of getting ideas before the legislature, an important component of the institutionalization and maintenance phase of group development.

Overall, AAM's legislative proposals are still regarded as radical by the majority of the two agriculture committees. According to one committee member, highly sympathetic to AAM goals, part of the problem is the group's insistence on emphasizing the parity concept, which is viewed as "archaic, inflationary, and detrimental to the competitive position" of the United States in the world grain markets.

AAM officials are aware of the criticism, but are convinced that the real problem is the legislators' inabilities to understand the concept. Both leaders and support staff in the national office complain that a high proportion of their media time, for example, is spent trying to explain the concept of parity.

The group appears to be in the process of reconciling its ideology with political reality, and recent public statements that mention parity define the term in a manner that seems noncontroversial and understandable ("the cost of production plus a reasonable return on investment"). In practice, according to the national director, AAM "is willing to support anything that will in some way raise farm prices." But the term *parity* is so central to the group's ideology and collective material aims that it will likely remain a cornerstone of its rhetoric in spite of the negative reaction it causes in others.

According to one congressional staff member, AAM has proven to be "highly effective in getting ideas on the policy agenda. But it has yet to prove it can get them adopted." It was very active in the 1985 Farm Bill deliberations, and has carved out a "niche" as the representative of family farmers, particularly those in credit difficulty.

Organizational Resources: Leadership

The central moving force in the organization is the national director, David Senter. The voluntary character of AAM participation has contributed to the emergence of a distinct pattern of leadership. Senter has come to rely on certain individuals for help, and a cadre has emerged composed of existing officers, an ex-president, and key elected delegates from a number of state organizations.

If Senter is the group's organizational task leader, Wayne Cryts is the group's emotional and rhetorical leader. He is a national officer and president of the large Missouri chapter. Within many midwestern farm circles Cryts is a folk hero because of his run-in with the law. He is in great demand as a speaker at farm rallies and by the media as a spokesman for the American farmer.[44]

A common view among AAMers is, "I don't know what would happen to this organization if something happened to David or Wayne." Such views are probably well founded because AAM has found it difficult to recruit or develop new leaders in the middle of the farm crisis. For the current leadership, solidary benefits and the sense of mission are crucial, and most have been involved in AAM since its inception.

In a sense, AAM shares a problem common to expressive, voluntary groups—reliance on leaders they know and trust with little effort to involve others. It is not that others would not be welcome, but the economic crisis atmosphere that pervades the group appears to mitigate against any long-range thinking about future leadership needs.

Organizational Resources: Money

Operating an interest group in Washington obviously takes money, even for an organization heavily dependent upon volunteers. AAM, Inc., has an annual budget of less than $350,000, and operating funds come from dues, interest, income from the sale of AAM memorabilia, and contributions from interested individuals and corporations.

The volunteers and sometimes even the national president pay their own expenses while operating as AAM representatives. State organizations help their national delegates, and group officials who travel around the country on business usually receive food and lodging from sympathetic farmers and help with other expenses (often involving passing the hat at a picnic or a rally). Some leaders, including Cryts and Senter, have lost their farming operations.

Group leaders, aware of the narrow and precarious funding base, have sought to develop a stable source of funding separate from membership dues. A promising venture is a financial rebate relationship with American Hybrids, marketers of hybrid corn, grain sorghum, and forage sorghum seeds. AAM members currently are serving as regional sales managers, district sales managers, and dealers in twenty-three states, and the group receives a small commission on every bag of grain sold. Officials are optimistic that the program will raise at least $150,000 for the AAM national office in 1986. The group also is in the process of developing a health and life insurance policy program with Peoples Life of Texas that would rebate to AAM a portion of the monthly premium for all policies sold to members.

Conclusion: Will AAM Survive?

From an incentive theory perspective, AAM's prospects for becoming a permanent interest group representing family farmers may not appear promising. The group still relies on expressive and collective material benefits to attract members, and it has not developed the selective benefits incentive theorists believe essential to overcome the free-rider problem. Moreover, the group's difficulty in developing an image as a mainstream group has posed problems both for membership expansion and public policy success. However unfairly, AAM still is viewed as a radical group by many policy makers, the media, and some farmers, but not radical enough by many farmers upset with the economy. In short, expressive costs are too great for some, but expressive benefits are no longer great enough for others.[45] If the farm crisis continues to worsen, both the group's credibility as an effective political force and its natural constituency will decline as well. Much of the group's future is dependent upon forces it cannot control.

While AAM's eventual success as a general membership farm organization is in doubt, the AAM may well survive as a staff organization representing family farmers. Indeed, it is already such an organization, with its narrow funding base and its cadre of policy makers. The annual meeting has become more a reunion than a policy-making body. Nevertheless, the group gradually has developed a stronger financial base, and soon it may not depend on membership dues.

The group has other strengths as well. Large numbers of dedicated individuals do not want to see AAM join the long list of abandoned farm groups. The core leadership is able and experienced. In spite of limited financial resources, the group is effective in using the free media to publicize and dramatize the plight of the farmer and in refining the grass-roots lobbying technique.

Few in Washington thought the AAM would survive after the 1979 tractorcade debacle, and fewer still thought the group could overcome the factional disputes of the early 1980s. But as a congressional aide noted in the spring of 1985, "As long as there is a farm problem there is room for AAM." On these terms, AAM may be here for a long time.

Notes

Special thanks to John Mark Hansen for his contributions throughout this project. The research was partially funded by a grant from the General Research Fund of the University of Kansas.

1. The American Farm Bureau Federation, the National Farmers Union, the National Farmers Organization (NFO), and the National Grange are considered the "big four" farm membership groups.
2. The material presented in this chapter represents some of the findings of a long-term project dealing with the evolution of AAM. Included is material gathered from personal and telephone interviews with group officials and other members, members of Congress and their staffs who deal extensively with AAM, as well as former members and opponents of the group. Interviewees, with few exceptions, were promised anonymity. The interviews were conducted by the author at various times between the spring of 1983 and the spring of 1986.

   The initial phase of the project, focusing on AAM's mobilization, was a collaborative effort with John Mark Hansen. See Allan J. Cigler and John Mark Hansen, "Group Formation through Protest: The American Agriculture Movement," in *Interest Group Politics*, 1st ed., ed. Allan J. Cigler and Burdett A. Loomis (Washington, D.C.: CQ Press, 1983), 84-109.
3. Major incentive theory works include the following: Mancur Olson, *The Logic of Collective Action* (Cambridge, Mass.: Harvard University Press, 1971); Peter Clark and James Q. Wilson, "Incentive Systems: A Theory of Organizations," *Administrative Science Quarterly* 6 (September 1961): 126-166; James Q. Wilson, *Political Organizations* (New York: Basic Books, 1973); Terry Moe, *The Organization of Interests* (Chicago: University of Chicago Press, 1980); Moe, "A Calculus of Group Membership," *American Journal of Political Science* 24 (November 1980): 593-623; and Robert Salisbury, "An Exchange Theory of Interest Groups," *Midwest Journal of Political Science* 13 (February 1969): 1-32.
4. Salisbury, "An Exchange Theory of Interest Groups."
5. See, for example, John Mark Hansen, "The Political Economy of Group Membership," *American Political Science Review* 79 (March 1985): 79-96.
6. External threats to a group may exist as well. See, for example, Gary T. Marx, "External Efforts to Damage or Facilitate Social Movements: Some Patterns, Explanations, Outcomes, and Complications," in *Social Movements: Development, Participation, and Dynamics*, ed. James L. Wood and Maurice Jackson (Belmont, Calif.: Wadsworth, 1982), 181-200.
7. AAM's early development drew the attention of a number of researchers. An insider's perspective is found in Gerald McCathern, *From the White House to the Hoosegow* (Canyon, Texas: Staked Plains Press, 1978); and McCathern, *Gentle Rebels*, (Hereford, Texas: Food for Thought Publications, 1982). Academic studies focusing upon the context within which the group arose and the nature of group leaders and supporters include: Cigler and Hansen, "Group Formation through Protest"; William P. Browne, "Mobilizing and Activating Group Demands: The American Agriculture Movement," *Social Science Quarterly* 64 (March 1983): 19-35; William P. Browne and John Dinse, "The Emergence of the American Agriculture Movement, 1977-1979," *Great Plains Quarterly* 5 (Fall 1985): 221-236; and Aruna Nayyar Michie and Craig Jagger, *Why Farmers Protest* (Monograph, Kansas State University Agricultural Experiment Station, 1980).
8. Browne, "Mobilizing and Activating Group Demands," 15.
9. Ibid., 16
10. Parity is an Agriculture Department index of the purchasing power of one unit of a farm commodity, originally based on 1910-1914 prices, but now on a ten-year average. When commodity prices are at full parity, a bushel of grain will buy the

same quantity of nonfarm products as it did in the base period. In September 1977, when AAM was founded, the parity prices for wheat and corn were $5.04 and $3.45 per bushel, respectively. The market prices were $2.16 and $1.60. In February 1986 the parity prices for wheat and corn were $6.83 and $4.98, while the market prices were $3.07 and $2.29.

11. Browne, "Mobilizing and Activating Group Demands," 16.

12. There is really no way to ascertain how many farmers were involved in AAM's early activity. *Doane's Agriculture Report,* December 1977, 4, reported a survey-based "estimate" that 9 percent of the nation's farmers were AAM participants. A study completed in western Kansas (an area of high AAM sympathy) reported that 18 percent of respondents considered themselves participants in the movement. See Cigler and Hansen, "Group Formation through Protest," 90-102.

13. AAM officials and participants believed that reported damage was greatly exaggerated by the press and the Department of Interior to discredit the efforts of farmers. See, McCathern, *Gentle Rebels,* 415-431.

14. Because many important industry, financial, government, and media leaders are members, the Trilateral Commission, the Council on Foreign Relations, and the Council on Economic Development are said to control government policy by monopolizing economic and political resources. According to J. C. Lewis, a prominent speaker at early AAM rallies, these groups, dominated by the Rockefeller family, are "scheming to submerge the United States politically and economically into a one-world socialistic government."

15. Wilson, *Political Organizations,* 295.

16. For more conservative farmers, solidary costs for AAM involvement were closely tied to expressive costs. Many felt "unease" around AAM participants, felt that involvement in the group would compromise their independence, and felt discomfort in associating with a group involved in picketing and protest. See Cigler and Hansen, "Group Formation through Protest," 100-101, 108.

17. "After Mushrooming, Farm Movement Slowing a Bit," *Topeka Capital,* July 2, 1979.

18. Reported quotes of Marvin Meek, AAM national chairman, at the July 16, 1980, national delegate meeting held in St. Louis.

19. Ibid.

20. Marcia Zarley, "Washington Report," *Successful Farming* 11, October 1979, 4, 10.

21. See, for example, Anne N. Costain, "Representing Women: The Transition from Social Movement to Interest Group," *Western Political Quarterly* 34 (March 1981): 100-113.

22. Theodore Lowi, *The Politics of Disorder* (New York: W. W. Norton, 1971).

23. "A Comprehensive Public Affairs Program for the American Agriculture Movement," Martin Haley Companies mimeograph, Sept. 8, 1981.

24. Ibid.

25. Ibid.

26. Ibid.

27. The publishers repeatedly claimed that they needed six thousand subscriptions to break even. Their figures indicated that during only two of the five years the paper was published did they have more than six thousand subscribers. When the paper ceased publication in December 1983, subscribers numbered less than three thousand.

28. Alden Nellis and Micki Nellis, "Complete Report of the Delegate Meeting,"

American Agriculture News, Feb. 16, 1982.

29. Ibid.
30. Letter to the Editor, *American Agriculture News,* March 9, 1982.
31. Ibid.
32. Alden Nellis and Micki Nellis, "How the Parity Fund Money Is Spent," *American Agriculture News,* Aug. 10, 1982.
33. Alden Nellis and Micki Nellis, "Farmers Liberation Army Emerges," *American Agriculture News,* Aug. 24, 1982.
34. Alden Nellis and Micki Nellis, "Alvin Jenkins Elected Grass Roots Spokesman by Overwhelming 93%," *American Agriculture News,* Nov. 30, 1983.
35. Deborah Frazier, "Springfield Bullied by AAM Radicals," *Rocky Mountain News,* Jan. 16, 1983.
36. Alden Nellis and Micki Nellis, "AAM Inc. and Grass Roots Agree to Co-Exist," *American Agriculture News,* Jan. 25, 1983.
37. William R. Ritz, "Farmers Turning Militant: Movement Teaches Combat, Bomb-Making," *Denver Post,* Feb. 13, 1983.
38. Mimeographed press release from AAM Inc., Feb. 16, 1983.
39. Grass Roots AAM, as an official entity, seemed to collapse when the *American Agriculture News* ceased publication in December 1983. However, certain remnants of the organization still exist in parts of the Midwest, and very active Grass Roots AAM groups are in operation in Missouri and Kansas. Not surprisingly, the public and the media still confuse the two groups, and the existence of Grass Roots AAM interferes with AAM, Inc.'s desired image.
40. AAM, Inc., Constitution, Article IV, Section 3.
41. AAM does not disclose its membership, but it can be estimated from a variety of sources, especially circulation figures from AAM publications. AAM activities, including rallies and marches, often attract many nonmembers.
42. Occasionally the group cooperates with nonfarm groups when farming interests are affected. For example, the group worked closely with environmental groups and the railroads in 1983 to defeat the Coal Slurry Pipeline Bill, which was seen by farmers as potentially increasing grain hauling costs.
43. The group works especially closely with a number of farm state representatives and senators including Sen. Tom Harkin, D-Iowa; Sen. John Melcher, D-Mont.; Rep. Glenn English, D-Okla.; and Rep. Berkley Bedell, D-Iowa.
44. In the spring of 1986 Cryts became a candidate for the Democratic nomination for Congress from Missouri's Eighth Congressional District. The district is in the rural bootheel region of Missouri, where both farming and mining are the major industries. William Emerson, the three-term incumbent Republican representative from the district, is a member of the House Agriculture Committee and has the strong support of the Missouri Farm Bureau Federation.
45. "Image" may still be the biggest problem for AAM. An especially troubling aspect is the bad publicity generated by some of the new radical farm and rural rightist groups that seem to be arising to appeal to alienated farmers. For example, on Aug. 15, 1985, the television show "20/20" aired a special about how anti-Semitic Christian identity groups were gaining strength in the Farm Belt. Many of the farmers interviewed on the show prominently displayed the AAM cap, and the link between AAM and the extremists groups seemed a reasonable inference for the viewer. But those interviewed were not connected to AAM, Inc., and the group was embarrassed by the telecast. AAM, Inc., received an apology from the network, but the damage had been done.

4.   PACs and Congressional Elections in the 1980s

M. Margaret Conway

Observers of politics would be hard pressed to name a feature of interest group and electoral politics over the past decade that has attracted more attention and aroused more emotion than campaign spending by political action committees (PACs). The growth of PACs in numbers (from 608 in 1974 to more than 4,000 in 1984) and in total spending (more than $100 million in direct candidate contributions in 1984) clearly represents a major force in American politics, with the potential to affect both electoral outcomes and public policy. Defenders of PACs see them as offering legitimate opportunities for representation and actually leading to greater citizen participation. Critics see these organizations as contributing to both the overrepresentation of business interests and the fragmentation of American politics by encouraging groups that focus on narrow issues.

In this chapter, Margaret Conway surveys the rise of PACs as potent political forces and assesses their impact upon electoral and legislative politics. The arguments of PAC defenders and detractors are outlined, and a number of recent proposals directed at "reforming the reforms" are examined. Conway suggests that most of the PAC reform proposals would have unintended consequences and would result in the channeling of PAC funds into politics in other ways.

The changing role of interest groups in American politics is reflected in the growth and influence of political action committees (PACs) in campaigns for national office. The number of PACs increased 560 percent between 1974 and 1984, and they have become a significant factor in financing campaigns for the U.S. House of Representatives and Senate. This chapter examines PACs, focusing particularly on the part they play in congressional elections and lobbying.

Political action committees operating at the federal level can be divided into two types: affiliated and independent. An affiliated PAC is created by an already existing labor union, corporation, or other type of organization as a separate, segregated fund to collect and spend money. Money is given voluntarily to the fund by individuals associated with the group to be used for political purposes. The second kind of political action committee is officially independent of any existing organization. These unaffiliated or nonconnected PACs usually focus on a specific issue or advocate a particular ideology.

Federal Law and the Growing Number of PACs

The principal federal laws governing the operation of political action committees are the Federal Election Campaign Act (FECA) of 1971 and the amendments to it enacted in 1974, 1976, and 1979, and the Revenue Act of 1971.[1] PACs are also guided by regulations issued by the Federal Election Commission (FEC) and its advisory opinions. In addition, several court decisions brought about significant changes in campaign finance practices.

Individuals and most organizations are limited by these laws in the amount of money they can contribute to political campaigns in any one year. The currently accepted limits are $1,000 per election to a candidate for federal office, $20,000 per year to national political party committees, and $5,000 to another political committee. No individual or organization may contribute more than $25,000 directly to candidates for federal election in any one year. Federal campaign finance laws give a distinct advantage to multicandidate PACs—those contributing to five or more candidates for federal office—whether they are affiliated or independent. A multicandidate committee may contribute as much money as it is able to raise but still is restricted to giving no more than $5,000 directly per candidate in each election. There is no limit on the total amount a PAC may spend on behalf of a candidate as long as the PAC does not coordinate its activities in any way with the candidate, his or her representatives, or the campaign committee. Because they can funnel enormous sums of money to political campaigns, PACs have grown in influence and number since the laws favoring them were passed.

The Federal Election Campaign Act, enacted in 1971, authorized the creation of separate, segregated funds by labor unions, corporations, and other organizations; these funds would be collected through voluntary contributions by members, employees, or stockholders and used for political activities. Neither corporations nor labor unions may make direct campaign contributions from their treasuries. Treasury funds may be spent for communications to persons associated with the corporation or labor union and to members of their families. Corporation or union treasury funds also may be spent for voter registration and mobilization and to establish a political action committee, administer it, and solicit funds for it.

The 1974 amendments to the FECA permitted government contractors to establish political action committees, which greatly expanded the universe of businesses and unions eligible to establish PACs. In April 1975 the FEC approved the Sun Oil Company's proposal to create a political action committee (SunPAC) and to use corporate funds to administer the PAC and to solicit contributions from employees and stockholders. The FEC opinion also legitimized the use of payroll deduction plans as a means of raising funds.

Thus, the FEC decision on SunPAC provided the basis for the extensive growth in the number of corporate PACs.[2]

Another major factor in stimulating the creation of PACs was the *Buckley v. Valeo* decision by the Supreme Court in January 1976.[3] Among other things, this decision indicated that the 1974 FECA amendments did not limit the number of local or regional PACs that unions or corporate divisions and subsidiaries could establish. Moreover, *Buckley v. Valeo* clarified the right of PACs to make independent expenditures (those not authorized by nor coordinated with a candidate's campaign) on behalf of a candidate. In 1976 further amendments to the FECA restricted corporate and labor union political action committee donations (regardless of the number of PACs created by a corporation's divisions or subsidiaries or a union's locals) to one $5,000 contribution per candidate in each election.

Obviously, the process of clarifying what is permissible in campaign finance continues. But we can examine the impact of these laws, regulations, and court decisions on the growth in numbers of PACs and their effect on congressional elections.

Political action committees have existed for years, but their number and impact were limited, and, prior to 1974, they were used more often by organized labor than by business interests. Between the end of 1974 and the end of 1984, the number of labor PACs increased by 95 percent, and trade association PACs increased by 120 percent. But the number of corporate PACs increased by an astonishing 1,780 percent. Thus, the first notable effect of the SunPAC decision has been the creation of many more corporate political action committees, as indicated in Table 4-1. Although the number of PACs has increased significantly, many might not be considered major figures in campaign finance. During the 1983-1984 campaign cycle, only 488 raised more than $100,000, and only 249 contributed more than $100,000.

After further refinements in the laws, other types of PACs were created. Of these, the independent or nonconnected PACs have become more prominent, growing from 110 in December 1977 to 1,053 in December 1984.

Political action committees can have enormous power, affecting both electoral outcomes and public policy. Because PACs have become a major source of campaign funds for congressional candidates, inability to win PAC support may mean a candidate cannot afford to mount an adequate campaign. If elected, the successful candidate will be reminded by lobbyists from the interest groups sponsoring the PACs of the financial assistance provided in the past. Implied is the potential threat that senators and representatives who do not support the legislative action desired by the interest groups will be unlikely to receive support from their PACs in the future.

Because independent PACs operate outside the official campaigns and can spend unlimited amounts for or against candidates, their participation is sometimes unwelcome, even by the candidate the PACs favor. In the 1982 congressional elections, a backlash developed in a few states (Iowa, Utah, and Vermont) where the PAC-backed candidates did not want the PAC to campaign for them. The candidates believed that identification with a single

Table 4-1 The Increasing Number of Political Action Committees

PAC Type	12/74	11/75[a]	5/76[b]	12/76	12/77	12/78	12/79	12/80	12/81	12/82	12/83	12/84	12/85
Corporate	89	139	294	433	550	784	949	1,204	1,327	1,469	1,538	1,682	1,710
Labor	201	226	246	224	234	217	240	297	318	380	378	394	388
Trade/Membership/ Health	318	357	452	489	438	451	512	574	608	651	645	698	695
Nonconnected	—	—	—	—	110	165	250	378	539	723	793	1,053	1,003
Cooperative	—	—	—	—	8	12	17	42	41	47	51	52	54
Corporation w/o stock	—	—	—	—	20	24	32	56	68	103	122	130	142
Total	608	722	992	1,146	1,360	1,653	2,000	2,551	2,901	3,371	3,525	4,009	3,992

[a] On Nov. 24, 1975, the Federal Election Commission issued Advisory Opinion 1975-23, "SunPAC."
[b] On May 11, 1976, the president signed the Federal Election Campaign Act Amendments of 1976, P.L. 94-283.

Source: Federal Election Commission press releases, Jan. 17, 1982, Aug. 19, 1985, and Jan. 20, 1986.

issue or with the particular PAC would do them more harm than good.

The Role of PACs in Campaign Finance

PAC receipts, expenditures, and contributions to congressional candidates have increased significantly since the early 1970s. Receipts grew from $19.2 million in 1972 to $287.8 million in 1984. PAC expenditures increased from $19 million in 1972 to $265 million in 1984.[4] Contributions from PACs to congressional candidates increased from $8.5 million for the 1972 elections to $112.6 million for the 1984 elections. PAC contributions accounted for 26 percent of all funds *raised* by all candidates for Congress for the 1983-1984 campaign cycle, compared with 17 percent of all funds raised during the 1977-1978 campaign. In 1984 PAC funds represented 18.8 percent of contributions received by Senate candidates, but 36.5 percent of campaign funds given to House candidates (Table 4-2). PAC contributions equalled 28 percent of all funds *spent* by congressional candidates in 1983-1984.[5]

Total spending in contests for the Senate increased by 23 percent in 1983-1984, with Senate candidates spending $97.5 million, compared with $68.2 million in 1981-1982. Candidates for the House of Representatives spent $126.5 million in 1983-1984, compared with $114.7 million in 1981-1982.[6] There are several reasons for the smaller increase in spending for House campaigns. One is the smaller number of open seats contested in 1984 as compared with 1982; more money usually is spent in contests where no incumbent is seeking reelection. More incumbents were seeking reelection in 1984 than in the two previous elections, and a higher percentage of incumbents were involved in contests that proved to be "safe" (the winner received 60 percent or more of the vote). Incumbents running in safe seats spend less money, on average, than incumbents who are facing a stronger challenge.[7]

Since 1974 approximately 65 percent of PAC contributions to congressional candidates has gone to candidates for the House. Senate campaigns usually are much more expensive than House contests, and the $5,000 restriction limits the impact of the contribution. Moreover there are a finite number of PACs strongly interested in any one contest; concern varies with the committee assignments of the members, their voting records, and the nature of the states or districts they represent. Affiliated PACs tend to be associated with a particular business, industry, or other economic or social entity and focus on contests in states where the sponsoring interest group is particularly strong, although there are exceptions to this. Last, several wealthy senators have played a major role in funding their own campaigns. But independent PACs, with their ideological interests, do play a role in senatorial campaigns.

The limited role of political parties in funding congressional campaigns is significant; political parties ranked last as a source of direct contributions to congressional candidates, and their relative proportion declined to its lowest level in 1984. The data in Table 4-3, however, understate the role of political parties because the data do not include expenditures by national political

Table 4-2 PAC Receipts and Amounts Contributed to Congressional Candidates, 1972-1984 (in millions of dollars)

PAC Type	1972 Receipts	1972 Contributions	1974 Receipts	1974 Contributions	1976 Receipts	1976 Contributions	1978 Receipts	1978 Contributions	1980 Receipts	1980 Contributions	1982 Receipts	1982 Contributions	1984[a] Receipts	1984[a] Contributions
Corporate	—	—	—	—	5.8	—	15.2	9.8	33.9	19.2	47.1	27.5	66.1	32.8
Labor	8.5	3.6	11.0	6.3	17.5	8.2	18.6	10.3	25.6	13.2	37.5	20.3	51.2	26.2
Trade/Membership/ Health	—	—	—	—	—	—	23.8	11.3	33.9	15.8	43.3	21.9	59.1	23.2
Nonconnected	2.6	—	.8	.7	—	1.5	17.4	2.8	40.1	4.9	64.7	10.7	102.2	15.3
Business-related	8.0	2.7	8.1	4.4	—	10.0	—	—	—	—	—	—	—	—
Other	—	2.2	1.1	1.0	29.6	2.8	2.4	1.0	4.1	2.0	6.8	3.2	9.2	4.1
Total[b]	19.2	8.5	20.9	12.5	52.9	22.6	77.4	35.2	137.7	55.1	199.4	83.6	287.8	112.6

[a] 1984 receipts not adjusted for transfers between committees.
[b] May not add up because of rounding.

Source: 1972, 1974, 1976, and 1978 data: Joseph E. Cantor, *Political Action Committees: Their Evolution and Growth and Their Implications for the Political System* (Washington, D.C.: Congressional Research Service, Nov. 6, 1981). 1980 data: Federal Election Commission press release (Washington, D.C.: FEC, Feb. 21, 1981); 1982 data: Federal Election Commission press release, Nov. 29, 1983; 1984 data: Federal Election Commission press release, May 19, 1985.

Table 4-3 Sources of Funds for House and Senate Candidates in General Elections, 1972-1984

	House Source					Senate Source				
	Candidate Receipts (millions of dollars)	PACs	Indivi-duals	Parties	Candidates	Candidate Receipts (millions of dollars)	PACs	Indivi-duals	Parties	Candidates
1972	$ 38.9	14.0%	59.0%	17.0%	—	$ 23.3	11.9%	67.0%	14.0%	.4%
1974	45.7	17.1	73.0	4.0	6.0%	28.2	11.0	76.0	6.0	1.0
1976	65.7	22.4	57.0	8.0	9.0	39.1	14.8	68.0	4.0	12.0
1978	92.2	24.8	57.0	7.0	9.0	66.0	13.5	60.0	6.0	8.0
1980	124.6	28.9	n.a.	3.6	n.a.	76.9	20.7	n.a.	1.5	n.a.
1982	185.0	31.1	n.a.	3.1	n.a.	117.2	18.4	n.a.	1.0	n.a.
1984	202.6	36.5	48.4	2.7	6.5[a]	151.0	18.8	65.0	0.7	10.7[a]

[a] Includes both contributions and loans made by candidates.

Source: 1972 through 1978 data: Joseph E. Cantor, *Political Action Committees: Their Evolution and Growth and Their Implications for the Political System* (Washington, D.C.: Congressional Research Service, Nov. 6, 1981), Tables 6 and 7. 1980 data: Federal Election Commission press release, March 7, 1982; 1982 data: Federal Election Commission press release, May 2, 1983; 1984 data: Federal Election Commission press release, May 16, 1985.

party-affiliated committees on behalf of congressional candidates. These expenditures totaled $19 million in 1984, with $13.1 million of that amount being spent by Republican national campaign committees.[8] In addition, both major parties channeled funds from accounts not subject to FEC reporting requirements to state and local party organizations. The total amount of these so-called "soft money" funds is difficult to estimate but undoubtedly many millions of dollars have made their way into both parties' campaign organizations at the state and local level since 1980. This soft money includes corporate and union treasury monies in states that permit such contributions to their political parties.[9]

Some incumbent members of Congress have created their own PACs. These PACs can be used not only to support the political activities of the incumbent who sponsors them, but also to assist other candidates for elective office. These candidate PACs therefore enable an incumbent to build support for future political goals, such as attaining a leadership position in Congress, or winning another elective office, such as the presidency. Candidate PACs have been used by Rep. Jack Kemp, R-N.Y., Sen. Robert Dole, R-Kan., Sen. Edward Kennedy, D-Mass., and both Ronald Reagan prior to the 1980 presidential campaign and Walter Mondale prior to 1984.

Strategies: Access and Replacement

Political action committees pursue two types of strategy to seek results from their contributions. One strategy is to give contributions to gain access to members of Congress. Money often is given to incumbents who serve on committees in which program legislation or appropriations crucial to a PAC's policy interests are considered. Contributions also may be given to facilitate gaining access to other members of Congress whose votes may be important in obtaining preferred legislative outcomes. The second strategy is to use contributions and expenditures on behalf of or against candidates to alter electoral outcomes, seeking to replace those members of Congress who are unsupportive of the PAC's interest. This strategy may be used in a narrowly targeted fashion, focusing on those representatives who occupy key party and committee leadership positions, or it may be used more broadly, as in efforts by some PACs to change partisan control of Congress.

Many types of PACs appear to employ an access strategy. Eighty percent of corporate and trade PAC contributions to House campaigns in 1984 went to incumbents, indicating that these types of PACs tended to pursue a "seeking access" strategy. In Senate elections, more than 70 percent of the funds contributed by these types of PACs went to incumbents. PACs associated with cooperatives and corporations without stock also tended to allocate funds to incumbents (90 percent of House contributions and 65 percent of Senate contributions in 1984). In contrast, labor-affiliated PACs tended to support incumbents in House contests (70 percent of their contributions went to incumbents, mostly Democrats), but these PACs support challengers or candidates for open seats in Senate elections, with only

30 percent of labor funds in 1984 going to Senate incumbents. More than 90 percent of labor PACs' contributions to Senate candidates went to Democrats; helping challengers and candidates for open seats was part of labor's attempt to return control of the Senate to the traditionally prolabor Democrats. A mixed strategy is pursued by nonconnected PACs, which in 1984 allocated slightly more than half their contributions in Senate contests to incumbents and slightly less than half their contributions in House contests to incumbents.[10]

Nonconnected PACs rank first in the amount of funds collected in the 1983-1984 campaign period, receiving a total of $102.2 million, and they spent more than $95 million. Because they are not part of a union or corporation, nonconnected PACs spend a higher proportion of the money collected on administrative and fund-raising costs. Of the $95.9 million disbursed by the nonconnected PACs, only $15.1 million went to candidates, with an additional $4.9 million being used for independent expenditures on behalf of or against congressional candidates running in 1984, although a total of $22.2 million was used for independent expenditures in both presidential and congressional campaigns.[11]

Nonconnected PACs traditionally spend far less in direct contributions (Table 4-2) and allocate more of their money for fund-raising activities and for direct expenditures in support of or against particular candidates. Media campaigns, such as the National Conservative Political Action Committee's (NCPAC) televison ads against several incumbent Democratic senators, can be conducted without having a large grass-roots organization. All that is required are the services of a few media consultants and lots of money to pay for the ads.

Nonconnected PACs have focused on defeating incumbents whose policy preferences and voting records are displeasing to the PACs. The primary criteria used by nonconnected PACs in selecting candidates for support or opposition are the ideology and voting records of incumbents and their potential vulnerability. Incumbents who are perceived as unlikely to be defeated would usually have only limited amounts spent against them or in support of their challengers.[12]

Sometimes, however, other criteria are involved in targeting. In 1982 Sen. Paul Sarbanes, D-Md., was selected by NCPAC to serve as an object lesson to other members of Congress. NCPAC assumed that other senators and representatives would see the ads against Sarbanes broadcast on the Washington, D.C., area television stations. The implied threat was that, if their voting records vexed conservative PACs, they might also be the targets of negative campaigns. Negative ads can use a single vote as the basis for the media campaign; for example, Sarbanes consistently opposed busing for the purposes of school desegregation, yet voted to provide funding for the enforcement of court-ordered busing. On the basis of that vote, Sarbanes was depicted as a supporter of "forced busing." These ads had a significant impact on the electorate's perceptions of Sarbanes's policy stand.[13] But when the 1982 election results were in, it was clear that the campaign against Sarbanes had not worked; he retained his seat in the Senate with 63 percent of the vote. The NCPAC campaign proved to be so unsuccessful that the anti-Sarbanes ads were withdrawn before the general election campaign. Of the twenty senators and three representatives NCPAC leader Terry Dolan had announced as his targets, only one, Sen. Howard W. Cannon, D-Nev., was defeated.

Because several PACs have engaged actively in senatorial campaigns through independent expenditures for or against selected candidates, the role of PACs in senatorial campaign financing is understated by the data presented in Table 4-2. The backlash against negative independent expenditures in the 1982 campaigns stimulated a change to a more positive strategy in 1984, with only 44 percent of independent expenditures being used for negative campaigns in 1984, compared with 80 percent in 1982.[14]

Independent expenditures can be important in influencing election outcomes. For example, in 1984 more than $1.1 million was spent to persuade the Illinois electorate to vote against incumbent Sen. Charles Percy, R-Ill., who subsequently lost the general election by 1 percent of the vote. Independent expenditures also can provide important support for a candidate. Phil Gramm, R-Texas, benefited from more than $500,000 spent on his behalf in the 1984 Senate contest. Both conservative and liberal groups have used independent expenditures to attempt to affect outcomes in congressional contests. While they are used more in presidential elections, independent expenditures in congressional elections increased from $2.3 million in the 1979-1980 election cycle to $6 million in 1983-1984.[15]

Partisan Allocation of PAC Contributions

In 1984 Democratic House candidates as a group received substantially more money from PACs than did Republican House candidates ($46.2 million versus $29.3 million).[16] With many PACs pursuing an "access to incumbents" strategy and because the Democrats controlled the House of Representatives, Democratic House candidates benefited, receiving contributions from both labor and business PACs. In 1984 labor-affiliated PACs targeted 95 percent of their contributions in House campaigns to Democrats, while 44 percent of corporate PAC contributions in these contests went to Democrats. Less than 5 percent of the corporate PAC funds given to Democratic candidates flowed to nonincumbents.

Republican Senate candidates received slightly more from PACs than did Democratic candidates ($15.4 million compared with $13.9 million). Corporate PACs allocated 27 percent of their contributions in Senate contests to Democratic candidates in 1984, 29 percent of which went to nonincumbents. An incumbent support strategy also is apparent in corporate PAC contributions to Republican candidates. In contrast, in 1984 labor-affiliated PACs channeled 70 percent of the funds given to Democratic candidates to challengers for Republican-held seats and to candidates in open races. Two other types of PACs—the nonconnected and those affiliated with trade or professional associations—as a group divided their contributions rather evenly between Democratic and Republican candidates, although individual PACs varied significantly in partisan giving. Trade PACs heavily favored incumbents in their contribution patterns. Nonconnected PACs gave more to incumbents of the party controlling the legislative chamber, and, in the party not controlling the legislative chamber, tended to allocate more funds to challengers and open seat candidates.[17]

The Democratic Study Group (DSG), an organization of liberal and moderate Democratic members of the House, reported that incumbent House Democrats elected in 1984 received more money from PACs than from individual donors and were more dependent on PACs for campaign funds than were the Republican incumbents. Democratic incumbents received an average of $151,202 from PACs and $144,868 from individuals; in contrast, Republican incumbents received an average of $128,474 from PACs and $174,402 from individuals. The congressional campaign committees of the two parties also differed in their dependence on PAC contributions, with the Democratic Congressional Campaign Committee and Democratic Senatorial Campaign Committee receiving 25 percent of their funds from PACs, while the equivalent Republican committees received less than 1 percent of their funds from PACs.

The role of the individual contributors in funding political campaigns appears to be declining, with "the problems being particularly acute with respect to individual members of the House, particularly Democratic incumbents." The effects foreseen by the DSG report include the displacement of grass-roots funding of political campaigns within the representative's district.[18] The problem of dependency on PAC contributions exists in the Senate as well, with 28 percent of Democratic incumbents' funds and 21 percent of Republican incumbents' contributions coming from PACs during the 1983-1984 election cycle.

PACs and the Policy Process

One important way that PACs affect policy is through influencing who serves in Congress. PAC campaign contributions can have several effects on election outcomes. The first is to help an incumbent ward off effective competition. Potential candidates are faced with having to raise large sums of money, and the larger the incumbent's campaign fund early in the election cycle, the more herculean the task of defeating that incumbent appears. This very early accumulation of large sums of money is intended by the incumbent to intimidate good-quality potential challengers from entering either the primary or the general election; the large campaign fund is being used as a preemptive strike.

The early accumulation of large campaign war chests by incumbents now permits them to begin campaigning earlier in the election cycle than in the past. For example, several senators seeking reelection in 1986 began media advertising campaigns in the summer of 1985. The goals of early media campaigns vary, ranging from increasing the popularity of weak incumbents, to increasing incumbents' fund raising, to shaping the electorate's perceptions of the issues and candidates in the impending electoral contest.

Because media messages must be repeated to be effective, the media campaign must be repeated periodically with new ads emphasizing the incumbent's campaign themes. Thus, an incumbent's early accumulation of a large campaign fund and its skillful use can play a significant role in establishing the themes and tone of the campaign. Robert Goodman, a leading media consultant who works with Republican candidates, stated that "running early, before the contest is formed, you can run unopposed. There's not a lot of clatter. Your message is positive. It achieves greater credibility." Larry McCarthy, another campaign consultant, also views positively the early use of media. "You can try to influence some of the variables in a race that you might not be able to do later." [19] A clear example of the effectiveness of a preemptive strike occurred in 1985. Sen. James Abdnor of South Dakota, considered to be the most vulnerable Republican incumbent seeking reelection in 1986, ran a series of image-building ads, each repeated an average of ten times; subsequent polls showed an unprecedented gain in the approval ratings given Abdnor by South Dakota voters. One goal of the ad campaign was to persuade Republican governor William Janklow not to challenge Abdnor in the primary.

Once the campaign is under way, do challengers and incumbents benefit equally from campaign expenditures? Because a challenger uses campaign funds to establish name recognition and to create candidate awareness, which an incumbent usually already has, the challenger benefits more than the incumbent from initial campaign expenditures. However, a diminishing returns effect occurs in congressional campaigns; during the 1970s challengers' campaigns began to lose their effectiveness after expenditures of about $160,000, with less impact on vote outcome per dollar spent after that. The diminishing returns effect occurs at a lower figure for incumbents, who are already well known when the campaign starts, than for challengers, and varies for challengers depending on political conditions in that particular year. Additional expenditures cannot do much to increase the incumbent's name recognition or awareness of his or her competence and issue stands among the electorate.[20] Incumbents, however, spend to match the spending patterns of their challengers. Because election outcomes are often uncertain, and events can change the expected outcome, uncertainty increases the willingness of the incumbent to spend, even when faced with a predicted victory.

The effectiveness of challenger expenditures also varies with whether political trends are favorable or unfavorable to the challenger's party. During the period from 1972-1982, one-third of the challengers who spent $250,000 or more were victorious, with those spending smaller amounts being less likely to win. However, when the data are analyzed in terms of the kind of year it was for the challenger's party, a different pattern emerges. Almost half of those challengers spending more than $200,000 won when it was a good year for the challenger's party, while in a bad year for the challenger's party,

10 percent or fewer were victorious regardless of the amount of money expended in the campaign.[21]

PAC contributions can affect public policy in several ways other than helping to determine who serves in Congress. First, contributions make it easier for PAC members to gain access to members of Congress to present their views. Second, contributions can aid in gaining support for PACs' views where the issue is not of great concern to the member of Congress or the member's constituency. While PACs may contribute to incumbents primarily to ensure more open-minded attention to their point of view, those making contributions may also hope that their views will be persuasive. Do PAC contributions appear to influence legislative outcomes? Unfortunately, insufficient research exists to permit generalization about the relationship between PAC contributions and committee policy decisions, and it is at this stage of the legislative process that crucial decisions about the content of legislation are often made.

Several studies have examined the relationship between PAC contributions and legislative roll-call voting patterns. Some conclude that PAC contributions affect members' support for legislation. Support for this view is provided by analysis of congressional roll-call voting patterns on issues such as minimum wage legislation,[22] the B-1 bomber,[23] the debt limit, windfall profits tax, wage and price controls,[24] trucking deregulation,[25] and legislation of interest to auto dealers and to doctors.[26] One study that looked at both general issues and urban issues reported that labor contributions had a significant impact on House roll-call voting on five of nine issues relating to urban problems and five of eight general issues, but business contributions were related to House roll-call votes in only one issue of each type.[27] Other research suggests that campaign contributions may not have had a significant impact on roll-call votes on issues such as the Chrysler loan guarantee and the windfall profits tax[28] or on dairy price supports.[29]

Whether campaign contributions influence votes is a function of a number of factors. Constituency interests may coincide or conflict with those of a PAC making a contribution to a representative's campaign. If the interests conflict and the issue is highly salient to the constituency, the probability of a contribution influencing a vote is substantially reduced. Party ties and ideological preferences may also influence members of Congress to vote contrary to PAC preferences on specific legislation. As Diana Evans notes (see Chapter 6) PAC contributions may have more impact on low visibility issues when party, ideology, and constituency interests are not important.

Criticism of PACs

The representation of interests in a large, complex society is simplified by organization, and PAC activities in funding congressional campaigns can be considered a legitimate representational activity. But several issues must be addressed. First, do the present campaign finance laws unduly promote single-issue politics? Second, should individuals be permitted to make larger contributions to a particular candidate? Third, should political parties be permitted—even encouraged—to play a larger role in campaign finance?

One criticism leveled against PACs is that they may create obligations on the part of congressional candidates to an interest group or to coalitions of interest groups that cooperate informally in channeling PAC money. Coalition formation is quite common in lobbying on legislation, whether the issue is funding for higher education, energy policy, environmental policy, deregulation of financial institutions, or anything else, and the coalitions formed may be quite diverse. Targeting of support by coalitions usually is based on shared interests and can be a less costly way of making the potential recipient aware of the groups' policy preferences.

PACs also are criticized as operating primarily to protect incumbents. But the proportion of contributions flowing to incumbents varies among the types of PACs.

The rapid increase in the number of business-related PACs and the potential for their considerable future growth, as contrasted with the number of labor PACs and the limited potential for *their* future growth, suggests that a significant imbalance of power between business and labor PACs has been created by the campaign finance law.

Some argue that business PAC funds merely represent money formerly provided to candidates by other means, such as individual contributions from business executives and contributions in kind—free services, for example.[30] The amount being contributed to congressional candidates during the 1980s, however, is substantially greater than in earlier elections, even when the increased costs of campaigning are considered. Turning to the business-labor imbalance in campaign contributions, a counterargument is that organized labor has the advantage in politics because of its historic ability to mobilize union members and their families to work in campaigns and to vote for endorsed candidates. It is interesting to note, however, that in recent elections the mobilized union supporters have not always supported union-endorsed candidates.

Another major criticism of PACs is that they weaken the role of individual citizens in politics. This criticism rests on the disparity between the amount that may be contributed to a congressional candidate by a PAC ($5,000 per election) and by an individual ($1,000 per election). To enhance the role of individuals, one proposed solution is to increase the maximum amount an individual may give. This change might reduce the channeling of funds through PACs. But increasing the maximum amount an individual is allowed to contribute to any one campaign could simply result in a partial shift in the way single-issue groups exercise political influence. Individuals would contribute more money directly in support of a single-issue cause. Critics charge that such a change would only enhance the influence of major economic interests because they have more discretionary income to allocate to political contributions.

Before passage of the campaign finance reform legislation in the early 1970s, any individual could give an unlimited amount of money to a candidate. Clement Stone, a wealthy Chicago insurance executive, contributed $2 million to the campaign of Republican presidential candidate Richard Nixon in 1972. Richard Mellon Scaife, heir to oil (Gulf), aluminum (Alcoa), and banking (Mellon National Bank) fortunes, contributed more than $1 million to Republican candidates in 1972. Current legislation limits an individual to giving no more than a total of $25,000 to *all* candidates for federal office in any one year. Thus, no individual can play such a large role in funding the candidacy of another person as occurred in 1972 and earlier; of course, some argue that the present limits are too stringent.

Increasing the amount an individual may contribute to any one candidate could reduce the burden of fund raising placed on candidates by, for example, enabling them to collect the same amount of money through fewer fund-raising efforts. Whether this should be the goal or whether the goal should be to force candidates to depend on wide financial support remains unresolved.

The tendency for a congressional candidate's financial support to be drawn more heavily from outside the constituency now than in the past raises the issue of accountability. To the extent that a successful campaign depends on financial resources and those resources come from outside the district, the winning candidate will be less accountable to the district constituency. Political action committees' activities in congressional campaign finance also are criticized because they make it more difficult for candidates to assess individuals' policy preferences. This criticism ignores the fact that PAC funds are raised from individual contributors who presumably share the set of beliefs and values embodied by the group. PACs do operate to nationalize campaign funding, and their utility as a mechanism for expressing constituent policy preferences is weakened if the organization members' policy views vary across congressional constituencies or if a particular group does not have significant membership in the recipient's constituency. In addition, diversity of views might present a problem in assessing the concerns of members of a broad-based interest group; for example, members of the American Farm Bureau Federation would have a more diverse set of interests than would members of a more narrowly focused group such as the American Dairy Association.

Argument can be made that the method of raising funds in many PACs works against centralized decision making in the allocation of PAC funds and pursuit of the strategy most likely to achieve the PAC's policy goals. A study of five PACs that raise money through local or state affiliates indicates that the fund-raising affiliates' suggestions for allocation of contributions are followed 80 percent to 90 percent of the time. These suggested allocations may not be in accord with the best strategy for the PAC. For example, the PAC may support an incumbent who is facing no serious opposition and does not need the help, or the PAC may support an incumbent who has little influence over policy of primary concern to the PAC.[31]

A frequent criticism made of PACs is that they undermine political parties, usurping the party's role in political campaigns. By providing funds to buy professional campaign services, the PACs decrease a candidate's reliance on the party organization. Those candidates who are supported by the PACs with a large membership base that can be targeted in a constituency also have less need for support in the form of voter mobilization by the party organization and, therefore, could operate more independently of the party.

A number of responses have been made to this criticism, including the arguments that (1) the decline of political parties' role in political campaigns began before the rise of PACs;[32] (2) anything that increases the role of television will weaken the role of the political parties;[33] and (3) PAC money facilitates purchase of modern campaign technology that substitutes for campaign assistance no longer provided by the political parties in many areas. Political parties were significant sources of campaign funds prior to the 1970s, but their relative share of the campaign funds contributed to congressional candidates has declined.

Since 1977, however, the Republican party's national-level committees have demonstrated the role that political parties could play through making direct contributions to targeted congressional contests and supporting a number of activities that could have a significant impact on election results.[34] National party funds have been used to develop state and local party organizations' ability to organize and conduct modern political campaigns. The funds used for these purposes do not come under the limits imposed by federal law; hence, this so-called "soft money" provides a mechanism for an increased party role in congressional as well as state and local campaigns. Furthermore, the political parties' congressional campaign committees play a major role in establishing credibility with the PACs for their candidates. An endorsement by the parties' campaign committees is crucial for obtaining PAC support; if the party campaign committee writes off a contest as poorly managed or unwinnable, few PAC funds will flow to the candidate.[35]

Increasing the amount that political party committees may spend on behalf of congressional candidates could bring about an increased role for the parties in these campaigns and reduce candidate dependence on interest groups.

Conclusions

The Federal Election Campaign Act and its amendments have had effects not envisioned by their original sponsors. The growth in the number of PACs, their role in campaign finance, and their varying potential for future activity all raise questions about the roles of different actors in the political process. The increasing power of PACs has led to several proposals that would alter their role in campaign finance.

Several different approaches to "reforming the reforms" have been suggested; most have as their goal reducing the dependency of congressional candidates on PAC money. All, however, would have unintended consequences that raise questions about their desirability.

One proposed reform is to limit the amount of money a candidate may accept from a PAC. This proposal is sometimes combined with a plan to increase the amount of money an individual may give to a candidate or with a program of direct subsidies to congressional candidates from a government campaign fund.

A proposal in the 96th Congress by Reps. David Obey, D-Wis., and Thomas Railsback, R-Ill., included a $75,000 limit. A similar proposal in the 97th Congress by Reps. Dan Glickman, D-Kan., Jim Leach, R-Iowa, and Mike Synar, D-Okla., included the same limit for House candidates and limits of from $75,000 to $500,000 for Senate candidates, depending on the size of the state. Such limits might be challenged as an unconstitutional violation of freedom of association or freedom of speech. Efforts to enact these limits have been unsuccessful, both because of their partisan consequences and because of their implications for campaign fund raising by incumbents and challengers. Republicans serving in Democratic controlled Congresses viewed efforts to limit both PAC contributions and party expenditures as an effort to restrict the activities of their candidates.

Another suggestion is to limit voluntarily the amount of money a candidate for Congress may spend; those who accept the limit would receive campaign money from a government fund. If the candidate accepts a limit but his or her opponent does not, then the amount of money received from the government fund would increase substantially, and the limit on what may be spent would also increase substantially.

The amount an individual may contribute to any one candidate also could be raised. The current limit of $1,000 per candidate per election increases the effort candidates must invest in fund raising and may discriminate against individuals in the political process. Furthermore, failure to adjust the amount for inflation has reduced the real value of the contribution being made.

Increased individual contributions could be encouraged by allowing individuals who contribute money to candidates or parties to deduct up to a maximum of $100 from their federal income tax. Some proposals would permit the tax credit to be claimed only for contributions made to political parties or candidates within the contributor's own state.

A bill that reflected several of these proposals was introduced in the 99th Congress by Sen. David Boren, D-Okla. The proposed bill would limit to $100,000 the funds a House candidate could accept, while the amount a Senate candidate could accept would vary with the state population, ranging from a low of $150,000 to a high of $750,000. The Boren proposal would lower the amount that a PAC could give one candidate from $5,000 to $3,000 and increase the limit on contributions by individuals from $1,000 to $1,500. Boren blames PAC money for stimulating the almost 400 percent increase between 1976 and 1984 in the cost of winning a Senate seat and the more than 200 percent increase in winning a House seat.[36]

Some proposals also have been made to create mechanisms for countering independent expenditures by PACs. One would be to give candidates whose opponents are assisted by independent expenditures access to a specified amount of free radio and television time. Those candidates whose opponents are the beneficiaries of independent expenditures would also be entitled to a campaign subsidy from a publicly financed campaign fund.

One proposal involves strengthening the role of political parties in the campaign process, as in other developed democracies. Technical assistance, such as production and distribution of mass media announcements and provision of professional campaign management services, is offered by the national parties' committee staffs or by the consultants hired by the national committees. In the United States, direct contributions by the national party to political candidates on a larger scale also is feasible, but until such time as the Democrats have modernized their fund-raising activities and services to a level more competitive with that of the Republicans, an enhanced role for political parties is not likely to gain Democratic support in Congress.[37] Offering such services and financial support would bring back the party's traditional role of joining specific issue interests within a more broadly based set of policy proposals.

All of these proposals have unintended consequences. Any bill that seeks to limit PAC expenditures would result in the channeling of PAC funds into politics in other ways, such as the funding of voter registration and mobilization drives, organizing grass-roots lobbying, or stimulating campaign contributions directly from individuals to candidates, conveyed in some fashion that makes clear to the candidate the policy interest and preferences of the contributors.

Imposing spending limits on campaigns probably would tend to favor incumbents, who start their campaigns with a significant advantage in resources and name recognition. Any limit likely to be enacted by Congress would be so low as to disadvantage challengers, who usually must spend a substantial amount of money to establish adequate name recognition among the voters.

The proposal for an increased tax credit would be the simplest change, but in the face of substantial budget deficits and demands for the elimination of tax credits and shelters of various kinds, this plan probably would encounter substantial opposition and be difficult to enact.[38]

In sum, the politics of PACs and PAC reform is beset by all the problems that historically have beset the combination of money and politics. PACs are here and are likely to remain. And we will continue to analyze, evaluate, and debate their appropriate role in the political process.

Notes

1. See Herbert Alexander, *Financing Politics,* 3d ed. (Washington, D.C.: CQ Press, 1984).

2. See Edwin Epstein, "The Emergence of Political Action Committees," in *Political Finance,* ed. Herbert Alexander (Beverly Hills, Calif.: Sage Publications, 1979), 159-197.

3. *Buckley v. Valeo,* 424 U.S. 1 (1976).

4. Federal Election Commission press release, May 19, 1985.

5. Calculated from data contained in Federal Election Commission press release, May 16, 1985.

6. Ibid.

7. Ibid., Appendix IV.

8. Ibid., Appendix I.

9. Elizabeth Drew, *Politics and Money: The New Road to Political Corruption* (New York: Macmillan, 1983), 101-108.

10. Federal Election Commission press release, May 16, 1985, Appendix I. Access money also can increase the intensity of support received from a member of Congress. See Larry J. Sabato, *PAC Power: Inside the World of Political Action Committees* (New York: W. W. Norton, 1985), 136.

11. Federal Election Commission press release, May 19, 1985.

12. Exceptions exist, such as Republican targeting of the chair of the Democratic Congressional Campaign Committee in 1980 and 1984.

13. Polls conducted by the *Baltimore Sun* indicated that the proportion of the public approving of Senator Sarbanes's job performance remained stationary, while the proportion disapproving increased from 20 percent to 29 percent between October 1981 and February 1982. During that period several NCPAC ads critical of Sarbanes's performance were shown on television stations broadcasting to Maryland residents. See Karen Hosler, "Voter Shifts Favor Hughes, Hurt Sarbanes," *Baltimore Sun,* Feb. 22, 1982, A1.

14. Federal Election Commission press release, Oct. 4, 1985.

15. Ibid.

16. These analyses of 1984 contribution patterns are based on data contained in the Federal Election Commission press release, May 16, 1985.

17. Ibid.

18. Thomas Edsall, "PACs Outpacing Individuals," *Washington Post,* Oct. 24, 1985, A8.

19. Paul West, " 'Early Media' Push Puts '86 Campaign on the Air," *Baltimore Sun,* Dec. 12, 1985, 1A.

20. See Gary C. Jacobson, "Money and Votes Reconsidered: Congressional Elections, 1972-1982," *Public Choice* 47 (1985): 43-46.

21. In the analysis done by Jacobson, all data were adjusted for inflation, with 1982 = 1.0. See Jacobson, "Money and Votes Reconsidered," 43.

22. Jonathan I. Silberman and Garey C. Durden, "Determining Legislature Preferences on Minimum Wage: An Economic Approach," *Journal of Political Economy* 84 (1976): 317-329.

23. Henry W. Chappel, Jr., "Campaign Contributions and Congressional Voting: A Simultaneous Probit-Tobit Model," *Review of Economics and Statistics* (February 1982): 77-83.

24. James B. Kau and Paul H. Rubin, *Congressmen, Constituents, and Contributors: Determinants of Roll Call Votes* (Boston: Martinus Nijhoff, 1982), Table 7.5, 96-97.

25. John P. Frendreis and Richard W. Waterman, "PAC Contributions and Legislative Behavior: Senate Voting on Trucking Deregulation," *Social Science*

Quarterly 66 (June 1985): 401-412.
26. K. F. Brown, "Campaign Contributions and Congressional Voting" (Paper presented at the Annual Meeting of the American Political Science Association, Chicago, Ill., Sept. 1-4, 1983).
27. Kau and Rubin, *Congressmen, Constituents, and Contributors.*
28. Diana E. Yiannakis, "PAC Contributions and House Voting on Conflictual and Consensual Issues: The Windfall Profits Tax and the Chrysler Loan Guarantee" (Paper presented at the Annual Meeting of the American Political Science Association, Chicago, Ill., Sept. 1-4, 1983.)
29. W. P. Welch, "Campaign Contributions and House Voting: Milk Money and Dairy Price Supports," *Western Political Quarterly* 35 (December 1982): 478-495.
30. Michael Malbin, "Of Mountains and Molehills: PACs, Campaigns, and Public Policy," in *Parties, Interest Groups, and Campaign Finance Laws,* ed. Michael Malbin (Washington D.C.: American Enterprise Institute, 1980), 152-183; Bernadette A. Budde, "Business Political Action Committees," in *Parties, Interest Groups, and Campaign Finance Laws,* 9-25; and Joseph E. Cantor, *Political Action Committees: Their Evolution and Growth and Their Implications for the Political System* (Washington, D.C.: Congressional Research Service, 1981).
31. John R. Wright, "PACs, Contributions, and Roll Calls: An Organizational Perspective," *American Political Science Review* 79 (June 1985): 400-414. For another view of the degree of centralization in the decision-making processes of various types of PACs, see Theodore J. Eismeier and Philip H. Pollock III, "An Organizational Analysis of Political Action Committees," *Political Behavior* 7 (1985): 192-216.
32. David W. Adamany, "PACs and the Democratic Financing of Politics," *Political Action Committees and Campaign Finance: Symposium, Arizona Law Review* (1980): 2.
33. Austin Ranney, "The Political Parties: Reform and Decline," in *The New American Political System,* ed. Anthony King (Washington, D.C.: American Enterprise Institute, 1978), 213-247.
34. In 1974 further changes in campaign finance law were enacted. These changes limited national party spending on behalf of candidates to $10,000 per candidate in each election for the U.S. House of Representatives and $20,000 or 2 cents per eligible voter as adjusted for inflation (whichever is greater) in U.S. Senate elections. A national or state party organization also may contribute $5,000 to each House candidate for each election and $17,500 in each election to a U.S. Senate candidate.
35. Alan Ehrenhalt, "Political Parties: A Renaissance of Power?" *Congressional Quarterly Weekly Report,* Oct. 26, 1985, 2187.
36. "Senate to Vote on Limiting PAC Contributions," *Congressional Quarterly Weekly Report,* Nov. 23, 1985, 2445-2446.
37. In the 1979-1980 election cycle, the three most prominent Republican national-level committees (congressional, senatorial, and national) raised a total of $128.1 million, while the Democrats' three equivalent committees raised only $18.8 million. During the first 18 months of the 1981-1982 election cycle, the Republican committees raised $146.25 million, while the Democratic committees raised $18.88 million (Federal Election Commission press release, Aug. 30, 1982). During the 1979-1980 election cycle, the principal Republican campaign committees spent $120.5 million, and the equivalent Democratic committees spent

$18.4 million (Federal Election Commission press release, Feb. 21, 1982, as corrected March 30, 1982). During the 1983-1984 campaign cycle, the national Republican party committees raised $300.2 million and spent $303.2 million, while the Democratic party raised $96.8 million and spent $97.2 million. The Republican Senate campaign committee had net disbursements of $83.6 million, and the Republican House campaign committee spent a net total of $61.7 million; the comparable figures for the Democratic committees were $8.7 million and $10.2 million (Federal Election Commission press release, May 7, 1985).

38. For a discussion of proposed reforms and their advantages and disadvantages, see Michael J. Malbin, "Looking Back at the Future of Campaign Finance Reform: Interest Groups and American Elections," in *Money and Politics in the United States: Financing Elections in the 1980s*, ed. Michael J. Malbin (Washington, D.C.: American Enterprise Institute, 1984), 232-276. See also Sabato, *PAC Power*, 173-186.

5. Big Bucks and Petty Cash: Party and Interest Group Activists in American Politics

John C. Green and James L. Guth

One major criticism of political action committees (PACs) is that they contribute to the destruction of American party politics. Critics contend that not only have PACs usurped the parties' role in campaign finance, but also that they have made it more difficult for parties to moderate conflict through the coalition-building process. From this perspective, ideological and single-issue PACs compete with parties for the loyalty of both voters and elected officials, to the detriment of the public interest.

The relationship between parties and PACs remains an empirical question, and in this chapter John Green and James Guth examine a key aspect of this linkage. They analyze the attitudes of contributors to more than sixty campaign committees, including the best-known ideological and single-issue PACs. Contrary to conventional wisdom, they find that the advent of PACs may be changing politics less fundamentally than many contend and that the bulk of PAC contributors do not harbor antiparty sentiments. The parties and their historical allies still dominate political finance, and between party and group activists the real conflict is over the party's issue agenda. Green and Guth suggest that such conflict has always been a part of American politics and that the party system has acted, time and again, to absorb a variety of special interests and social movements.

American politics is a politics of organization. Political scientists traditionally have distinguished between two types of representative institutions, parties and interest groups, but recently many new kinds of organizations have arisen. Not only do we have the Democratic and Republican parties, but also quasi-party organizations, such as ideological and presidential candidate political action committees (PACs). Older economic interests have been joined by single-issue groups with concerns as varied as the environment, consumerism, abortion, prayer in schools, gay rights, gun control, and nuclear disarmament.

This expansion of the interest group universe has created enormous problems for those seeking to build governing coalitions. The 1984 election provides good examples. Ronald Reagan's victorious coalition, the "Reconstituted Right," was an alliance of Republican regulars, the business community, New Right groups such as the National Conservative Political Action Committee (NCPAC), and single-issue activists in the antiabortion and Christian Right movements. No sooner was the election over, however, than the Right began to "deconstitute." Republican stalwarts and their business allies wanted Reagan to pursue economic issues, as he had done so successfully in his first term, but New Right leaders demanded top priority for social issues.[1]

Disputes were even more numerous within the Democratic camp, always an "alliance of antagonists." [2] Here the battle raged long before the election. While labor supported Walter Mondale early, conservative Democrats rooted for John Glenn, and many New Politics activists preferred Gary Hart. Democratic regulars complained that special interests and liberals dominated the party, to the detriment of its image; New Politics forces and the Reverend Jesse Jackson chided party leaders for being unresponsive to minorities, environmentalists, feminists, and peace advocates. About the only thing the party regulars and New Politics groups had in common was unease over the pivotal role of the AFL-CIO in Democratic politics.

These disputes run deeper than particular issues or candidates. They involve rival styles of organizing political competition. The Republican and Democratic parties and their business and labor allies are proud of their pragmatic, moderate politics. They resent the strident and ideological style of the new issue-conscious organizations, to which they ascribe a litany of ills: raising divisive and unpopular issues, polarizing politics, undermining party loyalty, encouraging cynicism and intolerance, and discouraging compromise. The new groups deny these charges, arguing that they merely seek to infuse politics with principles and to raise important issues that older organizations evade.

How are these new groups changing American politics? One way to answer this question is to look beyond the tactics and quarrels of political leaders to those who actually "speak" through these organizations: the activists who run the campaigns, recruit the candidates, set the agenda, and pay the bills. If new ideological and single-issue PACs are transforming American politics, the direction of change should be apparent from the attitudes and activities of their key supporters. And a good place to find large numbers of such activists is among campaign contributors. As lobbyist Charls Walker puts it, "There is now a financial channel or opportunity for virtually every political enthusiasm." [3]

In this chapter we examine data collected in our 1982-1983 survey of contributors of $200 or more to over sixty campaign committees, including almost all the largest and best-known ideological and single-issue PACs. Also included are important labor and business peak associations and major party committees (see Appendix for a list of examples).

The evidence we present on campaign contributors certainly reveals the great diversity of activists and organizations, but it also suggests that the advent of PACs is changing politics less fundamentally than many suppose.

Conflict among them is primarily over the control and direction of the major parties, a struggle between traditional and more issue-oriented, "responsible" partisans.

Organizations and Donors

For purposes of analysis we have combined contributors into six categories. The first three include donors to party-oriented committees: party (Republican, Democratic), allied economic groups (business, labor), and presidential candidate PACs (Reagan's Citizens for the Republic and Mondale's Committee for the Future of America). The other three categories are issue-oriented and include donors to conservative and liberal PACs (such as NCPAC and the National Committee for an Effective Congress) and two groups with more specific concerns: single-issue donors who support only one PAC and multiple-issue donors who support more than one PAC as well as other types of committees.[4] We thought these donor groups would differ on several aspects of political style: issue focus, ideology and partisanship, civility, political motivations, membership in social and political networks, and types of activism. What follows is a brief summary of what we expected to find based on our reading of scholars and journalists.

Party-oriented Donors

The major parties are known for brokered politics, a style given to accommodation and compromise, which seeks to satisfy as many groups as possible. And, as party alignments still reflect the New Deal, we expected their financial backers to care most about economic issues, be relatively moderate, and have strong partisan commitments. Many of these supporters will be party "professionals," activated by material and social incentives, rather than by expressive, or policy, incentives. Their most important goal will be winning elections. As part of the establishment, party contributors probably belong to broad, partisan networks and engage in a wide variety of conventional political activities, particularly campaigning.[5]

The historic allies of the parties, business and labor, are also a part of brokered politics, although their objectives are more limited. The "special interest" style involves pursuit of tangible goals, mostly economic. On such issues they may hold extreme positions, but, like party donors, they are otherwise relatively moderate and strongly partisan. These contributors are probably motivated by material incentives; they belong to business and professional networks and specialize in insider politics, especially fund raising and lobbying. As this description suggests, the longstanding and intimate ties between the parties and their allies reflect considerable similarity in political styles.[6]

We expected donors to candidate PACs to exhibit a "personalistic" style: strong attachment to the principles, policies, and personality of one leader. While their issue focus varies with the candidate, they are probably more ideological and less partisan than party donors. On the other hand, their involvement in party politics hints that they will be less ideological than issue-oriented donors. Likewise, they exhibit a variety of incentives: many will be "vocationalists" who promote their own political careers, and others will be "avocationalists," attracted to causes their candidate supports. They are most likely to be entrenched in electoral networks and to specialize in campaigning.[7]

Issue-oriented Groups

If party-oriented donors seek power by accommodation, then issue-oriented groups seek policy through confrontation. Conservatives and liberals exemplify an ideological style. They want their strongly held political philosophies embodied in public policy. Thus, their hallmark is consistent and extreme views on all kinds of issues. They are "amateurs" or "purists," motivated by expressive incentives, preoccupied with new social and foreign policy issues, and only loosely attached to the major parties. Being part of insurgent movements, they belong to narrow, ideological networks and specialize in both campaigning and outsider activities, such as letter writing, protesting, and supporting minor parties.[8]

Our last two categories of donors are variants on a single-issue style: intense commitment to one emotion-laden, top-priority issue that admits of no compromise (see Chapter 2). They probably hold consistent and extreme views on "their" issue, but may be less intense on others. They distrust parties and other institutions and are wary of joining coalitions. Motivated exclusively by expressive incentives, they belong to isolated issue networks and may resort to unconventional political tactics.[9]

We divided donors to single-issue PACs into two categories, single-issue and multiple-issue, for a very important reason: many of them (75 percent of those on the Right and 50 percent of those on the Left) also gave to other committees, usually conservative or liberal PACs. As multiple-issue donors violate the single-issue model—having more than one political concern—we felt this separation was warranted. And, as we shall see, single-issue PAC donors do conform to media caricatures, while multiple-issue donors often do not.[10]

In Tables 5-1 through 5-7, we divided the groups into two basic categories: those donating to Right-oriented PACs and those donating to Left-oriented PACs. In addition, the tables contain information on the relative size of each group, weighted by the amount of money raised in each category (weighted N).[11] As the tables show, donors to party-oriented organizations far outnumber issue-oriented contributors, accounting for more than 70 percent on each side of the political spectrum. The Right is dominated by the GOP: Republicans make up almost half of its donors (48 percent), with business and candidate committees providing roughly a quarter (17 percent and 10 percent, respectively). The issue-oriented categories are much smaller: conservative, 17 percent; multiple-issue, 6 percent; and single-issue, 2 percent. In contrast, the Left is dominated by party allies: Democrats make up nearly a quarter of donors (23 percent), and labor and candidate contributors account for half of the total (33 percent and 17 percent, respectively). Issue-oriented donors are slightly more numerous than on the Right: liberals, 13 percent; multiple-issue, 9 percent; and single-issue, 6 percent. Thus, while issue-oriented groups may be the wave of the future, their supporters are still clearly in the minority.

Competing Agendas: Parties, PACs, and Priorities

Like other insurgent movements in American history, issue-oriented PACs are vehicles for a new political agenda, shifting attention from New Deal economic issues toward social and foreign policy concerns.[12] Indeed, many accuse these groups, especially the single-issue PACs, of reducing politics to one set of issues that are not of paramount concern to most voters. How accurate is this critique? To find out, we asked contributors to name the "two or three most important problems facing the United States."

Party-oriented and issue-oriented donors do have different agendas. As Table 5-1 shows, business and labor emphasize economic issues, with

Table 5-1 Salient Issues: Most Important Problems Facing the Country

	Contributors to Right-oriented PACs					
	Repub-lican Party	Business	Presidential Candidate	Conserv-ative	Multiple-issue	Single-issue
(Weighted N)	(1260)	(434)	(262)	(448)	(162)	(51)
Percentage naming						
Economic issues	64	75	64	62	53	29
Social issues	17	7	18	17	29	51
Foreign policy	13	11	13	18	17	14

	Contributors to Left-oriented PACs					
	Demo-cratic Party	Labor	Presidential Candidate	Liberal	Multiple-issue	Single-issue
(Weighted N)	(277)	(390)	(203)	(161)	(105)	(72)
Percentage naming						
Economic issues	71	78	50	54	37	32
Social issues	7	5	18	8	12	14
Foreign policy	17	13	27	36	45	49

Source: Survey conducted by the authors.

Republicans and Democrats not far behind, but issue-oriented contributors are more concerned with social issues and foreign policy. This is especially true of single-issue activists: on the Right they are three times as likely as Republicans to name a social issue, while on the Left, they list foreign policy nearly three times as often as Democrats. Thus, on priorities at least, the conventional portrait of the new activists holds true, but the effect is not the same on both sides of the fence: social issues divide the Right and foreign policy splits the Left. Although this pattern reflects in part the PACs studied (e.g., the Moral Majority on the Right, peace activists on the Left), it holds even without these groups.

Although single-issue donors concentrate on social concerns and foreign policy, not all focus intensively on one issue. In fact, if a single issue is, in political scientist Marjorie Hershey's words, "one defined by its proponents as so basic to their value system, so deeply rooted and compelling, that it cries out for priority," then many donors to single-issue PACs do not qualify.[13] Feminists, abortion rights groups, gay rights advocates, tax protesters, gun owners, and donors to prodefense PACs do not name their issue more frequently than do other contributors. But some PAC contributors do give their issue top billing. Antifeminists, right-to-lifers, Christian fundamentalists, gun controllers, environmentalists, and, particularly, peace donors fit the single-issue stereotype. The asymmetrical effect here, where activists on only one side put highest priority on their issue, may be a common feature of single-issue politics.[14]

The urgency that social-issue conservatives and foreign policy liberals feel no doubt reflects the indifference of many Republican and Democratic leaders, who may have a more realistic assessment of public concerns. At the time of our study, 89 percent of Gallup Poll respondents named economic issues as most important, an agenda much closer to that of party donors and their business and labor allies than to that of donors to issue-oriented PACs.[15] Thus, critics of "unrepresentative" single-issue and ideological PACs may have a point: these new groups speak for the priorities of very few voters.

Ideology and Issues: Moderation versus Extremism?

Issue-oriented PACs often are accused of polarizing politics by their strident rhetoric, which drowns out the moderate, pragmatic voices of the parties. Political scientist Gary Jacobson points out that PAC appeals are most effective when they "excite emotions of fear, anger, outrage, and righteous indignation." The byproduct of such appeals, journalist Elizabeth Drew argues, is that "our politics has become more ideological."[16]

We measured donors' ideological orientations in three ways.

(1) We determined contributors' "consistency" by their responses on twenty-four issues, divided into economic, social, and foreign policy domains. A donor was defined as "ideological" if he or she took conventional liberal or conservative stances on at least two-thirds of the

Table 5-2 Ideology: Issue Positions and Self-identification

	Contributors to Right-oriented PACs					
	Repub-lican Party	Business	Presidential Candidate	Conserv-ative	Multiple-issue	Single-issue
(Weighted N)	(1260)	(434)	(262)	(448)	(162)	(51)
Percentage taking conservative position						
Economic issues	50	60	57	58	68	42
Social issues	25	25	35	39	47	55
Foreign policy	25	21	30	39	44	36
Percentage identi-fying as						
Conservative	88	80	91	91	95	83
Very conservative	30	30	55	60	58	44

	Contributors to Left-oriented PACs					
	Demo-cratic Party	Labor	Presidential Candidate	Liberal	Multiple-issue	Single-issue
(Weighted N)	(277)	(390)	(203)	(161)	(105)	(72)
Percentage taking liberal position						
Economic issues	29	60	40	32	58	32
Social issues	49	44	59	68	80	76
Foreign policy	31	35	37	41	50	45
Percentage identi-fying as						
Liberal	50	69	59	60	82	72
Very liberal	15	29	19	34	42	38

Source: Survey conducted by the authors.

issues in each area. To judge their intensity, we also looked at how strongly donors felt about these issues.

(2) We asked donors for their ideological self-identification, using a scale ranging from extremely conservative to extremely liberal.

(3) We used a proximity measure, asking donors how close they felt to a number of liberal and conservative groups and leaders.

Issue-oriented activists are indeed far more ideological, as indicated in Table 5-2. In general, multiple-issue donors are the most consistent ideologues, followed by liberals and conservatives. These groups, plus single-issue donors, are particularly consistent in the social and foreign policy realms, reflecting their priorities. As we expected, business and labor are more consistent only on economics, where single-issue donors show remarkable diversity. Party donors, Republican and Democratic alike, live up to their reputation, holding relatively mixed opinions across the board. For all groups, intensity accompanies consistency. Donors who are most consistent in a policy area also hold these views strongly—issue-oriented donors on social issues and foreign policy; business and labor on economics. Party donors are not only less consistent, but also less intense in their beliefs.

The strong ideological bent of issue-oriented groups extends to individual issues. Although single-issue donors are not always preoccupied with their issues, they do hold, as expected, monolithic views. Feminist donors overwhelmingly support ERA and abortion, the gun owners unanimously spurn gun control, and peace PAC contributors uniformly back arms reduction. And, with almost no exceptions, those with strong views on each issue are most numerous among single-issue donors, decline somewhat among ideological and candidate contributors, and reach a low point, as expected, among the party activists. For example, 78 percent of right-to-lifers strongly want government to limit abortions, but only 11 percent of Republicans do.

Party donors' moderation is confirmed by their self-identification. On the Right, nearly all activists call themselves conservative, but Republicans and business donors least often identify themselves as very conservative. Almost twice as many conservative and multiple-issue donors identify themselves that way. But single-issue donors are less conservative than either of the latter, suggesting that some have not linked their cause to an ideological world view. On the Left, Democrats are much less often liberal, or, for that matter, very liberal, while the issue-oriented are much more inclined to take those labels. Again, as on issues, we find multiple-issue activists the most extreme.

Proximity measures reveal a similar pattern. We asked contributors how close they felt to fourteen political groups and leaders. Table 5-3 reports net positive or negative ratings. Clearly, party-oriented donors on the Right have quite negative or, at best, neutral feelings toward the John Birch Society, the right-to-life movement, the Moral Majority, and antifeminist leader Phyllis Schlafly, all part of the recent New Right infiltration of the GOP. With the partial exception of the Birch Society, issue-oriented donors feel much closer to New Right groups and the National Rifle Association, which gets only mildly favorable reviews from party-oriented contributors. On the other hand, single-issue donors are not as positive toward mainstream conservatism, whether represented by Sen. Barry Goldwater or the Chamber of Commerce, both favorites of party-oriented groups. Thus, we find distinct constituencies for both the traditional Republicanism of Sen. Robert Dole and the New Right style of Sen. Jesse Helms.

The Left is even more diverse. All groups feel distant from the Socialists, although the margin is largest among Democrats and smallest in the labor and issue-oriented camps. The moderation of "checkbook Democrats," a

Table 5-3 Proximity Measures: Degree of "Closeness" to Selected Groups and Leaders

	Contributors to Right-oriented PACs					
	Repub-lican Party	Business	Presidential Candidate	Conserv-ative	Multiple-issue	Single-issue
(Weighted N)	(1260)	(434)	(262)	(448)	(162)	(51)
Net percentage close to						
John Birch Society	−47	−34	−25	−24	−17	−11
Right-to-Life	−14	−16	−4	7	33	52
Moral Majority	−9	0	16	47	63	56
Phyllis Schlafly	−5	16	24	44	73	57
National Rifle Assn.	19	11	24	43	71	37
Senator Goldwater	53	54	60	55	59	23
Chamber of Commerce	57	58	56	53	35	16

	Contributors to Left-oriented PACs					
	Demo-cratic Party	Labor	Presidential Candidate	Liberal	Multiple-issue	Single-issue
(Weighted N)	(277)	(390)	(203)	(161)	(105)	(72)
Net percentage close to						
Socialist party	−55	−20	−40	−32	−25	−28
Sierra Club	30	25	34	35	68	74
Ralph Nader	13	32	38	30	55	51
ACLU	33	40	42	61	62	72
Common Cause	38	41	54	66	70	71
Senator Kennedy	19	60	46	33	53	36
AFL-CIO	2	81	15	8	19	−3

Source: Survey conducted by the authors.

Note: A minus sign represents a negative rating; the larger the number, the more positive or negative the group's rating.

recurrent theme of earlier contributor studies, shows up in lukewarm ratings of liberal groups and figures, including the AFL-CIO and Sen. Edward Kennedy (both enthusiastically backed by labor).[17] Multiple- and single-issue contributors admire the Sierra Club, Ralph Nader, the ACLU, Common Cause, and Kennedy, but lack warmth toward organized labor. These disparate preferences for allies certainly underlie the bitter divisions among Democratic leaders, union chiefs, and New Politics advocates in Washington.

The coolness of both Republicans and Democrats toward would-be ideological allies is accompanied by some affection for the opposition: 38 percent of Republicans feel close to at least one liberal group or leader; 36 percent of Democrats to at least one conservative group or leader. Only 24 percent of single-issue donors on the Right and 17 percent on the Left ever cross the ideological divide.

Thus, issue-oriented activists appear as likely as the party-oriented to join coalitions, although each has an affinity for a different set of partners. The issue-oriented belong to alliances based on newer issues, while the party-oriented partake of older, economics-based alignments. Only a few single-issue donors stand aloof from either grouping. There seems to be little doubt, however, that these new organizations have contributed to ideological polarization. If the behavior of issue-oriented PACs is sometimes extreme, this reflects not only the preferences of their managers, but also the consistent and strongly held views of contributors.

Partisanship: Are PACs Killing the Parties?

Many observers believe that the simultaneous decline of parties and the rise of PACs are connected. Issue-oriented PACs are often accused of usurping the role of political parties, undermining efforts of party leaders, and thereby contributing to declining partisan loyalty among voters. Such activists, political scientist Frank Sorauf wrote, "reject the relatively issueless politics of traditional party organizations . . . and the broad omnibus loyalty to a political party that their parents and grandparents were comfortable with." [18] If PACs are indeed the organizational new wave, partisanship may become obsolete. To test this possibility, we looked at three indicators of activists' partisanship: evaluations of party performance, partisan self-identification, and confidence in party leadership (Table 5-4).

Our findings suggest that parties have a future. When asked which party would do a better job in handling each of sixteen issues, issue-oriented donors approved their allied party's performance more often than party donors, especially on social issues and foreign policy. Even on economics, where business and labor donors are most pro-party, issue-oriented donors match Republicans and Democrats. A look at individual issues is even more revealing: contributors to each single-issue PAC are more likely than party donors to approve of party performance on their pet issue, whether it is gun control, abortion, prayer in schools, or the ERA. For example, 39 percent of peace activists rated the Democratic party "much better" than the GOP on SALT talks, while only 15 percent of Democrats did.

Still, the new activists have not translated this approval into strong identification with the parties. For instance, all Right groups are heavily Republican, but strong Republicans are most numerous among GOP and conservative activists. Fewer single-issue donors are Republicans and many fewer are strong Republicans. This tendency may reflect the newness of GOP affiliation: 45 percent report having moved away from the Democrats. Indeed,

Table 5-4 Partisanship: Issue Evaluations, Self-identification, and Trust in Leaders

| | Contributors to Right-oriented PACs | | | | | |
	Republican Party	Business	Presidential Candidate	Conservative	Multiple-issue	Single-issue
(Weighted N)	(1260)	(434)	(262)	(448)	(162)	(51)
Percentage evaluating Republicans better on						
Economic issues	67	83	74	80	72	57
Social issues	33	29	46	40	52	47
Foreign policy	78	93	88	90	88	84
Percentage identifying as:						
Republican	97	94	95	94	92	83
Strong Republican	61	56	51	61	56	27
Percentage trusting Republican leadership	52	35	39	41	57	25

| | Contributors to Left-oriented PACs | | | | | |
	Democratic Party	Labor	Presidential Candidate	Liberal	Multiple-issue	Single-issue
(Weighted N)	(277)	(390)	(203)	(161)	(105)	(72)
Percentage evaluating Democrats better on						
Economic issues	47	73	60	59	69	46
Social issues	52	49	58	69	71	67
Foreign policy	43	56	56	56	58	52
Percentage identifying as:						
Democratic	77	88	80	86	90	69
Strong Democratic	51	65	53	48	39	20
Percentage trusting Democratic leadership	24	35	23	27	23	7

Source: Survey conducted by the authors.

such deserters comprise at least 30 percent of all donors to Right issue-oriented committees. They may well bear witness to party realignment among activists, precipitated by Democratic stands on abortion, school prayer, national defense, and other issues.

Once again, the Left exhibits much greater diversity. Both Democratic and candidate donors are actually less likely to profess Democratic loyalty than labor or issue-oriented donors—in fact, many Republicans are found in both groups (15 percent in Democratic party committees, for example). Labor PACs have the greatest number of strong Democrats; multiple- and single-issue groups, the fewest. Given the Democrats' recent electoral misfortunes, it is not surprising that the Left counts fewer GOP converts, but, as on the Right, party switchers abound among the issue-oriented PACs, indicating that New Politics issues, such as ERA, nuclear disarmament, and environmentalism, may have moved some Republicans from their traditional party home.

Activists also differ in their trust of party leaders. The Right has much more confidence in GOP leaders than the Left has in the Democrats. And Republicans have more faith in GOP leaders than do Right issue-oriented groups, with the exception of multiple-issue donors. On the Left, labor trusts Democratic leaders most, party donors are matched by most other groups, and single-issue contributors are very skeptical. For their part, issue-oriented donors are more-likely to trust PACs and public interest groups. With the exception of labor, which trusts PAC leaders, party-oriented donors are quite critical of these same people. Thus, party-oriented and issue-oriented donors share a common trait—distrust of the other's leadership.

Hence, the new activists are clearly not intent on destroying the parties; only single-issue donors exhibit a strong antiparty bias. Rather, the new PACs reflect more a transformation than a diminution of partisanship. As journalist Sidney Blumenthal argues, an ideological movement "inhabits the party in order to advance the ideology." [19] Such activists view parties as vehicles for issues, but not yet as objects of real loyalty or commitment. They are "responsible" partisans, who seek to make the parties "stand for principle." [20]

Political Civility: Trust, Optimism, and Tolerance

Americans' declining confidence in their political, social, and economic institutions has been a repeated theme of journalists, pollsters, and even chief executives over the past two decades. To many observers, the appearance of new PACs and the behavior of their leaders both expresses and encourages growing cynicism, loss of civic hope, and mounting intolerance. As one PAC leader observes, issue-oriented contributors "tend to be very, very frustrated . . . but there's not very much they feel they can do to turn the country around." [21]

To determine whether these activists represent the disenchanted, we asked contributors how much confidence they had in several institutions: organized religion, charitable groups, the news media, universities, business,

Table 5-5 Trust and Optimism: Trust Major Institutions and Optimism for Country

	Contributors to Right-oriented PACs					
	Repub-lican Party	Business	Presidential Candidate	Conserv-ative	Multiple-issue	Single-issue
(Weighted N)	(1260)	(434)	(262)	(448)	(162)	(51)
Percentage trusting more than four institutions	59	56	47	49	67	45
Percentage trusting federal government	46	27	41	31	21	24
Percentage optimistic about future of country	81	72	68	64	60	57

	Contributors to Left-oriented PACs					
	Demo-cratic Party	Labor	Presidential Candidate	Liberal	Multiple-issue	Single-issue
(Weighted N)	(277)	(390)	(203)	(161)	(105)	(72)
Percentage trusting more than four institutions	50	33	36	45	29	17
Percentage trusting federal government	42	35	43	22	20	24
Percentage optimistic about future of country	87	74	83	76	72	65

Source: Survey conducted by the authors.

organized labor, the bar, and the medical profession. Of course, each institution has its unique constellation of supporters and critics; Table 5-5 reports a measure of generalized trust, the proportion of activists claiming at least some confidence in four or more institutions.

Two tendencies emerge. First, all Right groups express greater institutional trust than their Left counterparts. This difference is understandable; the Left often advocates policies to correct deficiencies in private institutions, and activists on the Right are often denizens of these same institutions. Second, Republicans and Democrats usually are more trusting than other

Right and Left groups. Not only do they score higher on generalized trust, but also they have more confidence in individual institutions, with single-issue donors having the least. For example, 47 percent of Republicans have a great deal of confidence in the United Way, compared with only 24 percent of single-issue contributors. These findings, interestingly, parallel the conclusions of political scientists Seymour Martin Lipset and William Schneider's study of voters. They found that strong partisans are more trusting than independents, and that ideologues, especially those on the Left, are less trusting than moderates.[22]

Whatever their reservations about private institutions, both Left and Right have even less confidence in the federal government. Table 5-5 also reports the percentage of donors who trust the federal government at least some of the time. Republicans, Democrats, and their associated candidate contributors score highest (more than 40 percent), with business and labor somewhat lower. Issue-oriented donors are uniformly disenchanted. Though all donors are much more optimistic about the future of the country, here as well optimism declines steadily from party to single-issue donors, with the Right less sanguine than the Left. Again, business and labor donors deviate, being somewhat less hopeful than we might expect, given their establishment status.

Many scholars argue that survival of the democratic process and civil liberties depends on the attitudes of political elites. Is the greater cynicism of issue-oriented groups accompanied by more political paranoia or less tolerance? We measured these by first asking contributors to name the most dangerous group in the country and then asking if such a group "should be allowed" to run a candidate for president, speak in a public place, or teach in a public school.[23] Table 5-6 reports both the types of dangerous groups named and the proportion of each donor group that is fully tolerant; that is, allowing members of the groups they named as dangerous to engage in all three activities.

Party-oriented and issue-oriented contributors certainly have different enemies. Not only are party-oriented donors more likely to say that there are no dangerous political groups in America, but also they more frequently name one on their own side! As single-issue PAC fund-raising tactics often emphasize threats from opposing single-issue groups, it is not surprising that many donors see such groups as most dangerous. On the whole, the Right tends to fear Left extremists more (e.g., Communists and Socialists), while the Left focuses on Right single-issue groups (e.g., the Moral Majority)— although all donors often name extremists on the other side.

Whatever the choice of enemy, the Left is markedly more tolerant. Few Right donors are fully tolerant, although Republicans are more tolerant than conservatives and single-issue activists. On the Left, all donors are quite permissive, but labor lags behind multiple- and single-issue donors. No doubt the Left's greater tolerance reflects both Democratic party tradition and practical need for protection of its own unorthodox views and unconventional political activities.

Table 5-6 Political Tolerance: "Dangerous Groups" and Respect for Civil Liberties

	Contributors to Right-oriented PACs					
	Republican Party	Business	Presidential Candidate	Conservative	Multiple-issue	Single-issue
(Weighted N)	(1260)	(434)	(262)	(448)	(162)	(51)
Percentage naming as dangerous						
Left extremists	27	30	34	29	39	25
Left single-issue	21	19	13	28	30	44
Other Left groups	16	16	20	32	18	16
All Right groups	18	14	8	9	2	7
No political group	18	21	25	2	11	8
Percentage fully tolerant of dangerous group	37	32	30	29	25	26

	Contributors to Left-oriented PACs					
	Democratic Party	Labor	Presidential Candidate	Liberal	Multiple-issue	Single-issue
(Weighted N)	(277)	(390)	(203)	(161)	(105)	(72)
Percentage naming as dangerous						
Right extremists	14	10	26	18	21	14
Right single-issue	35	37	32	37	37	47
Other Right groups	14	20	15	15	22	16
All Left groups	22	14	6	9	10	3
No political group	15	18	14	16	8	15
Percentage fully tolerant of dangerous group	63	53	61	63	76	68

Source: Survey conducted by the authors.

Our findings, in this instance, confirm some widespread suspicions: issue-oriented PACs on both sides represent those who have less trust in social and political institutions than party activists (especially on the Left), are more pessimistic about the nation's future, and—on the Right—are less willing to grant unpopular minorities their constitutional rights.

Incentives for Political Activity:
Merging Motivations

To this point, party-oriented activists have largely conformed to their image: they are moderate, partisan, and civil—traits often associated with professional activists, who are in politics for material or social reasons and who are preoccupied, above all, with winning elections. While issue-oriented activists sometimes have surprised us, they bear the unmistakable markings of amateurs, who demand fidelity to the cause, even if it means defeat at the polls. Are they amateurs? We asked our respondents the most important reasons for their political involvement.

As it turns out, all groups consider influencing policy and winning elections far more important than furthering political or business careers. As Table 5-7 shows, the expected differences appear between party-oriented and issue-oriented activists, but often they are muted. On the Right, issue-oriented

Table 5-7 Incentives for Political Involvement: Reasons Listed as "Very Important"

	Contributors to Right-oriented PACs					
	Republican Party	Business	Presidential Candidate	Conservative	Multiple-issue	Single-issue
(Weighted N)	(1260)	(434)	(262)	(448)	(162)	(51)
Percentage naming						
Influencing policy	45	51	50	60	51	60
Winning elections	47	47	49	69	63	63
Furthering career	19	20	26	27	38	15
Business reasons	19	24	13	10	14	7
	Contributors to Left-oriented PACs					
	Democratic Party	Labor	Presidential Candidate	Liberal	Multiple-issue	Single-issue
(Weighted N)	(277)	(390)	(203)	(161)	(105)	(72)
Percentage naming						
Influencing policy	59	58	59	45	70	61
Winning elections	48	61	57	36	49	50
Furthering career	36	23	48	26	28	22
Business reasons	17	29	7	6	4	4

Source: Survey conducted by the authors.

donors do want to influence public policy, but they are just as interested in electoral victory, supposedly a professional trait. Indeed, on the whole they score higher on both motivations—and on advancing political careers—than party-oriented donors. Only business reasons are cited more frequently by Republican and business donors.

On the Left, the pattern is slightly different. All groups are about equally likely to mention policy goals, except for multiple-issue donors, who score much higher than the others. Winning elections, on the other hand, is less vital to the issue-oriented (especially in comparison with their Right counterparts) and, surprisingly, to Democrats. Democrats and candidate donors place highest importance on careerism, as expected, exceeding their Right counterparts and reflecting, perhaps, the Democratic party's greater residual professionalism. Democrats and labor contributors are also most prone to cite business- or job-related motivations.

Thus, traditional patterns hold in part, but professional groups are much more expressive than expected, and amateurs reveal some markedly professional traits. Why the similarity in incentives? Perhaps direct mail and other mass fund-raising techniques rely on expressive appeals and, whatever their sponsorship, attract mainly policy-oriented activists. Material and social incentives might draw other types of activists, although studies of county party chairmen, state convention delegates, and national party conventions have discovered the same pattern we have. The paucity of professionals may also reflect a steady disappearance of material incentives from the parties' arsenals, while expressive incentives have, if anything, become more available. Whatever the cause, there has been a homogenization of incentives, producing responsible partisans in all kinds of organizations.[24]

Networks and Activism: The Struggle for Access

Perhaps the residual professionalism of party-oriented donors derives from their access to traditional party organizations. Many studies emphasize the networks to which activists belong: the web of social and political organizations that provide contacts and information and support specialized political activities. There is evidence that party-oriented activists belong to establishment organizations rather than narrow political groups; receive their political information from public sources, which reflect mainstream views; and engage in conventional activities to take advantage of their access to political leaders. On the other hand, the insurgent issue-oriented activists belong to more specialized organizations and draw their information from less public (and more congenial) sources. Lacking access to political elites, they pursue unconventional politics.[25]

To what extent do donors fit these profiles? Though we cannot present all of the evidence here, responses on organizational membership, sources of political information, and kinds of political activity are informative. Party-oriented donors do, in many ways, fit their establishment image. They are quite likely to belong to professional and civic organizations and participate less often in narrow political groups. Few party donors claim membership in PACs or public interest groups, although business, labor, and candidate contributors often do. In accord with their preference for mainstream organizations, party-oriented donors get political information from public sources, especially television news, which business and labor donors supplement with professional publications. As expected, party donors engage in a broad range of conventional activities; those giving to business and labor are particularly active in lobbying and fund raising, candidate donors in campaign work.

Issue-oriented donors, as expected, have many insurgent traits. Single-issue donors on both the Right and the Left are less likely to join professional and civic associations, but conservatives and liberals are not far behind party donors in their willingness to join these groups. They do belong to narrow political organizations in large numbers: the Right claims PAC membership, the Left belongs to public interest groups. Issue-oriented donors also rely on more private information sources: family and friends, books, opinion magazines, and political mail. The Right donors disdain the mass media, but listen to their clergy; activists on the Left have little use for religious leaders, but read newspapers and listen to public radio. And all issue-oriented groups specialize in outsider activities: demonstrating, writing letters to the editor, and backing alternative parties. For example, 33 percent of Left single-issue contributors provided some support for a minor party—mostly for John Anderson or the Citizens Party—in the 1980 presidential race.

Although such evidence conforms to the traditional pictures of party-oriented and issue-oriented activists, other findings do not. On the whole, issue-oriented donors are not more isolated socially or less active politically. In fact, they belong to more organizations and use more information sources than their party-oriented fellows. For instance, only 30 percent of Republican donors belong to four or more organizations, compared with 45 percent of single-issue activists. Similarly, only 19 percent of Democratic donors use four or more sources of political information, whereas 29 percent of the single-issue activists do. The biggest difference, however, is in total political participation: issue-oriented donors are simply more active. For example, only 16 percent of GOP donors engaged in seven or more political activities in 1980, compared with 36 percent of multiple-issue contributors.

Ironically, Republicans are the least involved group. The Right multiple-issue donors take up the slack, assisted by candidate and other issue-oriented groups; all campaign and engage in insider activities as often as Republican donors do. Indeed, issue-oriented donors are just as likely as Republicans to join party clubs, and single-issue donors are twice as likely to attend GOP conventions. As before, the Left is a little different. Democratic donors are slightly more active than the Left issue-oriented activists (and fall between the Republicans and their more active allies). The real dynamos of the Left, however, are labor donors, who engage in virtually every kind of activity. Indeed, labor and Left candidate donors equal the participation rates of the Right multiple-issue activists.

Thus, differences between party-oriented and issue-oriented donors are more modest than expected: not only do these activists share many attitudes, alliances, and incentives, but also they operate in overlapping networks and engage in many of the same activities. Perhaps the relative inactivity of the party donors results from their broad contributor base; the GOP, especially, may have tapped donors with only a marginal interest in politics. On the other hand, the greater intensity and minority status of issue-oriented donors may compel greater involvement. Their numerous group memberships, extensive use of information sources, frenetic and varied activism may be an attempt to gain the degree of political access party-oriented activists already enjoy.

Conclusion

The diversity of party, special interest, candidate, ideological, and single-issue PACs can be understood in simpler terms. Although the range of organizations certainly offers activists a smorgasbord of choices, the real struggle boils down to one between traditional and responsible partisans. Despite the advent of direct mail fund raising, with its purported ideological bias, Republicans and Democrats still conform well to the broker model of moderate, pragmatic New Deal politics. The parties have been infused with greater concern for ideology, though not, as some have argued, with ideological extremists. The special interest style of business and labor is still largely intact, with these donors representing the New Deal agenda even more than their Republican and Democratic allies. The personalistic candidate PAC donors are still best thought of as partisans, but as the most ideological partisans.

The role of single-issue donors is also clarified by our discovery that most are not the emotional, single-minded, isolated activists often portrayed. To a large degree we concur with political scientist Sylvia Tesh's contention that "virtually all the presumed single issues are revealed as multiple. Their supporters and opponents link them . . . to other issues and thus to the varied convictions supporting liberalism and conservatism." [26] While there are many single-issue PACs, there are few single-issue contributors. Although often more intense, the multiple-issue donors resemble conservative and liberal ideologues: they perceive themselves as part of a larger ideological coalition, are distrustful of politics-as-usual, remain aloof from traditional party loyalties, but are hopeful of transfusing the parties with new visions of the public good.

In this struggle, issue-oriented activists may be slowly gaining in the battle of the agenda, but party-oriented cadres are winning the war of organization. As the number of cases in the tables indicates, those most dissatisfied with politics-as-usual are the least successful in attracting money. On the Right, pure single-issue activists represent only a small fraction of donors, and, even when added to the multiple-issue group, they account for fewer activists than Right candidate PACs. And though conservative contributors are twice as numerous as the multiple- and single-issue groups together, they only match business donors. Republicans still dominate the Right, with nearly three times the supporters as any other group and almost twice the number of the issue-oriented categories combined. Because of their frantic activism, issue-oriented donors constitute a vital factor in GOP politics, but the party itself can certainly resist their demands, although the greater homogeneity of attitudes on the Right reduces the likelihood that many such claims would be considered "extreme." [27]

The Democratic party's difficulties are highlighted by the financial pastiche of the Left. Although the party-oriented groups contain almost three-quarters of the Left's donors, the Democrats' weakness in fund raising increases the influence of labor and candidate activists. And while Democratic donors outnumber every issue-oriented category by large margins, they are outweighed by all these groups combined. The wide gaps in attitudes among Left constituencies greatly intensify the Democratic party's problems in managing conflict between its traditional and responsible partisans. As journalist Elizabeth Drew argues, "The problem the Democrats have had in defining themselves stems in some part—perhaps a substantial part—from their dilemma over where to turn for money." [28]

Thus, the advent of new ideological and single-issue PACs may not transform American politics as thoroughly as some anticipate. Not only do the parties and their historic interest group allies still dominate political finance, but also the very success of the ideological and single-issue groups requires getting their issues added to a larger agenda still dominated by economic issues. Historically, the party system has absorbed many special interest groups and new social movements. This process may well be occurring again. As political scientist Joseph Schlesinger notes, "Groups with broader policy concerns . . . must follow the lines held out to them by the competitive party system." [29] Although the organizational content of politics may change, the partisan framework remains.

Notes

1. Cf. Benjamin Ginsberg and Martin Shefter, "A Critical Realignment? The New Politics, the Reconstituted Right, and the Election of 1984," in *The Elections of 1984,* ed. Michael Nelson (Washington, D.C.: CQ Press, 1985), 15-23.
2. Ibid.
3. Quoted in Frank J. Sorauf, *What Price PACs?* (New York: Twentieth Century Fund, 1984), 18. For an excellent discussion of PAC diversity, see Larry J. Sabato, *PAC Power* (New York: W. W. Norton, 1984), chap. 1.
4. Our categories were suggested by Gary R. Orren, "The Changing Styles of American Politics" in *The Future of American Political Parties,* ed. Joel L. Fleishman (Englewood Cliffs, N.J.: Prentice-Hall, 1982), 4-41. Also see Sorauf, *What Price PACs?* 76-79. For good descriptions of organizations in our

categories, see *Money and Politics in the United States,* ed. Michael J. Malbin (Chatham, N.J.: Chatham House, 1984).

5. Samuel J. Eldersveld, *Political Parties: A Behavioral Analysis* (Chicago: Rand McNally, 1964).

6. Cf. Terry M. Moe, *The Organization of Interests* (Chicago: University of Chicago Press, 1980), chap. 5.

7. Xandra Kayden, *Campaign Organization* (Lexington, Mass.: D. C. Heath, 1978).

8. James Q. Wilson, *The Amateur Democrat* (Chicago: University of Chicago Press, 1962).

9. Marjorie R. Hershey, *Running for Office* (Chatham, N.J.: Chatham House, 1984).

10. Sylvia Tesh, "In Support of 'Single-Issue' Politics," *Political Science Quarterly* 99 (Spring 1984): 27-44.

11. For practical reasons we surveyed roughly equal numbers of donors to small and large PACs, although some single-issue PACs, such as the Gun Owners of America, raised much less money than very large PACs, such as NCPAC. To compare and contrast all contributors we needed to correct for the vast overrepresentation of donors to small PACs and the vast underrepresentation of donors to large PACs. Hence we weighted each group of respondents according to the amount of money their PAC raised in 1982. The weighted N approximates the number of donors that would be in each category had we randomly sampled a master list of donors to all the PACs studied.

12. A. James Reichley, "The Rise of National Parties," in *The New Directions in American Politics,* ed. John E. Chubb and Paul E. Peterson (Washington, D.C.: The Brookings Institution, 1985), 179-195.

13. Hershey, *Running for Office,* 12.

14. See John E. Jackson and Maris A. Vinovskis, "Public Opinion, Elections, and the 'Single-Issue' Issue," in *The Abortion Dispute and the American System,* ed. Gilbert Y. Steiner (Washington, D.C.: The Brookings Institution, 1983), 69.

15. Gallup Poll "Most Important Problem Trend," *Gallup Report* 198, March 1982, 27.

16. Gary C. Jacobson, "The Republican Advantage in Campaign Finance," in *New Directions,* 152; and Elizabeth Drew, *Politics and Money* (New York: Macmillan, 1983), 130.

17. Edmond Costantini and Joel King, "Checkbook Democrats and Their Copartisans," *American Politics Quarterly* 10 (January 1982): 65-92.

18. Sorauf, *What Price PACs?* 41.

19. Sidney Blumenthal, "Building a Conservative Elite," *Washington Post Weekly Edition,* Oct. 14, 1985, 6.

20. See Reichley, "The Rise of National Parties," 195-197. "Responsible" parties take explicit and distinct stands on issues and carry out policy promises once in office. See Austin Ranney, *The Doctrine of Responsible Party Government* (Urbana: University of Illinois Press, 1954).

21. Drew, *Politics and Money,* 132.

22. Seymour Martin Lipset and William Schneider, *The Confidence Gap: Business, Labor and Government in the Public Mind* (New York: The Free Press, 1983), chap. 4.

23. Cf. John L. Sullivan, James Piereson, and George E. Marcus, *Political Tolerance and American Democracy* (Chicago: University of Chicago Press,

1982), chap. 1.

24. This trend has been under way for some time. See Dwaine Marvick, "The Middlemen of Politics," in *Approaches to the Study of Party Organization*, ed. William J. Crotty (Boston: Allyn & Bacon, 1968), 341-374; Jeane C. Kirkpatrick, *The New Presidential Elite* (New York: Russell Sage Foundation, 1976); and Alan J. Abramowitz and Walter J. Stone, *Nomination Politics* (New York: Praeger, 1984), 45-55.

25. Cf. Kirkpatrick, *The New Presidential Elite*, 80-88; John H. Kessel, *Presidential Parties* (Homewood, Ill.: Dorsey Press, 1984), chap. 10; and Ruth S. Jones and Warren E. Miller, "Financing Campaigns: Macro Level Innovation and Micro Level Response," *Western Political Quarterly* 38 (June 1985): 187-209.

26. Tesh, "In Support of 'Single-Issue' Politics," 34.

27. David Adamany makes a similar point in "Political Parties in the 1980s," in *Money and Politics*, 108.

28. Drew, *Politics and Money*, 52. Also see Richard L. Rubin, *Party Dynamics: The Democratic Coalition and the Politics of Change* (New York: Oxford University Press, 1976).

29. Joseph A. Schlesinger, "The New American Political Party," *American Political Science Review* 79 (December 1985): 1168.

Appendix

Below are examples of organizations included in each category in Table 5-1 through Table 5-7. The sample was weighted together according to the amount of money each organization raised in the 1982 election cycle. All analyses were performed using unweighted data with very similar results.

Right

Republican party — Republican National Committee
National Republican Congressional Committee
National Republican Senatorial Committee

Business — Business and Industry Political Action Committee (BIPAC)
U.S. Chamber of Commerce

Candidate — Citizens for the Republic (Reagan)
Gerald Ford Leadership Committee (Ford)

Conservative — National Conservative Political Action Committee (NCPAC)
Fund for a Conservative Majority

Multiple-issue — (Contributors to conservative PACs and single-issue committees)

Single-issue — Right-to-life committees
Gun Owners of America

Eagle Forum
Moral Majority
American Security Council

Left

Democratic party	Democratic National Committee
	Democratic Congressional Campaign Committee
	Democratic Senatorial Campaign Committee
Labor	AFL-CIO Committee of Political Education (COPE)
	United Autoworkers
	Teamsters
Candidate	Fund for a Democratic Majority (Kennedy)
	Committee for the Future of America (Mondale)
Liberal	National Committee for an Effective Congress (NCEC)
	Democrats for the 80's
	Independent Action
Multiple-issue	(Contributors to liberal PACs and single-issue committees)
Single-issue	National Abortion Rights League
	Handgun Control
	National Organization for Women
	Human Rights PAC
	Council for a Livable World,
	Sierra Club

6. PAC Contributions and Roll-call Voting: Conditional Power

Diana M. Evans

The well-documented growth of political action committees (PACs) has led to widespread fears that PAC expenditures will unduly influence members of Congress. Especially worrisome are the reports that recipients of large contributions have voted overwhelmingly in favor of policies advocated by the PACs, as in the case of gun control legislation and the National Rifle Association. Many journalists, public interest advocates, and some legislators have called for reforms to curtail the impact of PACs on campaigns for office. As of 1986, a decade after Supreme Court decisions cleared the way for the expansion of PACs, scholarly research has not answered basic questions about their impact. No unambiguous linkages between contributions and congressional voting have been unearthed, nor should we expect any such discoveries. Rather, the role of money in politics is, as ever, complex and contingent.

In this chapter Diana Evans seeks to sort out the relationships between PAC contributions and legislative actions on two specific policies—the Chrysler loan guarantee program and the windfall profits tax. Her results will disappoint those who expect PACs to exert great influence over legislative decisions. She finds no simple, direct effects. At the same time, PAC contributions do appear to make a difference at the margins—when legislators may have no strong preferences and where PACs make a strong commitment of resources. Evans's research reflects the kind of careful, detailed work essential to building a firm understanding of the effects of PACs within the policy process.

One of the central questions in the current debate about reforming campaign finance laws concerns the possibility that contributions from political action committees (PACs) corrupt the people who receive them. Specifically, the question is: Do PAC contributors buy members of Congress? Common Cause has been answering yes for years. One of their recent publications portrays congressional voting on several bills as auctions at which the final decisions were sold to the highest bidders.[1] The same year, the *Wall Street Journal* ran a series on the role of PACs in the political process, the general tone of which is illustrated by the following:

When Rep. Joseph Addabbo [D-N.Y.] changed his mind about encouraging the Army to buy M1 tank engines from a second supplier, he surprised his liberal colleagues. But he delighted Avco Corp., which had just donated $5,000 to his 1984 reelection campaign.[2]

Although that series was reasonably balanced, the message was not reassuring. The clear implication was that, despite protestations of public spiritedness by PAC directors and impartiality by members of Congress, large contributors do indeed influence the decisions of members of Congress.

However, there are good reasons for questioning such conclusions. Consider, for example, the basis of Common Cause's inference in the same publication that members of the U.S. House of Representatives sold out to dairy producers on a vote that would have reduced dairy price supports: "Members who voted for the dairy industry received on the average six times as much money from dairy PACs as those who didn't." No doubt. But who were those members who supposedly sold their votes? Were they people who would have voted that way without dairy contributions? In a more thorough analysis of voting on milk price supports in 1974, William Welch found that the amount of dairy production in the districts and the members' party and ideology influenced their voting far more than dairy PAC contributions. "In 1976 dairy PACs gave substantial amounts of money to candidates who were compelled to vote in favor of price supports by constituency, ideology, and party. In a sense, such congressmen did the lobby no favor." [3]

Nevertheless, Welch found a statistically significant, though relatively small, effect for PAC contributions. The point is that ignoring the likelihood that PACs contribute heavily to members who would support them anyway leads to serious overestimation of the impact of PAC contributions on roll-call voting. Existing scholarly studies on the impact of PAC contributions take into account other possible influences. The results, however, are conflicting, suggesting that contributions sometimes do and sometimes do not affect roll-call voting.

For example, PAC contributions apparently had little effect on voting on auto emissions standards, B-1 bomber appropriations, or a cargo preference bill. On the other hand, contributions evidently had large effects on roll-call voting on trucking deregulation, on a congressional veto of an FTC rule requiring used-car dealers to inform potential buyers of a car's defects, and on the exemption of professionals from antitrust legislation.[4]

What conclusions can we draw from the accumulated results of these studies? First, it must be said that no precise generalizations are possible, as few of the studies use both exactly the same explanatory variables and statistical techniques. Second, with that caveat in mind, it seems safe to say that the impact of PAC contributions differs from one bill to another. It appears that on some bills, contributions have little or no impact relative to the factors that normally influence legislative behavior, such as party and ideology; on others, however, PAC money probably does have an effect on members' decision making. After all, roll-call votes differ in a number of ways. Some are more important to an interest group than others; some are highly publicized, and others receive no public scrutiny; some are obscure and technical, while others have clear policy or symbolic implications. Thus, if PAC contributions have any effect at all, they probably have more effect on some bills than others.

In fact, the major question that these studies raise is this: Under what circumstances do PAC contributions affect the roll-call voting decisions of members of Congress? Although there are several circumstances that might moderate or enhance the effect of PAC contributions, a critical dimension is the existence of conflict as opposed to consensus on a bill. Specifically, if a consensus exists among interest groups lobbying on a bill, contributions will have more impact than when there is conflict among groups. This chapter examines that hypothesis by comparing the effects of PAC contributions on House members' voting on the Chrysler loan guarantee, a bill that enjoyed a consensus among lobbying groups, with voting on the windfall profits tax, a bill that generated a great deal of conflict among groups.

PAC Money and the Legislative Environment

The broad outlines of the argument are as follows: PAC contributions are more likely to affect members' voting on consensual issues than on conflictual issues, because on consensual issues, any reasons that a member might have for voting *against* a contributor are not reinforced by groups active on that side, as they are on conflictual issues. Moreover, we can understand the basis for conflict or consensus on a bill by analyzing the characteristics of the bill, focusing on whether a bill offers concentrated or dispersed costs and benefits.

First, consider consensual bills, where PAC contributions are most apt to influence voting. Consensual bills are likely to be those that offer concentrated benefits and dispersed costs; the milk price-support program is a perfect example. That is, a relatively small group, usually an economic interest group, seeks a benefit for its members at the expense of a large portion of the general public. Protective tariffs, special tax treatment, and most subsidies fall into this category.

To predict that such bills will be consensual is not to say that there will be no congressional opposition to them, rather that the opposition outside Congress is likely to be either unorganized or poorly organized. It is difficult, even irrational, for the public to organize to fight this kind of special interest legislation precisely because of the huge number of people involved.[5] In fact, the public normally is unaware that such legislation is pending. Therefore, members of Congress who are inclined to oppose the group and champion the public on ideological grounds may do so, but unless such members' hostility to the proposal is intense, the lack of reinforcement from groups representing the public may result in weak opposition that can be undermined by campaign contributions from the other side.

Thus, in spite of the wide dispersion of people affected by the legislation in many or all congressional districts, the fact that they typically are not organized makes it difficult for them to counteract the power of campaign contributions. Members of Congress themselves show concern over this phenomenon. For example, Rep. Dan Glickman, D-Kan., worried about PAC influence on consensual issues:

> I do not think any member of Congress votes because of how a PAC gives him money on El Salvador, or the MX missiles, or some of what I call the broader, abstract national issues. But those are not the ones I am really worried about. The ones I worry about are the specialty issues on which nobody is on the other side. . . . Where was the public last year before the dramatic rate increases that we are now seeing as a result of divestiture of the telephone company? The public wasn't there; AT&T [American Telephone and Telegraph Company] and CWA [Communications Workers of America] were there. Where has the public been on dairy legislation when we raise dairy price supports? . . . The public generally is not there; the dairy lobby is there. Where is the public on banking policy? On pharmaceutical legislation? . . . The public doesn't know, and I think the smaller specialty issues, where no one is on the other side, are the heart of the dramatic problem of special interest contributions.[6]

Conversely, PAC contributions are less likely to be effective when legislation is considered in an environment of interest group conflict, especially if groups on both sides have PACs. Bills are likely to generate conflict in two cases: (1) when both costs and benefits are concentrated, as they are on labor bills, which pit business against organized labor; and (2) when costs are concentrated and benefits are dispersed, as they are, for example, on environmental legislation. The reason for conflict in the first case is obvious: one group tries to get something at the other's expense and both have the resources for a fight.[7] In such cases, many representatives will have to oppose a supporter no matter what they do, and, by and large, contributions by PACs on one side may be matched by PACs on the other side. Hence, the contributions may effectively cancel each other out.

The second case (concentrated costs and dispersed benefits) might appear at first glance to be essentially the same as the situation that generates consensual bills. But note that this time someone is imposing costs on an organized group for the benefit of the public. The very fact that such a bill has gotten on the congressional agenda guarantees a fight. Indeed, getting such bills on the agenda historically has been no mean feat,[8] largely because it is so difficult to organize widely dispersed interests. When they do organize, they tend to remain financially weak compared with more concentrated economic groups. For example, all of the affiliated environmental PACs put together contributed $12,135 to House and Senate races in 1979-1980, while Exxon alone contributed $55,535 during the same period. Additionally, labor unions such as the AFL-CIO and the United Auto Workers (UAW), which are organized primarily to promote the economic well-being of their members, frequently lobby on behalf of the public, but labor's interest in such issues is always secondary.

Thus, where costs are concentrated and benefits are distributed, the competing groups are not likely to cancel each other out, because the stakes are higher for one side than the other. The groups that are being asked to bear the costs are more likely to try to trade on their campaign contributions than the other side because they have more to lose. So it is likely that contributions from PACs for whom the stakes are higher have a greater effect on voting than those for whom the stakes on the same bill are lower.

Even so, contributions from PACs for whom the stakes are highest will have less effect in this situation than they would on a consensual bill. On a conflictual bill, representatives who are inclined to oppose a group hear from organized groups that agree with them and may feel that there is so much public interest in the issue that they can gain more politically by taking a public position against a contributing PAC than by supporting it in return for a $500 contribution.

The case studies of the Chrysler loan guarantee and the windfall profits tax test two hypotheses: that PAC contributions have more effect on voting on consensual bills than conflictual bills, and that PAC contributions from those with the most at stake on a bill have more effect than money from PACs with less at stake on the same bill.

Issues and Tactics: Chrysler

The year 1979 was a very bad one for Chrysler Corporation. By the end of the third quarter, it had lost $721.5 million, the most money any U.S. corporation had ever lost.[9] Private lenders, fearing that Chrysler's cash problems were terminal, were reluctant to lend it more money for fear Chrysler would go bankrupt anyway and they would never be paid.

Chrysler's initial strategy was to attack government regulations on pollution, safety, and fuel economy as the cause of its problems; it sought a special five- to ten-year delay in the implementation of the environmental regulations and a cash advance against future tax credits for investment costs. The company argued that the interest on the research and development costs to meet the regulations was $125 per car, whereas the cost to General Motors, which sold more than five times as many cars as Chrysler, was only $27 per car. Moreover, Chrysler argued that, because it had no profits, that expense, instead of being deductible, came directly from its cash flow.

However, when it became clear that Congress was not buying its arguments, Chrysler asked for loan guarantees, a strategy that got a much friendlier reception on the Hill and in the White House. In fact, the Chrysler loan guarantee was largely a consensual issue. Very few groups testified against it in House hearings; more important, all of the active groups with PACs were in favor of the loan guarantee. The supporting lineup was impressive: Chrysler, the UAW, the National Automobile Dealers Association, United Technologies, National Steel Corporation (both Chrysler suppliers), and the Carter administration. The bill provided federal guarantees for private-sector loans to Chrysler, meaning that if Chrysler defaulted on the loans, the federal government would repay them. Thus, the benefits were concentrated, while the costs, if Chrysler had failed, would have been distributed among all taxpayers.

The tone of the testimony in House hearings indicated that the opposition that did exist was largely unorganized outside of Congress. Among Congress members, opposition was primarily based on ideology; in other words, conservatives did not believe that the government should bail out a business that was not efficient enough to survive on its own. The hypothesis developed earlier suggests that in such a situation, conservative members would be influenced by PAC contributions if anyone was; the liberal, prolabor members who favored the bill anyway would not need to be influenced.

Chrysler argued that without the loan guarantee, it would be bankrupt by the end of the year. The company claimed that 600,000 jobs were on the line in the short term, and that 400,000 jobs would be lost for good. Those claims clearly persuaded the Carter administration, whose officials argued that a Chrysler failure would be intolerably costly in terms of unemployment and welfare payments as well as tax losses.

Although the UAW had not wholeheartedly backed Chrysler's attempt to delay the implementation of regulations, the threat of massive unemployment among its members motivated the union to work hand-in-hand with Chrysler for the loan guarantee. A UAW lobbyist said in an interview, "We didn't try to make excuses for management's mistakes"; instead, they based their arguments on the massive consequences of a Chrysler failure.

Indeed, in their lobbying campaign, Chrysler and the UAW worked to assemble the largest coalition possible, asking not only Chrysler workers, but all UAW members to lobby for the bill, to demonstrate that the union's members did not consider it exclusively a Chrysler issue, but a broad labor issue. A Chrysler lobbyist felt that Douglas Fraser, president of the UAW, was especially helpful, not only for his obvious political clout, but also because he had "tremendous respect on the Hill from friends and foes alike" for his integrity and candor.

As the final vote in the House approached, Chrysler followed a grassroots strategy, periodically assembling one hundred dealers at the Capitol Hill Club for breakfast and sending them out to lobby their representatives. These dealers were armed with lists not only of Chrysler plants and employees, but also all Chrysler suppliers and their employees, as well as all of *their* suppliers and employees, all grouped by congressional district. With that approach, they managed to demonstrate that a Chrysler failure would affect every district in the country. This not only showed members "the massiveness of the problem," according to the Chrysler lobbyist, but also gave members a justification for voting for the bill.

The strategy worked. The House passed the Chrysler loan guarantee by a vote of 271-136, after beating back two attempts to weaken it. The final conference committee bill, signed by the president, authorized $1.5 billion in federal loan guarantees, provided that Chrysler got another $2 billion in aid from dealers, creditors, and workers (by selling them stock, for example). In retrospect, one can argue that the policy was a spectacular success: in July 1983 Chrysler president Lee Iacocca announced that Chrysler was paying off the last of its loans, seven years ahead of schedule.

The saturation lobbying campaign conducted by Chrysler and the UAW is a good illustration of the kind of political environment that exists on consensual bills. Members of Congress heard from only one side, and the principal actors on that side, Chrysler and the UAW, both had PACs that had contributed to members in the preceding (1978) election. Thus, although the laissez-faire sentiments of conservative members normally would have led them to vote against a government bailout for a foundering corporation, in this case such members had not had their position reinforced by campaign contributors who agreed with them. They were, instead, pressed by a contributor to vote against their ideological inclinations. The statistical analysis in the next section tests the hypothesis that those who got contributions were more inclined to go along than those who did not, and that they were more likely to be influenced on such a bill than they would be on a conflictual bill when their predisposition was reinforced by other groups.

Issues and Tactics: Windfall Profits

The bill to impose a windfall profits tax on the oil industry falls into the category of conflictual bills; it imposed concentrated costs and provided dispersed benefits. This bill, like the Chrysler loan guarantee, was considered and passed in the House of Representatives in 1979. Proposed by President Jimmy Carter as part of his energy program, it was designed to recapture for the public a large portion of the additional profits oil companies would receive when domestic oil prices were allowed to rise to world price levels. Carter's energy policy was intended to promote conservation by ending price controls. To ease the pain (as well as the public opposition), the resulting tax revenues would be devoted to an Energy Security Trust Fund, which would provide fuel assistance for the poor, subsidies for the development of synthetic fuels, and aid to mass transit systems.

Carter's windfall profits tax proposal was rather complex, but its two major features were a 50 percent tax on the price increase on "old" oil (already in production) that would occur as a result of decontrol of domestic oil prices, and an "OPEC tax," which provided that the government would take 50 percent of any price increase by U.S companies that resulted from an OPEC price hike that exceeded the rate of inflation.

Not surprisingly, the oil industry was in favor of decontrol, but opposed to the windfall profits tax, and, of all of the bill's provisions, the industry hated the OPEC tax the most. Although their friends in the House advised them to accept the tax and work toward weakening it, oil companies publicly opposed it on the grounds that it would hinder exploration, development, and production of new oil supplies. At the same time, however, the industry was reporting record profits amid a new round of shortages and soaring prices, all of which was reflected in the wide range of groups that testified before the House Ways and Means Committee in favor of the tax.

Groups that expected to benefit directly from the Energy Security Trust Fund, including the American Public Transit Association and the National Oil Jobbers Council, testified for the tax, as did a variety of environmental groups, such as the Sierra Club and Friends of the Earth. However, only two supporting groups, the UAW and the AFL-CIO, had PACs that were active in the 1978 elections. This issue was not of primary importance to either group, as it was not a labor issue per se. But a top UAW lobbyist said in an interview that a position in favor of the tax fit in with the union's general policy. In fact, both unions opposed domestic price decontrol, but argued that if prices were allowed to rise to world levels, the resulting windfall profits should be taxed heavily; otherwise, according to the lobbyist, the result of decontrol would be a "massive transfer of income from consumers to multinationals." Implementation of the tax, on the other hand, would provide additional funding for social programs they favored.

Unlike Chrysler and the UAW, the oil companies did not conduct a highly coordinated lobbying campaign. One House staffer described the process as "every man for himself." Although that may be an exaggeration, the companies did not all take the same position. Some were hungry for decontrol even with the tax; at the other extreme was Mobil, which went so far as to bolt the ranks, calling for continued price controls on domestic oil in return for death to the OPEC tax. Moreover, majors and independents fought over who would get the best breaks if the tax did pass. Nevertheless, all companies, majors and independents alike, opposed the tax; the only disagreements were over which part of the legislation they disliked the most.

The Ways and Means Committee reported the president's bill with its own amendment. The amendment was to be voted on during consideration of the bill by the full House, and provided, among other things, that the tax rate on old oil be raised from the 50 percent rate proposed by President Carter to 70 percent. That amendment passed, thus making even more critical the industry's attempts to weaken the legislation, which by then appeared certain to pass.

The compromise that eventually passed as a substitute to the Ways and Means bill was offered by Democratic representative James R. Jones of Oklahoma and Republican W. Henson Moore of Louisiana, both friends of the oil industry. Their bill indeed killed the permanent OPEC tax and eliminated the windfall profits tax altogether after 1990; however, it set the tax on old oil at 60 percent, even higher than Carter's request, but lower than that set by the committee's amendment.

In the end, the bill that emerged from Congress raised the rate on old oil to 70 percent; oil discovered after 1978 was taxed at 30 percent. Independent producers in some cases were taxed at lower rates. Certain wells, such as those owned by Indian tribes and state and local governments, were exempt altogether. The bill also ended the tax in the early 1990s, the exact year to depend on revenues.

The windfall profits tax bill is different from the Chrysler loan guarantee on the conflict-consensus dimension. There was a great deal of conflict, and members of Congress were lobbied on both sides. More important, there were PAC contributions on both sides; thus members were more likely to receive reinforcement for whatever position their ideology or partisan loyalties drew them toward. However, the stakes for the two sides were different. They were clearly very high in economic terms for the oil companies, whereas the groups with PACs on the other side, the UAW and AFL-CIO, lobbied mainly for ideological reasons. The next section tests the hypotheses that the oil PACs influenced members more than the unions and that even the influence of the oil PACs was less than the effect of the PACs active on the Chrysler bill, as the latter was a consensual bill and the windfall profits tax was conflictual.

The Effect of PAC Contributions
on Voting on the Bills

To test the two hypotheses about the effects of PAC contributions on House members' votes on the two bills, it is important to take account of other variables that commonly affect members' voting on legislation, especially the member's party, ideology, and district interests.[10] Failure to do so often produces the strong, but misleading, relationships between contributions and voting observed by Common Cause. For example, labor PACs give money to liberal Democrats, and liberal Democrats then vote for labor legislation. However, at least some of those members would certainly vote for such bills whether or not they received labor PAC contributions. The important questions are, therefore, the following: Do PAC contributions influence members' roll-call voting? If so, on what kinds of issues? What are the effects of PAC money relative to the effects of party, ideology, and district needs? And finally, how much *more* likely is a member who has received a PAC contribution to vote with the PAC than an otherwise similar member who has not received such a contribution?

To answer those questions and test the hypotheses about the answers to the first and second questions, I estimated a logit equation for each non-unanimous vote on both bills. Logit analysis estimates the relative effects of several independent variables, such as PAC contributions and party, on a dependent variable, such as a roll-call vote, which has two values (the member voted either yes or no). Thus, we can draw inferences about whether the independent variables have a significant effect on the dependent variable and which has the greatest effect. In addition to including campaign contributions from each group that testified or lobbied, or clearly had an interest in the bill, I included the member's party, ideology as measured by his or her ADA rating (a measure of the liberalism of the member's voting record) or COPE rating (the AFL-CIO scale that is based partly on labor issues), and a measure of the member's constituents' interest in the bill—for Chrysler, the existence of a Chrysler plant in the district; for the windfall profits tax, the per capita petroleum production in the member's state. It is essential to include the party, ideology, and district variables as controls, as PACs commonly give to those most inclined to support them anyway; labor gives to Democrats, business gives to conservatives, and so on.[11] Thus, if these variables were not included, the effect of contributions would be overestimated by including the effects of the omitted variables.

There were three non-unanimous votes on the Chrysler loan guarantee. In addition to the final vote on the bill (called LOAN in the tables), there was a recommittal motion (WAGE), which instructed the committee to add a three-year wage freeze for Chrysler workers, and a substitute bill (SUBSTITUTE) that would have doubled Chrysler workers' wage concessions relative to those in the final bill. Both Chrysler and the UAW opposed the latter two attempts, and both failed, while LOAN passed.

There were five major non-unanimous votes on the windfall profits tax. JONES was the vote on the Jones-Moore substitute that defeated the Ways and Means Committee bill; WPT70 was the vote on the committee's amendment that raised the tax rate on old oil from 50 percent to 70 percent; OLDOIL was an amendment that would have increased the amount of old oil subject to the tax; PLOW would have given companies a tax credit for "plowing back" their windfall profits into exploration for and development of new oil sources; and EXIND would have exempted from the tax some of the oil produced by the independents. The last three amendments failed. The statistical analysis measured the relative effects of party, overall liberalism or prolabor leanings, district interests, and PAC contributions on voting on each of those bills or amendments.

We expected certain results on both issues. Apart from any PAC influence, Democrats and other prolabor members were likely to support the Chrysler loan guarantee because it would save many jobs; Republicans would not be so inclined because such support would conflict with laissez-faire principles. Members from districts with Chrysler plants and those who received contributions from any of the groups that testified for the bill were expected to support the loan guarantee and oppose the other two measures to a greater degree than other members.

On the windfall profits tax, Democrats and other liberals were expected to support the tax; Republicans, other conservatives, and those with oil production in their states were expected to oppose it and any amendments to strengthen it, as were those who received contributions from any of the major oil companies or independents. Those who received contributions from the UAW and AFL-CIO, which supported the tax, were expected to support it.

The logit analysis of each vote indicated, as is usually the case on roll-call votes, that the party and ideology of members had more influence on their voting than any of the other variables. The results were in the expected direction—Democrats and liberal or prolabor members were most likely to support the loan guarantee and the windfall profits tax and any strengthening amendments. Those whose districts had a direct economic interest in the bill also voted as expected. Indeed, party and ideology were both more important than PAC contributions in all of the votes but one.

However, PAC contributions did affect members' voting on both issues to some degree. Moreover, the effects were somewhat greater on the consensual bill, the Chrysler loan guarantee, than on the conflictual windfall profits tax. On the Chrysler bill, contributions from Chrysler ranked behind only party and ideology in importance, whereas on the windfall profits tax, contributions from the major oil companies were usually the least important influence on members' votes when they had any impact at all.

One of the most surprising results is that UAW contributions had no effect on voting on the Chrysler bill. The reason is that the bill was of such importance to labor that generally prolabor members voted for it regardless of whether they received UAW money. Indeed, the lack of an effect of UAW contributions is testimony to the success of their lobbying strategy, which went well beyond the recipients of union money.

Moreover, as expected, contributions were effective only for those PACs for whom the stakes were highest. Contributions from the major oil companies had an effect on voting on the windfall profits tax; the UAW and AFL-CIO, for whom the issue was secondary, did not. Contributions from Chrysler suppliers and others who testified for the loan guarantee had no effect on the roll-call voting.

Tables 6-1 and 6-2 make clear the impact of PAC contributions on the two bills. The figures are calculated from the logit results and show the probability of a typical Republican or Democrat voting with the PAC at various contribution levels. For Chrysler, the average contribution (calculated on the basis of members who received contributions) was $326; $546 and $766 represent amounts at one and two standard deviations above the mean, respectively. That is, approximately 98 percent of all Chrysler contributions were less than or equal to $766. The same rationale applies to the summed contributions from the major oil companies: $1,414 was the average contribution given by all of the major oil companies added together to each member who received contributions.

The probabilities in the table potentially range from zero (that is, there is *no* probability that the member will vote with the relevant PAC) to one (that is, it is a certainty that the member will vote with the PAC). Thus, 0.5 is the critical point; once a member crosses that threshold she or he is more likely than not to vote with the PAC. All of the Chrysler votes are included in Table 6-1 because contributions had an effect on voting on each of those roll calls. Table 6-2 contains probabilities only for those votes on which contributions from anyone had any substantial effect.

The tables show that members who had no direct interest in the votes (in other words, their districts had no economic stake in the bill and the members received no contributions from concerned PACs) voted as expected. Democrats favored the loan guarantee, supporting both Chrysler's and the United Auto Workers' positions, and the windfall profits tax in opposition to the oil

Table 6-1 Conditional Probabilities of Voting with Chrysler[a]

Chrysler Corporation	LOAN		WAGE		SUBSTITUTE	
	Dem.	Rep.	Dem.	Rep.	Dem.	Rep.
0	.79	.33	.91	.34	.98	.30
$326	.89	.53	.96	.52	.99	.41
$546	.94	.66	.97	.64	.99	.49
$766	.96	.77	.98	.75	.99	.57

[a] Conditional upon having the mean COPE rating for one's party, not having a Chrysler plant in the district, and receiving no UAW contributions.

Source: Campaign contribution data supplied by the Federal Election Commission.

Table 6-2 Conditional Probabilities of Voting with the Major Oil Companies[a]

Major Oil Company Contribution	OLDOIL		EXIND		JONES	
	Dem.	Rep.	Dem.	Rep.	Dem.	Rep.
0	.20	.94	.10	.70	.20	.92
$1,414	.50	.98	.18	.82	.37	.96
$2,788	.80	.99	.31	.90	.57	.98
$4,162	.94	.99	.47	.95	.76	.99

[a] Conditional upon having the mean ADA score for one's party, no petroleum production in the state, and no contributions from independent oil companies.

Source: Campaign contribution data supplied by the Federal Election Commission.

companies. By the same token, Republicans who had no direct interest in the bills opposed Chrysler's position and favored the major oil companies.

Thus, the most interested PACs needed to influence Republicans on the loan guarantee and Democrats on the windfall profits tax. Table 6-1 shows that Chrysler was successful on all three votes in turning around the votes of Republicans to whom they contributed, though that was just barely true on SUBSTITUTE. The major oil companies were somewhat less successful than Chrysler, but did not fail altogether to influence the Democrats to whom they contributed. Major oil PAC contributions raised Democrats above the threshold of support on the vote for the Jones-Moore bill and the OLDOIL amendment. Even though Chrysler also contributed to Democrats and the oil companies to Republicans, those contributions were superfluous because those people were already strongly inclined by party or ideology to support them on these issues.

Rewards for Good Behavior

Although PAC contributions were usually among the less important influences on House members' voting on the two bills, roll-call voting greatly influenced campaign contributions by Chrysler and the major oil companies. A number of factors influence a PAC's decisions about whom to fund, but quite sensibly, they generally give prime consideration to a member's past support for their interests.[12]

OLS regression equations produced estimates of the effects of votes cast by members in favor of the Chrysler loan guarantee and against the windfall profits tax on contributions from Chrysler and the major oil PACs, respectively, for the 1980 elections, with a number of other variables included as controls (see Appendix for results). (OLS regression, like logit analysis, produces estimates of the effects of several independent variables on a dependent variable; in this case, PAC contributions. This technique is used when the dependent variable is a continuous interval-level variable. Thus, contributions might range from zero to $10,000.) For Chrysler, support for the loan guarantee was the second most important influence on contributions; the most important was the existence of a Chrysler plant in the member's district. For the major oil companies, a record of opposition to the windfall profits tax was the most important consideration; members' overall conservatism was second in importance.

Apart from that similarity, however, the contribution strategies of Chrysler and the major oil companies for the 1980 elections differed in one important way: Chrysler gave mainly to incumbents, and the oil companies contributed heavily to nonincumbents. In 1977-1978, 82 percent of the recipients of Chrysler contributions were incumbents; for the election following the passage of the Chrysler loan guarantee, 85 percent of the recipients were incumbents. The major oil companies selected a list of recipients, of whom 73 percent were incumbents in 1978; in the 1980 election, which followed the passage of the windfall profits tax, only 60 percent of their beneficiaries were incumbents.

Those reactions are not surprising. Chrysler had every reason to be happy with Congress and thus followed a pragmatic strategy of rewarding those who had already helped them and those in influential positions, especially members on key committees. On the other hand, the oil companies, while helping their friends in Congress, followed a more aggressively ideological strategy of trying to change the composition of a Congress they had perceived as hostile from the beginning of the oil crisis of 1973-1974.[13] Thus, the type of legislation passed by Congress as well as the voting behavior of its members evidently influenced the contribution strategies followed by those political action committees. Indeed, House members' voting behavior on these bills influenced the PACs' subsequent contribution decisions more than the PACs' earlier contributions influenced the members' voting.

Conclusions

The results of the case studies support several of the arguments made earlier. First, PAC contributions do have more effect in some cases than in others, and, if we want to understand fully those effects, we need to take into account the circumstances under which a bill is considered. Although two case studies cannot provide completely satisfactory evidence for any hypothesis, in the cases considered here, the hypotheses put forth were supported: PAC contributions had more effect on voting on the consensual than the conflictual bill, and contributions from groups with the most at stake were the most influential.

Another way of looking at the latter statement is to say that groups that had the most reason to back up their contributions with intense lobbying were the most effective. Indeed, the UAW's influence on the Chrysler loan guarantee exceeded the broad reach of their PAC contributions; prolabor members voted for it even if they received nothing from the UAW. On the other hand, although the UAW and AFL-CIO were active on the windfall profits tax, they had little reason to exploit any sense of obligation to them that members might feel; the issue was not, by comparison, critical to the unions.

One remaining feature of this research deserves comment. Although the Federal Election Campaign Act allows multicandidate PACs to contribute up to $10,000 to a candidate in an election cycle, the corporate PACs considered here contributed nowhere near that amount. Chrysler's average contribution to House incumbents in 1978 was less than $500, and the average contribution of all of the major oil companies put together in that same year was only $1,414. A frequent and plausible speculation is that business PACs do not want to be perceived as trying to buy either election outcomes or members.

Finally, lest the point be lost in the glare of the spotlight on PAC contributions, it is still true that in most cases PAC money has less effect on members' voting than their partisan and ideological persuasions. Future research will, of course, take those variables into account, but should also focus on the circumstances under which the legislation is considered to determine what other factors, in addition to conflict and consensus, condition the effects of PAC contributions on Congress members' roll-call voting.

Notes

An earlier version of this paper was delivered at the annual meeting of the American Political Science Association, Chicago, Ill., Sept. 1-4, 1983, under the name Diana Evans Yiannakis. Thanks to Gary Jacobson and Stephen Weatherford for many helpful comments on previous incarnations of this paper.

1. Common Cause, *People Against PACs* (Washington, D.C.: Common Cause, 1983).

2. Brooks Jackson, "Avco Corp. Makes Judicious Use of Gifts to U.S. Congressmen," *Wall Street Journal,* Oct. 13, 1983.

3. W. P. Welch, "Campaign Contributions and Legislative Voting: Milk Money and Dairy Price Supports," *Western Political Quarterly* 35 (December 1982): 493.

4. Henry W. Chappell, Jr., "Campaign Contributions and Congressional Voting: A Simultaneous Probit-Tobit Model," *Review of Economics and Statistics* 64 (February 1982): 77-83; John Frendreis and Richard Waterman, "PAC Contributions and Legislative Behavior: Senate Voting on Trucking Deregulation," *Social Science Quarterly* 66 (June 1985): 401-412; and Kirk F. Brown, "Campaign Contributions and Congressional Voting" (Paper presented at the Annual Meeting of the American Political Science Association, Chicago, Ill., Sept. 1-4, 1983). See also James B. Kau, Donald Keenan, and Paul H. Rubin, "A General Equilibrium Model of Congressional Voting," *The Quarterly Journal of Economics* (May 1982): 271-293; Benjamin Ginsburg and John Green, "The Best Congress Money Can Buy" (Paper presented at the Annual Meeting of the American Political Science Association, Washington, D.C., Aug. 31-Sept. 3, 1979); and Candice Nelson, "Counting the Cash: PAC Contributions to Members of the House of Representatives" (Paper presented at the Annual Meeting of the American Political Science Association, Denver, Colo., Sept. 2-5, 1982).

5. For a more complete development of this line of analysis, see Michael Hayes, *Lobbyists and Legislators: A Theory of Political Markets* (New Brunswick, N.J.: Rutgers University Press, 1981); Mancur Olson, *The Logic of Collective Action* (Cambridge, Mass.: Harvard University Press, 1971); and James Q. Wilson, "The Politics of Regulation," in *Social Responsibility and the Business Predicament,* ed. James W. McKie (Washington, D.C.: The Brookings Institution, 1974).

6. Quoted in "Looking Back at the Future of Campaign Finance Reform: Interest Groups and American Elections," by Michael J. Malbin, in *Money and Politics in the United States,* ed. Michael J. Malbin (Chatham, N.J.: Chatham House, 1984).

7. Hayes, *Lobbyists and Legislators,* and Wilson, "Politics of Regulation."

8. See Mark V. Nadel, *The Politics of Consumer Protection* (Indianapolis: Bobbs-Merrill, 1971) for a discussion of the history of consumer legislation.

9. The background on the Chrysler bill in the House comes from the 1979 *Congressional Quarterly Almanac* (Washington, D.C.: Congressional Quarterly, 1980), 285-292; from hearings before the Economic Stabilization Subcommittee of the Banking, Finance, and Urban Affairs Committee, entitled "The Chrysler Corporation Financial Situation"; from interviews with lobbyists for Chrysler and the UAW; and Robert B. Reich and John D. Donahue, *New Deals* (New York: Times Books, 1985). Background for the windfall profits bill is taken from the 1979 *CQ Almanac,* 605-632; from hearings before the Ways and Means Committee, May 9-18, 1979; and from interviews with a staff attorney for the Ways and Means Committee and the legislative assistant for a House member who worked closely with the oil companies on the windfall profits tax.

10. For studies of roll-call voting decisions, see, for example, *Party and Constituency: Pressures on Congress* by Julius Turner, revised by Edward V. Schneier (Baltimore: Johns Hopkins University Press, 1970); and Aage R. Clausen, *How Congressmen Decide: A Policy Focus* (New York: St. Martin's Press, 1973).

11. See, among others, David A. Gapoian, "What Makes PACs Tick? An Analysis of the Allocation Patterns of Economic Interest Groups," *American Journal of Political Science* 28 (May 1984): 259-281.

12. See, for example, Gapoian, "What Makes PACs Tick?"; Brown, "Campaign Contributions and Congressional Voting"; and Welch, "Campaign Contributions and Legislative Voting."

13. Edward Handler and John R. Mulkern, *Business in Politics* (Lexington, Mass.: D. C. Heath, 1982).

Appendix

Table 6-3 Determinants of Voting on the Chrysler Loan Guarantee

	WAGE			SUBSTITUTE			LOAN		
	Estimated Coefficient	Standard Error	Partial R	Estimated Coefficient	Standard Error	Partial R	Estimated Coefficient	Standard Error	Partial R
Intercept	−1.860[a]	.295		−2.405[a]	.356		−1.554[a]	.259	
DEM	1.110[a]	.332	.140	2.200[a]	.383	.262	.668[b]	.304	.079
CHRYS IMP	2.068	1.150	.052	1.380	.983	.000	2.197[b]	1.102	.063
COPE	.046[a]	.008	.268	.057[a]	.010	.267	.032[a]	.006	.224
CHRYS	.002[b]	.001	.078	.0016	.001	.034	.003[a]	.001	.104
UAW	.0006	.0004	.034	.0005	.0005	.000	.0001	.0001	.000
	$R^2 = .387$			$R^2 = .494$			$R^2 = .243$		

[a] $P \leq .01$
[b] $P \leq .05$

DEM = 1 if the member is a Democrat; 0 if the member is a Republican;
CHRYS IMP = 1 if the member has a Chrysler plant in the district; 0 otherwise;
COPE is the member's COPE score for 1979-1980;
CHRYS is the contribution from Chrysler for the 1978 election;
UAW is the contribution from the UAW for the 1978 election.

Note: Appendix Table 6-3 presents the results of the logit analysis of each of the roll-call votes. A positive coefficient is associated with a tendency to vote in favor of the Chrysler loan guarantee.

Source: Campaign contribution data supplied by the Federal Election Commission.

Table 6-4 Determinants of Voting on the Windfall Profits Tax

	JONES			WPT 70		
	Estimated Coefficient	Standard Error	Partial R	Estimated Coefficient	Standard Error	Partial R
Intercept	3.2719[a]	.4670		2.9530[a]	.4639	
DEM	−1.6226[a]	.4232	−.149	−2.8478[a]	.4075	−.287
ADA	−0.0527[a]	.0069	−.315	−0.0611[a]	.0090	−.277
PETPRO	0.0266[a]	.0080	.125	0.0365[a]	.0079	.184
MAJORS	0.0006[b]	.0003	.070	0.0004	.0002	.040
INDEP	−0.0002	.0004	.000	−0.0001	.0003	.000
	$R^2 = .520$			$R^2 = .645$		

	OLDOIL			PLOW		
	Estimated Coefficient	Standard Error	Partial R	Estimated Coefficient	Standard Error	Partial R
Intercept	3.6134[a]	.5289		3.6048[a]	.5158	
DEM	−1.8205[a]	.4811	−.148	−3.3338[a]	.4305	−.319
ADA	−0.0557[a]	.0074	−.313	−0.0592[a]	.0089	−.272
PETPRO	0.0252[a]	.0084	.111	0.0392[a]	.0079	.200
MAJORS	0.0010[a]	.0003	.117	0.0001	.0002	.000
INDEP	−0.0004	.0004	.000	−0.0001	.0003	.000
	$R^2 = .560$			$R^2 = .645$		

	EXIND		
	Estimated Coefficient	Standard Error	Partial R
Intercept	1.4700	.3279	
DEM	−1.3516[a]	.3373	−.157
ADA	−0.0414[a]	.0065	−.262
PETPRO	0.0300[a]	.0071	.166
MAJORS	0.0005[a]	.0002	.097
INDEP	−0.0001	.0002	.000
	$R^2 = .461$		

[a] $P \leq .01$
[b] $P \leq .05$

ADA is the member's ADA score for the 96th Congress.
PETPRO is the petroleum production per capita in the member's state;
MAJORS is the summed contributions from all major oil companies in the 1978 election;
INDEP is the summed contributions from a number of associations of independent producers.

Note: Appendix Table 6-4 presents the results of the logit analysis of each of the roll-call votes. A positive coefficient is associated with a tendency to vote against the windfall profits tax.

Source: Campaign contribution data supplied by the Federal Election Commission.

Table 6-5 Determinants of 1980 Campaign Contributions by Chrysler and the Major Oil Companies

	Regression Coefficient	Standard Error	Standardized Regression Coefficient	
Chrysler=a	31.910	32.601		
DEM	−46.539	24.689	−.126	
ADA	−0.086	0.355	−.016	
CHRYSIMP	225.261[a]	36.719	.305	Adjusted R^2=.162
ELECT80	0.175	0.369	.023	
PRIM	23.192	19.650	.059	
SENIORITY	1.761	1.170	.074	
CHRCOM	44.300[b]	17.751	.123	
CHRYSUP	26.457[a]	6.842	.241	
Majors=a	1180.743[b]	486.256		
DEM	−161.690	259.278	−.040	
ADA	−11.379[b]	4.706	−.187	
PETPRO	2.912[b]	1.189	.115	
ELECT80	−2.100	3.812	−.025	Adjusted R^2=.265
PRIM	460.714[b]	203.893	.106	
SENIORITY	−27.484[b]	12.129	−.105	
OILCOM	533.327[a]	195.856	.126	
OILSUP	263.208[a]	73.841	.295	

[a] $P \leq .01$
[b] $P \leq .05$

ELECT80 is the member's actual vote in 1980, which here represents the expected vote;
PRIM=1 if the member had a primary in 1980; 0 otherwise;
SENIORITY is the number of years the member had been in office by 1979;
CHRCOM is the number of committees important to Chrysler that the member served upon: Ways and Means, Commerce, Judiciary, and Banking, Finance and Urban Affairs;
CHRYSUP is the number of votes cast by the member in favor of the loan guarantee; (Range=0 to 3);
OILCOM is the number of committees important to the oil industry that the member served on: Ways and Means, Commerce, and Interior;
OILSUP is the number of votes cast by the member against the windfall profits tax (Range=0 to 5).

7. The New Group Universe

Michael T. Hayes

Interest groups are typically portrayed as organizations that seek to mobilize members to influence public policy. Numerous groups formed in recent years, however, do not conform to this traditional conception of a mass-based membership group. Many have no members at all, and those that do often make little or no attempt to provide outside opportunities for personal interaction. Some organizations are composed of nothing but staffers in Washington and are funded entirely by sources such as private foundations, large gifts from individuals, or grants and contracts from government agencies.

In this essay Michael Hayes surveys the contemporary interest group universe and develops a group typology that relies on variation in funding sources and opportunities for face-to-face contact among members. He suggests that the emergence of outside funding has enabled a wide variety of interests to organize. Indeed, more interests are represented than ever before. Hayes raises questions of whether a more representative set of groups has been the result of these changes. Wide gaps often exist between the leaders and followers in many of the new groups, and the organizations frequently see themselves as pressured to conform to funding conditions set by powerful outside forces. Hayes reminds us that the proliferation of groups may not lead directly or necessarily to some realization of the American pluralist ideal.

The number of organized interest groups active at the national level has expanded dramatically over the past twenty-five years. It is ironic that the lion's share of this growth has occurred in those very large and diffuse interests previously thought to be least likely to mobilize (see Chapter 1). A wide variety of groups have emerged to represent previously unorganized segments of society: consumers, environmentalists, women, senior citizens, and others.

This chapter will attempt to bring some order to this rapid proliferation of groups by advancing a typology of group forms. Groups may be classified in a variety of different ways, depending upon the purposes of the researcher.

For example, a wide variety of authors have found it useful to classify groups according to the nature of the benefits they seek: material, expressive, solidary, or some combination of these.[1] Similarly, in a major empirical survey of contemporary interest groups, political scientist Jack L. Walker distinguished between groups with some professional or occupational prerequisites for membership and citizens' groups that are open to anyone taking an interest in a group's activities. Walker further subdivided his occupational group category to distinguish between private sector and not-for-profit groups.[2]

My focus here will be somewhat different. The vast majority of the new groups formed in recent years fail to conform to the traditional conception of a mass-based membership group. Many of these groups are staff organizations, lacking any real membership base. Others have a membership consisting of "checkbook" members, affiliated with the group only by virtue of monetary contributions and lacking any face-to-face contacts with other members in a common setting.[3]

This chapter will begin with an examination of the traditional conception of interest groups within group theory. That conception will be seen to rest on certain characteristics—in particular, an extensive formal membership and a network of local chapters permitting widespread personal contact among individual members—that cannot be taken for granted. Rather, these characteristics must be understood as variables that interact to produce distinct organizational forms.

The Traditional Conception of the Group

Almost without exception, group theorists have viewed interest groups as organizations seeking to mobilize a membership in order to influence public policy. According to political scientist David Truman, for example, "We do not, in fact, find individuals otherwise than in groups; complete isolation in space and time is so rare as to be an almost hypothetical situation."[4] Similarly, to political scientist Bertram Gross, the importance of individuals "stems from their actual or potential relationships to groups. They are the bedrock materials from which groups are organized."[5] More recent theories of group formation, building on economist Mancur Olson's analysis of the free-rider problem, have emphasized the obstacles facing interest groups pursuing collective benefits for their memberships.[6] While countering earlier views that mobilization of shared interests would be more or less automatic, these theorists nevertheless treat group formation as a problem of attracting and retaining *members* (whether individuals, business firms, or other associations) for collective action.

Moreover, the early group theorists emphasized the need for at least a minimal degree of interaction among individual members as a prerequisite for the formation of a group. To Truman, individuals sharing some common characteristic properly qualified as an interest group only if they interacted with some frequency on the basis of their shared characteristics.[7] More recent theorists would not go quite this far; following Robert Salisbury, most would now treat solidary rewards as only one of several potential benefits available to group leaders seeking to mobilize a membership.[8]

Although interaction among rank-and-file members may not be a necessary precondition for group formation, as Truman believed, regular opportunities for personal contact are nevertheless important. Conventional pluralist theory has long emphasized the pivotal role of overlapping memberships in tempering the pursuit of narrow group interests. According to this view, multiple affiliations produce a heterogeneous membership in most groups, reducing group cohesion and forcing at least some semblance of internal democracy in group decision making. The pursuit of group interests is thus moderated by the inevitable process of internal compromise and adjustment. For these moderating tendencies to operate, however, rank-and-file members typically must have regular and frequent contact with other group members.[9]

At worst, the proliferation of groups in which members have little or no contact with their fellow members can signal the development of what sociologist William Kornhauser termed a "mass society." Such a society has its roots in the centralization of the communications media, a corresponding nationalization of politics, and the increasing isolation of individual citizens. Where the community is no longer the locus of major decisions, distant events take on ever increasing importance. Under such circumstances, interest groups tend to become "mass organizations": large, centralized, national groups lacking local subunits through which individual members can influence group decision making. Individuals within such organizations are faced with a remote and impersonal national leadership. Increasingly isolated and alienated, they become vulnerable to manipulation by group leaders and governmental authorities competing for their allegiance.[10]

By contrast, traditional mass-membership groups serve a necessary function as mediating institutions between individuals and the state. Such groups are built upon a network of vigorous and autonomous local chapters that provide both opportunities for member interaction and avenues for influencing group decision making. Kornhauser argued:

> Where proximate concerns are meaningful, people do not spend much time or energy seeking direct gratification from remote symbols. They may try to understand and influence the course of distant events, but they do so by means of and in relation to their face-to-face relations, at home, in the neighborhood, at work, in their club or union, and so forth.[11]

Breakdown of the Traditional Conception

Clearly, the traditional conception of interest groups rested upon assumptions that cannot be taken for granted. Groups were seen as attempting to mobilize a mass membership. Equally important, they were seen as providing frequent opportunities for face-to-face relationships among individual members.

Given such a conception, it is not surprising that political scientists largely failed to anticipate the emergence of an almost bewildering variety of new groups organized to represent large and diffuse interests.[12] These new groups have not conformed to the traditional model. Many have no real memberships in any sense of the word. Others have a membership base, but make little or no attempt to provide opportunities for interaction among members. These two pivotally important group characteristics—a membership base and an extensive network of local chapters—must instead be understood as variables.

Membership Base

Group theory traditionally has assumed that entrepreneurs will rely heavily, if not exclusively, on member dues for funds sufficient to sustain their operations. The free-rider problem was seen as posing a serious obstacle to organization precisely because it was assumed that large, diffuse groups had no recourse but to mobilize a membership to get off the ground. Successful entrepreneurs might accomplish this by offering a mix of benefits, both economic and noneconomic, to attract and hold members.

More recent empirical research suggests, however, that most of the new citizens' groups have not so much overcome the free-rider problem as circumvented ·it by securing alternative sources of funding outside their memberships. Eighty-nine percent of the groups in Walker's sample required at least some outside funding to get started, and many of these groups remained heavily dependent on outside sources even after becoming firmly established.[13] In this regard, political scientist Jeffrey Berry's survey of public interest lobbyists found almost a third of these groups dependent on foundation support for more than half of their current income.[14] Other major sources of outside funding include contributions from wealthy philanthropists, grants from government agencies, and grants or loans from previously organized interest groups. According to Walker, the largest single factor contributing to the veritable explosion in the number of citizens' groups active in Washington has been the emergence of such sources of patronage for new groups since 1960.

Face-to-face Contact

The second variable emphasizes the opportunities offered by the group for interaction with other members. As noted above, this typically requires an extensive network of local chapters. While some of the new citizens' groups hold annual or biennial conventions, these gatherings are realistically open to only a small percentage of the group's membership, and then only on a very infrequent basis.[15] Meaningful face-to-face relations would seem to require regular meetings realistically available to a large percentage of the organization's membership. For a large organization concerned with national issues, it is hard to envision how this could take place without a network of local chapters.

In this regard, many of the newer groups offer few, if any, real opportunities for member interaction. Among the public interest lobbies in Berry's sample, two-thirds of the groups had no local chapters whatsoever. Another 12 percent had twenty-five or fewer chapters, translating into less than one chapter for every two states.[16] While systematic data are lacking for other kinds of groups, it is apparent from the best available evidence that this phenomenon is by no means limited to public interest lobbies.

A Typology of Groups

These two variables are readily operationalized. For example, reliance on a membership base can be measured in straightforward fashion as the percentage of the group's annual revenues deriving from member dues rather than outside sources. Opportunities for membership interaction might be similarly measured as the number of local chapters currently in operation for each group. For ease of exposition, I will treat these two variables as dichotomous. Cross-tabulation of the two dimensions thus gives rise to four distinctively different kinds of groups.

A Typology of Interest Groups

		Primary Source of Financial Support:	
		Membership	Outside Sources
Opportunity for Face-to-face Relations:	High	Pure membership groups	Subsidized solidary groups
	Low	Mass groups	Pure staff groups

Mass-membership Groups

The first category consists of traditional mass-membership based groups. Truman and Kornhauser regarded these groups as effective mediating institutions within a pluralistic society, combining a reliance on a membership base for primary funding with an extensive network of local chapters that provide realistic opportunities for rank-and-file interaction and influence on group decision making. Among the older groups currently in existence, the Farm Bureau Federation, the Chamber of Commerce, the Sierra Club, and the League of Women Voters all would fall in this category.

Among the more recently formed citizens' groups, the National Organization for Women also would qualify. As of 1978, NOW had 125,000 members and 700 chapters, with at least some chapters in all fifty states. Member dues accounted for almost 70 percent of NOW's revenues that year, with most of the remainder coming from large individual contributions. As the largest women's group focusing on feminist issues, NOW lobbies on a wide range of issues affecting women, including abortion, the Equal Rights Amendment, and legislation ensuring equal credit opportunities. Because of its large and heterogeneous constituency, NOW often finds its membership divided on controversial issues. To help ease internal divisions, the organization has delegated a great deal of latitude to local chapters. The autonomy of local chapters is further reinforced by NOW's policy of rebating 4 percent of its national revenues to the state chapters.[17]

Staff Groups

At the other extreme are the pure staff groups. These are groups consisting almost entirely of a small, Washington-based staff. Lacking any mass-membership base, these groups must rely on outside sources of funds to survive. In addition to the sources identified by Walker—foundation grants, large individual gifts, grants from government agencies, and assistance from previously established groups—these organizations may pay their own way by contracting to do consulting work. In any case, with no real membership, staff groups cannot credibly claim to speak for a larger constituency and thus must typically confine themselves to litigation or the provision of technical information to policy makers.

One example of such an organization is the National Council of Senior Citizens, at least in its early years. This group was founded in the early 1960s for the primary purpose of lobbying for the passage of Medicare legislation. The NCSC began as a small, very specialized staff organization; it built on the infrastructure left from the Senior Citizens for Kennedy group, set up by the Democratic National Committee during the 1960 election. The DNC hoped to draw a major constituency group away from its traditional Republican leanings. During its first five years, the NCSC drew approximately two-thirds of its income from labor unions and the DNC, with the remainder coming from dues paid by a small membership.

The NCSC has evolved over time and is no longer a staff group. Following passage of the Medicare bill in 1965, the group decided to expand its membership and its range of political activities. There are currently more than 250,000 members nationwide, with more than three thousand affiliated senior citizens' clubs. The NCSC nevertheless remains heavily linked to the Democratic party and to labor unions, relying on these two sources for supplementary funding and, in many cases, leadership cadres as well.[18]

Another example of a pure staff group is the Center for Women Policy Studies. This group was founded in 1972 to provide technical expertise to policy makers on a variety of women's issues, ranging from equal credit opportunity legislation to the problems of battered women. In 1978 its small Washington staff consisted of ten professionals who supported themselves almost entirely through government contracts.[19]

Mass Organizations

A third category consists of groups that centralize decision making in the hands of a small Washington staff, but nevertheless remain heavily dependent on a mass membership for financial support. For all practical purposes, such groups resemble pure staff groups in their internal decision making. Individual contributors typically have little or no opportunity for interaction with other members. Rather, they are merely checkbook members whose only link with the national organization consists of occasional legislative alerts, periodicals, and appeals for funds. Following Kornhauser's definition, these groups may thus be termed mass organizations:

> In general, formal organizations are to be identified as mass organizations, not by their size, but when they lack intermediate units which have some autonomy from the central leadership. In the absence of a structure of smaller groups, formal organizations become remote from their members.[20]

As noted above, most of the public interest lobbies and law firms organized in recent years fail to provide realistic opportunities for interaction through a network of local chapters. In this same vein, the vast majority provide few, if any, avenues for members to influence group decision making. An example of this type of group is the Ralph Nader group, Congress Watch. Although dependent on direct mail solicitation for the bulk of its revenues, Congress Watch consists largely of a small, Washington-based staff, with Nader making the key decisions himself. A similar example is the Fund for Animals. Founded in 1967 to combat the inhumane treatment of animals, the group depends almost entirely on member dues and periodic fund-raising appeals for revenues. While the organization could boast a membership of more than thirty-five thousand in 1972, it provides no avenues for membership interaction or influence in group decisions. There is no annual convention, and members receive no voting rights.[21]

Many unconnected political action committees also would fall into this category. Made possible by the rise of direct mail techniques, ideological PACs serve as political investment brokers for small individual contributors. In distinct contrast to the political parties, which sponsor candidates across the political spectrum, ideological PACs channel campaign funds to a much narrower range of candidates, enabling contributors to express ideological preferences with much more precision. While such PACs are thus an attractive form of political participation for many individuals, rank-and-file contributors have no direct say in how the group's revenues are spent, as decisions regarding campaign strategy are made by a small central staff.[22]

Subsidized Solidary Groups

The final category consists of groups offering a network of local chapters while, paradoxically, remaining heavily dependent for survival on outside sources of funding. At a glance, such groups would seem to constitute something of an anomaly. However, subsidized solidary groups are more common than might be expected.

All groups seeking to mobilize a mass membership face very high start-up costs. This is particularly true for groups attempting to establish a network of local organizations spread over a large geographic area. Many contemporary membership groups were subsidized solidary organizations in their early years. The Farm Bureau Federation provides a good example of this type of group. The Farm Bureau had its origins in the Department of Agriculture's efforts to disseminate scientific knowledge about farming techniques. The department sought to reach small groups of farmers through a network of county agents. Out of these government-sponsored efforts the Farm Bureau was born. The Chamber of Commerce, with its network of affiliates in local communities throughout the United States, had a similar origin in the federal government's desire early in this century to establish a single institution to represent the business community.[23]

Among the citizens' groups formed in recent years, perhaps the best example is the National Council on Aging. Founded primarily to champion the expansion of senior citizens' centers throughout the United States, the organization sponsors more than five thousand affiliated senior citizens' centers and lobbies to preserve federal funding for such centers. Throughout its life, the group has been forced to rely on foundation and government grants for most of its revenues. In its early years, NCOA obtained substantial grants from the Ford Foundation and the Alma Schipper Foundation. Then the group shifted to reliance on federal government grants and contracts, moving its headquarters from New York to Washington accordingly in 1969. In 1971 member dues accounted for less than $28,000, as compared with almost $2 million in fees and grants from government agencies. At the same time, NCOA remains an unusually pure case of a solidary organization, in view of the group's almost exclusive focus on maintaining a network of senior citizens' centers. NCOA is not a multiple-issue group; its board of directors normally eschews group involvement on broadly defined national policy issues. Two-thirds of the group's membership cited the maintenance of senior citizens' centers as their primary reason for joining the group.[24]

Group Evolution

The foregoing examples clearly show that interest groups cannot be classified in static fashion. All groups go through a life cycle and must address certain common problems: the death or retirement of a founder, the need to secure stable, long-term sources of financial support, a consequent change in emphasis from early concerns with mobilization to a longer-term focus on group maintenance, and so on. As groups evolve, they may significantly alter their organizational form, moving from one category to another in the above typology. For example, the Farm Bureau and the Chamber of Commerce, both now self-supporting membership groups, began as subsidized solidary organizations. The National Council of Senior Citizens began as a pure staff group and later became a membership group, although it is heavily, but not primarily, reliant on outside sources of funding.

The pattern followed by the NCSC is a particularly common one. Citizens' groups face high initial costs and often find it virtually impossible to establish a network of local chapters at the outset. Some groups find it too expensive even to cultivate checkbook members in view of the need to provide publications or other incentives to satisfy members' interests in expressive rewards. Moreover, a membership can be confining, making it difficult to engage in necessary compromises on highly emotional or symbolic issues.[25]

Nevertheless, staff organizations often find it a serious disadvantage not to be able to speak credibly for a mass-based constituency. For this reason, a number of citizens' groups have worked hard to acquire a membership base once their survival was assured. For example, NOW expanded its membership from 1,122 and fourteen chapters in 1967 to 125,000 members and seven hundred chapters in 1978. Similarly, the National Abortion Rights Action League (NARAL) dramatically expanded its membership base from 20,000 to 90,000 during the 1970s through an intensive direct mail recruiting effort. Some groups have established a two-tier membership system, falling somewhere between the mass organization's reliance on checkbook members and the pure membership group's provision of significant opportunities for member participation. The National Women's Political Caucus, which focuses on nominating and electing more women to public office, expanded its membership from a mere 271 in 1971 to 50,000 in 1978. Of this expanded membership, however, most are only checkbook affiliations. A smaller core of 11,000 "governing" members play a more participatory role within the organization.[26]

While the above pattern is particularly common, a wide variety of life cycles is possible, as different groups attempt to mobilize very different constituencies and find it rational to offer different mixes of incentives accordingly. Along these lines, a particularly instructive example is provided by the American Agriculture Movement's change from a loosely organized membership group in the late 1970s to a staff organization by the mid-1980s (see Chapter 3).

Implications for Pluralism

Traditionally, interest-group theorists have viewed group activity as a desirable way for individuals to exert influence on the policy process. These theorists took it as axiomatic that there is ordinarily no clearly defined and agreed upon conception of the public interest on most issues. Rather, the public interest was seen as emerging from the contention of a multiplicity of self-interested actors, with the group struggle serving as a kind of adversary process giving rise to a degree of rationality that otherwise would be unattainable. For this to happen, however, all groups with a stake in the issue must be represented and group leaders must faithfully represent the collective interests of their memberships.

The proliferation of citizens' groups since the 1960s goes a long way toward satisfying the first condition. The emergence of outside funding sources has enabled a wide variety of previously unorganized potential groups to circumvent the free-rider problem. Some critics have observed that business groups seem better organized than ever before, while a variety of interests still remain unrepresented.[27] Even so, there seems little doubt that more groups are active at the national level than at any previous time in our history.

If Gross was correct in asserting that the concept of policy making as group struggle will eventually prove as powerful a tool to political science as the concept of competition has proved for economics,[28] then what is needed to evaluate properly the rise of the new citizens' groups is some concept of workable competition. To the economist, monopoly and perfect competition constitute ideal types, theoretically interesting but often unrealistic end points on a continuum of alternative market structures. In between lies the more practical realm of workable competition, where the number of competitors falls short of the atomistic ideal, but is still large enough to prevent any firm or combination from exerting market power. While the political analogue of perfect competition likewise seems unattainable, this does not preclude a workable group struggle in which many interests are represented and none exerts disproportionate influence over policy making.

The new citizens' groups more clearly fall short of the pluralist ideal in their internal decision making, however. One of the great advantages of policy making by group struggle lies in the ability of individuals to communicate a wide variety of policy concerns through membership in a multiplicity of political organizations.[29] For this form of representation to occur, however, group leaders must be responsive to the shared attitudes of their memberships. This does not mean that group leaders must mirror group preferences exactly, for rank-and-file members will be poorly informed on many issues and have no discernible opinions on others. Serious problems arise, however, when group leaders are attracted by entirely different rewards than their members, or when leaders come to recognize a vested interest in preserving their own power.[30]

At a minimum, the policy views of group leaders often will diverge from those of their members. In distinct contrast to the rank and file, group leaders tend to be attracted by the prospect of distant and intangible rewards.[31] This interest in expressive rewards may be rooted in self-interest as well as ideology. Too much success can be fatal to group leaders, as it calls into question the need for the group's continued existence. For group leaders, the ideal situation is rather to be perceived as making steady progress toward distant, intangible goals that are never quite achieved.[32]

This divergence between the views of leaders and followers is particularly serious in view of the lack of real accountability within most of the new citizens' groups. Many of these new groups have no members at all, freeing them from the imperative of satisfying the policy preferences of a mass constituency. Among those groups with large nominal memberships, there is frequently little or no opportunity for members to influence group decision making.

At the same time, it is not entirely clear that the new citizens' groups are less responsive to their memberships than the traditional membership groups. Although there is no pretense of formal democracy within many of the new mass groups, a democratic formal structure often conceals a high degree of oligarchy within the traditional membership groups. Most of the new citizens' groups are forced to compete with a variety of rival groups for potential contributors. Such market pressures ultimately may prove more effective in forcing responsiveness to rank-and-file preferences than formally democratic mechanisms.[33]

In any case, freedom from a mass membership does not mean that these new groups are fully autonomous. Rather, such groups must instead be responsive to some set of interests outside their memberships. Walker observed that virtually all support for interest groups arrives with some set of policy strings attached. The strong correlation between the receipt of government grants and support for an expansion in the level of government activity among groups active at the national level suggests that agencies "are unlikely to sponsor groups that do not share their fundamental political sympathies."[34] At a somewhat less Machiavellian level, Joyce Gelb and Marian Lief Palley found women's groups significantly hampered by the need to secure foundation support:

> Several groups examined have become involved in projects they would not have undertaken had special funds not been made available for specific studies or conferences. Many group leaders feel that foundations prefer to fund educational programs and are loathe to fund litigation. Leaders of other groups indicated that foundations were fond of funding such things as internship programs, which were sometimes of limited value in contributing to the fulfillment of organizational goals. Some groups have accepted money for "earmarked" projects and have sought to utilize them "loosely" in order to gain flexibility. In general, funding may shape a group's entire focus and distort its initial priorities. Project-by-project funding fragments an organization and hinders a holistic approach to policy development.[35]

In the final analysis, then, it remains unclear whether these new groups have made for a more representative group struggle. At one level, more interests than ever before are effectively organized. At the same time there is often a wide gap between leaders and followers within these organizations; decision making typically is centralized in a small national staff. Lacking a network of independent local chapters, the majority of these groups become remote from their members, as leaders are forced to conform to conditions for continued funding set by powerful outside patrons. The vast majority of the new citizens' groups thus fail to conform to the traditional membership-based model. The continuing susceptibility of such large and diffuse constituencies to the free-rider problem suggests, however, that if alternative organizational forms had not emerged, most of these interests would remain unorganized today.

Notes

1. See Robert H. Salisbury, "An Exchange Theory of Interest Groups," *Midwest Journal of Political Science* 8 (1969): 1-32; James Q. Wilson, *Political Organizations* (New York: Basic Books, 1973); and Terry M. Moe, *The Organization of Interests* (Chicago: University of Chicago Press, 1980).
2. Jack L. Walker, "The Origins and Maintenance of Interest Groups in America," *American Political Science Review* 77 (1983): 390-406.
3. On "checkbook" organizations, see Michael T. Hayes, "Interest Groups: Pluralism or Mass Society?" in *Interest Group Politics*, 1st ed., ed. Allan J. Cigler and Burdett A. Loomis (Washington, D.C.: CQ Press, 1983), 110-125.
4. David B. Truman, *The Governmental Process* (New York: Alfred A. Knopf, 1951), 48.
5. Bertram M. Gross, *The Legislative Struggle* (New York: McGraw-Hill, 1953), 5.
6. Mancur Olson, Jr., *The Logic of Collective Action* (New York: Schocken Books, 1970).
7. Truman, *The Governmental Process*, 24, 35-36.
8. See Salisbury, "An Exchange Theory"; Wilson, *Political Organizations;* and Moe, *The Organization of Interests.*
9. Truman, *The Governmental Process*, 157-164.
10. William Kornhauser, *The Politics of Mass Society* (New York: Free Press, 1959). See also Murray Edelman, *The Symbolic Uses of Politics* (Urbana: University of Illinois Press, 1964).
11. Kornhauser, *The Politics of Mass Society,* 60-61.
12. On the failure of political science to adequately recognize—and properly emphasize—the explosion in interest group formation in the past quarter century, see Jack L. Walker, "The Mobilization of Political Interests" (Paper delivered at the Annual Meeting of the American Political Science Association, Chicago, Ill., Sept. 1-4, 1983).
13. Walker, "Origins," 397-401.
14. Jeffrey M. Berry, *Lobbying for the People* (Princeton, N.J.: Princeton University Press, 1977), 72.
15. Ibid., 186-195.
16. Ibid., 42.
17. Joyce Gelb and Marian Lief Palley, *Women and Public Policies* (Princeton, N.J.: Princeton University Press, 1982), 28-30, 44.
18. Henry J. Pratt, *The Gray Lobby* (Chicago: University of Chicago Press, 1976), 56-73, 88-89.
19. Gelb and Palley, *Women and Public Policies,* 32, 44.
20. Kornhauser, *The Politics of Mass Society,* 95.
21. On the various Ralph Nader groups, see Andrew S. McFarland, *Public Interest Lobbies* (Washington, D.C.: American Enterprise Institute, 1976), 70-71. On Fund for Animals, see Berry, *Lobbying,* 110-140.
22. The discussion here applies only to ideological, or nonconnected, PACs. Business and labor PACs are political arms of parent organizations and thus would not constitute mass organizations in Kornhauser's terms. For a full discussion of PACs, see Larry J. Sabato, *PAC Power* (New York: W. W. Norton, 1984).
23. Grant McConnell, *The Decline of Agrarian Democracy* (New York: Atheneum, 1969).

24. Pratt, *The Gray Lobby,* 92-94, 97.
25. Gelb and Palley, *Women and Public Policies,* 51-52.
26. Ibid., 29-36. See also 50-52.
27. Kay Lehman Schlozman, "What Accent the Heavenly Chorus? Political Equality and the American Pressure System," *Journal of Politics* 46 (1984): 1006-1032.
28. Gross, *Legislative Struggle,* 5.
29. Truman, *The Governmental Process,* 508-524.
30. Robert Michels, *Political Parties* (New York: Free Press, 1962).
31. Group leaders may secure "surplus profits" to lobby for their own personal policy preferences. See Salisbury, "An Exchange Theory."
32. Mayer N. Zald and Roberta Ash, "Social Movement Organizations: Growth, Decay, and Change," *Social Forces* 3 (1966): 327-341.
33. For a slightly different view of market forces, see Jeffrey M. Berry, *The Interest Group Society* (Boston: Little, Brown, 1984), 57-58.
34. Walker, "Origins," 401-402.
35. Gelb and Palley, *Women and Public Policies,* 49.

8. Washington Lobbyists: A Collective Portrait

Robert H. Salisbury

As the scope and substance of government programs have grown since the mid-1960s, the number and diversity of Washington-based lobbyists have similarly expanded. Lobbyists' offices have filled up buildings in the K Street corridor and spilled over into Georgetown and Capitol Hill. In the decade following 1975, the number of registered lobbyists doubled, and the number of lawyers in Washington more than tripled between 1973 and 1983, rising to more than 37,000 from 11,000.

Given the intense and often value-laden media attention devoted to lobbying in the mid-1980s, it is difficult to develop an objective perspective about the process and practitioners of interest representation. In this chapter Robert Salisbury examines data from a large new study of Washington interest representatives and outlines some salient features of the capital's lobbying community. He finds, for example, that continuity is the norm in representational relationships and that the core actors in various policy domains have remained relatively constant over time. Although lobbyists work in various settings, most represent only a few organizations. They are not, on the whole, the "guns for hire" often portrayed in the press. Salisbury sees the "expansion of policy domain participation" as the most notable feature of contemporary interest group politics. Many lobbyists do not specialize. Rather, they play a part in several policy domains, albeit for a limited number of interests.

The First Congress of the United States included in its first proposed amendment to the Constitution the right to petition the government for redress of grievances. Americans were already thoroughly familiar with the

This essay is one result of a collaborative project in which the author is associated with John P. Heinz of Northwestern University and the American Bar Foundation, Edward O. Laumann of the University of Chicago, and Robert L. Nelson of Northwestern University and the American Bar Foundation. Papers growing out of this research may be written by one or more of the investigators, but it is our practice to list all the names on each publication, identifying the person(s) chiefly responsible for drafting it but acknowledging the indispensable contributions of the others. In addition, we acknowledge with gratitude the financial support from the American Bar Foundation and the National Science Foundation.

practice of importuning the government, and they regarded it as essential to their liberties. Hence the First Amendment language. Quite often in the early days of the Republic, the right was literally expressed as a petition, drawn up and signed by concerned citizens and formally presented to elected representatives for their consideration. Despite the great difficulties in reaching Washington in those days and the discomforts involved in staying there, however, Americans soon began to arrive in person to press particular claims on the new government. Some wanted jobs, others sought pensions, and still others were concerned about broader issues of public policy. Once government buildings had been constructed that were sufficiently spacious to accommodate both officials and petitioners, the latter could congregate in the lobbies and were referred to as lobbyists.

Lobbyists have always seemed to descend on Washington in rough proportion to the scope and significance of the programs and policies of the national government. The more ambitious the proposed legislation the larger the number of people seeking to influence and benefit from the outcome. The expansion of government during the Civil War, in particular, attracted a horde of people to Washington intent on taking personal or group advantage of the situation. The permanent resident population of the city was still relatively modest in size, but a large number of visitors, including both the members of Congress and assorted job seekers and lobbyists, filled the hotels and boarding houses, patronized the restaurants and saloons, and enriched the proprietors of gambling establishments and other centers of entertainment. Much of the lobbying in nineteenth-century Washington was in fact not conducted in the lobbies and corridors of government buildings at all, but in the more salubrious environment of nocturnal pleasure palaces.

Sam Ward, the legendary "King of the Lobby," was one of a small army of advocates who, during and after the Civil War, made both fortune and reputation by convincing readily persuadable government officials to assist their client organizations.[1] Their clients consisted largely of the business corporations and trade associations, which had sprung up in ever-increasing numbers after mid-century. The story of Washington lobbying from the Civil War until World War I is thus one of growth: growth in the scope of government, growth in the number and variety of interest organizations in the nation, and, at least among some citizens, a deepening sense that the whole system had become corrupt and was greatly in need of reform.

Muckraking journalism and legislative investigations, such as the Pujo hearing in 1913 and the sensational inquiry led by Charles Evans Hughes into the insurance scandals of New York, gave dramatic publicity to the machinations of organized interests, and lobbying became one of the targets of Progressive Era reform. But World War I exacerbated the problem as once again the rapid growth of government attracted to Washington what seemed like throngs of hopeful lobbyists.[2] Apparently, the expansion of the lobbying system created by World War I remained a fact of life after the war. Political scientist Pendleton Herring, writing in 1929, estimated the number of interest group representatives in Washington at more than 500.[3] It is probable that the number increased again during the 1930s, perhaps rapidly in the early New Deal years of 1933-1935 when new federal programs were started and old ones grew dramatically. Certainly, World War II brought many new groups to Washington to assist in and/or extract from wartime policy development. Historian Arthur Schlesinger, Sr., put the number of private groups with Washington offices in 1942 at 628,[4] but by 1946 the number of Washington lobbyists was thought to be 1,180.[5] By then, in a very real sense, the shape, though certainly not the size, of the "modern" structure of lobbying in national policy issues was reasonably complete.

The 'Modern' System
of Washington Interest Representation

Several recent studies of American lobbying activity use 1960 as a baseline for describing the contemporary world of interest groups, primarily because so many organizations, especially citizens' groups and public interest advocates, have been formed since then. We argue instead that 1946 is the marker that divides the old from the new and that the main components of the present system have been in place since that time. Indeed, five such components can be identified. First, by 1946 there was a vast array of federal domestic programs that had generated a watchful constituency seeking to maintain or improve program benefits or reduce losses. Second, a relatively stable set of foreign commitments involving alliances, economic and military aid, international trade agreements, and military preparedness has evolved— all in a context dominated by the continuing rivalry with the Soviet Union and the unsettling problems of the Third World.

Third, there has been a steady, though very weak, pattern of interest group regulation. The Foreign Agents Registration Act of 1938 and the Regulation of Lobbying Act of 1946 still represent the principal efforts to bring lobbying into the open and thus perhaps induce restraint on the part of the interest groups affected. The only significant change in the legal environment of interest group activity has been the explicit authorization of political action committees (PACs) in the 1974 Amendments to the Federal Election Campaign Act of 1971. Although PACs have given lobbyists an additional arena in which to operate, they apparently have not altered substantially the contours of the interest group universe.

A fourth feature of the "modern" system of interest representation in Washington is the dependence on sophisticated methods of communication. Political scientist Lester Milbrath, writing in 1963, emphasized the role of communication in lobbying. Other observers of the 1950s agreed that communication and the interaction of lobbyists and decision makers, rather than pressure in the nineteenth-century sense, were the key elements.[6] The flamboyant feasts at which Sam Ward had entertained and persuaded officials were no longer much in evidence. Highly developed public relations techniques and the credible presentation of factual information—these have become the mainstays of post-1946 lobbying. For government officials as well as for lobbyists, jet-age travel has made direct contact with constituencies— members, voters, client organizations, or whatever—both more necessary and more feasible. "Farming the membership" is the interest group equivalent of "working the district" by a member of Congress. Both are enhanced by technology; both may result in the mobilization of mass support for a position; both have become standard features of American politics.

Finally, the Washington lobbying "community" has become just that, a community. No longer an in-and-out, hotel-based array of pleaders, using whatever forms of bribery and cajolery worked, without much concern for ethical niceties or much fear of damaging exposure, Washington lobbyists since World War II have tended to be permanent residents in the nation's capital. They employ information and arguments far more than the "booze and broads" of a century ago, and they are actively involved in a number of substantive, often esoteric and highly specialized policy issues, whose outcomes can be of momentous consequence to those—often, only a tiny group— with a stake in the matter. The permanent presence in Washington of interest representatives has many implications regarding the likely bases and sources of lobbyist recruitment, their career paths, and their interaction patterns, some of which we explore later in this discussion.

To be sure, the lobbying patterns of the 1980s are not identical to those of the 1940s. The interest group world has grown enormously in both size and complexity, as we will see in a moment. New groups have come into existence, new issues have assumed prominence, and some of the old concerns have faded. We would emphasize, however, that the essential structure today is much as it was shortly after World War II.

The Washington Lobbying Community Today

We can begin by summarizing what is known about the size and composition of the Washington interest group world.[7] By the early 1980s some 30 percent of all national nonprofit trade and professional associations had their headquarters in Washington. The number of people employed by the more than 2,000 organizations has been estimated to be as high as 80,000 and is at least in the 50,000 range. By 1978 more than 500 corporations had established public affairs offices in Washington, and the rapid growth of that category has continued. The number of lawyers in Washington, long regarded as a rough predictor of the number of lobbyists there, grew from not quite 11,000 in 1973 to more than 37,000 a decade later. In 1965 there were 45 out-of-town law firms with branch offices in Washington; the figure increased to 247 in 1984. The number of Washington-based consultants (a term covering a *very* wide variety of skills and claims to competence) is unknown but large.

The result of the most extensive effort to identify all the individuals who represent group interests of every kind is a list published annually that by 1984 included some 10,000 names.[8] By no means were all of these people officially registered as lobbyists, but even with the various loopholes that enable individuals to avoid registration, the number registered reached 7,200 by 1985, up from 3,400 just ten years earlier. Some 850 people registered in 1985 as agents of foreign governments and firms, more than 20 percent greater than in 1982.

Whatever the specific indicators we use, then, it is plain that the Washington lobbying scene is populated by large numbers of people, larger by far than just a few years ago. These individuals, moreover, work in many different organizational settings. Some, as noted, are employed by trade or professional associations. Some work in the public affairs or government affairs divisions of business corporations. Others hold equivalent positions in labor unions. Then there are the hundreds of interest groups composed of individual citizens—farmers seeking price support increases, reform-minded advocates of public financing of elections, religious fundamentalists trying to restore prayer in the public schools, and so on. Jack Walker classified 20.7 percent of the organizations he studied as nonoccupational in terms of the basis of their membership;[9] 31.7 percent were profit-seeking organizations, and the rest were occupation-based but nonprofit or mixed. Most of the citizens' organizations have relatively small staffs, but taken together they swell considerably the ranks of lobbyists. We have already noted the rapid growth of law firms in Washington, and the traditional lore on lobbyists locates many of the most influential in those firms. Public relations firms such as Robert Gray Associates or William Timmons have gained in both size and prominence, as have other types of consultants.

It is clear that the interest organizations in Washington are numerous, varied, and influential. What is less certain is which kinds of groups are more important than the others and what positions within their ranks the lobbyists occupy. To get a closer look at the Washington lobbyists—who they are, where they work, and what they do—we must turn to a different set of data that specifically address these questions.

The data reported here are drawn from a large study of interest representation in Washington in which a total of 806 individuals were interviewed at considerable length about their backgrounds, careers, activities, and attitudes.[10] The interviews were conducted in 1983. Most (776) of the respondents were selected through a rather complicated procedure designed, first, to identify the organizations that were actively involved in four broad areas of public policy (agriculture, labor, health, and energy) and, second, to pinpoint the individuals who represented the interests of those organizations. An additional 30 respondents were added to fill out a set of "notables," persons identified in preliminary interviews as especially influential in a particular field. From an original list of 72 such individuals, 42 already appeared in our sample. We added the other 30. Thus, although our sample does not cover the full range of Washington lobbyists, we do have a good deal of information about a large number of individuals who have been nominated for us by the groups whose interests they serve. This is important because it turns out that the kind of organization and the position of the individual within it makes a difference.

Further, we believe that the four policy areas we have chosen are sufficiently different from one another in the structure of group activity and involvement that our data are probably not far off what full representativeness would have produced. The advantage of our procedure is that we will be able to examine differences among policy domains to see whether lobbying practices vary from one to another. In this discussion we present a preliminary report and touch on only a few of our findings. Neverthless, our survey represents the most detailed and systematic report yet presented on who the Washington lobbyists are and what they do.

Who Are the Lobbyists?

Social Background

Washington lobbyists are surely a political elite. But do they come from elite backgrounds or are they more representative of society as a whole? Earlier studies of lobbyists have found that they were well educated and that most were white males.[11] This would imply that lobbyists, like other political elites, occupy relatively privileged niches in society. But their current high status may have been *achieved* and reflect upward social mobility, or they may in fact have been born into relatively comfortable circumstances.

Table 8-1 summarizes data relating to the social background of Washington lobbyists. In most respects the profile is similar to those of most

Table 8-1 Selected Social Characteristics of Washington Lobbyists (in percentages)

	Agriculture	Energy	Health	Labor	Total
Women	7.4	10.3	18.9	11.9	12.3
Minorities	1.6	2.2	2.4	5.2	2.9
Prestige Protestant	30.7	25.5	21.8	16.0	23.5
Catholic	12.0	20.1	21.4	22.7	19.1
Jewish	4.2	7.1	12.1	18.0	10.4
Metropolitan area origins	28.4	40.7	51.0	53.9	43.7
Northeast origins	19.1	28.9	49.0	42.2	35.2
Southern and Western origins	44.0	42.0	23.0	28.0	34.0
Blue-collar fathers	21.8	27.6	31.2	36.7	29.4
Professional and managerial fathers	45.7	60.2	59.5	47.6	53.3
Elite college graduates	21.9	26.6	29.6	31.4	27.5
(N)	(192)	(184)	(206)	(194)	(776)

other elites in the United States. Very few members of minority groups are present, women are substantially underrepresented, there are more Jews and upper status Protestants than in the nation as a whole, and more than half of the respondents come from relatively advantaged family backgrounds. The proportion who grew up in major cities is not much different from that of the rest of the population, nor do the regional patterns depart significantly.

There are some interesting differences among the four policy domains. Nearly twice as many lobbyist-representatives in labor and health come from metropolitan areas as do those in agriculture; agriculture and energy people generally come from the South and West, and labor and health advocates come from the Northeast. Not surprisingly, labor issues tend to attract people of somewhat lower status—more minorities and members of blue-collar households, fewer Protestants from prestige denominations. Even so, however, 47.6 percent of the lobbyists on labor issues, a category that includes both management and union representatives, had professional or managerial fathers.

Education

A second set of variables that help us locate Washington lobbyists in the broader structure of American society is their education. More than 90 percent (91.3) are college graduates, and 27.5 percent graduated from high-prestige colleges. More significant is the fact that 74.1 percent attended graduate or professional school. As we might expect from other studies of American political elites and from journalistic treatments of the Washington power structure, a sizable share (34 percent) have law degrees. That fraction is not much different from what Milbrath found in the 1950s, but there is some reason to think that lawyers do not hold quite the dominant position they did in the past. One-eighth of our sample held advanced degrees in science or medicine. Although such backgrounds are probably not usually thought of in connection with lobbying, they were relatively prominent in all our policy areas except labor. A full one-third of the sample held advanced degrees in nontechnical, nonlegal fields. Clearly, Washington representatives are an extremely well educated lot.

Career Patterns

Perhaps the most widely circulated hypothesis about Washington lobbyists is that they have moved "downtown" to the private sector to cash in on the contacts and experience they acquired while in government service. There are several variants on this general theme. One version suggests that there is a "revolving door" through which agency or regulatory commission officials move to more lucrative jobs with the firms or trade associations with which the agency regularly has done business. A second variation on the theme emphasizes the shift of former members of Congress and high-ranking staffers who capitalize on their familiarity with the people and processes of

Table 8-2 Previous Government Experience of Lobbyists

Federal government	45.0%
Congressional	16.9
Executive/Commission	22.0
Other (includes field offices, consulting positions, and miscellaneous others)	6.1
State and local	9.4
Total with government experience	54.4%

legislation to serve private clients. Still another, though somewhat less sinister, form of this hypothesis focuses on those for whom government service comes directly after school, especially law school, and serves as a kind of postgraduate apprenticeship, after which the individual moves to a downtown firm where his or her real career begins. The anecdotal literature is rich in supportive illustrations of each of these versions of the basic story.

How valid is this notion for the whole array of contemporary Washington representatives? The answer appears to be mixed; sometimes it is true and sometimes not. Table 8-2 summarizes the basic findings. Nearly half the respondents have had experience with the federal government, and the proportion is somewhat higher still if we look only at the outside lawyers and consultants and those organizational employees who concentrate on government affairs. Even among these groups, however, one-third to 40 percent have never worked for the government.

A second way of estimating how widespread the revolving door phenomenon might be is to ask how long the individual has been with his or her present organization, whether law firm, corporation, trade association, or citizens' group. Even though many interest organizations are themselves quite young, the mean number of years our respondents spent with their current organization is twelve. In addition, nearly half have held positions with other nongovernmental organizations, which means that whatever their public service may have been, they have had extensive careers outside the government. We will return to this issue later.

The Roles of Washington Representatives: Structure and Differentiation

Let us now look more closely at the way the positions the respondents hold are structured and at some key variables that help determine what kind of position a respondent might occupy. When we collected our data, we asked organizations active in a policy field to name up to four people *inside* the organization and up to four *outside* who represented their interests in the policy field. Our sample was then drawn from the list of more than 1,700 in-

Table 8-3   Organizational Positions of Washington Representatives

External lawyers	13.9%
External consultants	4.5
Organizational officers	43.4
Government affairs staff	22.3
Internal lawyers	6.1
Research staff	9.8
	100.0%

dividuals generated by this question. Table 8-3 groups the people we interviewed into the main categories of positions held.

The table provides some revealing data. First, it should be noted that fewer than one-fifth of the individuals identified as representing client organization interests in Washington are hired from the "outside," on a retainer or fee-for-service basis. This figure is surely smaller than popular images of the free-wheeling, hired gun lobbyist would lead us to expect. Second, the prominence of organizational executives may at first seem remarkable. Some of these (5.5 percent) are corporate chief executive officers (CEOs), but the largest number are trade association executives (144 out of 337, or 43 percent). Many trade associations have fairly small staffs, and policy representation is often a major function of such organizations. It is not surprising, therefore, that these association heads play a leading role as lobbyists. The generous sprinkling of government affairs staff among the lobbyists also might be expected. Government affairs programs have multiplied rapidly in recent years, as we noted earlier, among both corporations and other types of organizations. For example, as health issues have assumed a permanent place on the nation's agenda, involving vast outlays of money, many professional associations, medical schools, hospitals, and citizens' organizations have developed sizable government affairs staffs.

Other interesting differences exist among domains in the way the positions are structured and utilized in the representational process. Rather than pursue those variations here, however, we would emphasize the point that interest representation—lobbying, in its broadest sense—is carried on primarily, and we believe increasingly, by people for whom the task is the core of their work. They are specialists, who, for the most part, are employed by specific organizations rather than serving a variety of clients.

The argument that interest representation is increasingly a specialized responsibility located within organizations with public policy concerns can be supported further from data in Table 8-4. First, we should note that income is noticeably higher for the outside lawyers and consultants than for insiders, though of course the chief executive officers of business firms are also well paid. The large incomes of the outsiders suggest that the guns for hire may

Table 8-4 Selected Characteristics of Washington Representatives, by Organizational Position

Organizational Position	Mean Income (1982)	Mean Age	Percentage Resident in DC Area	Mean Years with Current Organization	Percentage Democrat	Percentage Republican
External lawyers	$166,742	49.2	77.8	13.2	47.2	25.0
External consultants	118,971	47.7	77.1	11.5	45.7	22.9
Organization Executives						
Business	154,975	52.5	30.2	15.4	20.9	51.2
Nonprofit	72,803	51.7	31.4	14.4	35.3	23.5
Trade association	102,309	51.3	68.8	12.9	23.9	48.6
Unions	57,500	56.3	40.0	21.1	83.3	4.2
Professional association	88,943	50.8	52.6	8.8	36.8	34.2
Citizens'	48,058	48.2	61.5	9.9	62.0	10.0
Government Affairs Staff						
Business	79,632	48.3	74.3	14.1	22.9	57.1
Trade association	52,115	43.0	87.0	7.5	33.3	42.6
Unions	47,286	47.0	96.7	14.3	86.7	00.0
Professional association	57,885	45.1	96.3	9.3	33.3	25.9
Citizens'	36,907	44.0	92.6	7.2	66.7	14.8
Internal lawyers	72,386	42.8	57.5	11.5	46.8	31.9
Research staff	52,625	47.0	63.2	11.7	40.8	31.6
Total Sample	$ 90,489	48.5	67.5	12.0	46.4	32.0

still be the "rainmakers," brought in for special tasks that routine lobbying cannot manage.

A second factor is that policy expertise is cultivated primarily in the Washington context, as Table 8-4 demonstrates. Although the CEOs are much less likely to live in Washington—they tend to come to town only when it is necessary—the government affairs staffs are located there permanently, and, as we noted earlier, a high proportion of the trade association population has moved there. External lawyers and consultants also are largely concentrated in the nation's capital, readily available to represent public policy interests.

The length-of-service figures are less expected. Popular notions of lobbyists, as mentioned earlier, emphasize the "revolving door" image, implying constant movement from government service to the private sector, where the government experience and contacts can be capitalized on. As Milbrath observed, "There is an aura of impermanence and non-professionalism about lobbying." [12] Yet more than half the respondents had been out of the government since 1976. Moreover, as Table 8-4 shows, the average length of service with the present organization is twelve years; in addition, nearly half the respondents have held positions with other private organizations. Thus, the total career time spent outside government is substantial.

As Table 8-2 indicated, nearly half the respondents (45 percent) have had some experience with the federal government, and this proportion is highest among external lawyers (67 percent) and consultants (60 percent). But for both these groups government work was completed, on average, more than eleven years earlier. Experience on Capitol Hill is most common among government affairs staff, which, as Table 8-4 shows, tends to be less well paid, younger, and somewhat newer on their jobs. Experience in the executive branch, including the regulatory commissions, is more common than Hill experience, especially for organization executives, and is especially significant for consultants and external lawyers.

These findings suggest three important points. First, although many lobbyists have had federal government experience, the role of interest representative has considerably more stability in organizational location than is generally recognized. Indeed, the majority of those thought to be most influential have been plying their trade at the same stand and often for the same clients or employers for a good many years. Second, despite the publicity attendant on moves by former senators or executive officials to lobbying jobs, recruitment from the ranks of government to the private sector occurs primarily at the lower levels, most often to positions with government affairs staff.

Third, the most notable exception to these two findings occurs among that loosely bounded category of consultants. They tend to move employment locations more often and to draw upon government experience more heavily than do those in positions that are more sharply defined by an organization or law firm. The term *consultant* can cover a multitude of characteristics and activities, of course, but our data show that on average they are a somewhat different lot from other lobbyists and policy representatives in Washington. One further point is suggested by preliminary data on the more than three hundred government officials we interviewed in our study. It appears that a substantial fraction of these people, especially those in the executive branch, have previously held positions as policy representatives. In other words, the revolving door between the private sector and public service appears to work both ways!

The partisan coloration among Washington representatives contains few surprises. Business firms and trade associations are predominantly Republican, unions and citizens' groups are Democratic, and professional associations are evenly split. Government affairs staffs generally mirror the party preferences of organizational executives. It is only with respect to the lawyers and consultants that eyebrows might be raised. Both groups are strongly Democratic. Compared to the other groups in our study, they are not particularly active in politics, and they do not seem to regard their party preferences of organizational executives. It is only with respect to the lawyers and consultants that eyebrows might be raised. Both groups are strongly among these presumed movers and shakers is striking.

In fact, Washington representatives generally have been quite active in party politics. For example, 25 percent have held office in a partisan political organization, and 42.3 percent have been significantly involved in political campaigns. Our findings are similar to those Milbrath reported, but he interpreted his data differently.[13] According to Milbrath, the fact that nearly half his respondents had never been much involved in party affairs indicated a low level of party activism. We think that, given the lower rate of participation among the general public, our findings and his both suggest that lobbyists are highly political in terms of their backgrounds, though we, like Milbrath, find that partisanship does not substantially affect their current representational work.

Policy Representation: How Much and What Kinds?

How much attention do Washington representatives devote to public policy matters and how much do they devote to other aspects of their jobs? Put differently, what proportion of the total work carried out by policy representatives is actually devoted to policy issues? Table 8-5 summarizes our data, again differentiating among several kinds of organizational executives, government affairs staff, research staff, lawyers, and consultants. The central finding is that, among these respondents, half their time is taken up by policy issues, state and federal, and one-third by matters within the individual's organization or firm (including law firms for lawyers). While important differences exist among the various organizational positions, it is significant that, if they choose to play a public policy role, even chief executives spend nearly half their time on policy issues. External lawyers stand out, not only because of their private law practice but because they alone are comparatively free from worry about managing the internal affairs of an organization.

Table 8-5 Policy Representatives and the Allocation of Time

Organizational Position	Percentage of Time on Conventional Law Practice	Percentage of Time on Federal Policy	Percentage of Time on State Policy	Percentage of Time on Organization Duties	Percentage of Time on Other
External lawyers	47.7	39.4	4.7	10.3	3.9
Consultants	0.6	46.4	8.8	22.9	21.3
Organization Executives					
Business	1.3	32.7	10.8	46.8	8.5
Nonprofit	0.1	31.6	10.1	47.5	10.6
Trade association	1.1	43.2	9.2	39.2	7.3
Unions	0.4	22.6	7.3	65.5	4.2
Professional association	2.4	30.0	9.2	43.3	15.2
Citizens'	3.5	28.2	18.7	43.5	6.1
Government Affairs Staff					
Business	0.0	57.1	9.5	31.1	2.3
Trade association	0.3	55.6	9.5	28.2	6.7
Unions	0.0	59.8	5.5	29.2	5.5
Professional association	1.1	53.7	6.4	33.7	5.2
Citizens'	0.2	55.4	11.4	28.9	4.1
Internal lawyers	22.9	34.5	11.5	28.1	2.9
Research staff	0.8	41.9	10.3	35.9	11.0
Total Sample	8.1	41.7	9.4	33.4	7.4

When they are involved in public policy matters, what do interest representatives do? Kay Lehman Schlozman and John Tierney have reported the response to a list of twenty-seven techniques or tactics.[14] They found that at least three-fourths of their respondents engaged in seventeen of the twenty-seven possible tasks, ranging from talking to the press to engaging in protest demonstrations. Our data are somewhat different in form. We asked people to indicate on a scale of one to five the importance of each of eighteen separate activities. The data are sufficiently complex to call for considerably more extended analysis than can be presented here. We will confine our attention to one general finding.

By subjecting the responses to our questions about the eighteen tasks to the statistical procedure of factor analysis, we could sort them out into four distinct groups. One set of activities involved the development of policy positions within the client organization and their formal presentation as testimony at official proceedings. A second set of activities comprised various types of monitoring of the policy process—maintaining contacts with other organizations working on the same issues, securing political contributions, and mobilizing grass-roots support. The third group consisted of two associated tasks—developing informal contacts and cultivating good connections. The fourth involved the more narrowly lawyerly activities of bill drafting, brief writing, and litigation.

It will surprise no one that the lawyers virtually monopolized the fourth category. What was unexpected is that lawyers, especially those from the "outside," are *not* very much involved in either policy development or in monitoring and mobilization. This set of tasks, which might be thought of as the heart of day-to-day professional lobbying, was dominated by the government affairs staffs of the interest organizations. Policy development, the first factor, was the province of organizational leaders, especially those who headed trade associations and government affairs programs. Informal contacting was undertaken by nearly everyone, but those who were lower in the organizational hierarchies spent more of their time keeping up good working relations with officials.

Evidently, according to these data, interest groups and other organizations concerned with public policy are complex enough in their structure to display rather clear patterns of role and task differentiation. We cannot be certain of what changes have been occurring over time, but our strong impression is that more and more of the policy representation tasks are being performed *within* the organizations rather than being "contracted out" to lawyers, consultants, or other free-lance operatives. The latter may still attract much of the journalists' hyperbole, but their importance on the lobbying scene is diminishing.

Some Tentative Conclusions

Although it is dangerous to venture judgments from research that is still very much in progress, we can offer some tentative conclusions that may be different, at least in part, from most standard interpretations. First, in recent years the number of organizations active in Washington has expanded greatly, but the core actors in each policy domain have been at their work for a considerable length of time. Continuity in representational relationships is far more characteristic than the sort of single shot "ad hockery" portrayed in some of the more lurid case studies of Washington lobbying.

Second, as we have just noted, the "business" of interest representation in Washington involves a fairly complex structure of differentiated roles, most of which are located *within* the participating organizations rather than outside as free-standing guns for hire. This structure, moreover, appears to be similar in form in all four of the policy domains we have examined.

Third, Washington lobbyists do not spend all their time trying to influence public policy. Moreover, many of those who are active in a given policy domain tend to participate, to some extent, in other domains as well. Thus the degree of specialization in task or subject matter is not as complete as might have been expected. One corollary of this relative lack of specialization is that the policy domains themselves are not as sharply bounded as the literature on iron triangles would have led us to assume. Hugh Heclo's conception of "issue networks" is closer to the mark,[15] but even that metaphor may imply a consistency of group participation within a given policy area that is seldom observed. It may be premature to coin a phrase to express our conception of how these issue spaces are organized, but at the very least we should recognize that they are permeable; in other words, all kinds of groups may get involved, at least as occasional participants.

Finally, the participation of nontraditional actors in the various policy domains is perhaps the most notable feature of the contemporary interest group universe. Schlozman has emphasized the continuity of business domination,[16] and, in terms of the total number of groups participating in all policy areas, it is true that business is the most active. Within a given domain, however, it is the presence in recent years of considerable numbers of citizens' groups, environmentalists, and other such forces, in addition to the traditional self-interested producers, that is most striking. Don Hadwiger has described the transformation of agricultural politics brought about by the advent of what he calls the externality/alternative coalition, made up of nonfarmers concerned about issues such as pesticides and conservation rather than farm production and price supports.[17] Something of this kind has occurred in other policy areas as well. War has long been regarded as too important to leave to the generals. Today it may be said that virtually every policy area has come to be regarded as too important to be left to the specialists and the narrowly self-interested.

Notes

1. See the biography of Ward by Lately Thomas, *Sam Ward, King of the Lobby* (Boston: Houghton Mifflin, 1965).

2. E. Pendleton Herring, *Group Representation Before Congress* (Baltimore: Johns Hopkins University Press, 1929), 51.
3. Ibid., 19.
4. Arthur Schlesinger, Sr., *Paths to the Present* (New York: Macmillan, 1949), 46.
5. Donald C. Blaisdell, *American Democracy Under Pressure* (New York: Ronald Press, 1957), 59.
6. Lester Milbrath, *The Washington Lobbyists* (Chicago: Rand, McNally, 1963).
7. For a useful recent survey of the "fugitive" materials on this matter, see Jeffrey M. Berry, *The Interest Group Society* (Boston: Little, Brown, 1984).
8. Arthur C. Close and Jody Curtis, eds., *Washington Representatives, 1985* (Washington, D.C.: Columbia Books, 1985).
9. Jack Walker, "The Origins and Maintenance of Interest Groups in America," *American Political Science Review* 77 (1983): 390-406.
10. A full description of the project design and sampling procedure is contained in Robert L. Nelson et al., "Interest Representation in Washington," mimeo, 1986.
11. Milbrath, *Washington Lobbyists;* Jeffrey M. Berry, *Lobbying for the People* (Princeton, N.J.: Princeton University Press, 1977).
12. Milbrath, *Washington Lobbyists,* 67.
13. Ibid., 26ff.
14. Kay Lehman Schlozman and John T. Tierney, *Organized Interests and American Democracy* (New York: Harper & Row, 1985), 148ff.
15. Hugh Heclo, "Issue Networks and the Executive Establishment," in *The New American Political System,* ed. Anthony King (Washington, D.C.: American Enterprise Institute, 1978), 87-124.
16. Kay Lehman Schlozman, "What Accent the Heavenly Chorus? Political Equality and the American Pressure System," *Journal of Politics* 46 (1984): 1006-1032.
17. Don F. Hadwiger, *The Politics of Agricultural Research* (Lincoln: University of Nebraska Press, 1982).

9. Interest Group Responses to Partisan Change: The Impact of the Reagan Administration upon the National Interest Group System

Mark A. Peterson and Jack L. Walker

The organizational strength and policy impact of interest groups are often tied to the fates of political parties and presidential administrations. Organized labor traditionally has enjoyed much closer ties to Democratic regimes; business has had a closer relationship with Republican presidents. Environmentalists, the evangelical Right, and many other groups also have direct stakes in partisan and presidential ascendancy. At the same time, groups can and do find ways to deal with hostile administrations. In some circumstances, as with environmentalists and Secretary of the Interior James Watt, groups may prosper, at least in terms of membership growth, when confronted with an inhospitable regime.

Building on two waves of group-based surveys, Mark Peterson and Jack Walker offer an interpretation of the evolution of interest groups during Reagan's first term. They see the increasingly polarized politics of parties and officeholders as framing the context within which groups must develop. Groups and interests have proliferated, to be sure, but this expansion has gone hand in hand with the emergence of a more contentious politics, as articulated by an administration with a reasonably well-defined ideological perspective. Peterson and Walker's findings and interpretations foresee major changes in the process of representation within the United States. Partisan realignment, regardless of its ultimate shape, has profound, long-term implications for the nature of interest group politics.

As bargaining concluded in 1981 between members of the White House staff and congressional leaders over the massive tax cut that was the legislative hallmark of "Reaganomics," David Stockman, one of the chief architects of the administration's political and economic strategy, was dismayed. He was shocked at the lack of regard by Washington lobbyists for equity or fairness in the tax system. The bill's avowed purpose was to provide incentives for individuals to save and invest, but, once serious bargaining began in Congress, representatives of special interests—the "piranhas" as Stockman called them—demanded amendments that would provide millions of dollars of privileges for their clients in exchange for their support. "Do you realize the greed that came to the forefront?" Stockman asked almost in wonder in a con-

162

versation with a reporter. "The hogs were really feeding. The greed level, the level of opportunism, just got out of control." [1]

Complaints about the harmful influence of greedy special interests certainly did not originate with Stockman. Even U.S. presidents have found themselves stymied by the interest group system. George Washington, in his farewell address in 1796, warned of the "baneful effects of the spirit of party" that through "selfish misrepresentations" tend "to render alien to each other those who ought to be bound together by fraternal affection." [2] Two hundred years later, Jimmy Carter echoed these sentiments in his farewell address by warning that the scramble of organized interests "tends to distort our purposes, because the national interest is not always the sum of our single or special interests. We are all Americans together, and we must not forget that the common good is our common interest and our individual responsibility." [3] Looking back on his experiences in Washington, Carter found that even his liberal supporters were major obstacles because "when you don't measure up a 100 percent to those so-called liberal groups, they demand a gallon of blood. There's no compromise with them. If they get 90 percent of what they want, that's not important. It's the 10 percent that they didn't get that becomes a driving political force." [4]

President Ronald Reagan, of course, prefers that liberal groups receive as little as possible of what they want, especially in the form of direct support from the federal government. Exploiting the widespread criticism of single-interest groups and the frustration generated by the Carter administration's alleged inability to take decisive action in the face of group demands, the Reagan administration launched a campaign to "defund the left" that is designed to reduce the number and influence of interest groups in Washington. To permanently shrink the size of the federal establishment—the president's fundamental, overriding goal—the Reagan administration believes that the much-heralded "iron triangles" binding congressional committees, federal bureaus, and interest groups into close-knit, impenetrable policy communities have to be broken. To achieve this goal, the Reagan administration during its first term sought to inhibit the growth and reduce the financial resources available from the government for interest groups operating in Washington. Strenuous efforts were made to prevent federal agencies from providing grants, contracts, or consultancies to interest groups. In collateral moves, the Office of Management and Budget (OMB) sought to change regulations concerning the political activities of federal contractors, and the Internal Revenue Service (IRS) altered the bases under which tax exemption was granted to make it more difficult for nonprofit groups to engage in anything resembling partisan political activity. [5]

For the political scientist, Reagan's first term presents a rare opportunity to study how the U.S. system of government reacted to an unusually determined effort by a partisan leader to effect a sharp change in public policy. Acting in the name of the presidency and the Republican party, Reagan challenged the representative system that had set the policy agenda in Washington for more than thirty years. In this chapter we seek to measure

the success of one aspect of this challenge. Has the Reagan administration reduced the number of interest groups operating at the national level or forced
major changes in the way they are maintained? How has the interest group
system responded to this strong thrust from the partisan political leadership?
Has the central target of the Reagan budgetary strategy—the social welfare
policy community—suffered especially serious policy setbacks or has the
number of interest groups working in this area been reduced? Does the
Reagan administration represent a dramatic shift in the way public policy is
made in Washington, or have the organized advocates been able to roll with
the punches and continue operating much as they did before Reagan was
elected?

There have been few previous studies concerned with the interactions of
political parties and interest groups, and those usually contrast the partisan
political system with the narrowly focused, issue-oriented world of interest
groups. The vitality of one system is often thought to come at the expense of
the other.[6] We believe, however, that the two systems are engaged in a
symbiotic relationship, each being molded by the same social forces.

By assessing the impact of the "Reagan Revolution" on the Washington
political establishment, we have a unique opportunity to study some of the
fundamental characteristics of the relationship between political parties and
interest groups. Reagan has played a central role in transforming the national
party system into a more centralized, ideologically based instrument of mass
persuasion.[7] Each party is coming to resemble some of the larger interest
groups that emerged from the civil rights, environmental, or other social
movements. We will show that because of the general political forces linking
the parties and the group system, the Reagan administration, with its potent
partisan base, has in many respects reinforced rather than weakened the
interest group system.

Using data collected in two surveys conducted by mail in 1980 and 1985,
we examined the link between parties and interest groups within the
governmental arena from the perspective of interest group leaders, assessing
the impact of the Reagan administration upon the system of interest groups.
Included in the sample were associations that are open to membership and indicate their concern with public policy at the national level by maintaining
some kind of formal presence in the nation's capital.[8]

Given the vast size and complexity of the modern interest group system,
our surveys could not include a variety of other organizations that now
provide representation for elements of the American public. For example, the
surveys did not cover trade unions or business corporations, both of which
greatly increased their concern with national public policy since the mid-
1960s. The surveys also excluded hundreds of nonprofit corporations, public
interest law firms, university-based research centers, independent commissions, newsletters, consulting firms, and the increasingly active national
lobbying efforts of public agencies and state and local governments. All these
entities are integral parts of the representative system, and a truly comprehensive survey of changes in the system of conflict resolution in America would

have to include them all.[9] This study would be stronger if data were available on the entire system of interest aggregation, agenda setting, and influence, but the data we have collected allow us to assess the impact of the Reagan administration's policies upon a large and important segment of the representative system.

We contacted a total of 902 membership organizations in 1980 as part of the survey, and 558 of them returned questionnaires, producing a response rate of 62 percent. In 1985, 799 of 1,501 membership groups that were contacted responded, for a rate of 53 percent. The 1985 dataset allows us to create a panel of 448 respondents to both surveys. For approximately 59 percent of those who responded to our 1980 survey, we have readings at two points in time. Using these data, we are able to compare the state of the interest group system prior to Reagan's inauguration with the state of the system at the end of his first term.

Growth in the Number of Groups under Reagan

All administrations try to reward their friends and frustrate, if not punish, their political enemies. Democratic administrations during the 1960s used several methods to funnel financial support to liberal political entrepreneurs who were trying to create interest groups to promote new social welfare programs and support the Democratic legislative agenda. The Carter administration revised the provisions in the tax code concerning nonprofit organizations to foster campaigns of grass-roots lobbying and, using an invigorated Office of Public Liaison in the White House, encouraged contacts between those organizations and Congress. The Reagan administration differs from these earlier efforts only in that it has placed far greater emphasis on challenging directly its liberal opposition. While Democrats did not threaten the organizational base of their opponents, the current administration has made such efforts an important part of its policy agenda. The first question we must ask in assessing Reagan's impact upon the group system, therefore, is whether the system's growth had been affected in any significant way.

One of the most distinctive features of American politics in recent years has been the rapid increase in the number of interest groups.[10] Our data indicate that the Reagan administration's efforts have done almost nothing to reverse this trend. As shown in Section A of Table 9-1, 16 percent of the total number of groups in our 1980 survey were founded during the ten years prior to the survey, compared with 17 percent of the groups responding to the 1985 questionnaire. So far we also have been able to determine that fewer than 5 percent of the groups responding in 1980 have left the scene either by merging with other organizations (1.4 percent) or ceasing their activities (3.2 percent). These data suggest that the rate of growth in the number of groups probably has leveled off, but the system still seems to be expanding briskly. There were more interest groups in Washington in 1985 then there had been five years before.

Table 9-1   Growth in Number of Membership Associations, for the Whole Sample and by Sector, 1980 and 1985

Sector	1980		1985	
	(N)	Percentage of Groups Ten Years Old or Younger	(N)	Percentage of Groups Ten Years Old or Younger
A. Whole Sample				
	(412)	16	(858)	17
B. By Sector				
Profit	(140)	15	(325)	14
Mixed	(44)	11	(50)	14
Nonprofit	(151)	12	(279)	12
Citizens	(75)	27	(204)	30

Source: The Michigan Interest Group Study. See Appendix for details.

Not only has the system continued to expand, but also growth is taking place in much the same way as it has in the recent past, as shown in Section B of Table 9-1. In previous articles, we have developed a typology of the group system that distinguishes among associations based upon occupational communities and those that are organized around an idea or cause.[11] Section B of the table displays the growth patterns characterizing these four categories of organizations: (1) groups whose members engage in the same profession or commercial activity in the profit-making segments of the society (e.g., the American Trucking Associations); (2) groups whose members are employed mainly by institutions in the nonprofit sectors of the society (the National Association of Public Hospitals); (3) "mixed" groups whose memberships come about equally from the profit and nonprofit sectors (the National Association of Broadcasters); and (4) citizens groups organized around a cause or idea whose members need not share any common occupational characteristics (the Sierra Club or Common Cause).

Our earlier reports demonstrated that the citizens groups were the fastest growing segment of the group system, and the 1985 results indicate that this trend continued unabated. In both the 1980 and 1985 surveys, only 12 percent of the groups made up of nonprofit professionals were created in the ten years immediately before the survey was conducted, but, in 1980, 27 percent of the citizens groups were ten years old or less, and that number increased to 30 percent in the 1985 data. Citizens groups are more likely than those based in the occupational sectors to go out of operation, but their five-year death rate of 6.9 percent is not high enough to fully counteract their vigorous overall rate of growth. The surge in the formation of citizens groups began in the early 1960s, and the appearance of these boisterous newcomers has led to increasing conflict and polarization within the American system of representation.[12] Our data indicate that nothing done by the Reagan administration during its first term has altered these broad trends in the development of the group system.

Ideological Polarization in the New Group System

The new groups founded during the past twenty years have not merely reinforced the interests that were already represented in Washington. Beginning with the civil rights movement in the 1950s and 1960s, wave after wave of new groups were formed to represent elements of the population, or points of view, that had been given little voice in earlier periods. The national debate over all aspects of public policy became more balanced, but also more conflictual, heated, and ideological. Issues that once were settled without publicity in relatively obscure precincts of Congress or the executive branch became the subjects of widely publicized congressional hearings and public protests. As television became the major conveyor of news from the capital, many new interest groups emerged whose purpose was not only to represent an established interest but also to raise new, highly controversial issues, mobilize politically quiescent elements of the society, and promote the creation of broad new social programs.[13]

The increasing political polarization caused by the growth of the group system is clearly illustrated by the data presented in Table 9-2. Groups were asked whether they had experienced an increase or decrease in cooperation and consultation with federal agencies as a result of the Reagan presidency.[14] For both new and old groups, we present the results to this question for the entire 1985 sample (Section A) and for several subsamples based upon the reported policy interests of the groups (Sections B through F).

Table 9-2 illustrates, first of all, that many of the groups founded since 1965, in the years after the Kennedy-Johnson administrations and the mobilization engendered by the expanding Great Society programs, have experienced a decline in cooperation from federal agencies under the Reagan administration. In Section A of the table, where the whole sample is described, 26 percent of the groups founded before 1965 reported increased cooperation, and about the same number—22 percent—indicated a decrease in cooperation. Among those founded in 1965 or after, however, only 14 percent reported more federal agency cooperation under the Reagan presidency, while 37 percent, almost three times as many, experienced a decrease in cooperation. Our survey shows that the group system as a whole is about evenly balanced between those who perceive greater access under the Reagan administration and those who report a decline in their relationship with the government, but it is clear that the newer groups that arose during an era when a liberal political consensus prevailed in Washington are the ones whose collective position has declined most dramatically. It is also worth noting that the Reagan administration was not shooting at phantoms when it initiated its attack on the expanded group system. The groups founded since

Table 9-2   Perceptions of Changes in Federal Agency Cooperation Produced by the Election of Ronald Reagan, by the Founding Dates of Groups for the Whole Sample, and by Policy Area in the 1985 Dataset

Founding Date	(N)	More Cooperation	No Change	Less Cooperation	No Contact Prior to 1980	Row Total
		A. Whole Sample				
Up to 1965	(493)	26%	44	22	8	100%
Post-1965	(292)	14%	34	37	15	100%
		B. Agriculture				
Up to 1965	(78)	33%	39	26	3	101%
Post-1965	(37)	11%	35	38	16	100%
		C. Economic Development				
Up to 1965	(254)	35%	38	24	2	99%
Post-1965	(137)	20%	37	34	9	100%
		D. Social Welfare				
Up to 1965	(270)	21%	48	28	3	100%
Post-1965	(166)	11$	28	48	13	100%
		E. National Security				
Up to 1965	(94)	33%	44	19	4	100%
Post-1965	(59)	17%	29	32	22	100%
		F. Government Management				
Up to 1965	(86)	40%	37	23	0	100%
Post-1965	(54)	15%	22	54	9	100%

Source: The Michigan Interest Group Study. See Appendix for details.

1965 are more likely to desire an increase in social services than those created in earlier years.

Sections B through F in Table 9-2 provide evidence that the polarization created by the influx of new interest groups since 1965 has taken place in all areas of American public policy. The patterns discovered for the full sample are repeated in all policy areas.[15] It comes as no surprise that the groups expressing an interest in social welfare policy (Section D) experienced declines in cooperation with federal agencies under Reagan, given the Reagan administration's efforts to sharply curtail expenditures for social programs, but the most extensive declines in cooperation actually appear in Section F among groups interested in the management and accountability of the federal government, presumably because of the Reagan administration's efforts to limit regulatory procedures and reduce public access to decision making. The data reported in Table 9-2 make clear that the supporters and opponents of the Reagan administration exist in all policy areas. The modern system of interest representation is highly polarized and becoming more so as the system grows.

The trend reflected in these data is toward increased ideological differences within the group structure underlying the two political parties. Interest groups, as they struggle to advance their own programs, are steadily being drawn into the orbit of one of the two major parties. It is important to recognize, however, that many groups are still largely impervious to the outcomes of partisan elections. Many of the newer groups have not established any contacts with federal agencies, so they have no relationships that can be affected by the outcomes of partisan elections. Section A of the table, however, shows that 44 percent of the groups founded before 1965 reported that they have experienced no change in their relationships with federal agencies, and 34 percent of the groups founded since 1965 also made that claim. Some of these unaffected groups have objectives and engage in activities that are inherently nonpartisan, or even apolitical. Approximately 8 percent of the groups in our 1985 survey, for example, did not engage in any of the electoral, lobbying, legal, or public relations activities asked about in our questionnaires. Groups like the Naval Historical Society, the American Genetics Association, or the American Home Economics Association confine themselves to standard-setting, information exchanges, specialized midcareer training, or other purely technical functions for the professions they represent.

Other organizations that are unaffected by changes in the partisan control of the White House are highly political and well connected with the federal executive and congressional establishments, but operate within the remaining subgovernments that are largely isolated from the pressures of partisan politics. It seems that more than one-third of the groups in our 1985 sample are involved in subgovernments, but, to put these numbers in perspective, 63 percent of our respondents in 1980 reported that they saw no change in their governmental relationships when President Carter replaced President Gerald Ford. The Reagan administration clearly has had almost twice as large an impact on the world of interest groups as the Carter administration. There are still many groups who are able to conduct business as usual, no matter who is in the White House, but their numbers seem to be declining rapidly.

Ideology and Response to the Reagan Administration

It is a group's ideology, not the policy area with which it is concerned, that best explains the degree of cooperation it experienced with federal agencies during the first term of the Reagan administration. Evidence from our panel study substantiates this generalization. All groups in 1980 were asked whether they advocated an increase in the level of social services provided by the federal government, felt the level provided should stay as it

Table 9-3   The Relationship between a Group's 1980 Position on the Provision of Federal Social Services and Federal Regulation and 1985 Perceived Changes in Federal Agency Cooperation as a Result of the Election of Ronald Reagan, in the Panel Dataset

Desired Level	(N)	More Cooperation	No Change	Less Cooperation	Row Total
A. 1980 Position on the Appropriate Level of Federal Social Services					
Much more	(46)	4%	30	65	99%
Somewhat more	(98)	8%	43	49	100%
Present level	(51)	20%	55	26	101%
Somewhat less	(47)	34%	38	28	100%
Much less	(43)	54%	40	7	101%
B. 1980 Position on the Appropriate Level of Federal Regulation					
Much more	(17)	0%	6	94	100%
Somewhat more	(46)	4%	30	65	99%
Present level	(51)	6%	43	51	100%
Somewhat less	(124)	25%	55	20	100%
Much less	(74)	58%	28	14	100%

Source: The Michigan Interest Group Study. See Appendix for details.

was, or would like to see the level reduced. The same kind of question was asked concerning the level of regulation exercised by the federal government. The data displayed in Table 9-3 clearly show the strong relationship between group responses to these general ideological questions in 1980 and their perceptions five years later concerning the effect of the Reagan administration on the degree of cooperation and consultation they experienced with agencies of the federal government.[16]

Both sections of the table provide the same unmistakable clear result. In Section A, the positions taken by groups in 1980 on whether they desired increases in social services correlate strongly (gamma = .55) with reports of cooperation with federal agencies under Reagan. Those who desired higher levels of social services in 1980 reported that they experienced declines in cooperation with federal agencies once the Reagan administration came to power. In Section B, the group's 1980 position on the desirability of further federal regulation was an even better predictor of cooperation with the Reagan administration (gamma = .67). Groups that expressed a preference for greater federal regulation in 1980 tended to experience declines in cooperation in 1985.

These data highlight the stable and enduring ideological commitments of interest groups, and demonstrate that for many groups these commitments determine the amount of access they enjoy with the administrative agencies of government. In 1980 the relationships between these ideological commitments and reports of cooperation with the Carter administration were also strong (gammas = .53 and .55), although in these cases, groups expressing a preference for more social services or regulation enjoyed *greater* cooperation with federal agencies. The sharp swings in the experiences of interest groups caused by changes in administrations provide further confirmation of the importance of ideology and the outcome of partisan elections in structuring the relationships between interest groups and the executive establishment.

The ideological positions of interest groups are closely related to the elements of the society they represent. Trade associations and professional societies emerging from occupational communities in the profit-making sector of the economy are more likely to call for a reduction in the size and influence of the federal government. Groups advocating a larger regulatory role for government and an expansion of social programs usually are either citizens groups with financial backing from foundations, wealthy individuals, churches, or trade unions, or they emerge from occupational communities within the society's growing nonprofit realm that often service or administer many government programs. The contrasting organizational foundations of the group system are revealed in Table 9-4, in which the types of groups most opposed to the Carter and Reagan administrations, and those that are most supportive are compared.

In Section A of the table, groups that strongly supported an increase in social services at the federal level in 1980 (described as liberals) and also enjoyed more cooperation from federal agencies during the Carter administration are compared with those that called for reductions in federal social services (designated as conservatives) and experienced less cooperation from federal agencies under Carter. In Section B the contrast is between the conservative groups that wanted to reduce social services and experienced greater cooperation from the Reagan administration—presumably Reagan's strongest supporters—and those liberal groups who stood in 1980 for an increase in social services and experienced a *decrease* in cooperation from federal agencies under Reagan.

Table 9-4 shows quite dramatically that the strongest opponents and supporters of the two administrations represent different parts of the interest group world. Seventy-five percent of Carter's conservative critics came from the business-oriented groups in the profit-making sector, while his liberal supporters were among the citizens groups (48 percent) and groups made up of social service professionals in the nonprofit sector (33 percent). Five years later, in 1985, the situation was completely reversed. The conservative interest groups that were Reagan's strongest supporters came predominantly from the business-oriented, profit-making sector (69 percent), and his most determined liberal opponents were from nonprofit (41 percent) and citizens groups (46 percent).

These data bring into sharp focus the fundamental organizational and ideological cleavages that characterize the affairs of the contemporary interest

Table 9-4　The Distribution of Ideology and Partisan Sensitivity of Groups in Each Sector, in the Panel Dataset

Ideology/Partisan Sensitivity	(N)	Sector				Row Total
		Profit	Mixed	Nonprofit	Citizen	
A. Effect on Federal Agency Cooperation of Carter's Election						
Liberal/increased cooperation[a]	(46)	13%	7	33	48	101%
Conservative/decreased cooperation[b]	(28)	75%	0	14	11	100%
B. Effect on Federal Agency Cooperation of Reagan's Election						
Conservative/increased cooperation[c]	(39)	69%	3	15	13	100%
Liberal/decreased cooperation[d]	(70)	7%	6	41	46	100%

[a] Groups that in 1980 called for an increase in the provision of federal social services and perceived an increase in federal agency cooperation as a result of the election of President Carter.

[b] Groups that in 1980 called for a decrease in the provision of federal social services and perceived a decrease in federal agency cooperation as a result of the election of President Carter.

[c] Groups that in 1980 called for a decrease in the provision of federal social services and in 1985 perceived an increase in federal agency cooperation as a result of the election of President Reagan.

[d] Groups that in 1980 called for an increase in the provision of federal social services and in 1985 perceived a decrease in federal agency cooperation as a result of the election of President Reagan.

Source: The Michigan Interest Group Study. See Appendix for details.

group system in America. When Reagan replaced Carter in the White House, there was a virtual revolution in the access enjoyed by interest groups in Washington. In the past, many groups may have been able to maintain their contacts with the bureaucratic agencies of the federal government through politically isolated subgovernments or iron triangles, no matter what the outcome of the election, but it was difficult to build such safe enclaves around a group's favorite programs during the 1980s. While subgovernments may still exist, many more interest groups now find themselves affected by a partisan change at the White House. When candidates for the presidency employ broad ideological themes in their campaigns, as Reagan did, and threaten to fundamentally alter the direction of public policy, almost no governmental program is entirely safe. Even those groups with the most narrow commercial, occupational, or professional focus find themselves being drawn into alliances with one of the two major political parties, whether they like it or not.

The Maintenance of Interest Groups under Reagan

The Reagan administration's campaign to restrict the resources and influence of interest groups that receive financial aid and comfort from the federal government is a logical extension of its unusually sharp confrontational style. The policy makers in the White House are well aware that groups in the nonprofit and citizen categories are likely to be unsympathetic with Reagan's policy goals. The administration may have failed to reduce the total number of interest groups operating at the national level, but our data reveal that it has been very successful in cutting the amount of government funding that helped maintain the types of groups most likely to oppose the administration's principal goals. Using data from our panel study, Table 9-5 presents the sources of revenue for all four types of groups—profit, mixed, nonprofit, and citizens—in 1980, just prior to the beginning of the Reagan administration, and in 1985, during the first year of the president's second term.

Each type of group has been affected by the policy changes of the Reagan administration in slightly different ways. The groups in the profit-making sector—mainly trade associations and professional societies that are sympathetic to the Reagan administration—received most of their revenues in recurring payments from their members in the form of dues, publication subscriptions, and conference fees in both 1980 (82.9 percent) and 1985 (81.3 percent). These groups changed their mix of support slightly by relying less upon annual dues in 1985 and increasing the revenues they received from conferences, trade shows, and seminars. These business-oriented groups also have increased the proportion of their revenues coming from nonrecurring sources such as grants, contracts, and gifts from other associations, business firms, and, interestingly enough, from government agencies in the Reagan administration.

Government support is down substantially for other types of groups, however, and this has caused the nonprofit and citizens groups to seek out several new sources of revenue. Table 9-5 reveals that both nonprofit and citizens groups, unlike groups in the other sectors, maintained the same level of revenues from dues. Citizens groups, however, received only 31.3 percent of their support in 1985 from annual dues, down slightly from 34.9 percent five years before.

There was an uneven pattern of gains and losses in membership among the citizens groups that opposed the Reagan administration. Many of the groups from the environmental, peace, and women's movements reported sharp increases in the size of their memberships, but, overall, groups that were the strongest critics of the Reagan administration, those that supported increases in the level of social services in 1980 and reported a decline in cooperation with federal agencies in 1985 as a result of Reagan's election, on the average lost about 10 percent of their members between 1980 and 1985.

Gifts and contracts also were down for the citizens groups as sources of revenue, not only from government, but also from individuals and founda-

Table 9-5 Mean Percentage of Total 1980 and 1985 Revenues Received from Various Sources by Groups in Each Sector in the Panel Dataset

Revenue Source	Profit 1980	Profit 1985	Mixed 1980	Mixed 1985	Nonprofit 1980	Nonprofit 1985	Citizens 1980	Citizens 1985
Routine contributions from members and associates:								
Dues	67.9	63.1	58.1	47.6	47.7	48.2	34.9	31.3
Publications	6.2	6.4	10.2	9.6	10.3	11.2	5.7	7.7
Conferences	8.8	11.8	11.1	11.4	8.3	10.3	4.3	3.9
Subtotal	*82.9*	*81.3*	*79.4*	*68.6*	*66.3*	*69.6*	*44.9*	*42.9*
Nonrecurring contributions from non-member institutions and persons:								
Individual gifts	1.8	0.6	2.1	4.2	3.1	1.8	16.2	11.2
Private foundations	0.4	0.4	1.2	0.8	3.6	2.8	10.8	8.1
Government	3.4	3.2	4.1	6.0	12.2	7.8	11.9	8.0
Business firms[a]	n.a.	2.3	n.a.	5.9	n.a.	2.4	n.a.	7.2
Churches[a]	n.a.	0.0	n.a.	0.0	n.a.	1.2	n.a.	1.1
Unions[a]	n.a.	0.0	n.a.	0.0	n.a.	0.0	n.a.	2.3
Other associations	2.1	1.8	0.4	0.5	3.1	2.1	3.0	3.2
Subtotal	*7.7*	*8.4*	*7.8*	*17.3*	*22.0*	*18.1*	*41.9*	*40.9*
Miscellaneous recurring and nonrecurring contributions:								
Investments, sales, fees, commissions, events, rent, interest, etc.	7.4	10.4	7.3	12.1	9.5	10.8	10.3	15.1
Loans	0.3	0.1	0.4	1.9	0.6	0.2	0.6	0.8
Other	1.6	0.8	5.1	0.0	3.0	0.5	0.9	0.1
Subtotal	*9.3*	*10.4*	*12.8*	*14.0*	*12.7*	*11.5*	*11.8*	*16.0*
Total Percentage	99.9	100.1	100.0	99.9	102.3	99.2	99.2	99.8
(N)	(155)	(156)	(25)	(28)	(151)	(155)	(96)	(103)

[a] In the 1980 questionnaire, there were no specific categories for funds from business firms, churches, or unions. Respondents may have included these percentages in the categories for individual gifts, other associations, or other.

Source: The Michigan Interest Group Study. See Appendix for details.

tions. To compensate for these losses, the citizens groups were able to increase significantly the revenues they received in 1985 from business firms, churches, and unions. They also earned more by selling the services of their staffs, gaining greater return on investments, and staging other fund-raising events. Government support for most interest groups was reduced by the Reagan administration, but the data in Table 9-5 indicate that the types of groups most vulnerable to these reductions were able to diversify their sources of revenue, and thus stay in operation, even if some of the administration's strongest critics suffered membership losses and were forced to reduce the size of their staffs.

The data in Table 9-5 report average revenues for all the groups in our sample, but the Reagan administration's efforts to reduce the flow of government grants and contracts to interest groups has fallen most heavily upon a relatively small number of groups, mainly associations of social service professionals in the nonprofit sector, that were the most heavily dependent on government financial support. These groups suffered significant setbacks during the first term of the Reagan administration and may have been forced to dismiss large numbers of staff members and substantially reduce their activities. Their operations are smaller, but our data indicate that most of these groups have managed to remain in existence by finding new sources of revenue. This process of diversification is illustrated in Table 9-6 where we investigate the financial status in 1985 of the forty-three groups from our panel study that received 30 percent or more of their revenues from government sources during the last year of the Carter administration.

The groups examined in this table received, on the average, 50 percent of their revenues from government agencies in 1980, but by 1985 that proportion had been cut to about 33 percent. Almost all of these organizations were required to reduce their staffs. They also tried to raise more money from their members by raising dues and increasing publication and conference fees. These efforts raised the proportion of their revenues coming from recurring contributions from members to 40 percent in 1985 from only 31 percent in 1980. They also made vigorous efforts to find new sources of funds from private foundations and business firms, and, like most of the groups in our study, devised many new ways to raise money through benefits, social events, the sale of services from their staffs, and short-term investment of their cash balances. The Reagan administration has managed to reduce funding for groups that were heavily dependent on support from sympathetic government agencies, but they have not been able—at least at the end of Reagan's first term in office—to completely eliminate all funds flowing to these groups, or to force very many of them out of existence.

Interest Groups, Iron Triangles, and Partisan Politics under Reagan

The Reagan administration's effort to break the ties between government agencies and sympathetic interest groups has met with mixed results. To

Table 9-6   Mean Percentages of Total 1980 and 1985 Revenue Received from Various Sources for Nonprofit Sector Groups Receiving 30 Percent or More of Their 1980 Funds from Government, in the Panel Dataset

Revenue Source	1980	1985
Routine contributions from members and associates:		
Dues	23.1	32.6
Publications	3.6	3.9
Conferences	4.9	3.6
Subtotal	*31.6*	*40.1*
Nonrecurring contributions from nonmember institutions and persons:		
Individual gifts	4.7	2.4
Private foundations	5.0	7.0
Government	49.8	33.4
Business firms[a]	n.a.	6.3
Churches[a]	n.a.	0.3
Unions[a]	n.a.	0.0
Other associations	1.0	0.5
Subtotal	*60.5*	*49.9*
Miscellaneous recurring and nonrecurring contributions:		
Investments, sales, fees, commissions, events, rent, interest, etc.	5.6	8.3
Loans	0.6	0.3
Other	1.6	0.9
Subtotal	*7.8*	*9.5*
Total Percentage	99.9	99.5
(N)	(43)	(43)

[a] In the 1980 questionnaire, there were no specific categories for funds from business firms, churches, or unions. Respondents may have included these percentages in the categories for individual gifts, other associations, or other.

Source: The Michigan Interest Group Study. See Appendix for details.

begin with, our data show that the interest group system continued to expand during Reagan's first term. Some citizens groups concerned with topics such as international peace and security, environmental protection, and women's rights have challenged the central tenets of the Reagan program in an effort to polarize issues and draw sharp distinctions between themselves and the administration. In those cases where the president has responded with ideological broadsides of his own, he has brought these groups to center stage and aided them in attracting new members and patrons. Ironically, the groups most vulnerable to the administration's challenge were not the publicity-oriented, contentious citizens groups of the political Left, but rather the professional societies in the nonprofit sector, which, before Reagan became president, had always claimed to be nonpartisan.

Ronald Reagan made a much larger impact on the interest group system than Jimmy Carter, but in both cases many interest groups were able to continue with business-as-usual, no matter who was in the White House. A small number of groups, about 8 percent of those in our sample, are virtually apolitical and hardly ever try to exert influence. Business and trade associations—the largest segment of the interest group system—were not targets of the Reagan administration's campaign, and many groups in the nonprofit sector were able to remain aloof because of their ties with virtually independent subgovernments. The Reagan administration managed to affect the operations of a much higher proportion of the interest group system than the Carter administration; nevertheless, more than 40 percent of the groups still were able to maintain their political independence, at least where the programs and issues of vital importance to them were concerned.

Some of the groups that were able to insulate themselves from the effects of partisan elections supported the Reagan administration's policies and were useful political allies, but almost one-half of the unaffected groups supported an increase in the social services provided by the federal government and clearly were not sympathetic with the administration's principal policy goals. The determined effort by the Reagan administration to change the relationships between interest groups and the agencies of the executive branch revealed how complex and mutually supportive these relationships are. It would take years of consistent pressure and the expenditure of a lot of political capital to cut all the ties that bind interest groups with committees of Congress and the permanent agencies of government.

Ideology, Partisanship, and the Future of American Politics

Even though the interest group system underwent no fundamental changes, there is no doubt that during his first term Reagan had a powerful impact upon the Washington political universe. Government funding for interest groups clearly was reduced, especially for those groups of professionals in the nonprofit sector working in social welfare fields who were heavily dependent upon support from sympathetic government agencies. Very few groups, however, were put completely out of operation because new sources of support were discovered by enterprising group leaders who successfully turned to business firms, unions, churches, and to their members for increased financial aid.

The stubborn resistance of interest groups to the determined efforts of the Reagan administration to curtail their influence illustrates several underlying trends shaping American political institutions in the 1980s. The president and the leaders of interest groups all are responding to the same pressures that are leading away from the politics of regional, religious, and ethnic blocs toward the new politics of the postindustrial middle class, carried out through the mass media and dominated by provocative ideological themes. As both political parties build national staffs of media consultants, direct mail specialists, and fund-raisers to engage in this new form of political mobilization, they begin to resemble the staffs of some of the larger citizens interest groups.

Successful presidential candidates increasingly must make appeals on programmatic grounds to blocs of voters who do not share the kind of intense religious, ethnic, or regional ties that were prevalent in the earlier part of the century. As the ideological content of the national political debate intensifies, and as the attentive public grows, many different elements of the country's diverse population feel that their interests are threatened and are prompted to join associations pledged to protect them. These associations fill the mails with dire warnings of environmental disaster, the triumph of secular humanism, of the incineration of civilization in a nuclear war.

Technological breakthroughs in mass communication make it easier to create citizens groups whose members are scattered across the country. As these groups join the political dialogue, with all their ideological guns firing, other interests feel jeopardized, and new organizations are created to protect them. The political entrepreneurs who create these associations approach churches, government agencies, business firms, universities, and hospitals— agencies that would never have dared to engage openly in anything resembling political activity even twenty years ago—in search of both financial and moral support, thus increasing the pressure on these institutions to become active patrons of political action.

As the circle of participants in the dialogue over public policy grows, and the political system becomes increasingly polarized along ideological lines, each individual interest group will be under more pressure to encourage the fortunes of the political party that affords it the best access to government. Pressures will increase for liberal interest groups to form loose alliances during elections to work for the victory of the political party that best represents their views. For most citizens groups there will be no other pathway to influence. Groups that have developed close, co-optive relationships within subgovernments increasingly will be pressed to take sides in the partisan struggle. As ideological polarization pushes interest groups into large contending camps, political parties emerge as the only agencies logically capable of exercising leadership and providing coordination.

So far, the Republican party has led the way in invigorating its national organization and providing coordination for the groups in its electoral and governing coalitions. During the 1980s, however, the leaders of the Democratic party have faced a dilemma that has restrained their progress toward organizational renewal. They have been unable to develop a set of campaign themes around which their extraordinarily diverse constituency can rally, without at the same time being perceived by the public as a captive of "the special interests." No matter how the two major parties develop, the search for simple, compelling campaign themes will intensify and the enhanced prominence of the programmatic goals of the parties will pose new threats to more and more elements of the population, thus stimulating the continued expansion of the system of interest groups.

The same broad social forces are determining the future of both the political parties and the interest group system in America. The Reagan administration's efforts to reshape the rules under which the representative system is governed are harbingers of a new form of ideological politics in America. If these trends continue, both political parties and interest groups will alter their behavior, and those who control our governing institutions will be confronted with many severe tests of leadership.

Notes

This paper grew out of research on interest groups funded by grants from the Earhart Foundation and the National Science Foundation. Jack Walker also acknowledges the support of the Woodrow Wilson International Center for Scholars and the Guggenheim Foundation for fellowships that supported early phases of the study. Special thanks are due to Thomas Gais, who made important contributions to the conception of this study and the design of the questionnaire, and to Frank Baumgartner who assisted in the analysis of the data. We also wish to acknowledge the work of Gina Hoeffer, Brian Christjohn, David Ericksen, Barbara Lahr, and Mark Messura, who carried out the data collection and processing with care and precision. Thanks also are due to Joel Aberbach, Jeffrey Berry, Henry E. Brady, Morris Fiorina, Margaret Weir, James Q. Wilson, and Mayer Zald who commented upon an early draft of this chapter. The Institute of Public Policy Studies at the University of Michigan supported the survey upon which this research is based and met some other costs of the research.

1. William Greider, *The Education of David Stockman and Other Americans,* (New York: E. P. Dutton, 1982), 58.
2. Henry Steele Commager, ed., *Documents of American History,* (New York: Appleton, Century, Crofts, 1973), 169.
3. Commager, *Documents of American History,* 275.
4. Jimmy Carter, Interview with Mark A. Peterson, Plains, Ga., June 20, 1984.
5. C. R. Babcock, "Policies on Education Grants Become an Issue," *Washington Post,* Aug. 14, 1982, 5; Felicity Barringer, "OMB Releases Proposed Restrictions on Lobbying by Contractors, Grantees," *Washington Post,* Nov. 3, 1983, A19;

Arthur Mackenzie, "When Auditors Turn Editor," *Columbia Journalism Review* 20 (1981): 29-34; B. Peterson, "Coalition Pushes Block Grants to 'Defund the Left,'" *Washington Post,* July 2, 1981, 6; Rochelle Stanfield, "'Defunding the Left,'" *National Journal,* Aug. 1, 1981, 1374-1378; and for a description of the Reagan program, see, James T. Bennett and Thomas J. Dilorenzo, *Destroying Democracy: How the Government Funds Partisan Politics* (Washington, D.C.: Cato Institute, 1986). Also see Harold Wolman and Fred Teitelbaum, "Interest Groups and the Reagan Presidency," in *The Reagan Presidency and the Governing of America,* ed., Lester M. Salamon and Michael S. Lund (Washington, D.C.: Urban Institute, 1984), 297-329.

6. E. E. Schattschneider, *The Semi-Sovereign People* (New York: Holt, Rinehart & Winston, 1960).

7. Joseph A. Schlesinger, "The New American Political Party," *American Political Science Review* 79 (December 1986): 1152-1169.

8. See Appendix for a description of the surveys.

9. For a comprehensive review, see Kay Lehman Schlozman and John T. Tierney, *Organized Interests and American Democracy* (New York: Harper & Row, 1986).

10. Jack L. Walker, "The Origins and Maintenance of Interest Groups in America," *American Political Science Review* 77 (1983): 399-406.

11. For an elaboration of the typology and a discussion of its relevance for understanding various attributes of group development, maintenance, and activities, see ibid.

12. Thomas L. Gais, Mark A. Peterson, and Jack L. Walker, "Interest Groups, Iron Triangles and Representative Institutions in American National Government," *British Journal of Political Science* 14 (Spring 1984): 161-185.

13. Ibid.

14. The question was: "How did the change in 1981 from Democratic to Republican control of the Presidency affect the amount of cooperation and consultation between this association and federal agencies?"

15. Respondents were asked to indicate the level of interest their groups had in ten policy areas. The results of a factor analysis were used to reduce the number of policy areas to five.

16. There may be some concern that the question about federal agency cooperation is merely tapping in another way a group's ideological position rather than its actual behavior. In other words, liberal groups may report declines in cooperation simply because they dislike and distrust Ronald Reagan, not because of real change in their relationship with federal agencies. Our data suggest, however, that this concern is unfounded. For example, in both surveys we asked the groups whether they were regularly consulted by federal agencies when policy changes were being considered. For the groups wanting the government to increase social services, the percentage reporting that they were consulted on policy issues declined to 53 percent under Reagan from 87 percent under Carter, while the percentage for their ideological opposites increased to 85 percent from 73 percent. In the 1985 survey, conservative groups consistently reported more frequent and more cooperative interactions with federal agencies than did their liberal counterparts.

Appendix

The data reported in this chapter are from two general surveys of national interest groups conducted by mail at the Institute of Public Policy Studies of the University of Michigan. The first survey (which began in 1979, but with most questionnaires completed in 1980 and 1981) sampled membership associations found in Congressional Quarterly's 1980-1981 *Washington Information Directory* (Washington, D.C.: Congressional Quarterly, 1979). After reviewing other sources, we determined that this directory offered the best means for sampling associations in the United States that are open to membership, and are concerned with some aspect of public policy at the national level. The directory is produced by an organization with a long history of comprehensive coverage of national governmental affairs. Whatever sampling biases it possesses, such as its overrepresentation of large, Washington-based associations, should not badly distort our understanding of how interest groups relate to national government institutions.

Our general survey of membership associations mentioned in the *Washington Information Directory* was supplemented in 1980 with additional samples of groups representing various constituencies (women, blacks, Hispanics, and the handicapped), and policy communities (aging, antipoverty, housing, pharmaceuticals, and urban mass transportation). In each case, we sought to develop a complete list of all groups in these areas, reaching beyond the directory to sources such as *Encyclopedia of Associations,* the *New York Times Index,* lists of witnesses at congressional hearings, telephone books, and other specialized organizational directories.

The summaries of the datasets displayed in Table 9-7 show that the 1980 survey included 1,326 organizations of which 734, or 55.4 percent, responded. For this chapter, we generally utilize only the interest groups that were listed in the *Washington Information Directory*—not the groups picked up only in the supplementary samples—where we received 558 responses, for a response rate of 61.8 percent.

The 1985 survey involved a revised questionnaire and was sent to the 1,501 membership associations listed in the 1984-1985 edition of the *Washington Information Directory.* The first questionnaire in this survey was mailed on December 4, 1984. To produce a panel dataset with responses from both 1980 and 1985, including as many groups as possible, we also mailed questionnaires to the 135 associations that responded in 1980 who were not listed in the directory but remained active as of December 1984, and for which we had current addresses.

Table 9-7 shows that the 1985 dataset includes 863 respondents, 53 percent of the 1,636 organizations that were contacted in the 1985 study. Once again, for this chapter, we have used only the 799 respondents whose groups were listed in the directory. Our panel dataset, however, includes all

448 groups from whom we have responses at two points in time, no matter which 1980 sample they came from. This procedure was used to ensure that we had enough cases for analysis whenever the data were broken into several categories.

Table 9-7   Summary of 1980 and 1985 Surveys and Panel Dataset

Type of Group	1980[a]			1985[b]			Number in Panel Dataset
	Total Contacted	Total Responses	Response Rate	Total Contacted	Total Responses	Response Rate	
Voluntary associations in CQ Directory	902	558	61.8%	1501	799	53.2%	385
Voluntary associations not in CQ Directory	424	176	41.5%	135	64	47.4%	63
Total	1326	734	55.4%	1636	863	52.8%	448

[a] The entire project began with the questionnaire being mailed in 1978 to a small test sample of groups in the aging policy area. Those responses are included in the 1980 dataset. The remaining questionnaires were mailed between June 29, 1979, and August 4, 1981, with the bulk of responses coming in 1980.

[b] For the 1985 survey, the questionnaires were sent to groups in five subsets. The questionnaire for the first block of groups was mailed on December 4, 1984.

Source: The Michigan Interest Group Study.

10. Policy and Interests:
Instability and Change in a Classic Issue Subsystem

William P. Browne

Many models of the public policy process emphasize tightly knit, closed patterns of decision making, with small numbers of participants determining policy outcomes in a given issue area. The concept of an "iron triangle," for example, is widely utilized to describe the interaction among legislative committee members, bureaucratic officials, and interest group representatives that leads to policy outcomes. Such outcomes may reward the triangle's participants and their constituents, often at the expense of the broader public interest. The proliferation of special interests and their increasing visibility, the impact of a decentralized Congress, and the external pressures of national economic problems appear to have greatly opened up the policy process in recent years.

Using agriculture as an example, William Browne convincingly illustrates how the intrusion of policy participants from the White House, Office of Management and Budget, nonagricultural interest groups, and members of other congressional committees have broken the "cozy" triangle decision structure in this crucial policy area. Although the process has become more open, agriculture priorities remain hard to set, leading to an unstable political situation in which programmatic tinkering is routine. Long-term public policy planning is virtually nonexistent, and actual policy decisions often reflect reactions to a crisis atmosphere.

Of all the issue areas of American politics, agriculture has been the one most frequently labeled a classic example of a self-governing subsystem—a tight alliance of interest groups, program administrators, and legislative committees that formulates policy primarily for the benefit of a particular constituency. Since the 1920s, with the onset of the congressional "farm bloc," analysts have portrayed agricultural policy as removed from the centralized control and intervention of either the White House or Congress. Food and fiber policy was seen as the prerogative of a small cadre of farm state legislators, U.S. Department of Agriculture officials, and interest group representatives. Lobbyists from the general farm organizations, particularly the Republican-oriented American Farm Bureau Federation and the Democratic-oriented National Farmers Union, exercised most of the private-sector influence that was to be had in the subsystem. That influence, especially in blocking proposals the groups did not like, was considered to be extensive as well as pervasive within the subsystem.

Conditions have changed, however. Agriculture, agricultural policy, and related interest representation have each become more complex as the economic components of food and fiber production, manufacture, distribution, and marketing have been fragmented and specialized. Farms are larger, more capital intensive, and more often operated according to established business practices than had been the case earlier. Farming exists in a competitive world food market frequently characterized by commodity surplus. In addition to overproduction, farmers have been troubled by accelerating costs, high interest rates, national budget deficits, the high value of American currency, governmental intervention in international food trade, and declining land prices. The agribusinesses and related industries that provide inputs— equipment and raw goods—and outputs—transportation and retailing—are affected in different ways by these trends as well. Such conditions have combined in the late 1970s and through the 1980s to create hard times for agriculture and for many allied industries.

Predictably, financial hardship has generated public policies and public demands for the alleviation of what has been called the modern farm crisis. These policies, however, are not just the traditional ones of commodity price supports. They also encompass issues such as international trade agreements, debt restructuring, and national economic decisionmaking—none of which can be dealt with solely from inside the agricultural community.

It is within this context that a wide array of interests, too broad to bargain comfortably within a cozy subsystem, now interact. The general farm organizations—over the last four decades—have been joined by commodity organizations, trade associations, corporate representatives, and a collection of farm activists.[1] Also involved are industry lobbyists, consumer groups, rural-oriented social reform movements, and a variety of professional societies concerned, pro and con, with food-related programs.[2] The positions articulated by these diverse groups often are contradictory and in conflict, leaving policy makers wondering about the credibility of reports of farm conditions and desirable directions for future agriculture policy.[3] The degree to which changes in interest representation have occurred within agriculture and the extent to which such changes have reflected, and perhaps furthered, the emergence of new patterns of public policy making is the focus of this chapter.

The Subsystem: A Political Concept

The concept of a subsystem has been used to explain the political relationships that give rise to public policy decisions within a specific issue area.[4] Three elements characterize a subsystem: decision, structure, and outcome. First, policy decisions are seen as the byproduct of bargaining among partners with narrow interests whose participation seldom involves them with anyone other than this small cluster of policy makers. While

Figure 10-1   The Traditional Iron Triangle in Agriculture

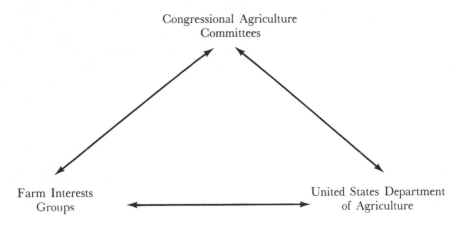

differences among the bargainers may exist, decisions are ordinarily resolv-
able without resorting to intervention or leadership of central authorities.
Second, the structure of a subsystem is made up of three sets of experienced
policy participants: legislative committee members, program administrators,
and interest representatives. These components often have been described as
the three sides of an "iron triangle," a term that nicely illustrates their tightly
structured tripartite interaction (see Figure 10-1). Finally, subsystems are
known by their self-serving results. The outcomes of policy decisions
specifically reward the primary constituencies of the triangle's participants,
often to the detriment of the public at large.

   Subsystems theory, as might be expected, evolved as a descriptive
summary of closed patterns of policy making. Observers of American politics
from a subsystem's perspective noted that few, rather than many, political
participants controlled the outcome of policy decisions in any given issue area.
Within iron triangles, it was believed, the prevailing pattern of political
relationships developed. Decisions were made most easily when ongoing
discussions among bureaucratic experts, long-time congressional committee
members, and established lobbies took place away from the public eye. The
primary goal of the subsystem was to mute policy conflicts and to ensure
consensual autonomy—their ability to make policy without interference from
outside the triangle—on the part of whichever specialists were concerned with
the decision at hand.

   Closed political relationships had a significant impact on American
politics. Above all, decentralization of policy leadership under these subsystem
arrangements took influence away from presidents and legislative leaders.
Centrally planned programs were diverted to subcommittees and agencies,
where renewed deliberations were dominated by those long in control of
existing programs. Substantive policy changes were infrequent, and few
programs were discontinued. Related programs, modeled on ones that had

found political favor, helped perpetuate the system. In short, subsystems made it easy for government to grow because policies in various issue areas were seldom subjected to comparative review.

Subsystems theory provided observers with a useful framework for understanding the politics and policies of agriculture. Here in a critical policy area, it seemed, was a perfect example of decentralized policy making, tripartite relationships, and self-serving results. Agricultural policy makers, it appeared, defied control, cared little about partisan divisions, spurned cutbacks in outdated programs, and continued to expand programs to advance farm interests and minimize farm risk.[5] Furthermore, these observations were rooted in a historical context that apparently gave them even more credibility. In his analysis of the evolution of American interest groups, Grant McConnell, an early and highly influential commentator on agrarian politics, had documented both classic subsystem behavior and similar self-serving policy results.[6]

The subsystems explanation, supported by the historical perspective provided by scholars like McConnell, has proven especially useful to those concerned with the political power of agricultural interests. American agriculture benefited from a tenfold increase in per worker federal budget expenditures between 1960 and 1982. Total farm payments increased from a 1970s average of $2.9 billion per year to $18.9 billion in 1983.[7] Despite these budgetary gains, agricultural programs were being increasingly criticized for their inability to safeguard farm workers, protect soil and water resources, and even maintain farm incomes.[8] This paradoxical situation came about at a time when the farm population, over a fifty-year period, had declined from approximately 25 percent of the United States population to less than 3 percent. Why, since fewer farms needed assistance, were program costs and demands for even greater outlays increasing in such dramatic fashion? Enter subsystem theory, with its emphasis on burgeoning expenditures and self-serving political relationships. Powerful interest groups, allied with their close friends on Capitol Hill and in the administration, were, in the opinion of many journalists and academicians, the obvious culprits.

While it seems logical that the continuing political prominence of agriculture rests on the support of interest groups within a political subsystem, several observations fail to square with that theory. As noted earlier, three elements—decision, structure, and outcome—define a subsystem's existence. Only the characteristic of self-serving policy outcomes, however, fits the realities of agricultural politics in the 1980s, and, even then, there are distortions in terms of who actually benefits. Many small and medium-sized farms gain very little from agricultural programs as supports go disproportionately to the largest farms and ranches.[9] In addition, the distribution of government supports to agriculture has produced a ready supply of food for consumers at relatively low prices. European countries, on the contrary, have achieved higher food prices by subsidizing small farms at adequate levels to keep these producers in business.[10] Obviously, not all U.S.

farmers benefit from agricultural policy outcomes—and some beneficiaries are not farmers at all.

The Complexity of the Agricultural Subsystem

In terms of decisions, bargaining on agricultural programs is far more complicated than the subsystems explanation allows. Since at least 1973, congressional farm bills have been passed by coalitions that include supporters of labor and of the cities.[11] These distinctly dissimilar participants have backed farm legislation because of the expansion of agricultural program benefits, such as food stamp programs, specifically intended for their clientele. It has taken brokers, in both Congress and federal agencies, to put and keep together broad but temporary coalitions of farm and labor, rural and urban politicians. Moreover, brokering has involved more than just the traditional subsystem partners. The intrusion of participants from the White House, Office of Management and Budget, nonagricultural interest groups, and members of congressional committees other than agriculture has caused these iron triangles to more closely resemble "sloppy hexagons."[12]

The complexity does not end with the increased variety of institutional participants, however. The interest group component of the presumed subsystem has become more fragmented than monolithic. Agriculture is no longer a policy arena in which general farm interests serve as advocates on all farm issues. Well over two hundred organized groups with a direct farm, agribusiness, or rural emphasis pursue their own public policy ends in 1980s-style national politics.[13] The efforts of their lobbyists are buttressed by paid consultants and activist members who complicate the bargaining process. In addition, bargaining occurs not only on behalf of farmers in general but also for the benefit of specific types of commodity producers and trade associations of marketing firms. Some of these groups are interested in government support programs but others concentrate their efforts on different issue areas such as exports, farm finances, environmental impact, conservation, and agricultural research. All these policy objectives could never be entirely complementary.

The claim is made, in fact, that the range of different and often competing groups throughout American government makes political interaction so confusing that the continued existence of subsystem politics becomes unlikely.[14] The proliferation of groups, at least, has destabilized the agricultural subsystem, making it harder for government to decide on policy choices. The political maneuverings surrounding the omnibus farm bills of 1973, 1977, 1981, and 1985 demonstrated how difficult it is to get agricultural interests to speak with any semblance of a single voice. The diversity of policy demands, evaluations of needs, and interpretations of farm conditions cause some farm state legislators each year to voice the fear that no farm bill may pass or that this might be the last one.

Under such conditions, it is hard for anyone to assert that a workable coalition of farm interest maintains—or even plays much of an effective role in maintaining—a viable agricultural subsystem. Some of the fragmentation in agricultural policy making results from organizations that will neither compromise nor deal with their commonalities of interest in policy outcomes. Blame must be shared by activists who create splinter organizations and pursue confrontational tactics, rather than cooperate under the auspices of established interests. In addition, lobbyists often seek to confuse the process and call into question the credibility of agriculture's own supporters in Congress and the administration.

It would be easy to understand these developments if interest groups were simple organizations where leaders did only the political bidding of a homogeneous membership. They are not, however, and their leaders are neither stupid nor shortsighted. To keep any interest alive involves far more than just cultivating the group's political relationships and maintaining the subsystem. Members must be recruited and retained, revenue raised, images created of the organization as unique and necessary, and strategies developed to publicize the group's goals. As a result, each organization, as it lobbies to influence public policy, is a creature both defined by its past and coping uncertainly with its present.

The Organization of Agricultural Interests: External and Internal Politics

The need to maintain a balance between past and present has led to a proliferation of both organized interests and styles of lobbies. A tightly structured subsystem might once have effectively served farm producers, but changing agricultural interests require styles of bargaining that meet the diverse needs of those who lobby.

Early political commentators saw interest group politics as a fairly easily understood phenomenon. Groups organized and lobbied government with whatever resources they possessed.[15] If resources were sufficient, groups were successful. Such an interpretation is far too simplistic, however. Interest groups do not mobilize all available resources in pursuit of their political goals. They are limited by two considerations: (1) acceptance by congressional and executive policy makers whom the group seeks to influence and (2) their lobbyists' perceptions of the way others will judge their tactics. The behavior of interest groups, in other words, depends on the attitudes of those with whom lobbyists interact. This "transactional theory" of interests suggests that group strategies and techniques—or the style of lobbying—vary dramatically under different political circumstances.[16]

How the group operates in the political arena also is affected by the interactions among the group's lobbyists and its leaders and members. Staff, officials, and members view political events differently, depending on their backgrounds and proximity to the action at hand. Political scientists have identified an exchange process that, in light of these diverse viewpoints, holds an interest group together.[17] In that process, the staff provides the members with services and benefits in exchange for their dues or other contributions.

While the membership may not be all that attuned to the political activities of the group and the political benefits of organization, they do expect the organization to meet two fundamental requirements. First, those who operate the group must not deplete all its resources in lobbying. Some time, attention, and money must go into the provision of selective benefits such as newsletters, insurance policies, conferences, and various personal services. Second, to remain true to loyal and politically idealistic members, the interest must continue to address the political issues and ideologies most members consider important. These will be highlighted in group periodicals and at conferences; and, at least symbolically, they will become part of the group's lobbying agenda.[18]

The disarray of agricultural interests in the 1980s can be accounted for in large part by both their external and internal relationships. Farm lobbyists interact with policy makers on a variety of agriculture and appropriations subcommittees in Congress and in several agencies, such as the Food and Drug Administration, which are also concerned with food and fiber issues. The transactions between diverse sets of organizers and members have created differing perceptions and beliefs about the needs of American agriculture and, more broadly, of American society. Members were initially attracted to the groups for varying reasons, some political and others not, which led to heterogeneous membership bases for the organizations. For example, the National Farmers Union and the American Farm Bureau Federation are both general farm groups, but they are quite different, in part, because the NFU disproportionately attracted wheat producers and the AFBF recruited more corn growers. As a result, there are now too many groups, too many viewpoints, and too many approaches for every interest to be accommodated comfortably within the confines of the old agricultural subsystem.

How Groups Choose Their Political Behaviors

The political behavior of agricultural interests encompasses the kinds of policies they seek from government and the specific strategies they use in pursuing their goals. Historically there has been wide variation in both of these areas. Although interests may differ from each other in the political approaches they employ, the choice of behavioral style of any group seems to change very little over time.[19] An interest selects strategies that will enable it to survive and that prove acceptable to those policy makers with whom it will interact. As a result, its staff does not decide on daily activities on the basis of a shopping list of all possible forms of lobbyist behavior.

Political observers have noted a link between agricultural group behavior and their policy involvement. Groups have usually been divided between those with a broad or diffuse policy interest—for instance, general farm organizations such as the American Farm Bureau Federation—and those with more restricted or intense concerns.[20] The latter category includes commodity producers such as the National Cattlemen's Association, market middlemen like the Fertilizer Institute, and organizations, like the Soil Conservation

Society, that are closely associated with government programs. Still other groups maintain specialized interests in rural issues such as poverty or development. But this distinction actually does little to explain the differences between the groups' political behavior. For example, the narrowly based commodity interests frequently are seen as more influential than the general farm organizations because specific support programs receive the greatest attention during farm bill debates. However, congressional agricultural committees have expressed the belief that, on comprehensive farm issues, the commodity groups are just as active as, and even more influential than, the general organizations.[21] Quite clearly, no specific issue areas separate the two kinds of farm groups.

Numerous questions have been raised about what the various specialized groups actually do. The answers are not always clear-cut. On milk issues, for instance, separate organizations exist for producers and marketers. But there are also large regional cooperative marketing associations of milk producers. Most of the specialty crops of fruits and vegetables are represented by large national organizations and commodity-specific regional groups that lobby on behalf of farm producers and also serve as commodity trade associations. However, nothing keeps any of these organizations, or for that matter the lobbyists for individual agribusiness firms, from being involved with what would be considered general farm issues or even with electoral politics. That is, the theoretical distinction between nominally generalist and specialist organizations breaks down in practice.

As a result, there is little use, from a policy perspective, in typing groups as either generalists or specialists and then subtyping the specialized groups according to a single facet of their agricultural interest. That typology simply does not predict which or how many issues will be of concern to the group, nor does it determine how the group will use its lobbying resources in attempting to exercise influence. More important, it does not explain why there are so many seemingly similar groups and why they frequently do not complement one another politically.

Perhaps a more helpful approach is to categorize farm interests according to their political behavior and interorganizational differences. To do so involves examining an organization's policy origins as well as any organizationwide redefinitions of its political interest and its ongoing relationships with political or financial supporters (see Table 10-1). Viewed from this perspective, four types of agribusiness and rural interests can be identified: rural protest groups, multipurpose organizations, single-issue organizations, and single-project organizations. In a reformulated fashion, their activities range along that still useful continuum from diffusely broad to intensely narrow involvement in agricultural policy issues.

Rural Protest Groups

The organizations with the most encompassing interests in public policy are the rural protest groups. They desire sweeping reform in either food

Table 10-1 A Typology of Contemporary Agricultural Interests

Organizational Policy Concerns

		Broad	*Narrow*
		Multipurpose Organizations:	Single-issue Organizations:
	Long-term	American Farm Bureau Federation	American Farmland Trust
		National Council of Farmer Cooperatives	National Peanut Growers Group
		National Cotton Council	National Soybean Processing Association
		American Seed Trade Association	Farm Credit Council
		Cargill	ADM Milling
		Women Involved in Farm Economics	National Food Processors
Interaction with Policy-makers and Supporters		National Farmers Union	
		Rural Protest Groups:	Single-project Organizations:
	Short-term	American Agricultural Movement	Agricultural Research Institute
		Family Farm Movement	Farmers for Fairness
		North American Farmers Alliance	Ralston Purina
		Prairiefire	Capital Legal Foundation
		National Rural Catholic Life Conference	Environmental Policy Institute
		Interfaith Action for Economic Justice	Food Research and Action Council

production or farm programs and adopt an adversarial style of participation. The groups in this category are diverse in what they emphasize but similar in their general condemnation of widely accepted agricultural practices. Many are farm groups, especially those organized during the late 1970s and early 1980s. A large number, like the National Catholic Rural Life Conference, are more broadly interested in rural problems. The policy ideals around which these farm groups are organized include price parity, reform of financial institutions, and family farm preservation. Some staff speak openly of the need for long-range changes such as Latin American-style land reform. An anticorporate ideology frequently plays an important role in the policy discussions of these organizations.[22] Similarly, they seek high-impact reforms such as chemical-use bans and the reversal of rural migration patterns.

Once they have made the initial, strong commitment to the issues and ideologies around which they developed, these groups tend to be persistent. In bargaining on major farm legislation, for instance, the American Agriculture Movement refuses to abandon applications of parity even though the continued use of that concept antagonizes policy makers.[23] Some farm groups, most notably the National Farmers Union, have moved away from this type of behavior and now belong in another category, either because they have achieved early political goals or because they modified their initial demands into more easily obtainable ones. Continuing as a protest-style group, clustered around a traditional goal such as preservation of the family farm, provides an interest with a clear and distinguishable label in discussions with policy makers. This has the advantage of legitimizing the organization's claims to familiarity with a particular facet of agriculture, but it places most of these groups at a disadvantage because busy policy makers feel they already know where each one stands. In addition, the pragmatism of most policy makers leads them to reject extreme positions. The result is that most protest groups have a difficult time gaining effective access to members of Congress and the administration.

In addition, protest groups may encounter difficulties because it is often unclear who has jurisdiction over their issues. The ascendency of congressional subcommittees and specialized agencies within the Department of Agriculture has divided agricultural policy responsibilities into highly specialized components. Policy makers within these institutions look for detailed information that is useful to their particular tasks, and, in consequence, they are seldom open to staff members and activists who want to discuss major reform.

The transactional relationships between the protest groups and policy makers are brief, irregular, and very limited. On the whole, these expressive organizations, which primarily serve the emotional needs of members, suffer from a lack of regular access, and they have little opportunity to discuss pending policy proposals with those who structure them. On most issues therefore, the protest groups remain outsiders.

The most important relationships for staff and officers of interest groups are those with members and other sources of funds. Because few protest groups offer any selective services, maintaining loyalty and affiliation is not easy. The strategy is usually to provide a sense of group cohesiveness and personal fulfillment to attract and retain people who are committed to work for the cause. This leads to highly visible participation but relatively small memberships, and a decided reluctance on the part of group representatives to discuss actual numbers of supporters. The strategy also may enable groups to do much more than protest. The greatest policy opportunity for the protest groups, indeed, lies in the hope that their activists will be able to link group goals to related but wider social issues. Legislation supporting alternative systems of agricultural production, for example, was tied to massive publicity about chemical contamination. The high levels of price supports proposed in so many versions of the 1985 farm bill owed their presence to the ability of farm protest groups to turn national media attention to farm strikes, tractorcades, forced farm sales, and foreclosures. Even with these successes, however, outsider protest groups have dictated little actual legislation.

Multipurpose Organizations

Multipurpose interest groups are defined by their involvement in numerous and widely different agricultural issues and by their heterogeneous memberships, supporters, and political contacts. These groups, as a consequence, formulate policy statements and actually lobby on a broad array of national legislative and administrative proposals.

This category of interest comprises some of the general farm organizations, several commodity groups, a few trade associations, many of the groups who represent both producers and marketing firms, and a small number of large agribusiness corporations. Examples include the Farm Bureau, the National Cotton Council, the American Seed Trade Association, and Cargill. In a given year, a typical group actively addresses general economic issues, agricultural financing, price supports, pesticide regulation, and worker-safety legislation. In addition, the group examines most farm policy proposals to judge their likely impact and their chances of becoming law. Unless the organization is unusually well staffed, like the Farm Bureau, the heavy workload normally precludes its lobbyists from doing much more than reacting on most issues. Group representatives will register their support or opposition, outlining their reasons and, perhaps, suggesting modifications. In a few instances, they may draft complete alternative proposals.

To compensate for the limited role they can play, lobbyists for multipurpose organizations attempt to maintain regular contacts with a wide range of policy makers in decentralized positions and, they hope, discover proposals at an early stage of discussion. This allows them greater opportunity to put their stamp on whatever legislative or regulatory proposals are being considered. As a result, these organizations place the greatest premium on lobbyists who have ready access to individuals throughout Washington. The transactional base is broad but, in general, the relationships between organization staff and policy makers are not strong. For most of these groups, their lobbyists, collectively, are seen as well qualified to do the job if they "know everyone" or "understand the terrain."

The same behavior characterizes relationships between staff and members. In most of the organizations, the membership expects the group to be politically active in all facets of farm or agribusiness life. In fact, sweeping agendas may emerge from membership meetings or corporate board rooms. Moreover, the staff must pay considerable attention to letting the agenda setters know which issues and problems need to be addressed, and must report on progress, explain new public policies, and, frequently, show why the organization was defeated on important issues. Because these activities require extensive, direct communication with supporters, the multipurpose groups have the most impressive range of magazines, newsletters, informational flyers, conferences, workshops, and seminars of any of the agricultural interests. While observers may take this as indicative of the groups' prominence and prestige, these pursuits actually reflect the difficulties faced in the internal management of the organizations as they slowly adjust to changing political conditions.

Although these groups constantly address new issues and problems, they often are better remembered for longer-term expressions of their views on general farm or business conditions. Many policy makers apply the label *liberal, moderate,* or *conservative* to these groups, but the designations are modified by orientations to free trade, populism, or other philosophical goals. Given the pragmatic and reactive approach the lobbyists take on policy issues, such sentiments seem to be based mostly on the proclamations made through organizational forums designed to involve their supporters. From these, by intent, the members gain a consistent and stable image of their organization's political purpose, yet they do so at some cost. Many policy makers are simply reluctant to get too close to lobbies that are seen as inflexible or unlikely to compromise their philosophical principles. The large number of organizations of this type, and the frequently contrasting viewpoints their images represent, have created a policy environment in which there is a good deal of caution concerning the motivations of any one of the multipurpose groups.

Single-issue Organizations

Most observers point to single-issue organizations when they comment on the political advantages of specialized expertise, the need for routine access to only a few policy makers, and the group's ability to focus on one item of interest. This began to change in the early to mid-1970s. As noted earlier, many commodity and trade groups have felt compelled to become involved in a broad range of policy issues. The turn-around should hardly be surprising, since problems of imports, farm credit, medication for dairy cows, and the like are nearly as important to milk producers as are their price support levels.

The largest number of commodity and trade groups, several large agribusiness firms, and a few rural interests have chosen not to address so many issues. These groups constitute the single-issue category. Most of these organizations decided to avoid other issues to make the most of their limited lobbying resources and maintain an image of expertise and experience. They have been able to do so because neither staff nor membership expectations about appropriate group action has escalated beyond the initial issue around which the interest organized.[24] Smaller and more homogeneous groups, for obvious reasons, have been best able over time to maintain this style of participation.

It is these organizations whose transactional political relationships can best replicate the subsystems model in which a few lobbyists work with highly specialized legislative subcommittees and relatively small federal agencies. A prime example is Sunkist, a grower-owned cooperative whose greatest political interest is in federal marketing orders for oranges. Lobbyists from organizations like Sunkist attempt to see policy makers regularly, engage them in ongoing policy dialogues, establish relationships of trust, and advance their own proposals early in the deliberative process. Such contact is especially important for lobbyists representing industries undergoing change. Groups concerned about foreign trade and farm income maintenance are most successful at this strategy, as are the client groups that have developed around USDA programs such as soil, research, reclamation, and rural electrification.

Other groups that pursue such a strategy are less fortunate, usually for one of two reasons. First, policy makers, because of personal and political considerations, may not want to provide access to the organization. Or, second, the policy makers themselves may be responsible for small or out-of-favor programs that currently do little to address the problems around which the group is organized. If noninfluential legislators and administrators are a group's primary contact with the government, the interest's interdependent status and limited opportunities to generate public support will prove to be a deterrent to any political goals. As was the case with the commodity groups prior to the greater fragmentation of power within subcommittees and agencies, many of the single-issue organizations must simply bide their time and hope for further structural changes in governmental decision making.

Single-project Organizations

The policy goals of single-project organizations are more sharply defined and immediate than those of the single-issue type. While single-issue interests have an ongoing, comprehensive concern for regulations that affect a commodity or product, single-project interests intervene intermittently to promote a needed reform or to block disadvantageous rulings. Because of their orientation the organizations can always approach policy makers to urge them to confront an immediate, if not a crisis, situation. Frequently, these organizations may be working for a group from one of the other types of interests. The representatives of these interests do not occupy—nor do they need to occupy—subsystem positions, although access to policy makers remains critical. These individuals, in effect, have entered the agricultural policy arena over specific, timely issues that both they and the policy makers hope to resolve quickly. A prime example is the farm credit situation, in which both lenders and producers are overextended financially and need relief.

To be successful in gaining the ear of legislators and administrators, single-project organizations must have useful and persuasive information about the issue, such as export grain quality. Because the transactional relationships with policy makers are short-term rather than long-term and dispersed throughout the agricultural arena, interest representatives seldom can rely on established personal contacts with individual public officials. Instead, they depend heavily on what they hope is their own or their organization's reputation for integrity.

For this reason, a large number of lobbyists who work for organizations of this type are retained representatives with their own Washington businesses and long careers dealing with agricultural issues. The consulting firms of Schnittker Associates and Abel, Daft, and Earley are good examples; other lobbyists work in large law firms. Like the multipurpose organization lobbyists, single-project representatives usually are hired because they know the right people and are familiar with the processes and the broad range of issues. The difference is that these individuals have only a single responsibility to their short-term contractor. They also enjoy the advantage of being able to use their own staff as well as the client's in presenting the appropriate case. A second advantage, the result of their status as hired experts, is the independence they have from the membership concerns of the group or firm. Seldom do they have to respond directly to diverse opinions within the organization. As one well-known agricultural consultant stated: "My job? I guess I'm like a commando landing on very familiar beaches." [25]

Not all the single-project organizations hire consultant lobbyists to do their work. Similar strategies are used by staff members of several trade associations and agribusiness firms who only rarely become involved in public policy decisions. Several interests more frequently identified with other policy arenas also intervene in this way—including, in the recent past, religious, social service, auto worker, and financial groups that have employed agriculture specialists. Unless these lobbyists work in cooperation with established agricultural organizations, as they often attempt to do, their efforts are likely to be poorly received. Some of the trade associations, business firms, and other group lobbyists, in fact, have reputations as being among the least effective representatives in the food and fiber policy arena. The complaint is that, while these lobbyists know what they want, they "don't know agriculture or what's good for it." [26] Single-project interests, it appears, have come to occupy a legitimate position in agricultural policy—as long as their representatives function with the finesse and knowledge of other agricultural insiders.

Effects on Subsystem Politics

The proliferation of agricultural interest groups, as they now exist, is in its fourth historical stage. Chronologically, however, these stages have not been separate and distinct. First, there were the decades of agrarian protest that ended early in the twentieth century but, nonetheless, were imitated by the National Farmers Organization in the 1950s and by many groups in the early 1980s. Then followed the years in which a few farm protest movements matured into general interest organizations and farmer cooperatives. These groups, along with the Farm Bureau, provided an array of economic, social, and political services to an agriculture that was as much a way of life as a business for the family farms that populated rural America. The stabilizing of large organizations with national political ties was nearly completed by the late 1930s.

In the immediate post-World War II era, commodity-based organizations grew in number as producers farmed increasingly greater acreage, specialized in one or a few commodities, and farm support legislation came to be more and more product-specific. It was during this third stage, especially in the 1960s, that farm group differences became more than partisan, regional, and ideological. The economic realities that pitted producers against one another (for example, when hog farmers applauded low corn prices) came to be rooted as much in the benefits of farm legislation as it did in the marketplace that had for so long created great uncertainty and risk for farmers. Larger farms, some with incorporated structures, the suppliers of equipment and raw materials, merchandisers of commodities, and retailers seeking stable and inexpensive goods all saw important economic reasons for becoming involved in the political affairs of agriculture. Good business practices demanded attention to the details of a political world that could positively or adversely influence profit margins. The scale of agriculture, competition between economic interests, and the specialization of its producer and middleman components had by this time made farming far more of a business than a way of life.

Developments of this magnitude promoted the fourth stage of proliferating interests in agriculture, one that has been particularly noticeable since 1975, with more Washington-based representatives in the capital for each new farm bill. In a competitive environment where small changes mean the difference between prosperity and financial losses, and where even minor public policy decisions often have had major impacts, lobbyists for many agricultural interests have had to select a participatory style that reflected their businesslike outlook. Single-issue and, especially, single-project organizations were well suited to these conditions, and the 1980s have become the era of political consultants, fine-tuned policy adjustments, and ever-increasing specialization. But because of political commitments, organizational investments, member support, and the simple fact that policy makers still respond to them, neither the protest nor multipurpose organization style has disappeared. Nor have imitators stopped reappearing with what they felt were new twists to a proven style. Simultaneously, therefore, the decade of the 1980s also is a time of agrarian protest, of concern for major policy overhaul, and of emphasis on various definitions of family farm protection.

The expanding interests, groups, and types of organizations have created an implosion within whatever remains of the agricultural subsystem. The subsystem's supportive structure collapsed as much from internally proliferating interest demands, claims, expressed beliefs, interpretations, and points of view as it has yielded to the external pressures of budget deficits and national economic woes. Policy makers, themselves scattered only somewhat more systematically throughout Congress and administrative agencies, can do little more than wonder who speaks for which policy, and which conditions are important in determining future agricultural programs.

What remains of subsystem relationships might better be characterized by what has been termed an issue network.[27] Like a subsystem, an issue network produces policy outcomes that are generally self-serving to the participants. But unlike a subsystem, networks involve so many different policy makers and interests that the structure must remain unspecified (see

Figure 10-2). It has all the substance of a cloud. Also network decisions are not just consensually bargained. Conflict, adversarial confrontation, and coercive behavior may be necessary to reach settlements as interests compete for policy leadership, member satisfaction, and political advantages. Because of the large number of participants, decisions will often not meet the needs of many of those attempting to exert influence.

Figure 10-2   The 1985 Farm Bill Issue Network: Price Supports

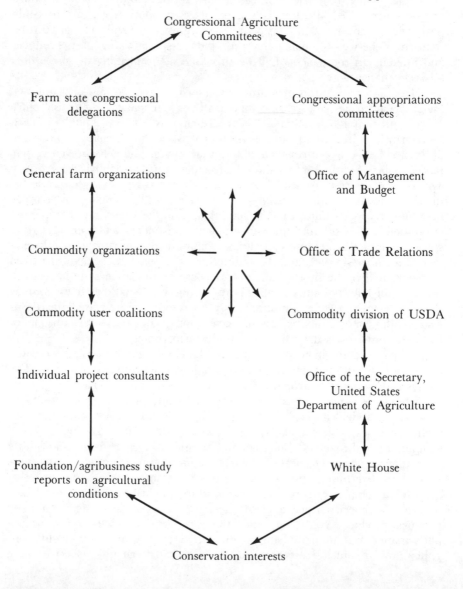

Agricultural politics in the 1980s, as a result, is hardly a tightly interactive arena. As a cozy iron triangle, the decisional structure has been outgrown rather than broken. The increasing number of fragmented interests have simply kept pace with the parallel decentralization of Congress and federal agencies and the impact of economic specialization. Would these organizations have emerged if the structural relationships provided in the many subcommittees and bureaus did not allow for entry? The research presented here indicates that they probably would not have.

The question that may be of greatest importance to those involved in the agricultural process is, what does the collapse of subsystem relationships mean for farm policy? There are two answers. On one level, it means that policy decisions often will be short-term reactions made in a crisis situation as previously excluded interests are suddenly recognized. These policies frequently will raise serious doubt among many policy makers who actually support them, simply because they have heard so many conflicting views. The result may be a rather unstable political atmosphere in which programmatic tinkering, or the threat of it, becomes routine.

For example, as the deliberations for the 1985 farm bill were concluding, many of the participants who had promoted this particular compromise were talking openly of the need for an emergency farm bill for 1986. There were questions on both sides of each issue, including the increase in direct support payments, further encouragement of trade, deficit reduction, and extension of more loan guarantees. No one, however, could venture to say specifically what would be accomplished through emergency legislation.

On a second level, the collapse of the subsystem most certainly does not mean the demise of agricultural policy as it provides a supportive environment for producers and agribusinesses. If anything, the increasing number and visibility of interests indicates that agricultural policy demands cannot be ignored. The high cost of the 1985 farm bill, in the face of many deficit-reducing initiatives in other policy areas, once again demonstrates that point most dramatically. Farm politics no longer occupies a hidden corner of American policy making. It is widely accepted that food and fiber production is a major component of the U.S. economy and everyone acknowledges that its products are vital resources for human survival. And there will continue to be farm bills, if for no other reason than the attractiveness of the issue to coalition partners with conservation, nutrition, and other interests who want to advance their own policy goals. The politics of those farm bills will be complex, tedious negotiations whose outcomes may well confuse and perplex many policy insiders as well as many interest representatives themselves. Nonetheless, as long as there are some, if fewer, American farmers, there will always be farm bills.

Notes

This chapter is part of a larger study of interest groups in agricultural politics, supported by the Economic Research Service (ERS) of the United States Department of Agriculture (USDA) and the Research Professorship program of Central Michigan University. Office space and assistance were provided in Washington during 1985-1986 by the Farm and Rural Economy Branch of USDA. An earlier version was presented at the annual meeting of the American Political Science Association, New Orleans, La., August 1985. Special thanks go to James T. Bonnen and Norman Reid, who provided commentary and insights along the way.

1. William P. Browne, "Farm Organizations and Agribusiness," in *Food Policy and Farm Programs,* ed. Don F. Hadwiger and Ross B. Talbot (New York: Academy of Political Science, 1982), 198-211.

2. Robert H. Salisbury, "Interest Representation: The Dominance of Institutions," *American Political Science Review* 78 (March 1984): 64-76; Jeffrey M. Berry, *Lobbying for the People* (Princeton, N.J.: Princeton University Press, 1977).

3. This has been noted by other scholars as a problem for national policy making. See Thomas L. Gais, Mark A. Peterson, and Jack L. Walker, "Interest Groups, Iron Triangles, and Representative Institutions in American National Government," *British Journal of Political Science* 14 (March 1984): 161-185.

4. J. Leiper Freeman, *The Political Process* (New York: Random House, 1955); and Ernest S. Griffith, *The Impasse of Democracy* (New York: Harrison-Hilton, 1939).

5. Theodore J. Lowi, *The End of Liberalism,* 2d ed. (New York: W. W. Norton, 1979).

6. Grant McConnell, *The Decline of Agrarian Democracy* (Berkeley: University of California Press, 1953); and McConnell, *Private Power and American Democracy* (New York: Alfred A. Knopf, 1966).

7. Clifton B. Luttrell, "Down on the Farm with Uncle Sam" (Los Angeles: International Institute for Economic Research, Original Paper 43, 1983): 12.

8. Anthony Grano, *Analysis of Policies to Conserve Soil and Reduce Surplus Crop Production* (Washington, D.C.: Economic Research Service, U.S. Department of Agriculture, No. 534, 1985); and Wayne D. Rasmussen, "Historical Overview of U.S. Agricultural Policies and Programs," *Agricultural-Food Policy Review* (July 1985): 3-8.

9. William Lin, James Johnson, and Linda Calvin, *Farm Commodity Programs: Who Participates and Who Benefits?* (Washington, D.C.: Economic Research Service, U.S. Department of Agriculture, No. 474, 1981).

10. C. E. Bray, Anne Marie del Castillo, and Eric Bjornlund, "Farm Structure Policy in Other Countries," in *Structure Issues of American Agriculture* (Washington, D.C.: Economics, Statistics, and Cooperative Service, U.S. Department of Agriculture, 1979), 290-305.

11. Weldon Barton, "Coalition-Building in the U.S. House of Representatives: Agricultural Legislation in 1973," in *Cases in Public Policy,* ed. James E. Anderson (New York: Praeger, 1976), 141-162; John G. Peters, "The 1977 Farm Bill: Coalitions in Congress," in *The New Politics of Food,* ed. Don F. Hadwiger and William P. Browne (Lexington, Mass.: Lexington Books, 1978),

23-35; John G. Peters, "The 1981 Farm Bill," in *Food Policy and Farm Programs,* 157-173.

12. Keith E. Hamm, "Patterns of Influence Among Committees, Agencies, and Interest Groups," *Legislative Studies Quarterly* 8 (August 1983): 379-426.

13. These were identified at the onset of the study from congressional hearings, media releases, and 1980-1985 newspaper clippings maintained by the Economic Research Service, U.S. Department of Agriculture.

14. Gais, Peterson, and Walker, "Interest Groups, Iron Triangles, and Representative Institutions."

15. See especially David B. Truman, *The Governmental Process* (New York: Alfred A. Knopf, 1951).

16. Raymond A. Bauer, Ithiel de Sola Pool, and Lewis A. Dexter, *American Business and Public Policy* (New York: Atherton, 1963); Michael T. Hayes, *Lobbyists and Legislators* (New Brunswick, N.J.: Rutgers University Press, 1981); and William P. Browne, "Variations in the Behavior and Style of Lobbyists and Interest Groups," *Journal of Politics* 47 (March 1985): 450-468.

17. Robert H. Salisbury, "An Exchange Theory of Interest Groups," *Midwest Journal of Political Science* 13 (February 1969): 1-32. This work builds on that of Mancur Olson, Jr., in *The Logic of Collective Action* (Cambridge, Mass.: Harvard University Press, 1965).

18. This does not mean that staff and officials do not attempt to set priorities for their own issues through these forums. Indeed they do.

19. Much of this material comes from a series of interviews conducted as part of a research project sponsored by the Economic Research Service of the U.S. Department of Agriculture in 1985-1986. Some of the information was collected in earlier research interviews between 1976 and 1982.

20. Ross B. Talbot and Don F. Hadwiger, *The Policy Process in American Agriculture* (San Francisco: Chandler, 1968), 90-98; Hadwiger, *The Politics of Agricultural Research* (Lincoln: University of Nebraska Press, 1982), 90-114; Browne, "Farm Organizations and Agribusiness," 198-211.

21. Paul Gardner, "The Effectiveness of Farm Lobby Groups: A Congressional Survey for Successful Farming" (Unpublished manuscript, Iowa State University, 1979).

22. William P. Browne and John Dinse, "The Emergence of the American Agricultural Movement, 1977-1979," *Great Plains Quarterly* (October 1985): 221-235.

23. Allan J. Cigler, "An Evolving Group in the Farm Crisis: Obstacles Facing the American Agriculture Movement" (Paper presented at the Annual Meeting of the American Political Science Association, New Orleans, La., August 1985).

24. These organizations best meet David Truman's observation that the group is defined in terms of its interest. That does not necessarily seem true of the two earlier cited types. See Truman, *The Governmental Process,* 33-39.

25. Quotations are from personal interviews with lobbyists, legislators, and legislative staff.

26. Legislative staff comment.

27. Hugh Heclo, "Issue Networks and the Executive Establishment," in *The New American Political System,* ed. Anthony King (Washington, D.C.: American Enterprise Institute, 1978), 113-115.

11. Reagan and the Intergovernmental Lobby: Iron Triangles, Cozy Subsystems, and Political Conflict

Charles H. Levine and James A. Thurber

Standing at the center of much research and theory on the roles of interests within the policy-making process are the ideas of 'iron triangles" and sponsored pluralism. The triangles (also labeled subgovernments) connect outside interests, congressional committees, and bureaucratic units in ways that routinize policy making and benefit those involved. Sponsored pluralism, best articulated in Theodore Lowi's *End of Liberalism,* describes how the government underwrites the activities of many societal interests, ranging from savings and loan institutions to legal services for the poor. During the 1960s and 1970s the federal government helped to create triangular policy relationships by sponsoring, through grants and contracts, the growth of numerous state and local interest groups. These groups, representing cities, counties, mayors, etc., became major actors in determining how federal programs were developed and funds spent.

Charles Levine and James Thurber pick up the story of the "intergovernmental lobby" as its members confronted a president dedicated to reducing the federal role in state and local policy making. This chapter details the "defunding" of the "SLIGs" (state and local interest groups) during the first five years of the Reagan administration. Not only have cutbacks occurred, but the politics of intergovernmental relations has changed dramatically during this period. As Levine and Thurber note, "When the president focuses on cuts, the level of conflict increases and interest groups ... must move into a battle for survival rather than expansion."

In his first inaugural address, President Ronald Reagan promised "to curb the size and influence of the federal establishment and to demand recognition of the distinction between the powers granted to the Federal Government and those reserved to the States or to the people." [1] With these words the president heralded a new era in intergovernmental relations; he made it a major priority of his administration to shift program development and funding responsibility from the federal government to state and local governments.

In exchange for assuming some or all of the responsibility for funding many programs, the president offered to loosen federal regulations on how these programs were to be administered. In his first State of the Union address, Reagan outlined his vision of federalism:

> Our citizens feel they've lost control of even the most basic decisions made about the essential services of government, such as schools, welfare, roads, and even garbage collection. And they're right. A maze of interlocking jurisdictions and levels of government confronts average citizens in trying to solve even the simplest of programs. They don't know where to turn for answers, who to hold accountable, who to praise, who to blame, who to vote for or against. The main reason for this is the overpowering growth of Federal grants-in-aid programs during the past few decades.
>
> In 1960 the federal government had 132 categorical grant programs, costing $7 billion. When I took office, there were approximately 500, costing nearly a hundred billion dollars—13 programs for energy, 36 for pollution control, 66 for social services, 90 for education. . . .
>
> The growth in these federal programs has—in the words of one intergovernmental commission—made the federal government "more pervasive, more intrusive, more unmanageable, more ineffective and costly, and above all, more [un]accountable." Let's solve this problem with a single, bold stroke: the return of some $47 billion in federal government programs to state and local government, together with the means to finance them and a transition period of nearly 10 years to avoid unnecessary disruption.[2]

Because of the large sums of money involved, the administration's new intergovernmental strategy was greeted with skepticism and resistance by many state and local officials, some of whom were struggling with severe fiscal problems in their own jurisdictions. Needless to say, they hardly welcomed the new challenge offered by the Reagan administration.

To overcome this resistance, the administration had to confront the Washington-based lobbying organizations of the affected subnational governments, many of which had measured their effectiveness in terms of their ability to channel federal funds downward to their state and local members. The intergovernmental philosophy of the Reagan administration and its political strategy in early 1981 had the net effect of destabilizing these organizations, causing several of them to face problems of finance, management, leadership, and direction.

Our focus in this chapter is on the impact of Reagan's new vision of federalism on the major state and local interest groups (SLIGs). Several dozen organizations represent state and local interests of one kind or another, and most of these governmental units belong to one or more comprehensive organizations that collectively are known as the "Big Seven": the U.S. Conference of Mayors (USCM), the Council of State Governments (CSG), the National League of Cities (NLC), the National Association of Counties (NACo), the International City Management Association (ICMA), the National Governors' Association (NGA), and the National Conference of State Legislatures (NCSL). We outline their story as a way of illustrating the high stakes involved in interest group politics and how cozy arrangements of subsystem politics can be dismantled when they stand in the path of major changes in policy direction.

To use the case of SLIGs to understand interest group politics, we first introduce the notion of policy subsystems, then describe the experience of the Big Seven, including their retrenchment and redirection in the 1980s. Next, we discuss some of the consequences of this episode for the organizations themselves, intergovernmental relations, and Reagan's New Federalism. Finally, we identify some lessons this case teaches us about the strategy and theory of interest group behavior in the American political system.

Interest Groups and Policy Subsystems

Interest groups play a critical role in public policy making in the United States. Groups focus their lobbying efforts on agencies, the White House, members and staff on congressional committees and subcommittees, other associations, the specialized media, and the attentive public in the program area of direct interest to their members.

The probability of an interest group's success and, thus, its power in a policy subsystem, is directly related to access to and participation with other actors in the subsystem. Interest groups try to develop close ties with staff and members of Congress and executive branch agency managers. These relationships range from total co-optation by groups of agencies and subcommittees to open political warfare. Competition among interest groups usually is not long lasting or extreme, often nonpartisan, and rarely ideological. In American politics there are few permanent friends or enemies. However, there are many examples of long-term friendly and supportive relationships among groups, agencies, and committees. These "subgovernments" were described in the late 1930s by Ernest Griffith, who observed that:

> The relationship among these men—legislators, administrators, lobbyists, scholars—who are interested in a common problem is much more real than the relationships between congressmen generally or between administrators generally.[3]

Information and analysis are important currency of interest group politics in policy subsystems. Groups carefully cultivate relevant members of Congress and agency executives over a long period of time. Making political action committee (PAC) campaign contributions, asking members or their staff to speak to a group for a fee, or simply providing excellent, timely information to agencies or members all help build reciprocal relations in a policy subsystem. Lobbyists appear before congressional subcommittees and committees, draft legislation to be introduced by friendly members, and build support from other interest groups and executive branch agencies for representatives who have sponsored bills. In addition, associations play an important role in the screening and selection of administrative appointees to agencies and commissions. Capturing an agency by having the power of final selection over its top appointed personnel is the goal of many powerful special interest groups. This practice helps develop close friendships with the bureaus and agencies that directly affect the program in which the groups have a special stake (e.g., mayors and officials of the Department of Housing and Urban Development).

One approach to explaining policy outcomes in the American system of government is to attribute them to the aggregate workings of these subsystems. Several political analysts have stressed that policy making in the subsystems ("iron triangles," subgovernments, etc.) was decentralized and segmented by issue or government program into different arenas composed of (1) interest groups, (2) the relevant administrative agency or section of the federal bureaucracy, and (3) the relevant congressional committees and subcommittees. In this conception of the policy process, access to these triangles is closed and difficult; even the president or a department head might have trouble penetrating these relationships.[4] Early scholarly research on iron triangles or policy subsystems focused on single public programs such as Arthur Maass's study of river development, J. Leiper Freeman's Indian affairs study, A. Lee Fritschler's study of smoking and politics, a study of merchant marine shipping policies by Samuel Lawrence, Douglass Cater's analysis of decision making in sugar subsidies and military affairs, and Roger Davidson's study of manpower programs.[5] In 1964 Theodore Lowi described this type of politics as built upon a trading pattern where, "each side of the triangle complements and supports the other two." [6]

The image portrayed by the iron triangle metaphor is of a closed and stable system of policy making broken down into small decision-making arenas with a limited number of participants. In such a system, the participants in each arena have final say over policy for that sector and the authority of the center—or in the case of the United States, the president—is weak or absent. In the world of the iron triangle, issues arise and are resolved among the participants, with little "leakage" into the wider political system.

The key characteristics of this image of policy making are its supposed dominance, stability, and closed nature. If these characteristics are accurate, critics charge, such a system would defy accountability and threaten democratic responsiveness. However, there is substantial evidence to suggest that this image of the entire American political system is simply incorrect; while triangles exist, they are hardly "iron," and they vary in policy areas from dominant and competitive to disintegrated and nonexistent (see Chapter 10).

Instead of a metaphor of fixed, rigid, and closed policy making, Hugh Heclo has posited a much more open decision-making system "where the 'set' of participants is unlimited and unpredictable, [and] decision-making is tending toward atomization." [7] In Heclo's image of "issue networks," the complexity of policy making and absence of final decision-making authority produce a consequent tendency to policy drift. While earlier literature acknowledged greater complexity than is suggested by the iron triangle image, Heclo argues that the transition from iron triangle to issue networks highlights the differences between American politics in the 1950s and 1960s and in the 1970s and 1980s.

According to A. Grant Jordan, the problem with the issue network metaphor lies in the degree to which this image extends to encompass "a pattern of atomization, fragmentation and disarray"⁸—a pattern fundamentally different *in kind* from iron triangles. Instead, Jordon argues, it is a matter of degree:

> [The] United States is not anarchical . . . while "iron triangles" have been invaded by more groups and value changing groups, much of the older, mutual learning and accommodation of the iron triangle imagery remains. Thus issue networks are not discreetly different arrangements from iron triangles, but are iron triangles with a greatly increased group population, with a further disaggregation of power, with less predictable participants, with reduced cohesion and homogeneity caused by the mobilization of value—changing groups, which in turn leads to the reduced capacity to "close" on a decision. *Different policies will be associated with greater or less movement from the iron triangle base.* Consequently some policies will not be handled by such structures at all. However, the twin ideas of issue network and iron triangle remain useful starting points *(emphasis added)*.⁹

The notion that the structure of policy subsystems is a variable with a range that extends from open and turbulent to closed and stable is an important aspect of policy making and politics: the successful resolution of a policy or issue conflict within a subsystem is essential to the subsystem's survival. Recent scholarly work has presented evidence that, if the actors in a subsystem cannot quickly and successfully resolve conflict among themselves, outsiders from other committees, agencies, bureaus, groups, and the media or the general public will take the issue away from them. These outsiders increase their influence and the probability of a policy change as the amount of internal subsystem conflict increases and becomes uncontrolled. Therefore, a primary goal of the actors in a policy subsystem is to control the *scope* and *level* of conflict associated with the programs and issues within its jurisdiction. Thus, subsystems resist externally generated forces of change, such as presidents and other "outsiders."

Subsystems are naturally closed, low-level operations in government, but they can be "opened" in several ways. Changing the scope of conflict, increasing the level of conflict, changing key personnel, reorganizing the jurisdiction over an issue, and using the regulatory process of administrative agencies and the courts are several important methods of changing the power of policy subsystems. The *scope of conflict* and the *level of conflict,* as argued by E. E. Schattschneider, are two primary factors that influence the nature of politics and, in this case, the power of the policy subsystem.¹⁰ More explicitly, the relationship between the scope and level of policy conflict and the influence of policy subsystems can be expressed in the following hypotheses:

— The wider the scope of policy conflict, the less influence policy subsystems have over policy outcomes.
— The wider the scope of conflict, the higher the level of conflict.
— The higher the level of conflict, the less influence policy subsystems have over policy outcomes.

These hypotheses suggest two questions: Who is most often left out at the level at which policy subsystems operate? What kinds of issues are too broad to be successfully contained by policy subsystems? Generally, closed policy subsystems work to exclude from their deliberations the general public, the popular press and the electronic media, political parties, congressional leaders, and even the president. Often, these "outsiders" are handed a policy already negotiated by participants in the policy subsystem. On the other hand, highly complex, broad public issues or highly emotional public policies are usually not within the power of specialized interest groups to submerge within closed subsystems. For example, before the 1973-1974 Arab oil embargo, energy policy of the United States was handled by well-defined policy triangles with clear, protected jurisdictions. When the oil embargo created a public awareness of an "energy crisis," the scope of the policy conflict was broadened rapidly, and it was impossible for the established energy subsystem to control either the nature of the conflict or the policy outcomes. Outsiders like the general public, the media, the president, and congressional leadership wanted to be involved in the development and implementation of energy policy; consequently, it took the federal government five years to establish the beginnings of a new energy policy. The lesson is clear. As the scope of the conflict expanded, the level of conflict increased, changing the nature and power of the subsystems handling energy policy in the United States. In fact, there was a disintegration of the traditional energy subsystems as a result of extreme political competition.

A complementary proposition can be advanced in the case of major policy changes. When a popular president attempts to redefine the role of government in a policy area, he automatically increases the level of conflict and widens the scope of political competition by focusing attention on that subsystem. How President Reagan's focus on a new pattern for intergovernmental relations widened the scope of conflict for the Big Seven and its consequences for their organizations and lobbying strategies is the focus of the rest of this chapter.

SLIGs in the Policy Process

Representing essential elements of the federal system, state and local officials need channels through which to communicate their policy preferences. As a result, over the past fifty years a number of organizations have been formed to represent their interests in Washington. State and local officials communicate most effectively through their special committees. Each of the state and local associations has developed committees and staff that are expert on a variety of topics and constitute a critical part of domestic policy subsystems. Over the past twenty years the SLIGs and their friends in policy subsystems have had varying roles in moving issues onto the public agenda, developing and passing legislation, making rules and regulations, preparing and passing budgets, administering and implementing programs, and evaluating and changing programs.

The seven major public interest groups (see Table 11-1), representing the general government interests of state and local government, evolved and

Table 11-1 The Big Seven: Major State and Local Interest Groups

	Headquarters	Number of Members	Distinctive Traits	Lobbies?
National Conference of State Legislatures (NCSL)	Denver (research) Washington (lobbying) (formed in 1975)	50 state legislatures, including legislators and staff	Union of three formerly competing legislative organizations; emphasizes policy development across states.	Yes
National Governors' Association (NGA)	Washington (since 1958)	50 governors	Created "Hall of States" where many state and local groups are housed.	Yes
National Association of Counties (NACo)	Washington (since 1958)	2,100 county governments	Large and effective interest group for county governments	Yes
National League of Cities (NLC)	Washington (since 1954)	1,175 small-to-medium cities	Highly developed research and professional staff	Yes
U.S. Conference of Mayors (USCM)	Washington (since 1932)	Mayors of 600 larger cities	Represents "big-city" interest; relies on direct lobbying by mayors	Yes
International City Management Association (ICMA)	Washington (since 1967)	7,000 city administrators	Professional organization for city managers	No
Council of State Governments (CSG)	Lexington, Ky. (Washington office since 1983)	50 states plus territories	Six regional offices; has many affiliate organizations, such as associations of chief justices, attorneys general	No

grew steadily between 1932, when the U.S. Conference of Mayors established a Washington-based office, and 1974, when the National Society of State Legislators located its lobbying staff in the capital. A recent survey shows fifty-nine SLIGs in Washington, D.C., representing 300,000 members, ranging from governors to state court administrators. These national associations have more than two thousand staff, and the seven largest SLIGs alone have annual total budgets of almost $34 million and staff totaling nearly five hundred. Each of the Big Seven began outside of Washington and moved to the capital to establish a more effective link with Congress and the executive branch of government.

The evolution and growth of the Big Seven were accompanied by the simultaneous development of functional interest groups and the creation of offshoots from the Big Seven. There are four other classes of SLIGs in Washington: umbrella functional interest groups, specific functional interest groups, affiliates of the Big Seven, and subsidiaries of the Big Seven. Functional interest groups represent specific policy areas or interests of specialists. The umbrella groups, such as the American Public Works Association (APWA), represent the broad spectrum of actors in the functional area of public works, while specific functional interest groups, such as the American Water Works Association or the American Association of Port Authorities, are examples of subgroups that might fall under the APWA umbrella. Over the past two decades, these groups located their headquarters in Washington to lobby for categorical grants during the growth years.

In addition to the functional groups, the Big Seven have contributed to the proliferation of SLIGs through affiliate and subsidiary groups. A number of groups share office space, staff, and resources with the Big Seven. For example, the NGA has sharing relationships with the Council of State Planning Agencies and the National Association of State Budget Officers. The Conference of Chief Justices, the Conference of State Court Administrators, the National Association of Attorneys General, and the National Association of State Auditors, Comptrollers, and Treasurers are all associated with and share the facilities of the CSG.

A 'Cozy Subsystem'

From the early 1960s to 1981, the relationships among the principal actors in the intergovernmental policy arena can be described as comprising a cozy policy subsystem, if not exactly an iron triangle. In this subsystem SLIG politics were organized around specific issues or programs primarily through a pattern of relationships among state and local government associations, congressional committees and subcommittees, and executive bureaus and agencies. The specialized professional media, such as journals and newsletters associated with the seven SLIGs, were often the only "windows" to their activities.

Implicit in many SLIG activities was the recognition that control of political turf, or jurisdiction over several federal programs or issues, was essential to their growth and long-term survival. This is especially important because, until the Reagan administration focused on them, the SLIGs were usually successful in thwarting challenges to their authority (from nonsubsystem players such as presidents) and in containing conflict. This was achieved by practicing a norm of reciprocity among SLIGs and their functional affiliates; in this way, they shared information, power, and influence over programs and public policy issues. In these subsystems, as in others, cooperation, supportive legislative oversight, and program evaluation were often hidden from public view.

Before Reagan, conflict in SLIG subsystems can be described as being at a low to middle level with the executive branch and among congressional subcommitees. In general, competition and conflict were managed within the subsystems through bargaining and compromise. Functional specialists, those persons with expertise and technical competence on particular issues or programs, dominated the subsystems. These specialists came from the SLIGs, academia, Congress, executive agencies, and the other subsystem institutions. Before the Reagan era, there was systematic and regular communication among the SLIGs and the functional specialists in the subsystem. During the 1960s and 1970s, professional careers were built around the issues and programs dominated by SLIG subsystems. Professionals often moved between the SLIGs, agencies, and Congress, building expertise and a reputation for knowledge about a subsystem and its programs. The number of critical actors with jurisdiction over an issue was usually less than one hundred people. Among this small community, surprises were not appreciated, and the sharing of information and knowledge was rewarded.

The growth and influence of the SLIGs closely parallel the change in the federal government's role in domestic affairs. During the 1960s there was a massive shift in the federal government's role in the intergovernmental system. President John Kennedy's New Frontier and President Lyndon Johnson's Great Society launched dozens of new programs aimed at financing programs to be delivered by state and local governments. During this period, the influence and size of the SLIGs grew enormously. Timothy Conlan reports, for example:

> In 1957, the National Association of Counties had a professional staff of one and a budget of $18,000. Twenty-five years later, its staff had swelled to 60 and its budget totaled $5 million. The U.S. Conference of Mayors, which had a budget of $88,000 in 1960, had grown to a $3.5 million operation by 1983 with a staff of 40. In 1954, the Conference of Mayors was joined in Washington by the American Municipal Association (now the National League of Cities), which by 1983 had a staff of 55 and a budget of $4.5 million. Perhaps the most dramatic change occurred in the case of the National Governors' Association (formerly the National Governors Conference), which did not open a Washington office until 1967. Fifteen years later the NGA had a staff of 70, a budget of $5.4 million, and had established a Washington center housing numerous individual states and affiliated organizations.[11]

However, this growth was not necessarily seen as a sign of strength for the SLIGs. For example, in 1974 Donald Haider noted:

> Although their direct channels of representation have been enhanced, state and local officials are now viewed increasingly in Washington—not as uniquely constituted co-governors—but as a few more voices among a multitude of special interest claimants.[12]

Haider's observation reflected changes that had developed in intergovernmental policy through the 1960s and 1970s. By the mid-1970s an unusual arrangement had developed between the Big Seven and the federal government. To carry out its state and local initiatives and stem the power of narrow, locally based interest groups promoting hundreds of categorical grants, the Nixon administration turned to the Big Seven to help implement federal grants programs and provide technical assistance. This mainly entailed the federal government providing grants and contracts to the SLIGs for programs to enhance state and local administrative capacity and to assist them in implementing and monitoring grant programs. In addition, program proponents called upon the organizations to advise Congress and the executive branch on the programs and to lobby for their continuation. According to B. J. Reed, the funding for capacity building and evaluation was so extensive that "by the mid-1970s federal dollars were funding (directly or indirectly) almost half of their employees," and programs covering policies in employment, environmental control, human services, community and economic development, transportation, and criminal justice were being administered by the SLIG organizations.[13]

The Breakup

The beginnings of the breakup of these cozy relationships can be traced to the Carter presidency. In addition to leveling off the growth in most federal grant programs and proposing declines in some others, the Carter administration changed some of the rules that had dominated politics in the intergovernmental arena. According to Reed:

> The Carter White House was not shy about appealing directly to NLC's board of directors to support an Administration position on a particular issue. According to NLC director Beals, Carter came to Washington running against the traditional insiders who dominated the policy process, including interest groups such as the League, Conference, and NACo.... Conference of Mayors executive director John Gunther believed that basic inexperience has a great deal to do with the Carter Administration's suspicion toward traditional *intermediaries* in Washington and that this spilled over into their relationship with local interest groups.[14]

The trends toward lower federal aid and reduced access to the White House that began during the Carter years were accelerated with Reagan's election. Not only was Reagan free of an obligation to the state and local groups for his election, but also his commitment to decentralize funding and administration of domestic programs meant that the provision of centralized technical assistance through SLIGs was seen as an unnecessary expense. Administration officials reasoned that a decrease in federal programs and regulations reduced the need to fund organizations that provided technical assistance aimed at helping their members cope with the requirements of those programs. Furthermore, because these funds were indirectly used to support lobbying by contributing to paying the overhead expenses of these organizations, "defunding" them as soon as possible was a way to reduce the pressure on the White House and Congress for more federal spending (or at least the maintenance of previous levels of funding).[15]

Explanations for the defunding of the SLIGs vary. Craig T. Ferris pointed out:

> Some association officials say the cuts in the grants, which are handed out at the discretion of the administration, have generally paralleled the overall cuts in domestic spending.
>
> But others say the groups that have most strenuously opposed the administration's plans are the victims of White House retribution and are bearing the brunt of the cuts.
>
> The biggest reduction in grants, according to figures, have been directed at the U.S. Conference of Mayors and the National League of Cities—the two organizations that have been the loudest critics of the administration's domestic spending cuts and the President's "New Federalism" plan, which would replace many grants to localities with so-called block grants to the states.[16]

Whatever the motive for the funding cuts, they were substantial. As shown in Table 11-2, in 1980 the U.S. Conference of Mayors received 64.3 percent of its budget from federal grants and contracts (out of a budget of $5.6 million). This funding was reduced to 34.2 percent (out of a total budget of $4.1 million in 1985). The National League of Cities experienced similar reductions; in 1980 the league received $3.7 million or 48 percent in federal grants and contracts out of a budget of $7.6 million, but by 1985 the total budget had been reduced to $5.4 million with no federal funds.[17] However, other major SLIG groups, representing governors, state legislatures and counties, fared better in the early Reagan years.

Even with the so-called "protective" posture of the Reagan administration toward the counties and state groups, their federal funding also fell, as shown in Table 11-2. In the case of the National Governors' Association, federal funding declined from 53.6 percent of total budget in 1980 to 38.2 percent in 1985, and from 28 percent federal funding in 1980 for NACo to 7.5 percent in 1985. The net reduction in federal funding from 1980 to 1985 for the seven state and local government associations was dramatic: 54.8 percent for NCSL, 28.7 percent for NGA, 73.1 percent for NACo, 100 percent for NLC, 46.8 percent for USCM, 72.7 percent for ICMA, and 64.6 percent for CSG.

The cutbacks in federal grants and contracts had a serious impact on the SLIGs. With no quick way to raise money to replace the federal grant funds, most of the groups rapidly began to diversify and retrench by cutting staff and administrative expenses. For example, the U.S. Conference of Mayors cut its staff by 55 percent (from 100 employees to 45). The conference was especially hard hit in 1982 when the U.S. Department of Housing and Urban Development cancelled the third year of a $1.2 million-a-year contract to provide technical assistance to cities for housing rehabilitation. The National League of Cities cut its staff from 125 in 1980 to 53 in 1985; the National Conference of State Legislatures cut its Washington and Denver headquarters staff from 120 in 1980 to 105 in 1985 and had nine lobbyists working four-day weeks rather than five.[18]

An exception to this general pattern was the National Governors' Association. Although federal grants were cut almost 29 percent, NGA suffered no staff reductions. Several years earlier the organization had decided to increase its own source revenues and rely less heavily on the federal government for funding.

The strategy of diversifying funding by turning to nonfederal sources has been forced upon all of the state and local interest groups as a key to their survival and effectiveness. Organizations like NACo, USCM, and NLC have redirected vital staff resources away from lobbying, research, and technical assistance to raise dues and fees, conduct membership drives, initiate business ventures, or hire fund-raisers. According to Ann Martino, "Even so, only a select few can thrive and flourish at pre-Reagan levels. As a result, many groups have no alternative except to eliminate member services previously financed by federal grants." [19]

Just as significant for the SLIGs as staff reductions, federal budget cuts, and changes of direction were the changes in leadership, which were caused in part by financial problems. Among those who left during 1981 and 1982 were Bernard F. Hillenbrand, the executive director of NACo, after twenty-five years with the organization; Stephen B. Farber, the executive director of NGA, after seven years; Mark Keene, the executive director of ICMA, after nearly fifteen years; and the executive directors of the Council of State Governments, the Municipal Finance Officers Association, and the National Association of State Budget Officers.

These organizations had energetically expanded their operations during the 1970s, become dependent on federal funds, had committed themselves to new buildings or long-term leases for office space, and found themselves unprepared to deal with the funding cuts of 1981 and 1982. Rochelle Stanfield reported:

> The immediate cause of Hillenbrand's departure was his assumption of responsibility for a mammoth $2 million cost overrun on NACo's new headquarters building, which precipitated the laying off of 21 staff members, a fourth of the organization's force.
>
> While lavish decorations and staff insubordination have been cited, an underlying problem was NACo's inability to fill the eight-story building with tenants. That was primarily because of the recession and cutbacks in federal contracts for the expected renters.[20]

Table 11-2 Vital Statistics of the Big Seven, 1975-1985 (annual budgets in millions)

	1975	1980	1981	1982	1983	1984	1985	Percentage Change 1980-1985
National Conference of State Legislatures[a]								
Total staff	20	120	120	120	105	105	105	−12.5
Total members	34	43	43	46	46	46	48	+11.6
Total budget	$0.8	$5.0	$5.7	$5.7	$5.4	$6.0	$6.5	+30.0
Percentage from federal government	31.5%	48.4%	50.1%	38.1%	26.1%	22.8%	21.9%	−54.8
National Governors' Association								
Total staff	—	70	70	70	70	70	70	0.0
Total members	54	55	55	55	55	55	55	0.0
Total budget	$2.1	$5.0	$5.7	$5.3	$5.4	$6.8	$6.2	+24.0
Percentage from federal government	40.2%	53.6%	58.3%	40.5%	43.0%	47.6%	38.2%	−28.7
National Association of Counties								
Total staff	87	—	120	120	58	58	58	−51.7
Total members	1,365	1,825	2,100	2,100	2,100	2,100	2,100	+15.1
Total budget	—	$5.8	$6.3	$6.0	$6.4	$7.0	$7.2	−20.7
Percentage from federal government	—	28%	26.2%	15.1%	11.7%	10.8%	7.5%	−73.2

National League of Cities								
Total staff	112	125	125	100	56	53	53	−57.6
Total members	15,000	950	950	990	1,100	1,175	1,175	+23.7
Total budget	—	$7.6	—	$6.5	$5.2	$5.0	$5.4	−29.0
Percentage from federal government	—	48.7%	—	30.8%	5.8%	0.1%	0.0%	−100.0
U.S. Conference of Mayors								
Total staff	5	100	100	65	55	45	45	−55.0
Total members	750	470	470	600	600	600	600	+27.7
Total budget	—	$5.6	$5.1	$3.6	$3.7	$3.9	$4.1	−26.8
Percentage from federal government	—	64.3%	49.0%	38.8%	32.4%	33.3%	34.2%	−46.8
International City Management Assn.								
Total staff	60	—	85	85	85	85	65	−23.5
Total members	6,500	—	7,000	7,000	7,000	7,000	7,000	0.0
Total budget	$2.6	$4.8	$4.8	$5.3	$5.1	$5.4	$6.0	+16.7
Percentage from federal government	30.7%	39.6%	33.3%	26.4%	18.8%	9.1%	10.8%	−72.7
Council of State Governments								
Total staff	100	—	120	100	100	100	100	−16.7
Total members	56	—	56	50	50	50	50	−10.7
Total budget	$3.4	$4.5	$4.1	$4.4	$4.1	$4.3	$4.1	−8.9
Percentage from federal government	52.4%	37.3%	33.7%	26.9%	21.5%	18.3%	13.2%	−64.6

[a] National Conference of State Legislatures as it exists today was founded in 1975 as a result of the merging of three organizations: the National Society of State Legislators, National Conference of State Legislative Leaders, and the National Legislative Conference.

Source: Data for each organization were collected from the respective executive directors in December 1985, except for 1975, which are taken from the *Encyclopedia of Associations for 1976*.

Note: A dash (—) indicates information not available.

The early 1980s were hard on the SLIGs, and the rest of the decade holds little promise for relief from fiscal and political difficulties. The Gramm-Rudman-Hollings deficit reduction law poses even greater challenges to the SLIGs, with massive cuts from grants to states and localities, primarily from services to the elderly, the handicapped, and poor, and other social programs. Under Gramm-Rudman-Hollings, the states and localities face major new cuts in discretionary federal spending. According to Office of Management and Budget (OMB) historical budget tables, federal aid to state and local governments hit its peak in 1978 at $75.6 billion. Using 1982 constant dollars, funding started to slip in Carter's last year in office and dropped sharply to $50.3 billion after Reagan's 1981 reconciliation bill. No matter what the outcome of the 1987 to 1991 budget battles, it seems certain that the states are being left on their own to fund many social programs previously paid for in whole or in part by the federal government.

As David Broder has observed:

> Whether he [President Reagan] succeeds in all of his ambitions or not, state and local governments are increasingly going to find themselves in a go-it-alone [situation]. . . . Is it any wonder that Jon Bragg [former president of the National Conference of State Legislatures] says, with some scorn, "The federal government has paralyzed itself and now it is going to paralyze the states"? [21]

The New Shape of Intergovernmental Relations

What have we learned about SLIG subsystem politics and intergovernmental relations during the Reagan years? Whether the full impact of the president's proposed budget cuts for FY 1987 through FY 1991 falls upon state and local governments, there can be little doubt that the structure and functioning of the intergovernmental relations system has taken on a new shape. For the Big Seven and their members, the cozy relationship they had enjoyed with the federal government during the period of growth in domestic spending from the 1960s to the late 1970s came apart.

This breakup occurred in several ways. First, instead of jointly lobbying with members of Congress and administration officials for more funding and new programs, the SLIGs found themselves in intense combat with the Reagan administration to maintain funding levels, influence administration appointments, and salvage old programs.

Second, instead of working cooperatively with familiar faces who share a common background and ideological view about domestic policy, the SLIGs faced adversaries in the Reagan administration who came from backgrounds different from theirs. Many of these officials came from conservative research organizations (think tanks) like the Heritage Foundation, CATO Institute, the Sequoia Foundation, and the Hoover Institution, and many others were conservative Republican party activists. Many of these new Reagan appointees lacked interest in continuing public service careers and did not spend time in the network of established public interest groups. As a consequence, few of the traditional sanctions and incentives available to the SLIGs have much influence on the behavior or policy preferences of these domestic policy officials. Reagan appointees generally did not accept the subsystem norm of system self-preservation, which calls for funding growth and expansion of subsystem turf.

Third, the adversarial posture of the SLIGs toward the administration's policy preferences forced them to rely far more on their memberships for financial support, and, in doing so, forced them to become more responsive to the nonmonetary aspects of their organizations' services (for example, educational, expressive, and solidary incentives). Membership services once were the second priority for many of the SLIGs, but in the 1980s they became the first priority and a primary source of revenue.

Fourth, the weakness of the Washington-based SLIGs, the growing importance of state governments as a source of financial aid, and the shift from direct categorical aid to local governments to block grants, which are divided and distributed to localities at the state level, have fostered an "every man for himself" strategy among state and local officials. During the 1960s and 1970s, state and local officials could rely on the SLIGs to provide them with a "fair share" of an expanding budget; in the 1980s, the scarcity of money dictated a more fragmented approach to lobbying to ensure that a state or local jurisdiction would receive at least part of the funding it was seeking.

This new structure of intergovernmental relations reflects the fragility of the so-called iron triangles of interest group politics. Interest groups have been put on the defensive by the Reagan administration's strategy of centralizing budgeting in OMB, and the 1981 reconciliation process bypassed the traditional sources of power in subsystem politics; that is, subcommittees and agencies. The new structure of intergovernmental relations also highlights some factors that foster the development of "cozy subsystems" and those that hinder them. Among these are the following:

Growing Budgets—A growing federal budget pie allows program expansion and the belief among policy makers that previously unfunded but worthwhile programs ought to be supported. This serves the interest of the lobbying organization (in this case, SLIGs) who are able to "deliver" these distributive programs for their membership and, therefore, can show their value to their membership by demonstrating influence in Washington. Declining or redistributive budgets jeopardize old programs and claims to effectiveness. Once a budget base is considered a target for redistribution or becomes frozen, subsystem politics become a zero-sum game and the norms of reasonable bargaining and compromise tend to disintegrate. Geographic redistribution of public goods, from the so-called Rust Belt to the Sun Belt also created cracks in the solidarity of SLIG systems. Harold Wolman and Fred Teitelbaum concluded in their study of interest groups in the Reagan years that groups became more reliant on mobilizing grass-roots support to fend off proposed budget cuts and block grants because:

First, to overcome the magnitude of the proposed cuts, groups have responded by increasing efforts to educate their own memberships and to mobilize public support against these proposals. Thus many interest groups have attempted to engage their memberships in letter-writing campaigns aimed at specific members of Congress. The hope was that as legislators have become more independent politicians and, consequently, more sensitive to constituent interests, this tactic might generate support in opposition to the cuts. Second, the budget process now results in a single floor vote on the reconciliation bill that contains almost the entire budget in one document. Consequently, to influence the decision on the budget, votes not just from key committee chairpersons but from all members of Congress have to be sought. This requires a grassroots campaign.[22]

Familiar Faces—A cozy policy subsystem usually means that people from interest groups will move in and out of government and eventually return to lobbying organizations. Once in a government agency or a congressional staff, they share norms, ideas, and careers with their former colleagues, making the job of the lobbyist (to gain access to key policy makers) relatively easy. Without familiar faces in government, jobs, access, and persuasion become much more difficult. Reagan understood this and tried to appoint new faces who did not accept the subsystem norms of career protection and reciprocity. This tactic caused substantial difficulties for the SLIGs during the first years of his administration.

Collective Benefits—When grants are given to a broad spectrum of an organization's membership, the incentive to pay dues to the organization is strong, particularly if the cost is incidental. If, however, the grants are targeted or are allocated at the state level and membership costs rise, the temptation increases for members to drop their support of the national organization and lobby alone or in more specialized functional or regional groups (e.g., the Northeast-Midwest Caucus). Putting membership services on a user-fee basis overcomes some of these problems, but it also increases the importance of more carefully fashioning services to meet member needs and the salience of marketing services to raise revenues.

Scope of Conflict—E. E. Schattschneider argued that, "one way to restrict the scope of conflict is to localize it, while one way to expand it is to nationalize it."[23] Schattschneider's dictum applies well to the Reagan strategy of cutting federal funds for state and local government and shifting responsibility for domestic programs to subnational units of government. By decentralizing program responsibility to the states, Reagan found a way of both cutting costs and shifting the scope of subsystem conflict and power away from Washington.

Presidential Support, Hostility, or Indifference—The president's power in domestic affairs is generally quite constrained by Congress and interest group activity. Nevertheless, armed with an election mandate and a budget-cutting tool like the Gramm-Latta Budget Reconciliation Act of 1981 or the Gramm-Rudman-Hollings Deficit Control Act of 1986, a popular president like Reagan can influence the domestic policy agenda substantially. Lobbying groups from state and local government have had little choice but to direct all their energies toward deflection of the cuts, rather than toward expansion of federal funds and promotion of new programs. When presidential support is present or is at least indifferent, lobbying groups can work with friendly congressional committees to promote new programs. When the president focuses on cuts, the level of conflict increases, and interest groups and congressional committees and subcommittees must move into a battle for survival rather than expansion.

Shared View of Policy Direction—A shared view of the existence of a problem and its solution is essential to cooperative policy making in a subsystem. When the White House, lobbying groups, and Congress agree that a problem exists—and a solution is readily available—action on policy comes easily. When there is a division about the existence of a problem, its causes, and the means for its solution, subsystem competition and, often, disintegration occur, as has been the case in the intergovernmental policy arena during the Reagan years.

In President Reagan's world view, the problems of states and localities are not those of the federal government; rather, where these problems exist, they are often caused by the federal government's regulation of intergovernmental grants-in-aid and the imposition of federal policies on state and local affairs. This view postulates that states should tax and spend for themselves. The solution that Reagan most often proposes—coupling "defederalization" and "defunding"—is often unattractive to state and local officials who must take up the slack in funding or cut the programs. Without a shared view of policy direction, it is little wonder that the intergovernmental policy arena has been transformed from a cozy to a contested subsystem.

Notes

Authors are listed alphabetically and the views expressed in this paper are those of the authors and not necessarily those of the Congressional Research Service or the Library of Congress.

1. Ronald Reagan, "Inaugural Address," Jan. 20, 1981.
2. Ronald Reagan, "The State of the Union," Jan. 26, 1982.
3. Ernest S. Griffith, *The Impasse of Democracy* (New York: Harrison-Hilton Books, 1939), 182-183.
4. A. Grant Jordon, "Iron Triangles, Woolly Corporatism and Elastic Nets: Images of the Policy Process," *Journal of Public Policy* 1 (February 1981): 95-123.
5. Arthur A. Maass, "Congress and Water Resources," *American Political Science Review* 44 (1950): 576-593; J. Leiper Freeman, *The Political Process: Executive Bureau-Legislative Committee Relations* (New York: Random House, 1965); A. Lee Fritschler, *Smoking and Politics* (New York: Appleton, Century, Crofts, 1975); Samuel A. Lawrence, *United States Merchant Marine: Policies and Politics* (Washington, D.C.: Brookings Institution, 1966); Douglass Cater, *Power*

in Washington (New York: Random House, 1964); and Roger H. Davidson, "Policy Making in the Manpower Subgovernment," in *Politics in America,* ed. M. P. Smith et al. (New York: Random House, 1975).

6. Theodore J. Lowi, "How the Farmers Get What They Want," *Reporter,* May 1964, 35.

7. Jordon, "Iron Triangles," 96. See Hugh Heclo, "Issue Networks and the Executive Establishment," in *The New American Political System,* ed. Anthony King (Washington, D.C.: American Enterprise Institute, 1978), 87-124.

8. Jordon, "Iron Triangles," 121.

9. Ibid., 103.

10. See E. E. Schattschneider, *Politics, Pressures and the Tariff* (New York: Prentice-Hall, 1935); and Schattschneider, *The Semi-Sovereign People* (New York: Holt Rinehart & Winston, 1960).

11. Timothy J. Conlan, "Transformation in Party Politics and Their Implication for American Federalism" (Paper prepared for the Annual Meeting of the American Political Science Association, New Orleans, La., Aug. 29-Sept. 1, 1985), 46. These and the following data are derived from Donald Haider, *When Governments Come to Washington* (New York: Free Press, 1974), chap. 1; Conlan, *Congressional Responses to the New Federalism: The Politics of Special Revenue Sharing and Its Implications for Public Policy Making* (Ph.D. diss., Harvard University, 1982), 11, 12; and *SIAM Intergovernmental News* 7 (Winter 1984): 4-6.

12. Haider, *When Governments Come to Washington,* 110, 111.

13. See B. J. Reed, "The Changing Role of Local Advocacy in National Policies," *Journal of Urban Affairs* (Fall 1983): 289.

14. Ibid., 290.

15. See "The Really Big PIGs Took a While Getting Corralled in Washington," *SIAM Intergovernmental News* 7 (Winter 1984): 6.

16. Craig T. Ferris, "State, Local Lobbying Groups Struggle to Live with Cuts in Federal Funds," *Weekly Bond Buyer,* July 6, 1982, 1, 59.

17. See Reed, "The Changing Role of Local Advocacy," 293. Also see Lawrence D. Brown et al., *The Changing Politics of Federal Grants* (Washington, D.C.: Brookings Institution, 1984).

18. Brown et al., *The Changing Politics of Federal Grants.*

19. Ann Martino, "PIGs Scramble for Fiscal Fitness After Reagan Game," *SIAM Intergovernmental News* 7 (Winter 1984): 7.

20. Rochelle L. Stanfield, "Hard Times Hit State, Local Groups Despite Shifts in Power," *National Journal,* Oct. 2, 1982, 1663-1686. While overexpansion might have been Hillenbrand's undoing at NACo, it has been a source of strength for the National League of Cities. The NLC has been able to reduce its occupancy from two-and-a-half floors of the eleven-story building to only a single floor, producing an unanticipated profit of around $200,000 for the sublease.

21. David S. Broder, "Leaving the States to Go It Alone," *Washington Post,* Feb. 9, 1986.

22. Harold Wolman and Fred Teitelbaum, "Interest Groups and the Reagan Presidency," in *The Reagan Presidency and the Governing of America,* ed. Lester M. Salamon and Michael S. Lund (Washington, D.C.: Urban Institute, 1981), 313.

23. Schattschneider, *The Semi-Sovereign People,* 10-11.

12. American Business and Politics

Graham Wilson

The American business community has not always sought great influence in national policy making. This is ironic because American business interests have not suffered from their inactivity—either in comparison with other U.S. interests or with business interests in sister Western democracies. Within the political science literature, Bauer, Pool, and Dexter's major 1963 study of international trade, *American Business and Public Policy*, downplayed the role and impact of business in the policy process. Thus, just as Lyndon Johnson's Great Society programs and the regulatory revolution of the 1960s and 1970s were beginning, academics tended to ignore the political stirrings of business interests.

In this chapter, Graham Wilson reviews the relative inactivity of American business and concludes that this apparent lack of action has been deceptive. Business interests in other nations have faced more profound and well-organized challenges than those confronted in the United States. In addition, Wilson's comparative perspective emphasizes the decentralization in American policy making and the representation of interests. The diversity of U.S. business interests makes it extremely difficult for any "umbrella" organization to represent the entire community. Nevertheless, since about 1970 business has become increasingly well organized and active in pursuing its policy goals. Indeed, the Chamber of Commerce of the United States and many political action committees have aggressively pursued business interests. At the same time, Wilson sees business political activity as more ad hoc and less "tidily structured" than in other democratic states.

Business: Just Another Interest Group?

A major recurring question about American politics is the degree to which it is influenced or controlled by business. Radical critics of the United States both at home and abroad have claimed that business has far more power than other interests in American society; placards at demonstrations against U.S. policies in Latin America, Iran, and many other parts of the world often have portrayed Uncle Sam as the agent of banks or large corporations. Despite the frequency with which the power of business in the United States is raised as an issue at home and overseas, political scientists until recently have conducted comparatively little systematic research on the topic. Even now, only a few scholars are actively studying aspects of the relationship between American business and politics—in large part because of the theoretical problems involved in assessing the role of business in political life.

The first theoretical difficulty stems from the tremendous variety of economic interests that are subsumed under the category of "business." The term includes organizations from a "mom and pop" grocery store to multinational corporations such as Exxon or General Motors, whose annual sales exceed the gross national product of many nations. Clearly, the interests of the grocery store and of Exxon do not always coincide. Moreover, large corporations disagree among themselves. For example, most textile firms favor greater protectionism in trade policy because they face severe foreign competition, but other large corporations with extensive overseas sales, such as Boeing or IBM, support free-trade policies. Even different companies in the same industry may have different interests at stake in a political issue. Ford and General Motors pressed for relaxed federal standards requiring new cars to attain a higher mileage per gallon of gas, because their cars did not reach the mandated average mpg. At the same time, Chrysler opposed any relaxation, because its products already complied with the federal target.

It follows that political scientists using a case study analysis of the power of business must be careful in selecting appropriate policies to examine. Some issues will pit one type of business against another; other issues will encourage different types of business to band together. Theodore Lowi's argument that different types of policy produce different types of politics is of general significance for political scientists, but is of particular importance for the study of business and politics.[1]

What is more, the nature of business interest groups is greatly influenced by the frequency with which different types of issues arise. When major public issues affect a wide variety of corporations in similar ways, businesses are motivated to strengthen trade associations, which represent the collective interests of businesses in the same industry, and umbrella groups that represent the collective interests of corporations in different industries. In contrast, when the dominant public issues divide corporations, because policy proposals will benefit some and hurt others, companies have no incentive to devote greater resources to the defense of collective business interests.

A second major theoretical problem can be summarized in the question: To what extent does the power of business depend on political action? It is reasonable to assume that the power of most interest groups derives from their use of directly observable techniques such as lobbying, contributing to campaigns, and seeking to influence voters. A number of writers have suggested that in the case of business, however, its sources of power are not necessarily to be found in such directly observable forms of influence, but rather are embedded in our socioeconomic system.

Matthew Crenson, for example, in explaining why Gary, Indiana, did not adopt air pollution control ordinances similar to those of comparable towns, has emphasized the degree to which employees of U.S. Steel dominated the power structure of that city.[2] U.S. Steel did not defeat possible pollution control regulations through observable political action, but its influence was nonetheless real. The firm's friends killed pollution control without being asked to do so by the company. Another writer, Steven Lukes, has stressed the role of dominant ideology.[3] In societies inclined to believe what is good for General Motors is good for the country, business is unlikely to be faced with fundamental challenges to its interests. Charles Lindblom has argued that business occupies a privileged position because of its control over the investment on which the prosperity of cities, states, and even nations depends.[4] Business does not need to rely on overt political pressure, in Lindblom's view, because the refusal of business to invest in localities whose governments are uncooperative will soon bring those governments to heel. Thus "antibusiness" policies will halt investment, and without investment, employment and even tax revenues will decline.

Assertions that the influence of business extends beyond visible political involvement have been keenly contested. There are readily available examples to show that the theories of Crenson, Lukes, and Lindblom either do not always apply or are based in part on assumptions that not everyone shares. Lukes, for instance, clearly believes that our true interest requires the abandonment of the capitalist system. Lindblom does not explain why other factors, such as the location of markets or of raw materials, would not prevent corporations from shifting their investment to avoid government policies they dislike.

Nevertheless, it would be naive to argue that the power of business in our society is limited to the resources it devotes to observable political action. Nor is it adequate to maintain that the power of business is based predominantly on one or more other potential sources of power. Rather, we will suggest in the following section that, as political circumstances have changed in the United States, so have the political strategies that business has adopted. In particular, as some of its less observable sources of influence have declined, so the overt political participation of business has increased.

Fluctuations in the Political Involvement of American Business

One of the most surprising findings by political scientists in the 1950s and 1960s was that business organizations in the United States were weak. The authoritative study by Raymond Bauer, Ithiel de Sola Pool, and Lewis Anthony Dexter into the politics of tariffs might have been expected to reveal extensive interest group activity by business.[5] Bauer and his colleagues found that, on the contrary, politicians felt that they heard too little rather than too much from business; few claimed to feel any real pressure, and many felt that they were insufficiently informed by businesses of their interest. Most important for our purposes, the trade associations representing whole industries were found, with few exceptions, to be particularly weak. These organizations were poorly staffed, often by people regarded as failed business executives, and they spent more time and effort in maintaining their membership than in influencing policy.[6]

Just as Bauer and his colleagues concluded that trade associations were surprisingly ineffectual, so too were business umbrella organizations. There was no strong, prestigious organization representing the collective interests of business in Washington in the 1950s or early 1960s. The two most plausible candidates for the title, the National Association of Manufacturers (NAM) and the Chamber of Commerce of the United States, were both regarded as suffering from obvious and major defects.[7] Neither, for example, was accepted as speaking authoritatively for big business. The Chamber of Commerce remained very much the voice of "Main Street" or small business, and NAM was dominated by medium-sized firms that belonged only out of a sense of corporate civic duty. Both NAM and the Chamber of Commerce were heavily identified with the right wing of American politics, enjoying little credibility on technical issues, among moderate or liberal politicians. Anxious to keep as many of their members as happy as possible, both organizations had to sit out debates on policies that affected different members unequally. For example, neither NAM nor the Chamber could express a clear view on foreign trade policy because some members were hurt by foreign competition while others benefited. As a result of their shortcomings, the Chamber and NAM were not often sought as allies in Washington; they were viewed as likely to bring the "kiss of death" rather than success to a proposal.

Nor was the weakness of trade associations and business umbrella groups offset by the strength of representation of individual corporations in Washington during the 1950s and 1960s. On the contrary, many large corporations maintained no permanent representation in Washington. General Motors did not have its own office in the capital until Ralph Nader began his onslaught on the safety of its products. ITT similarly opened its Washington office only in the late 1960s. Except for firms that depended heavily on the federal government for sales (for instance, defense contractors), big business generally felt that any matters that arose could be handled by Washington lawyers whom they retained to exert political influence.

American Business in Comparative Perspective

Until the late 1960s American business seemed remarkable for the degree to which it failed to use the standard techniques of interest group politics. This failure seemed all the more surprising in light of the development of successful organizations of employers in other countries. In both Austria and Sweden, for example, a single employers' organization was formed; civil servants regarded it as having considerable technical expertise, and the government accepted it as *the* voice of business, consulted it before any major policy decision was made, and entrusted it with managing certain key issues, such as counterinflation policy.[8] In Japan, too, the employers' organization, the Keidanren, was closely integrated with government—not only advising the government but sometimes actually substituting for it (for instance, in making trade agreements with other countries).[9] In West Germany, France, and post-1964 Britain, there existed a single employers' organization, which was regularly consulted by government. Even those who disagreed with this organization acknowledged its technical expertise. In addition, it was well staffed and, above all, was accepted as the sole legitimate representative of business interests.

To promote economic growth, the government in several of these countries worked closely with the business umbrella group and the trade associations representing individual industries. In Japan and France, employers' organizations became partners of the state, as government implemented what we would now call an industrial policy. Government money was funneled into those industries that were expected to have a promising future, and industries that were thought to have little future were encouraged to run down. Government influence or control over the allocation of private credit reinforced the importance of direct government intervention in industries.[10] Industrial policies were typically both formulated and implemented in close partnership between government and employers' associations.

As research on the relationship between business and government in other nations accumulated, the situation in the United States seemed more and more anomalous. Reviewing the innovative practices evolving overseas, Philippe Schmitter argued that in modern industrialized democracies there was a trend toward what he called *neocorporatism*.[11] Governments increasingly made and implemented policies in cooperation with prestigious, influential organizations that enjoyed the monopolistic right to speak for business or for labor. In contrast, the United States was distinctive by virtue of its weak, fragmented, and poorly regarded business organizations. Why were these U.S. groups so poorly developed by international standards? The theories offered at the beginning of this chapter help to answer the question. Most business executives saw no need for stronger organizations, and government similarly had no reason to promote their development.

Several factors explain why business leaders were not motivated to develop strong business interest groups. First, until the late 1960s, public attitudes toward business were highly favorable. Although Charles Wilson, Dwight Eisenhower's secretary of defense and a former auto industry executive, was criticized for saying that what was good for General Motors was good for the United States, many Americans, as noted earlier, tended to agree. Opinion polls showed a high level of trust in the integrity of business managers and in the degree to which corporations struck a reasonable balance between their desire to make money and a broader public interest.[12]

The apparent acceptance of business practices on the part of the general public was accompanied by the absence of challenges from economic groups or forces. In the years preceding the emergence of Japan as an economic power, American industries, such as steel and auto manufacturing, were world leaders in terms of scale and productivity. Labor unions, viewed with alarm by corporate America of the 1930s, had been accommodated by many large corporations, such as U.S. Steel and Ford, which had bitterly opposed their creation. The left wing of the union movement had been considerably weakened in the 1940s by fights between Communists and the democratic Left; there had certainly been no tendency to create an explicitly anticapitalist labor movement such as existed in Europe. Legislation, particularly the 1947 Taft-Hartley Act, had tilted the law more in management's favor. In fact, union membership in the United States peaked at about one-third of the work force in the 1950s, a low level compared with other countries, and then entered a long decline that continues in the mid-1980s. (Only 19 percent of the current American work force belongs to a union, compared with about 47 percent of the British work force and 85 percent of the Swedish.) Thus, although some isolated investigations, such as the inquiry by Sen. Estes Kefauver (D-Tenn., Senate 1949-1963), into the drug companies, perturbed individual industries, the average corporate executive had few political fears until the late 1960s. There were few incentives to create stronger interest groups to defend business.

Second, business benefited from the balance of power within government. The Eisenhower administration was most definitely a business executive's administration; "eight millionaires and a plumber" was the description applied to Eisenhower's first cabinet. Conservative dominance of Congress was secured by the alliance between Southern Democrats and Republicans. The commanding heights within Congress—especially the committee chairmanships—were held disproportionately under the seniority system by conservative Southern Democrats. In short, political elites as well as the public were inclined to be sympathetic to business. As a result, it would have been difficult to place on the political agenda policies that business opposed.

Third, with some significant exceptions, such as the defense industry, government and business have never been as closely integrated in the United States as in many other countries. Governments in the United States—federal, state, and local—spent a smaller proportion of national income than governments in most other industrialized democracies. The federal government did not aspire to lead the development of the economy through extensive intervention, nor did Washington try to run an incomes policy. Even the responsibility of the government for ensuring full employment and economic growth was less readily accepted in the United States than in other industrialized democracies. Richard Lau and David Sears have shown that Americans have been particularly reluctant to expect government to deal with economic problems because of their "ethic of self-reliance."[13]

It followed that government and business in the United States had less need to institutionalize their dealings than in most European countries or Japan. Needing the cooperation of interest groups in economic planning and perhaps, above all, in running an incomes policy, the governments of many industrialized democracies consciously built up a single organization to represent employers. In Britain the 1964-1966 Labour government helped create the Confederation of British Industry, in order to deal with a single, authoritative employers' group.[14] In Austria, governments more or less required an employer or even a trade association that wished to discuss an issue with government to operate through the employers' umbrella organization. Moreover, it is doubtful whether the fragmented executive branch and the even more fragmented Congress had the capacity—or the will—to promote the development of a single cohesive pressure group.

Thus, the comparative weakness of American business organizations noted by writers such as Bauer, Pool, and Dexter reflected not so much the weakness but the strength of business in the United States. The benefits to business embodied in the socioeconomic system allowed corporations the luxury of neglecting their overt political activities. In the nineteenth century, when some of the largest corporations in the world were based here, the only federal official most people would meet was the letter carrier. Political scientists have long argued that interest groups develop in response to a threat to their environment.[15] American businesses, experiencing few challenges to their interests or disturbances within their political and economic environments, had fewer incentives to develop strong interest groups than did businesses overseas.

The Upsurge of Business Political Activity

A particularly astute social scientist might have predicted that if the circumstances changed, if corporations in the United States were confronted with a less favorable environment, then stronger business involvement in politics would result. In fact, several severe shocks to American business did occur.

First, public confidence in business declined considerably, falling much faster than confidence in other institutions (for instance, government).[16] Major scandals of the 1970s brought to public attention as much illegal activity by business executives as by politicians. By the mid-1970s, many Americans no longer believed that business managers were striking a reasonable balance between the quest for profit and the public interest. The public distrust was reflected in the rise of a number of new public interest groups such as Common Cause, the Nader organizations (including Public Citizen), and a range of environmental defense groups.

Second, the balance of power in Washington shifted away from probusiness elected officials. The seniority system in Congress was somewhat weakened and, in any case, less consistently favored conservatives. The extensive Democratic victories of 1964 and 1974 showed that liberal and potentially antibusiness majorities could readily be mobilized. Partly as a result of the activities of the public interest groups and the shift of opinion against business, the Congresses of the early 1970s, and even the supposedly probusiness Richard Nixon, approved a flood of measures, such as environmental and workplace safety regulatory laws, that were hardly welcome to business.

Third, the era of American domination of industry passed. Because of the so-called economic miracles of West Germany, France, Japan, and, more recently, Taiwan and South Korea, American industries faced intense competition from higher productivity and lower costs abroad. Basic American industries such as steel, textiles, and auto manufacturing found it increasingly difficult to withstand foreign competition even within the American domestic market. Major industries and corporations were forced to turn to government for protection from imports (textiles and steel) or for financial help in staving off bankruptcy (Chrysler). Although the United States economy showed tremendous strength in certain areas, such as computers and aerospace, the days of American supremacy in business were gone. In the 1960s, the French had worried about *le défi americain,* the challenge posed by American products in European markets. In the 1970s, the French auto manufacturer Renault purchased the bulk of the stock of the fourth largest auto manufacturer in the United States, American Motors, and Japanese firms such as Nissan and Honda opened plants in the United States. *Le défi* was now often a challenge to American industries rather than by American corporations.

Fourth, between 1965 and the 1980s the federal government experienced remarkable growth—an increase in size that in many ways benefited business. The defense buildup of the late 1970s and 1980s, for instance, was a boon to defense contractors. The broadened involvement of government also served to awaken business' political awareness. Of particular importance was the creation, in response to the concerns of consumers and environmental activists, of a number of new regulatory agencies with extensive powers over business. Two agencies especially, the Occupational Safety and Health Administration (OSHA) and the Environmental Protection Agency (EPA), both created in 1970, brought the threat of strict federal regulation to almost every workplace in America. Other agencies created in the early 1970s and seen as a potential threat to business included the Consumer Product Safety Commission and the National Highway Traffic Safety Administration. Even the formerly moribund Federal Trade Commission was reconstituted by President Jimmy Carter in a form that seemed to challenge the interests of a wide range of businesses. David Vogel has argued that American business executives have generally been more distrustful of government than have their counterparts in other countries.[17] Much of the growth of government in the 1970s seemed threatening indeed to corporate managers.

Business Strikes Back

The increase in political activity by business since the mid-1960s has been impressive.[18] It is an upsurge that has taken many forms.

Individual firms have become much more likely to have their own representation in Washington. Most large firms, such as ITT and General Motors, now have Washington offices that monitor legislative developments and lobby Congress. These offices also keep an eye on the activities of executive branch agencies such as EPA or OSHA, whose decisions can be of momentous consequence to business. As in the past, the Washington offices also seek, through their own efforts or by enlisting the help of congressional delegations from states in which the company is located, to promote sales to the federal government of the firm's products. In 1985, for example, a particularly vigorous drive was made by Northrop to sell the F-20 fighter to the Air Force. In addition, Washington offices currently enjoy a higher status within corporations than they have historically.

The Washington bar also grew rapidly in the 1970s, not so much because of a rise in the number of lawsuits within the District of Columbia circuit, although that did happen, but because more corporations retained major law firms to represent them before Congress and the executive agencies. "Super lobbyists" such as Charls Walker or Tommy Boggs also prospered, attracting corporations through their links to powerful figures in the nation's capital. For his services Boggs earned more than $1 million during 1985.

Perhaps the best-known example of the upsurge in business' involvement in the Washington arena is the growth in the political action committees (PACs) run by individual corporations and trade associations (see Chapters 4 and 6). Business has taken considerable advantage of the rights given to it under federal election finance law to raise money from executives and stockholders. Business PACs are not the most affluent in terms of the money they raise, but they are substantial contributors to congressional campaigns. Because corporations and trade associations can pay the operating costs of their PACs out of general funds, almost every dollar donated to a business PAC is available as a campaign contribution. Business PACs (including both corporations and trade associations) significantly outspend other interest groups in campaign contributions, giving more than twice as much on elections as unions do, for example.[19]

Considerable controversy exists within the business community about how their PAC contributions should be distributed. Some corporate executives, such as Justin Dart, have argued that contributions should be given only to those conservatives, mostly Republicans, who can be counted on to defend the "free enterprise system." Many business PACs, however, contribute to Democratic congressional races, including the campaigns of some liberal Democrats. In fact, about half the contributions from trade associations and individual corporations go to Democrats.

Why do business leaders give money to politicians whose views they dislike or whose party they tend not to vote for? The answer is that campaign contributions often have as their goal the buying of access to powerful legislators, many of whom, especially in the House, are Democrats. Certainly corporations prefer to give to Republicans and conservatives; business PACs rarely if ever support liberal Democratic challengers or candidates in "open" congressional elections—that is, where there is no incumbent seeking reelection. Business PACs are usually pragmatic enough, however, to back Democratic incumbents, irrespective of their ideology, who are likely to win with or without business support. Business PACs are particularly likely to support incumbent Democrats who hold powerful posts, such as committee chairs.

An upsurge in campaign contributions has not been the only way in which business interest groups have made their presence felt in Washington. Some trade associations have increased the scale and quality of their activities, too, and not just through political action committees. Trade associations representing industries that have been extensively criticized (such as the American Petroleum Institute) or regulated (such as the Chemical Manufacturers Association) have raised subscriptions sharply in order to hire more staff, particularly more scientific and economic experts. Although no study comparable to Bauer, Pool, and Dexter's has yet been completed, it is unlikely that trade associations would emerge from such an analysis in as poor a light now as they did early in the 1960s. Indeed, in their survey of Washington representatives, Kay Lehman Schlozman and John Tierney found that few business organizations today are short of funds or resources.[20]

The changes at the level of the umbrella groups that seek to represent the collective interests of business have been equally dramatic. In the early 1970s, at the instigation of Irving Shapiro, the chief executive officer of Du Pont, many of the largest corporations in the United States set up the Business Roundtable to serve as their advocate in Washington. The creation of the Roundtable reflected the belief that existing umbrella organizations, including the Chamber of Commerce and the National Association of Manufacturers, were too closely identified with small and middle-sized businesses and with conservative ideological groups to be of value to large corporations. Thanks in large part to the activities of Shapiro and the Roundtable's insistence that chief executive officers of member corporations be involved in lobbying, the group soon developed a reputation among Democrats as a tough-minded organization with a more pragmatic approach than the Chamber of Commerce or NAM.

Naturally, the competitive pressure from the Business Roundtable as well as the changed circumstances that had encouraged its development prompted the Chamber of Commerce and NAM to improve their performance, too. The two came close to joining forces, which would have created an organization with a strong claim to be *the* voice of business. Although the merger did not go through, the two organizations lost the amateurish image that had handicapped them in the past. NAM has improved the quality of its technical and economic analyses, making them valuable even to politicians who don't like its policies, and the Chamber is now regarded as a pacesetter in lobbying. Borrowing and extending techniques of grass-roots lobbying from the public interest groups, the Chamber is unmatched in its ability to mobilize its members to let their representatives and senators know how they want them to vote on significant issues.

Trade groups and corporations also have tried to secure more favorable treatment for business in the world of ideas and among the general public. Foundations such as the American Enterprise Institute and the Heritage Foundation, which promote conservative views, have received generous support from executives who felt that existing "think tanks" such as the Brookings Institution were too critical of business. Corporations from industries with an adverse public image (for instance, Mobil Oil) have increased efforts to convince the public that they are good citizens. Mobil sponsors "Masterpiece Theatre" on public television, produces television ads promoting the company's image rather than its product, and presents its policy positions in ads in quality newspapers like the *New York Times*.

Such changes are examples of the adoption by business of the tactics of traditional pressure group politics. Business was in a sense forced to take such measures because it had lost some of the advantages it had previously enjoyed. Corporations and trade groups have been able, however, to command the resources of staff, expertise, and money sufficient to engage in conventional interest group politics very effectively.

American business, then, has become both more politically active and more effective in protecting its collective interests. But how far have these changes gone? Have the differences in the degree to which business is politically organized in the United States and in other industrialized democracies narrowed or even disappeared?

A Limited Revolution?

The tremendous growth in the number of corporate PACs and lobbyists should not lead us to assume that stepped-up political activity on the part of business has become the norm. Only about half the corporations listed in the *Fortune* 500, for instance, have PACs. Similarly, many large firms do not have their own representation in Washington. By and large, those that are not closely regulated by government or dependent on it for sales remain outside the political arena.

Trade associations, for their part, continue to vary significantly in the effectiveness of their activities. The vigorous role played by some interest groups, such as the American Petroleum Institute and the Chemical Manufacturers Association, does not mean that every trade association is now a skilled participant in the political process. Most trade associations, in fact, are still based outside Washington, an indication that these groups do not view participation in federal policy making as a primary concern. Indeed, the political endeavors of individual corporations in some cases undercuts the trade association for the industry in which the firm operates. The more effectively General Motors is represented in Washington, for instance, the less scope there is for the automobile trade association to establish itself as *the* voice of the industry.

Nor has the mobilization of business in the United States resulted in the creation of a single employers' umbrella organization to represent their collective interests. Ironically, the Business Roundtable has in some respects made matters worse, because its creation added a third organization to those aspiring to serve as business' advocate in Washington. NAM and the Chamber of Commerce, as noted earlier, did not merge. Differences in policy as well as in style are clearly visible, especially between the Roundtable and the Chamber of Commerce. American business is therefore no nearer to, and possibly further away than ever from, creating the single organization to function as the authoritative voice of business.

Indeed, the character of business politics in the mid-1980s is highly fragmented. Attitudes toward trade policy, for example, differ not only from industry to industry but from corporation to corporation. Tax reform proposals have pitted many industries that benefit disproportionately from existing tax arrangements against those that do not. In short, business interest groups in the United States are still not nearly as important in aggregating different business interests into a coherent set of policy objectives as would be the case in other industrialized countries. Business in the United States has become more politically active, but it remains organizationally split.

Why should this be so? In the first place some of the factors that have long inhibited the creation of authoritative, cohesive organizations retain their significance. In the continental-scale economy of the United States, the diversity of business remains considerable, particularly compared with a small country like Sweden, whose economy is dominated by a relative handful of companies. In the recession and recovery of the late 1970s to mid-1980s, striking differences occurred in the fortunes of American corporations. Firms engaged in basic manufacturing, the so-called smokestack industries, were especially hard hit by foreign competition. High-tech businesses fared better, and many service industries boomed. The Frost Belt, where many of the traditional manufacturing industries were located, suffered more severely from the recession than did the Sun Belt, the site of many of the newer industries.

Another factor has been the clear separation of government and industry in the United States. Even professionals working for business interest groups generally think of themselves as outside government trying to exert pressure on it. In contrast, business organizations in neocorporatist nations, such as France and Japan, tend to view themselves as partners with government. The psychological distance between Washington and the business community means that incomes policies or industrial policies, which governments can operate only with the assistance of strong interest groups, are still not used in the United States.

Strong arguments have been made in favor of the adoption of an industrial policy in the United States.[21] Whatever the merits of such arguments, they have been rejected in practice by the results of the 1980 and 1984 presidential elections. Tentative moves in the direction of an industrial policy during the Carter administration were brought to an abrupt halt by the election of Ronald Reagan. Reagan made clear his commitment to reducing the role of government in economic policy and resisted pressures for governmental intervention in support of declining industries. Advocates of an industrial policy maintain that those who reject the idea already have an industrial policy, one without intention or coordination. The sum of federal policies that protect the environment, provide lucrative defense contracts, and offer tax concessions to some industries and not others can be termed an industrial policy, even if it is not consciously created as such. Because of Reagan's lack of interest in specifically formulating such a policy, there was no need to establish more authoritative interest groups to participate in its creation and implementation. The persistence and indeed reassertion of the American belief in a limited role for government in economic policy has meant that the state has had no need for authoritative, cohesive business interest groups.

Further, the ability of the American state to force interests to coalesce into a limited number of groups in line with the pattern found in neocorporatist countries remained slight and may have declined. In neocorporatist nations, such as Austria, even large corporations are more or less required to present their views to government through the appropriate interest group. In the United States, the separation of powers, combined with the fragmentation of power within Congress and the executive branch, has always precluded any such simple system. It can be argued that representatives and senators are more attuned than ever, not to the needs of particular industries and groups, but to the interests located within their districts or states.[22] It is the perspective of the individual company, or even of the plant within the district, that attracts attention, not the view of the trade association speaking for the entire industry. Congress views trade and tax policies very much in terms of their impact on specific localities, thus preventing the consideration of industrial policy in broader terms.

One new factor did, however, have a surprisingly adverse impact on business interest groups. In the 1970s, American business, as we have seen, was impelled toward greater activity and greater unity by a perception that business was facing political challenges—especially by consumer groups and environmentalists— and was suffering severe setbacks to its collective interests. Reagan's election, and the upsurge of conservatism that his candidacy represented, demonstrated the decline of such threats. Reagan acted swiftly to weaken regulatory agencies such as OSHA, which business executives had perceived as dangerous. In addition, his appointments to key positions in these agencies were favorable to business. The decline in the political fortunes of liberal Democrats and the even sharper decline in the strength of unions encouraged many business leaders to believe that their major political problems had been solved. In particular, the very threats that had encouraged more collective political action by business receded.

It is possible, therefore, that the turn to the right in American politics will slow down the rate of increase in business political activity. Whether there will be an actual decline in the political activism of business is more problematic. In the early 1980s, when the recession was at its worst, the Reagan administration promised much to a hard-pressed business community. At that time the *Washington Post* detected signs that the increase in the number of business lobbyists in Washington had stopped and that there was even a slight decline. A more recent report in the *National Journal* argued that this development had been short-lived; the number of business lobbyists had increased again between 1981 and 1985.[23]

It is likely, however, that this rise illustrates the continuing growth in the importance of government to individual corporations. The willingness of companies to invest their money to defend the collective interests of their industry or of business in general probably peaked in the late 1970s, or, at the latest, in the tax cut policy making of 1981. Some foundations engaged in fighting the battle of ideas on behalf of business, such as the American Enterprise Institute, have had greater difficulty in raising money in the 1980s than in the 1970s. It is worth remembering that there have been other periods in American politics when organizations representing the unified voice of business seemed to have established themselves as a central element in policy making, only to fade later. During the New Deal, for example, trade associations were very important in the formation and operation of the National Recovery Administration. Fears that Franklin Roosevelt's administration was hostile to business gave a powerful boost to the National Association of Manufacturers. Yet, as we have seen, in the heyday of business in the 1950s, both the trade associations and NAM had begun to decline. Another drop in the standing of organizations that defend general business interests is a real possibility, especially (and ironically) if the conservative trend in public policy continues. At the same time, individual corporations may well remain very active.

Conclusion

American business has become much more politically active since the mid-1960s. Whether this degree of activism persists, especially in the defense of collective business interests, remains to be seen. In any event, the political endeavors of American business will remain much less neatly structured than those in many other industrialized democracies, particularly the neocorporatist nations. The boundaries between the responsibilities of trade associations, business umbrella groups, the Washington law firms, and the Washington offices of individual corporations remain unclear. When does a corporation turn to a trade association or business umbrella group for help and when does it rely on its own Washington lobbyists or a law firm? At present we are unable to predict what circumstances cause a company to choose a particular strategy. The untidiness of American business politics may or may not serve business well. It certainly leaves political scientists with much to explore.

Notes

1. Theodore Lowi, Review of *American Business and Public Policy* in *World Politics* 16 (1964): 677-715.
2. Matthew Crenson, *The Un-Politics of Air Pollution: A Study in Non-Decision Making in the Cities* (Baltimore: Johns Hopkins University Press, 1981).

3. Steven Lukes, *Power, A Radical View* (London: Macmillan, 1974).
4. Charles E. Lindblom, *Politics and Markets: The World's Politico-Economic Systems* (New York: Basic Books, 1977).
5. Raymond Bauer, Ithiel de Sola Pool, and Lewis Anthony Dexter, *American Business and Public Policy* (New York and London: Prentice-Hall International, 1964).
6. Ibid.
7. Richard Gable, "NAM: Influential Lobby or Kiss of Death?" *Journal of Politics* 15 (1953): 254-273.
8. See Gerhard Lehmbruch and Philippe Schmitter, eds. *Trends in Corporatist Policymaking* (London: Sage Publications, 1982).
9. Chalmers Johnson, *MITI and the Japanese Miracle: The Growth of Industrial Policy, 1925-75* (Stanford, Calif.: Stanford University Press, 1982).
10. John Zysman, *Governments, Markets and Growth: Financial Systems and the Politics of Industrial Change* (Ithaca and London: Cornell University Press, 1983).
11. Philippe Schmitter, "Still the Century of Corporatism?" *Review of Politics* 36 (January 1974): 85-131.
12. "Opinion Roundup," *Public Opinion* (April-May 1980): 21-31.
13. Richard R. Lau and David O. Sears, "Cognitive Links between Economic Grievances and Political Responses," *Political Behavior* 3 (1981): 279-302.
14. Wyn Grant and David Marsh, *The Confederation of British Industry* (London: Hodder & Stoughton, 1977).
15. David Truman, *The Governmental Process* (New York: Alfred A. Knopf, 1951).
16. "Opinion Roundup."
17. David Vogel, "Why Businessmen Distrust Their State: The Political Consciousness of American Corporate Executives," *British Journal of Political Science* 8 (January 1977).
18. For further details see Graham K. Wilson, *Interest Groups in the United States* (Oxford and New York: Oxford University Press, 1981); and David Vogel, "The Power of Business in America: A Re-Appraisal," *British Journal of Political Science* 13 (January 1983): 45-78.
19. See Larry Sabato, *PAC Power: Inside the World of Political Action Committees* (New York and London: W. W. Norton, 1984).
20. Kay Lehman Schlozman and John T. Tierney, *Organized Interests in Washington* (New York: Harper & Row, 1986).
21. For a convenient summary of the arguments, see *The Industrial Political Debate*, ed. Chalmers Johnson (San Francisco: Institute for Contemporary Studies, 1984).
22. "The Influence Industry," *National Journal*, Sept. 14, 1985.
23. Ibid.

13. One Nation, Many Voices: Interest Groups in Foreign Policy Making

Eric M. Uslaner

Although foreign interests historically have enjoyed representation within the American political process, this side of interest group politics has received an especially generous amount of attention in the 1980s. Trade, oil, and currency policies have demonstrated the extent of U.S. dependence on world economic conditions. In addition, many top-level Washington lobbyists have obtained large contracts to represent foreign interests (see Chapter 14). This trend is unlikely to end in the near future. The impact of American policy making on the rest of the world, coupled with the complexity of many major issues (for example, acid rain), will lead foreign interests, both governmental and private, to obtain professional representation on those policy matters of the greatest importance.

In this chapter Eric Uslaner discusses the general roles played by foreign interests within American politics as well as examining in detail the impact of the Israeli and Arab lobbies. Uslaner emphasizes the numerous ways in which foreign interests can intervene in domestic politics and policy making. Especially significant are the electoral possibilities afforded to sophisticated, affluent, and relatively numerous constituencies such as the Jewish and Greek communities. In the end, foreign interests often can have an impact for many of the same reasons that work to the advantage of domestic lobbies. Resources, constituency efforts, and political sophistication pay off over time.

When we think of foreign policy issues, we usually conjure up pictures of international crises. We remember the hostage incidents in Lebanon and Iran, the conflicts in El Salvador and Nicaragua, and the threat that other locales (including South Africa) might ultimately be the site of superpower confrontations. We recall the wars in Vietnam and Korea and the two great world wars. For most of us, this is the stuff of foreign policy.

In these crisis situations, we think of foreign policy in very different terms from domestic policy. The stakes are much higher. The entire world could be destroyed by nuclear weapons as a result of a decision that might take only minutes to make. Second, and obvious, is that foreign policy decisions are often irreversible. Even when decision making does not involve the threat of nuclear war, foreign policy choices generally produce effects that last for years, if not decades. A major crisis will set the tone for relations between nations, which then are not readily changed. In contrast, domestic policies that are found to be unpopular or simply do not work can be changed much more easily. If an administration proposes a policy to put more people to work and inflation rises dramatically, it can change the course and pursue a strategy that will slow down the pace of the economy.

In addition, relations with foreign nations are not entirely within the control of American policy makers. Once a decision was made in 1949 not to recognize the Communist regime in China, both domestic pressures and the attitude of the Chinese government precluded the establishment of ties for more than three decades.

Moreover, foreign policy decisions, particularly in crises, need to be made quickly. During the Cuban missile crisis in 1962, President John Kennedy had to set national policy in just a few weeks as the threat of a nuclear confrontation with the Soviet Union loomed over the world. Domestic issues rarely get resolved so rapidly; government provision of medical care to the elderly remained just an interesting proposal on the legislative agenda for more than half a century.[1]

The need for quick action on high-stakes issues that cannot be readily reversed means that at least crisis decisions on foreign policy must be centralized. It is the president who dominates foreign policy making. This is so for three reasons. First, there simply is not time for bargaining among affected groups. Second, expertise on foreign policy is much more centralized than on domestic policy, which limits the capacity of outsiders to claim credibility for their arguments. This is emphatically not the case on domestic policy, where even motion picture stars such as Jane Fonda and Jessica Lange testify before Congress about the problems of family farmers. Third, foreign policy issues take on a we-versus-them cast. The goals of all Americans are posited to be the same: at the very least, the survival of a democratic way of life against a hostile power that is not committed to individual freedoms. If the nation does not speak with a single voice, our adversaries might think that we lack the resolve to defend ourselves.

Foreign policy issues are of less concern to most Americans than domestic policy. Even on a war and peace issue such as the conflict in El Salvador, only a quarter of Americans in 1983 could correctly identify which side the United States was supporting, and just 13 percent knew that the United States backed the insurgents in Nicaragua.[2] Citizens find events in the international arena far more remote than domestic affairs. Many members of Congress thus seek to highlight their role in domestic policy and to play down any interest they have in foreign policy. One member of the Senate Foreign Relations Committee said of his assignment:

> It's a political liability.... You have no constituency. In my reelection campaign last fall, the main thing they used against me was that because of my interest in foreign relations, I was more interested in what happened to

the people of Abyssinia and Afghanistan than in what happened to the good people of my state.[3]

As if to bear this out, the two most recent Foreign Relations Committee chairmen, Frank Church, D-Idaho, and Charles Percy, R-Ill., lost their reelection bids after assuming the leadership post.

Most Americans are content to let the president make foreign policy and give virtually unchallenged support to the chief executive as long as crises do not appear to get out of hand. Presidential popularity jumps sharply in an international crisis. The public remains supportive if there is evidence that the president is taking firm action to bring the crisis to a quick resolution so that the nation can get on with its important domestic business. If a crisis drags on and begins to be felt at home, as when war casualties increased during the Korean and Vietnam conflicts,[4] or when the Iranian hostage crisis lingered on for more than a year,[5] the public gets restless and support for the president plummets. These events are unusual, however; the public generally supports the president in the international arena.

Congress also generally follows the president's lead, rarely overturning presidential initiatives in foreign policy. Partisan divisions do not disrupt international affairs the same way they affect most domestic issues.[6] Political leaders often are reluctant to appear to be leading U.S. adversaries to believe that the country is divided internally on key foreign policy issues. Because most citizens do not follow international affairs and because crises usually increase public support for the incumbent president, few political rewards can be reaped by challenging foreign policy initiatives. Traditionally, then, foreign policy has been marked by bipartisanship.

In this context, the capacity for interest groups to affect foreign policy is very limited. If there is a need for the nation to speak with a single voice, the bargaining among interest groups that is the hallmark of domestic politics seems very much out of place in the international arena. The conflict is posited as being between "them" (adversaries, generally the Soviet Union) and "us" (the West) rather than among contending groups in the United States. Many Americans conjure up a diabolical picture of how private interests affect international politics for their own advantage, putting any idea of a "national interest" distinctly to the background. If the nation is to speak with a single voice, many Americans feel that interest groups must not be permitted to seek out allies abroad in the hope of influencing foreign policy.

Interest Groups and Foreign Policy

The preceding discussion might lead one to suspect that there are no key interest groups on foreign policy questions. This is not so. The above scenario is not so much wrong as incomplete. Foreign policy involves much more than crises, and the nature of foreign policy decision making has changed dramatically over the past two decades. Consider three reasons why foreign policy might afford interest groups considerable opportunity to attempt to influence governmental decisions.

First, many foreign policy issues involve clear-cut economic stakes for Americans. Trade policies are perhaps the best example. Most analyses of trade politics find that interest groups are very active, although industries seeking protection have been largely unsuccessful in fighting presidents' commitments to low tariffs.[7] Often, however, administrations have had to compromise with unions and industries seeking limits on some foreign goods. President Ronald Reagan ultimately agreed to a quota on Japanese cars for an extended period after being pressured by American auto makers and automobile unions. Imported products often sell for considerably less than their American competitors and thus threaten jobs in the United States. A foreign policy issue thereby becomes a domestic politics concern.

Second, the world has become increasingly interdependent in the past half century. No longer can we say that certain policies are clearly domestic and others in the realm of foreign policy. Rather, most policies are now "intermestic."[8] The dramatic increase in oil prices in 1973-1974 (and again in 1979) radically changed our perception of energy policy. Before 1973, energy decisions were made strictly according to the domestic politics of specific fuels.[9] Thereafter our attention shifted to the producing nations. As the export market became more important to farmers, competition from abroad and broader foreign policy concerns entered this arena as well. When President Jimmy Carter forbade grain sales to the Soviet Union following that nation's invasion of Afghanistan in 1979, he met widespread criticism in the Midwest. Reagan made the embargo a key issue in his 1980 quest for the presidency and in 1981 announced the termination of these sanctions, even as he continued to criticize Carter for not being tough enough on the Soviets.

Americans traditionally have thought of banks as neighborhood bulwarks that were more worthy of confidence than even our governmental institutions.[10] In the 1980s, however, many banks faced severe financial problems because of loans to developing nations. One large bank, Continental Illinois, was forced into federal receivership. The worries over Third World debt helped to drive up domestic interest rates, making home mortgages more difficult to obtain and adversely affecting the domestic housing industry. The growing interdependence of the world economy has led new actors, including, of course, interest groups, to participate in foreign policy decision making.

Third, the Vietnam War changed the way Americans react to foreign policy. Protests against the war were widespread, particularly on college campuses. Support of the president's policies was no longer automatic. Various ideological interest groups sprang up to challenge some of the key assumptions behind our involvement in the war. To be sure, organizations such as the Committee for a Sane Nuclear Policy (SANE) on the Left and the Committee of One Million (pro-Taiwan) on the Right had long been active in attempting to influence foreign policy. However, their impact was minimal because they were proposing policies considerably at variance from those the government was pursuing and because their bases of support were not widespread.[11] Conversely, opposition to the war in Vietnam grew as the conflict dragged on. Crossing so many different segments of American society, opposition quickly became legitimized. Until Richard Nixon assumed the White House, however, both support for and opposition to the war crossed party lines. When the war became associated with a Republican president, many congressional Democrats felt free to make the conflict a partisan issue. The post-World War II era of bipartisanship in foreign policy had come to an end.

As parties were free to criticize each other on international affairs, so too did interest groups multiply. Church groups, which played an important role in war protest, branched out into concerns for nuclear disarmament, the conflicts in El Salvador and Nicaragua (some churches gave sanctuary to refugees from these countries), and the ending of apartheid in South Africa. Secular organizations formed for each of these policy areas as well, most prominently the nuclear freeze. Groups advocating a more aggressive foreign policy toward the Soviet Union also formed.

Since the Vietnam War, foreign policy has been marked by increasingly bitter and partisan wrangling in Congress. Many moral issues of government involvement in the international arena have divided the parties and interest groups according to the traditional Left-Right ideological split. Issues such as energy and agriculture, on the other hand, reflect constituency interests more than partisan or ideological considerations.[12] What is critical is that interest group participation on foreign policy has become legitimized. Americans no longer automatically accept the existence of a single correct foreign policy that commands bipartisan support. There continues to be a commitment to the Western alliance standing against the Soviet bloc, but the public seems considerably more reticent about using military force to defend other American allies (such as Israel, South Korea, Saudi Arabia, and even Japan) or even to ensure an adequate supply of oil for the United States.[13]

The growth of the role of interest groups in foreign policy parallels the sharp rise in the number of such organizations in domestic policy.[14] One indicator of how important interest groups have become in American society is the number of informal organizations that have formed in the Congress. In 1984 almost one hundred such groups were active, and about a dozen of them were concerned primarily with foreign policy issues.[15] Foreign policy making often appears more like a Tower of Babel than a clear voice telling friends and adversaries alike where the United States stands. Even in Congress, for every group advocating one side of an issue there is at least one other pursuing an alternative course. The Members of Congress for Peace Through Law, founded during the Vietnam era to seek an end to the conflict by legislative means, begat the defense-oriented Members of Congress for Peace Through Strength. The Ad Hoc Congressional Committee on Irish Affairs, chaired by Italian-American representative Mario Biaggi, D-N.Y., presses, through its 110 not-all-Irish members, for an American policy toward Northern Ireland that would be more favorable to the Catholic population; the 80-member Friends of Ireland advocates a more conciliatory approach.[16] The prominence of these caucuses indicates that foreign policy formation in the United States is becoming increasingly similar to the politics of domestic policy.

Ethnic groups have long been active on foreign policy issues. First, the United States is a nation of immigrants. Many citizens maintain strong affective bonds with the country of their heritage and thus have an interest in American relations with other nations. Indeed, many people have relatives abroad. Second, the nature of democratic politics in the U.S. system of government means that Congress plays an important role in checking executive decisions on foreign as well as domestic policy.[17] Because the legislative branch has been more hospitable to interest groups than the executive, ethnic groups focus on Congress. Many legislators come from the same ethnic background as the largest bloc of their constituents and are similarly concerned with American policy toward the "old country." Thus, these interest groups have a ready forum in Washington.

Ethnic Groups in Foreign Policy

How do Americans view interest groups that openly campaign for more favored treatment for other nations? Here I refer to "ethnic lobbies." These are interest groups organized largely on the basis of ethnic identification of members, pressing Congress and the White House for policies favorable to the "homeland" of the hyphenated Americans in question. In the remainder of this essay, I shall consider such groups. What do they seek, how do they go about organizing support in Congress and the executive branch, and how successful are they? First, I consider some ethnic interests active on foreign policy: Greeks, Turks, Eastern Europeans, Hispanics, and blacks. Next, I examine a group that is universally recognized as the most effective of all the ethnic lobbies: the "Jewish," or more accurately, the Israeli lobby, and its antagonist, representing the Arab cause. Finally, I consider a new element in ethnic lobbying that makes the linkage with domestic policy complete: the level of support for a foreign nation as an electoral litmus test. Does campaigning for or against a candidate on the basis of a single issue, particularly a single foreign policy issue tied to a foreign country, raise issues of divided loyalty? Some Americans, including very influential politicians, seem to believe that it does.

Major Ethnic Actors

Because of the importance of the Middle East to American foreign policy, the Israeli and Arab lobbies receive most of the attention in the American press. Many other ethnic groups also organize to influence foreign policy, although far less is known about these interests, largely because they are not nearly so active or as public in their activities.

The ethnic lobby generally considered to be second in effectiveness to the Israeli groups is that of Greek-Americans.[18] The lobby strives to pressure the United States to maintain a balance in foreign aid received by Greece and Turkey, both members of the North Atlantic Treaty Organization (NATO) but traditional rivals. Following Turkey's invasion of Cyprus in 1974, which led to a partition of Cyprus into Greek and Turkish communities and massive population dislocation, the Greek lobby successfully argued for an embargo on arms sales to Turkey. The embargo was repealed in 1978, when the Carter administration argued that Turkey was an important military site for the Western alliance. The administration also believed that action on ending the embargo was critical to convincing the Turkish government to slow the illegal export of drugs to the United States.

The administration's spokesman in the House of Representatives was Stephen Solarz, D-N.Y. Solarz's role was important because he is Jewish and a leading figure among pro-Israel members of Congress. Traditionally, the Greek lobby has worked closely with the Israeli lobby. The American Hellenic Institute Public Affairs Committee (AHIPAC), founded in the 1970s, was consciously modeled after the American Israel Public Affairs Committee (AIPAC). Furthermore, the Greek-American community, like American Jews, is clustered in large cities in the northeastern United States and has a strong tradition of electoral loyalty to the Democratic party. The Greek-Americans, however, are not as affluent or as numerous as the Jews, with a population that is variously estimated from 600,000 to three million. Thus, it has had to depend upon shrewd lobbying efforts and alliances with more potent groups.[19] Prominent Greek-Americans in Congress, including former majority whip of the House, John Brademas, D-Ind., and Sen. Paul Sarbanes, D-Md., helped espouse the cause. Nevertheless, when a lobby confronts a determined administration, as the Greek lobby did on repeal of the embargo in 1978 and as the Israeli lobby did on Arab military sales in 1978 and 1981, the president is likely to prevail.

Cracks in the Greek-Jewish alliance began to show in the 1970s as many supporters of Israel recognized the need to support administration initiatives on other aspects of foreign policy. Following the Yom Kippur War in 1973, the warm relations between Greece and Israel turned much cooler, reaching almost a freezing point in 1981 with the election of a strongly pro-Arab Socialist government in Greece. The Greek lobby's difficulties were compounded by the anti-American rhetoric of Premier Andreas Papandreou. The restoration of democracy in Turkey in 1983 further complicated the Greek-Americans' task. The strategic importance of Greece to the military alliance and the failure of Turkey to resolve the Cyprus issue helped to maintain support in Congress for giving Greece its traditional allocation of $7 in foreign aid for every $10 Turkey receives.

The Greeks maintain a much larger Washington presence than the Turks. There are only 200,000 Turkish-Americans, and they have no major ethnic lobbying group. The Turkish government plays an active role in pressing its cause, but it is not regarded as particularly effective; instead, it has benefited from the interest of the American Legion and the Veterans of Foreign Wars, who are concerned about the Turkish link to NATO.[20] The Turks, aside from constituting a small portion of the American population, are not as clearly associated in the national consciousness as being a significant force in either the United States or in NATO.

The Eastern Europeans have a congressional caucus and a long history of political activism. The bicameral Ad Hoc Congressional Committee on the Baltic States and the Ukraine has seventy-five members. There is no opposition lobby because the Eastern Europeans seek support for restoring democracy to the nations now dominated by the Soviet Union. A large number of ethnic lobbies focus on this issue, including the Polish National Alliance, the Albanian Federation of America, the Bulgarian National Front, and the National Committee for the Liberation of Slovakia. The Assembly of Captive European Nations, founded in 1954, is the umbrella organization. It seeks independence from Soviet influence for Albania, Bulgaria, Czechoslovakia, Hungary, Poland, Romania, and the Soviet republics of Estonia, Latvia, and Lithuania. In 1959, at the organization's urging, Congress enacted a law denoting the third week of July as Captive Nations Week, to be observed until these nations are liberated.

There are large numbers of Americans of Eastern European background. The Polish-American population alone is estimated to be between five million and seven million. Several midwestern states have large concentrations of Eastern Europeans, and both major political parties have recognized the importance of these groups by establishing divisions dealing with their affairs. Yet, these ethnic groups have had little impact on foreign policy. First, they are not united among themselves on precisely what they want Washington to do. Second, they have failed to convince administrations that Americans of Eastern European origin are preoccupied by the existence of Communist regimes in their native lands. In this sense, they have failed precisely where American Jews have succeeded: no American president needs to be convinced of the centrality of a homeland in Israel to American Jews. Third, many Americans of Eastern European ancestry believe that emphasizing their background would only stir the negative sentiments that many met when they emigrated here. Fourth, and most important, pursuing a tougher line on Eastern Europe would mean that the United States would have to sacrifice détente with the Soviet Union, a position that no American administration is willing to adopt. Captive Nations Week gathers many testimonials from members of Congress looking for political gain among their constituents of Eastern European background, but it leads to little direct action. Indeed, some observers argue that the strident anticommunism of these ethnic lobbies has become a political embarrassment for the United States.[21]

Opposition to a Communist government in their native land forms the basis for the foreign policy concerns of Cuban-Americans as well. Although many Cuban-Americans have played active roles in politics, particularly within the Republican party, they have not coordinated their activity with other Hispanics. Overall, Hispanic Americans number between fifteen million and twenty-three million or between 6 and 10 percent of all Americans. However, there is little unity among them. The largest group is the Chicanos, or Mexican-Americans, comprising 60 percent of all Hispanic Americans. They are most numerous in California and Texas. The second largest group is Puerto Ricans, who constitute 14 percent of all Hispanics and are concentrated in New York and New Jersey. Cubans are 6 percent of the Hispanics, and a majority of them live in Florida.[22]

This diversity of land of origin underlies a similar variety of political perspectives. Not all Chicanos have citizenship, so political action is precluded for many of them. Those who are citizens tend to be poorer than most other Americans, and most identify with the Democratic party. Their lower economic status means that they participate less in politics. When they do organize for political action, they are far more likely to be concerned with the more pressing economic issues of the moment than with foreign policy issues. Chicanos often have ambivalent feelings toward Mexico. Mexican governments have been more preoccupied with the welfare of their own citizens residing in the United States than with the affairs of Chicanos. Furthermore, some Chicanos fear that identifying too strongly with the motherland would stir up racial/ethnic antagonisms in the United States.

Puerto Rican groups are divided over the status of that island, which is a commonwealth of the United States. Some favor independence, others statehood, and still others the continuation of the present status. A 1985 meeting of the National Congress for Puerto Rican Rights could not reach a resolution over the issue of coordinating strategies with other Hispanic groups. Some Puerto Ricans resent other Hispanics because on average Puerto Ricans earn less although they have had American citizenship longer.[23] There is little talk by either Chicanos or Puerto Ricans of coordinating political activities with Cuban-Americans. The latter are much better off financially, and opposition to Fidel Castro's rule in Cuba forms the basis of most of their foreign policy concerns.

Hispanic groups thus do not play a key role on foreign policy. More important than their lack of unity is the lower economic status of Chicanos and Puerto Ricans, which limits their concern for foreign policy issues. The more affluent Cuban-Americans are handicapped by the same problem that plagues people of Eastern European extraction: the policies favored by Cuban-Americans—direct confrontation with Castro, for example—are regarded as too extreme by the American government. Equally important is the fact that issues relating to Mexico, Puerto Rico, or Cuba are not terribly salient to most Americans, in contrast to our role in the Middle East.

For countries such as El Salvador and Nicaragua where American policy is more controversial, foreign policy lobbies are dominated by religious organizations, such as the Washington Office on Latin America, with few ties to the indigenous communities. These organizations largely focus on human rights issues. Some have influence on Capitol Hill, but their lobbying activities tend to concentrate more on legislators who are already committed to their cause.[24] Altogether more than a half a dozen organizations operate on the Left, and one, the American Institute for Free Labor Development, on the Center-Right. The latter is funded by the United States Agency for International Development, is affiliated with organized labor, and seeks to counterbalance the human rights movement. These groups had only limited successes.

Blacks, like Hispanics, traditionally have been more concerned with domestic economic issues than with foreign policy concerns. Unlike some other groups, blacks' ties to a "home country" are weaker. First, blacks have been in the United States longer than most other ethnic groups active in foreign policy. Second, during slavery, black culture was deprecated. Third, most American blacks cannot trace their roots to a specific country. Given the diversity of the continent, even of black Africa, focused political action is more difficult. Instead, many blacks have concentrated on trying to persuade the government to impose sanctions on South Africa for its policies of racial separation, but until recently U.S. blacks have met with frustration more than anything else.

Blacks vote overwhelmingly for the Democratic party, and black leaders inside and outside Congress had problems dealing with the Republican administrations of Richard Nixon and Gerald Ford. Blacks in Congress resorted to trying to block administration appointments to executive branch positions and to filing lawsuits to curtail relations with South Africa.[25] The Carter administration was more willing to give financial aid to many African nations, but remained reluctant to impose sanctions on South Africa. The United States is dependent upon South Africa for key minerals used in defense. In 1984, however, protests against apartheid became widespread in the United States as racial violence escalated in South Africa. The impetus for the demonstrations came from the Congressional Black Caucus and TransAfrica, an ethnic lobbying organization with a budget of $325,000 in 1982 and a membership of ten thousand.[26]

Support from religious groups played a key role in the anti-South Africa demonstrations, as did support from leading black and white politicians and entertainers. In 1985, facing congressional pressures, the president imposed limited sanctions. Critical to the success of this drive was the force of public opinion: both blacks and whites had sharply negative attitudes toward South Africa and its racial policies, and the differences in public opinion by race were negligible.[27] Both blacks and whites opposed supporting any organization that advocated violence to change South Africa's policies, and both races expressed opposition to an American role if that meant either increasing violence or enhancing the prospect of a Communist role. The strong tide of opinion against the policies of the South African government broadened the scope of concern from a small ethnic lobby to key legislative leaders of both political parties. Even many of the most conservative Republicans in the Congress joined the call for sanctions.

The sudden thrust of the black ethnic lobby into foreign policy prominence indicates just how important the role of public opinion is to any group attempting to influence international affairs. Like the Israeli lobby, TransAfrica succeeded by mobilizing first its own ethnic community and then seeking and obtaining support from a wide range of actors in both political parties. Second, the foreign policy cause was made a moral issue. Just as Israel is to be supported because it is a democracy, South Africa is to be condemned because it purports to be one, but fails to make that claim believable.

The Israeli and Arab Lobbies

The best-organized, best-funded, and most successful of the ethnic lobbies, indeed perhaps of all foreign policy lobbies, is that representing the interests of Israel.[28] Jews, who form the bulk of the pro-Israel lobby, comprise 2.7 percent of the American population. However, as we shall see, they are strongly motivated in support of Israel's cause and are highly organized in the cause. They seek to provide U.S. financial aid (both economic and military) to Israel and to deny it to those Arab nations in a state of war with Israel. And they have been very successful indeed: the lobby, since its inception in 1951, is believed to have lost on only three key decisions. In 1978 it failed to prevent the sale of F-15 fighter planes to Saudi Arabia and Egypt, and in 1981 and 1986 it could not block arms sales to the Saudis.[29]

The primary goal of the lobby is financial aid to Israel. From 1948 to 1983, American aid to Israel totaled almost $27 billion in grants and loans. As of 1985, all of the assistance has taken the form of direct grants, which reach a figure of $7.1 billion for 1986 and 1987.[30] Israel receives by far the largest amount of foreign aid from the United States. Only Egypt even approaches the Israeli aid figure, and this is a relatively recent development. Following the 1979 Camp David peace treaty between the two nations, Egypt's aid dramatically increased, almost to parity with that for Israel. However, the financial crisis in Israel in 1985 led to additional emergency assistance from the United States.

Israel has also benefited from other provisions in American laws that provide it with unique forms of aid. In 1985 the two countries signed a free-trade pact that will completely eliminate all tariff barriers between them by 1995. The United States also has agreed to permit Israel to use a portion of the military credits it receives in foreign aid to finance the construction of the Lavi fighter plane, instead of having to purchase American military equipment. Furthermore, Israel annually benefits from large tax-exempt contributions from the American Jewish community, including some $500 million in direct charitable grants and a similar amount from the sale of Israel government bonds.[31] No other foreign nation is so favored.

The Israeli lobby is comprised of one organization devoted entirely to the cause of that country and of a wide-ranging network of Jewish groups that provide support. AIPAC, founded in 1951, has a staff of eighty and operates out of offices one block away from Capitol Hill as well as in other major cities.[32] Most employees are support staff, but the small group of lobbyists is regarded as among the most astute on Capitol Hill. AIPAC stresses that it is an American group and that it keeps its distance from the Israeli Embassy. The organization has an annual budget of $5 million, raised entirely from non-tax-deductible contributions and dues from its fifty-one thousand members. Sitting on the AIPAC board are the leaders of the largest Jewish organizations in the nation.

AIPAC concentrates its efforts on Congress. The White House and the State Department are the focus of the Conference of Presidents of Major Jewish Organizations, a coordinating body of forty Jewish groups throughout the nation. The conference does not lobby because most of its members are tax-exempt charitable organizations. It disseminates information and maintains a high profile. The American Jewish Congress and the American Jewish Committee, each with memberships of approximately fifty thousand, focus on religious matters and civil liberties issues, but also are concerned with Israel, as is the largest Jewish fraternal organization, the half-million-member B'nai B'rith.

The success of the Israeli lobby has been attributed to its political acumen. Sanford Ungar stated:

> In a moment of perceived crisis, it can put a carefully researched, well-documented statement of its views on the desk of every Senator and Congressman and appropriate committee staff within four hours of a decision to do so.[33]

AIPAC's current director, Thomas Dine, is a former Senate staff aide who specialized on military issues, thus giving him instant credibility when he argues either for arms sales to Israel or against them to Arab countries. The organization's close ties to many congressional staffers keep it well informed about issues affecting Israel on Capitol Hill. Its lobbying connections are so thorough that one observer maintained, "A mystique has grown up around the lobby to the point where it is viewed with admiration, envy, and sometimes, anger." [34] Not only is the Washington organization a master of legislative strategy, but also the network of Jewish organizations across the country is easily mobilized to put pro-Israel pressure on members of Congress in their constituencies. Furthermore, even though liberals (and Democrats) tend to be somewhat more sympathetic to Israel than conservatives (and Republicans),[35] the lobbyists are careful to maintain bipartisan support.

In contrast, the Arab lobbying effort has been singularly unsuccessful. There were no major Arab organizations operating at all before 1972, and a Washington presence did not begin until 1978.[36] The largest Arab group, the National Association of Arab Americans (NAAA) claims eighty thousand members, although even many Arab Americans regard this figure as highly inflated. NAAA seeks closer ties between the United States and the Arab world in political, military, and economic arenas. It also argues for a weakening of the United States-Israel bond and the creation of a Palestinian homeland. It always has, however, recognized the right of Israel to exist. The organization follows the AIPAC strategy of publishing research reports and issuing press releases, but its publication arm is considerably more far-reaching, including a business survey, a monthly journal, a biweekly commentary, and a quarterly newsletter. NAAA also conducts international trade seminars and arranges cultural exhibits; its focus is as much oriented to public relations as to influencing legislation. NAAA directly models itself on AIPAC, but with an estimated 1981 budget of $500,000, it commands far fewer resources. Unlike AIPAC, it makes no pretense of being free from "mother country" direct influence. For example, advertisers in the business survey are primarily Arab governments, the Palestine Liberation Organization (PLO), and firms doing business in the Persian Gulf.

The second major Arab organization is the American-Arab Anti-Discrimination Committee. Founded in 1980, it does not lobby on behalf of legislation, but focuses on battling the negative stereotypes of Arabs in the media and in government. The triggering mechanism for establishing the committee was the Abscam incident, in which FBI agents, dressed as Arab sheiks, sought to bribe members of Congress in exchange for immigration-related favors. The Anti-Discrimination Committee, like NAAA, is modeled directly on a Jewish organization, the Anti-Defamation League of B'nai B'rith, founded some fifty years ago to combat discrimination against Jewish Americans. While the committee does not lobby, it has some potential clout because its head is former senator James Abourezk, D-S.D. The organization seeks to mobilize not only Arab Americans, but also groups believed to be sympathetic to the Arab cause, including blacks and liberal churches. Another recently established organization is the Center for United States-European-Middle East Cooperation, founded by former NAAA lobbyist John Richardson. The center emphasizes the introduction of American decision makers to Europeans who are sympathetic to the Arab cause. Most of the other Arab groups are smaller and focus on education or refugee problems in the Middle East: Amideast, Americans for Middle East Understanding, Americans for Near East Refugee Aid, American Educational Trust, and the American-Arab Affairs Council. The Palestinian Human Rights Campaign and the Palestinian Solidarity Committee are among the more politically active, although they tend to concentrate more on demonstrations than on mainstream political tactics.

The heart of the difficulty of Arab-American lobbying efforts is found in the existence of another group, the American Lebanese League, which claims ten thousand members and seeks a democratic and pro-Western Lebanon. The group's leader commented, "How in the hell can NAAA have a constituency among the Lebanese when they support Syria, which is shelling Lebanese villages, and Saudi Arabia and Kuwait, which fund the Palestine Liberation Organization?" [37] The American Lebanese League represents Christian forces in Lebanon, which have little in common with the Muslims and Druze of that country. Even a past president of NAAA admits the central hindrance to Arab lobbying in the United States:

> We can't represent the Arabs the way the Jewish lobby can represent Israel. The Israeli government has one policy to state, whereas we couldn't represent "the Arabs" even if we wanted to. They're as different as the Libyans and the Saudis are different, or as divided as the Christian and Moslem Lebanese.[38]

Inter-Arab divisiveness thus accounts for some, but not all, of the difficulties that these lobbying organizations confront.

Public opinion plays a much larger role. Americans have for a long time taken a much more sympathetic view toward Israel than toward the Arabs. Most polls show that Americans favor the Israeli position by better than a 3-1 margin. Occasionally, as during the Israeli invasion of Lebanon or the 1985 TWA hostage crisis, public support for Israel drops sharply, but it has always rebounded. Sympathies with the Arab cause rise slightly in each case, but not enough to make a significant dent in the level of support for Israel.[39] The roots of the friendship between the two nations include factors such as: (1) a common biblical heritage (most Arabs are Muslim, an unfamiliar religion to most Americans); (2) a shared European value system (most Arabs take their values from Islam, which is often sharply critical of the moral tenor of the West); (3) the democratic nature of Israel's political system (most Arab nations are monarchies or dictatorships); (4) Israel's role as an ally of the United States (most Arab countries are seen as either unreliable friends or within the Soviet sphere of influence); and (5) the sympathy Americans extend toward Jews as victims (Arabs are portrayed as terrorists or exploiters of the American economy through their oil weapon).[40] The close connection of Arab lobbying efforts to the Middle East does not help to overcome such difficulties.

The smaller Arab-American population, some two million to three million in numbers compared with almost six million Jews, further limits the political clout of Arab Americans. Even more critical, however, is the much greater political mobilization of American Jews, particularly in support of Israel. Jews have a very high rate of participation in politics, Arab Americans a rather low rate. Futhermore, Arab Americans are more fully assimilated into American life and do not as readily identify with the Arab cause as American Jews do with Israel. Some Arab Americans own businesses with many Jewish customers and fear becoming too politically active lest they lose income.[41] There are also divisions between older, native-born Arab Americans and more recent immigrants. The latter, including many Palestinian refugees who emigrated in 1948, view the American government as an enemy of Arab interests and prefer confrontational tactics rather than public relations efforts and lobbying.[42]

While Arab groups are divided among themselves and have no common frame of reference, American Jews are united behind support of Israel. A 1982 survey of American Jews showed that 94 percent considered themselves either pro-Israel or very pro-Israel. Two-thirds often discuss Israel with friends and, by a 3-1 margin, reject the notion that support for Israel conflicts with one's attachment to the United States. Three-quarters of American Jews argue that they should not vote for a candidate who is unfriendly to Israel, and a third would be willing to contribute money to political candidates who support Israel.[43]

The Washington presence of the two lobbies also offers a striking contrast. AIPAC is regarded as extremely professional with close ties to legislators of both parties on Capitol Hill. On the other hand, the Arab lobbies are regarded as much more amateurish and too dependent on "hired guns," who are paid large retainers to push the Arab cause. Prominent public figures who have lobbied on behalf of the Arabs include former vice president Spiro Agnew, former secretary of state Edmund Muskie, former budget director Bert Lance, former attorney general Richard Kleindeinst, former Treasury secretaries John Connally and William Simon, and former senator J. William Fulbright.[44] Arab groups have found that this approach does not enhance coalition building in Congress. The major oil companies, which are among the largest American investors in the Middle East, have shied away from open alliance with the Arab cause most of the time because they fear the public impact of such a tactic.

On the other hand, in 1985 Jewish leaders formed an unlikely alliance with independent oil producers to work for the preservation of small petroleum companies' tax breaks in return for fund raising and exhortatory support for Israel. The common bond of the two groups was the reduction of American dependence on imported (Arab) oil. Organized labor, which has long applauded the central role of the labor movement in Israeli society and the nation's strong anticommunist position, has been a long-term ally of the Israeli lobby.[45] There is also resentment in Washington concerning overt displays of Arab money: Middle Eastern governments have endowed professorships and academic centers at several prestigious institutions, such as Harvard, Georgetown, Stanford, and the University of Southern California, leading to the impression that they were trying to purchase a more favorable image. NAAA also has modified its tactics to block assistance to Israel because many radio stations refused to air the organization's advertisements.[46]

In Washington, the Jewish presence is much more visible than that of Arab Americans. There are four times as many Jewish as Arab-American senators and ten times as many Jewish members of the House. Furthermore, the Arab Americans in Congress do not identify with their cause and do not caucus on Middle Eastern issues.[47] Indeed, both Arab-American senators (George Mitchell, a Maine Democrat, and James Abdnor, a South Dakota Republican) joined seventy-two other senators in sponsoring a resolution in 1985 opposing U.S. arms sales to Jordan until that nation began peace talks with Israel. In contrast, Jewish members of Congress seek out committee assignments that focus on the Middle East: in 1984, 25 percent of the members of the House Foreign Affairs Committee and 30 percent of that body's subcommittee on the Middle East were Jewish.[48]

Arab Americans did become more active in 1984, supporting the Reverend Jesse Jackson's quest for the Democratic presidential nomination. Jackson argued for a Palestinian homeland and included as one of his campaign vice chairmen a former director of NAAA. Arab Americans raised $300,000 for the Jackson campaign, a small figure compared with Jewish fund raising (see below) and one made less credible by the admission by the candidate that he had made anti-Semitic remarks.[49]

The greater success of the Israeli lobby thus can be traced to: (1) consistent American public opinion favoring Israel over the Arab nations; (2) the commitment of the American Jewish community to Israel and the resolve to take action on those goals, compared to the splintering of Arab-American opinion; (3) the capacity of the Israeli lobby to distance itself from the Israeli government compared with the inability (or unwillingness) of NAAA to do the same; and (4) the far greater sophistication of AIPAC in the ways of Washington compared with the Arab lobbies.

Organizational strength is important, but the underlying basis of the Israeli lobby's success is the force of public opinion. Members of Congress appreciate receiving the detailed research reports AIPAC provides, which gives them ammunition to challenge any administration attempt to be less favorable to Israel;[50] this information resource would be useless if public opinion were tilted toward the Arabs. As Bernard Cohen has argued, any foreign policy lobby will face formidable odds when its goals conflict with the official administration policy and the weight of popular sentiment.[51] This, then, is the predicament of the Arab lobby. Israel's supporters start with a decided advantage that would require an enormous effort to overcome.

The key elements in interest group success on foreign policy, then, appear to be public opinion and the established direction of American policy. However, even with the weight of public opinion and the administration on one's side, only victory on current issues can be assured. One way of making sure the longer-term success can be achieved is to affect the membership of the Congress itself. The Israeli lobby has pursued this strategy vigorously in recent years. I now move to a consideration of this tactic.

The Electoral Connection in Foreign Policy

Most lobbyists concentrate on legislation in Washington, but tactics have been shifting increasingly toward the electoral arena. Interest groups use political action committees to channel contributions to candidates for Congress (see Chapters 4, 5, and 6). If a sound presentation doesn't convince a legislator to accede to one's cause, the argument runs, perhaps a campaign contribution might. Or, indeed, perhaps money given to the legislator's opponent might work even better. At best, a legislator hostile to an interest group might be defeated and replaced by one sympathetic to the lobby's point of view. Almost as acceptable is the fear that might be engendered in the incumbent so that he or she will become more receptive to a group's position.

This strategy is widespread in domestic politics, if not approved by everybody. As noted in the introduction to this chapter, pluralism in domestic politics is accepted, if not exalted. Whatever the merits or lack thereof of the role of money in elections, few would actually go so far as to argue that any contributions are themselves illegitimate. Is this also the case on foreign policy? If the nation must speak with one voice rather than the many tolerated on domestic issues, what are the consequences if the single voice reflects political pressure rather than public opinion and the administration's view of the international arena?

Retiring senator Charles McC. Mathias, Jr., R-Md., worries about such issues. He wrote:

> Factions among us lead the nation toward excessive foreign attachments or animosities. Even if the groups were balanced—if Turkish-Americans equaled Greek-Americans or Arab-Americans equaled Jewish-Americans—the result would not necessarily be a sound, cohesive foreign policy because the national interest is not simply the sum of our special interest and attachments ... ethnic politics, carried as they often have been to excess, have proven harmful to the national interest.[52]

In particular, he is concerned about threats by the Israeli lobby about electoral retaliation against legislators who are not perceived to be sufficiently pro-Israel. He described instances of such threats against members of Congress and argued: "[A]s a result of the activities of the lobby, congressional conviction has been measurably reinforced by the knowledge that political sanctions will be applied to any who fail to deliver." [53]

The strategies of pro-Israel groups usually have focused on placing intense constituency pressure on legislators who make either anti-Israel or pro-Arab statements.[54] In addition to this grass-roots tactic, Jewish organizations and individuals have increasingly turned to raising funds in attempts to influence congressional elections. In 1980 and 1982 they concentrated their efforts and resources on a House race in Illinois involving Republican representative Paul Findley, an outspoken advocate of recognition of the PLO. The initial attempt to dislodge Findley failed, but another effort two years later met with success. Findley was defeated by Dick Durbin, a strong defender of Israel. According to AIPAC, $685,000 of the $750,000 that Durbin raised came from Jewish sources.

Two years later, AIPAC focused on two key senators. Percy had been a sharp critic of Israel. Jewish sources gave $322,000 to defeat him, and one donor from California spent more than $1 million of his own money in "uncoordinated expenditures" for the same cause. Percy defeated his pro-Israel rival in the Republican primary, but lost to an equally fervent pro-Israel candidate, Paul Simon, in the general election. Jesse Helms, R-N.C., an even more strident critic of Israel, faced a tough contest against James Hunt, the Democratic governor; after Simon, Hunt was the largest recipient of pro-Israel money in 1984. Helms won in a tight race, but apparently was chastened by the experience; his Middle East stance shifted 180 degrees.

In 1984, fifty-four pro-Israel political action committees spent more than $4.25 million, considerably more than the real estate industry, which has the single largest domestic PAC. The scope of the donations was broad: 29 of the 33 Senate races and 154 of the 435 House races received funds. Every state except Utah and Idaho was covered. The highest concentration was on races involving members of the Senate and House committees with Middle East jurisdictions and on opposition to five senators who supported the sale of AWACS aircraft to Saudi Arabia. Almost 80 percent of the contributions went to Democrats; more than a third of all donations to Republicans were focused on one campaign, that of Sen. Rudy Boschwitz, Minn., who is Jewish and chairs the Senate Foreign Relations Committee's Subcommittee on the Middle East.[55] In contrast, Arab Americans report only two political action committees. One, the Middle East Political Action Committee, reported no money raised or spent as of 1982. The other, Americans for Lebanon Political Action Committee, is related to the Lebanese League. It supports moderate candidates, some of whom are of Arab extraction, but in 1982 gave only $5,500 in total to six campaigns.[56]

The imbalance of resources between pro-Israel and pro-Arab groups is not the major reason for concern about the potential for campaign contributions to influence foreign policy. The pro-Israeli lobby, after all, had considerably more influence than the pro-Arab lobby long before the former began to contribute heavily to congressional candidates. Rather, the nature of ethnic group, and indeed interest group, participation in foreign policy may well change because of the heavy spending. What should the role of money in American politics be? Is political support to be given to the highest bidder? We need only recall the comment of Rep. John Breaux, D-La., when he was asked if his vote could be bought, he responded with an emphatic "no." "But," he added, "it can be rented." [57]

Even though ethnic lobbies do not stand to benefit financially from a foreign policy that suits their preferences, many Americans are simply so skeptical of the role of money in politics that they will worry that something is not right. Thus, it is conceivable that support for foreign policy initiatives will be seen as open to influence by campaign contributions. It is equally possible that the victorious group will be viewed with suspicion by the larger public, much as large corporations are. The strategy of influencing policy by shaping the membership of Congress may thus backfire. The public and members of Congress may strongly disapprove of winning policy debates by threats. This has happened in some election campaigns in which the New Right has attempted to discredit Democratic incumbents, and there are signs that some Jewish leaders have begun to worry that it might happen to them. An American lobbyist for the government of Jordan concluded about Arab strategies: "Israel-bashing is bad business. It doesn't work." [58]

It is even more disturbing that such tactics occur on foreign policy issues than on domestic concerns. Purely domestic issues have traditionally divided our parties, while foreign policy has been bipartisan. A strident electoral campaign by a foreign policy interest group might disrupt this pattern. Jewish groups, for example, have given far more money to Democratic candidates than to Republicans. Might pro-Israel sentiments become more identified with the Democrats than the Republicans? If this were to come to pass, then Republican administrations and members of Congress might feel free to take pro-Arab positions. Given the success that the Republicans have had in recent presidential elections, this policy might prove disastrous for pro-Israeli groups. American policy might be shaped through a tug of war between a Democratic Congress (or one house of that body) and a Republican president and might shift radically depending upon which party was in power in the White House.

Pro-Israeli groups seem to have recognized this problem. In 1985 and 1986 they shifted their political contributions to the Republican party, especially to those New Right senators who have backed Israel. In doing so, however, they have alienated many liberal Democrats who have long been staunch defenders of Israel. Moreover, when contributing to the ultraconservatives, pro-Israeli groups are ignoring many issues about which the New Right and American Jews strongly disagree, especially prayer in public schools. Some observers see this strategy as leading to a situation in which concern for Israel's security will be the only issue for American Jews; this will ultimately make political alliances between members of Congress and pro-Israeli forces into little more than contests for campaign contributions (not unlike some domestic political issues) rather than bonds based on long-term philosophical commitments.[59]

As unsettling as this is for the Middle East, there is little reason to believe that electoral politics would be confined to this foreign policy issue alone. Our relations with the Soviet Union and our allies in Western Europe, Canada, and Japan might also become greater concerns in national elections. While there are relatively few interest groups focusing on these matters now, this is likely to change dramatically if an electoral bidding war begins on *any* aspect of foreign policy.

The bipartisan nature of our foreign policy is thus threatened by making international politics too much like domestic issues. We can afford to be contentious at home. The stakes are much greater abroad, where indeed the future of the whole world is at stake. Already Soviet leaders complain that negotiating with American presidents is difficult because our leaders cannot ensure that agreements reached will be approved by Congress. These problems could only increase if foreign policy issues became important in election campaigns marked by heavy expenditures and threats. In such contests, complex issues become reduced to ideological slogans, and candidates on the "wrong" side may even be accused of disloyalty. What the correct policy ought to be becomes less important than which group can yell the loudest, and the volume is affected by the purchasing power of television advertising. Causes that have heretofore enjoyed widespread, and bipartisan, support among the public, such as support for Israel, might become objects of great conflict. The very groups that spawned this effort might ultimately regret such tactics.

Notes

Support of the General Research Board, University of Maryland-College Park, is gratefully acknowledged, as is the assistance of Fred Augustyn and Rodger Payne. The comments of Allan J. Cigler, Burdett A. Loomis, and George H. Quester are greatly appreciated.

1. See John Spanier and Eric M. Uslaner, *American Foreign Policy Making and the Democratic Dilemmas*, 4th ed. (New York: Holt, Rinehart & Winston, 1985), chaps. 1 and 7; and Theodore J. Lowi, "Making Democracy Safe for the

World," *Domestic Sources of Foreign Policy,* ed. James Rosenau (New York: Free Press, 1967), 295-331.

2. Adam Clymer, "Poll Finds Americans Don't Know U.S. Positions on Central America," *New York Times,* July 1, 1983, A1-A2.
3. Richard F. Fenno, Jr., *Congressmen in Committees* (Boston: Little, Brown & Co., 1973), 141.
4. John E. Mueller, *War, Presidents, and Public Opinion* (New York: John Wiley & Sons, 1973), 53-55.
5. Spanier and Uslaner, *American Foreign Policy Making,* 158-160.
6. See Aage R. Clausen, *How Congressmen Decide* (New York: St. Martin's Press, 1973).
7. See Raymond A. Bauer, Ithiel de Sola Pool, and Lewis Anthony Dexter, *American Business and Public Policy,* 2d ed. (Chicago: Aldine-Atherton, 1982); and Robert Pastor, *Congress and the Politics of U.S. Foreign Economic Policy, 1929-1976* (Berkeley: University of California Press, 1980).
8. Bayless Manning, "The Congress, the Executive, and Intermestic Affairs: Three Proposals," *Foreign Affairs* (January 1977): 306-324.
9. David Howard Davis, *Energy Politics,* 3d ed. (New York: St. Martin's, 1982).
10. Seymour Martin Lipset and William Schneider, *The Confidence Gap* (New York: Macmillan, 1983), chap. 3.
11. Spanier and Uslaner, *American Foreign Policy Making,* 143.
12. On energy, see Eric M. Uslaner, *Everyman Out of His Humor: Energy Politics and Legislative Leadership* (forthcoming), chaps. 5 and 6; on agriculture, see Barbara Sinclair, *Congressional Realignment* (Austin: University of Texas Press, 1982), chaps. 7 and 8.
13. John E. Rielly, "American Opinion: Continuity, Not Reaganism," *Foreign Policy* (Spring 1983): 99.
14. Jack L. Walker, "The Origins and Maintenance of Interest Groups in America," *American Political Science Review* 77 (June 1983): 390-406.
15. Roger H. Davidson and Walter J. Oleszek, *Congress and Its Members,* 2d ed. (Washington, D.C.: CQ Press, 1985), 363-365.
16. Ibid., 363.
17. Paul Y. Watanabe, *Ethnic Groups, Congress, and American Foreign Policy* (Westport, Conn.: Greenwood Press, 1984), chaps. 1 and 2.
18. Thomas M. Franck and Edward Weisband, *Foreign Policy by Congress* (New York: Oxford University Press, 1979), 191ff.
19. Ibid., 192-193.
20. Ibid., 191-193.
21. Stephen A. Garrett, "Eastern European Ethnic Groups and American Foreign Policy," *Political Science Quarterly* 93 (Summer 1978): 301-323.
22. Eli S. Rivera, "Hispanic Americans: So Much to Offer," *Engage/Social Action,* December 1983, 10-17.
23. Rodolfo O. de la Garza, "Chicanos and U.S. Foreign Policy: The Future of Chicano-Mexican Relations," *Western Political Quarterly* 23 (December 1980): 571-572; and Jesus Rangel, "Puerto Rican Need Discussed at Home," *New York Times,* June 3, 1985, B18.
24. Bill Keller, "Interest Groups Focus on El Salvador Policy," *Congressional Quarterly Weekly Report,* April 24, 1982, 895-900.
25. Jake C. Miller, "Black Legislators and African-American Relations, 1970-1975," *Journal of Black Studies* 10 (December 1979): 245-261.

26. Michael Beaubien, "Making Waves in Foreign Policy," *Black Enterprise,* April 1982, 37-42.
27. Milfred C. Pierce, "Black and White American Opinions Toward South Africa," *Journal of Modern African Studies* 20 (1982): 669-687.
28. Franck and Weisband, *Foreign Policy by Congress,* 186.
29. Ben Bradlee, Jr., "Israel's Lobby," *Boston Globe Magazine,* April 29, 1984, 64. For a case study of the AWACS sale, see Spanier and Uslaner, *American Foreign Policy Making,* 145-148. Since the Camp David peace treaty between Israel and Egypt was signed in 1979, the Israeli lobby has not made a strenuous effort to block foreign aid to Egypt. For 1986, see Steven Pressman, "Reagan Finally Carries the Day," *Congressional Quarterly Weekly Report,* June 7, 1986, 1262-1263.
30. Ellen B. Laipson and Clyde R. Mark, "Israeli-American Relations," Issue Brief IB2008, Congressional Research Service, Library of Congress, updated June 1983; Don Oberdorfer, "Will U.S. Dollars Fix Israel's Economy?" *Washington Post,* June 9, 1985, D1, D4.
31. Cheryl A. Rubenberg, "The Middle East Lobbies," *The Link* 17 (January-March 1984): 4.
32. This section is based upon Bradlee, "Israel's Lobby"; Bill Keller, "Supporters of Israel, Arabs, Vie for Friends and Influence in Congress, at White House," *Congressional Quarterly Weekly Report,* Aug. 22, 1982, 1523-1530; Sanford J. Ungar, "Washington: Jewish and Arab Lobbyists," *Atlantic,* March 1978, 6-22; and Steven V. Roberts, "Lobbyists Line Up the Power on Arms for Jordan," *New York Times,* Oct. 21, 1985, A16.
33. Ungar, "Jewish and Arab Lobbyists," 10.
34. Bradlee, "Israel's Lobby," 64.
35. Robert H. Trice, "Congress and the Arab-Israeli Conflict: Support for Israel in the U.S. Senate, 1970-1973," *Political Science Quarterly* 92 (Fall 1977): 443-463.
36. This section is based upon Rubenberg, "The Middle East Lobbies"; Keller, "Supporters Vie,"; and Steven L. Spiegel, *The Other Arab-Israeli Conflict* (Chicago: University of Chicago Press, 1985), 8.
37. Quoted in Keller, "Supporters Vie," 1528.
38. Quoted in Spiegel, "Other Conflict," 8.
39. Spanier and Uslaner, *American Foreign Policy Making,* 154-155.
40. Keller, "Supporters Vie," 1523.
41. Ibid., 1528; Bradlee, "Israel's Lobby," 76.
42. Keller, "Supporters Vie," 1528; Robert A. Trice, *Interest Groups and the Foreign Policy Process* (Beverly Hills, Calif.: Sage Publications, 1976), 54-55.
43. Leon Hadar, "What Israel Means to U.S. Jewry," *Jerusalem Post,* International Edition, June 19-25, 1982), 11; Bradlee, "Israel's Lobby," 8.
44. Robert Sherill, Review of *The American House of Saud,* by Steven Emerson, *Washington Post Book World,* May 5, 1985, 4.
45. Keller, "Supporters Vie," 1530; Dale Ruskoff, "Oil Producers, N.Y. Jewish Leaders Join Forces," *Washington Post,* May 15, 1985, A9; Spiegel, "Other Arab-Israeli Conflict," 5.
46. Bradlee, "Israel's Lobby," 76.
47. Ungar, "Jewish and Arab Lobbyists," 12.
48. Bradlee, "Israel's Lobby," 76.
49. *New York Times,* "Arab Americans Take an Increased Political Role," Nov. 4, 1984, 74.

50. Speigel argues that the Israeli lobby is not a notable success in influencing the White House and that its clout lies more with the Congress in "Other Arab-Israeli Conflict," 388-394.
51. Bernard C. Cohen, *The Public's Impact on Foreign Policy* (Boston: Little, Brown & Co., 1973), 98-104.
52. Charles McC. Mathias, Jr., "Ethnic Groups and Foreign Policy," *Foreign Affairs* 59 (Summer 1981): 981.
53. Ibid., 993.
54. Cf. Alan Ehrenhalt, "Congress and the Country: Mideast Politics a Local Issue in New York," *Congressional Quarterly Weekly Report,* July 13, 1985, 1407.
55. John J. Fialka and Brook Jackson, "Jewish PACs Emerge as a Powerful Force in U.S. Election Races," *Wall Street Journal,* Feb. 26, 1985, 1, 16; *New York Times,* "Study Finds Pro-Israeli PACs Active in '84 Races," Aug. 16, 1984, B10.
56. Rubenberg, "Middle East Lobbies," 12.
57. Thomas B. Edsal, "Democrats' Lesson: To the Loyal Belong the Spoils," *Washington Post,* Jan. 14, 1983, A7.
58. Roberts, "Lobbyists Line Up." Cf. Jack W. Germond and Jules Witcover, "Cracks in the Jewish Lobby?" *Washingtonian,* December 1981, 82.
59. See Robert Kuttner, "Unholy Alliance: How Jewish PACs May Save the Republican Senate," *New Republic,* May 26, 1986, 19-25; and Paul Taylor, "Pro-Israel PACs Giving More to GOP," *Washington Post,* Nov. 4, 1985, A1, A11.

14. Coalitions of Interests: Building Bridges in the Balkanized State

Burdett A. Loomis

The growth of organized interests has paralleled the more general fragmentation or "Balkanization," in Kevin Phillips's terms, of American society. This condition has increased the difficulty of formulating, enacting, and implementing coherent policy initiatives across the whole of American politics. For some complex and difficult issues, a virtual "gridlock" has developed. On immigration, for example, no suitable policy has emerged to deal with the current glut of undocumented workers and a sieve-like Southern border. From a group perspective, neatly ordered policy subsystems have broken apart.

American interests, however, have proven themselves extremely adaptable to changing conditions. One key adaptation of the 1980s is the rapidly rising use of coalition strategies. Regardless of the subject at hand, coalitions are organized to speak for broad groupings of interests. On a case by case basis, this tactic represents no great innovation, but, as Burdett Loomis observes, the major change has come in the pervasiveness of coalition building—at all stages of electoral, legislative, and administrative politics. The continual reshuffling of interests into a series of coalitions may offer special opportunities to brokers and entrepreneurs whose stock in trade is to organize such groupings. In addition, the emphasis on coalitions illustrates the centralizing tendencies that necessarily arise to cope with the fragmentation of the Balkanized state.

What do 7-Eleven stores, Kingsford charcoal, amusement parks, and lawn and garden outlets have in common? They all want more daylight in the evening hours—the better to snack, grill, play, and till the soil. How to stretch out the day? Pass legislation to extend the months covered by daylight saving time, of course. And to do so, these diverse interests formed the Daylight Saving Time Coalition. The group's executive director, who claims credit for getting the pending legislation to cover Halloween, explains that this is the first time ever that "business has taken a look at this and realized it means money in their pockets." [1]

Bringing widely diffuse interests together was crucial because no single group had enough clout to place the extension of daylight saving time, into

March and through November, on the crowded legislative agenda. When the barbecue lovers joined the gardeners and the candy lobby—voila!—an impressive ad hoc grouping was born.

The collaboration on daylight saving time illustrates a fast-growing trend in interest group politics. Increasing numbers of complex and difficult issues have bred seemingly innumerable coalitions, which range from ad hoc groupings of a few interests to long-term arrangements among a great many. This chapter does not adopt any strict definition of the term *coalition*. Rather, it interprets coalition building, collaboration, and cooperation as overlapping notions that all express a joining together of several interests, for at least a measurable period of time. One meeting would not qualify, but a series of meetings and communications, no matter how loosely structured, would. This is a far cry from formal models of coalition behavior, but it does reflect the practices of contemporary interests and groups.

Coalition building scarcely represents an innovative tactic in the United States, nor in any other nation. Cooperation among interests and groups has been integral to American politics from the inception of the Republic. The framing and ratification of the Constitution exemplifies an early collaboration among interests, all with their own reasons (e.g., strong currency, trade, land claims) for endorsing the experiment in nation building.

Most attention on intergroup cooperation has been focused on its impact on legislative decisions. This is appropriate and understandable, for it is on Capitol Hill that coalitions are most visible, as they openly lobby for their favored legislation. Since the mid-1970s, however, as interest advocacy has "exploded," [2] groups have joined together in a variety of other settings, ranging from alliances on campaign finance to think tank conferences to policy implementation negotiations with agency personnel.

The cooperative activities of interests reflect Kay Lehman Schlozman and John Tierney's conclusions that groups currently do "more of the same" in comparison with past endeavors, but that "more of the same" may, at some point, become a qualitatively different phenomenon.[3] An occasional instance of ad hoc coalition building may be one thing for a group, but participating in a series of long-term cooperative efforts represents something quite different.

This chapter argues that more collaboration among interests demonstrates real and important departures from lobbying efforts of the past —a past as recent as the Eisenhower and Kennedy administrations. These changes result from many circumstances, but the central causes include (1) increased policy complexity; (2) the growth and decentralization of government, especially within Congress; (3) improved communication capabilities, both among interests and with their grass-roots constituents; and (4) the growing politicization of interests that were either nonexistent (antiabortion), poorly organized (consumers), or relatively inactive (business).

The Context of Coalition Building

Coalitions have always been important, and often essential, for interests to prevail within the policy-making process. The legislative majorities almost automatically produced in strong party systems (usually parliamentary) have existed only rarely in American politics. Rather, the ordinary context of group politics is framed by the Constitution's mandates of bicameralism and the separation of powers. As V. O. Key concluded, the rules of the game often produce the politics of deadlock:

> Pressure groups cannot well assume the function of general legislative leadership. Yet they may be extremely influential in the prevention of action when party or presidential leadership is weak. The power to obstruct is for many special interests the power to prevail, for their goal is the prevention of action in the general interest.[4]

In the main, politics under the Constitution virtually demands coalition building among interests that seek new policies. Majorities must be constructed at a series of stages within the legislative process—from the first subcommittee decision to the last vote on final passage. One virtue of broadly based coalitions is that such alliances, by their mere development, may well convince members of Congress that a consensus exists on a given legislative proposal, thus easing the way for its passage.[5]

Contemporary fragmentation, however, may well exceed the historical capacities of interests to build effective coalitions. Labeled "Balkanization" by political observer Kevin Phillips, this decentralization reflects traditional structural problems, compounded by weakening political parties and increased awareness and activism on the part of individual interests.[6] He asserts first that

> The U.S. Constitution's notion of "separation of powers," borrowed by the Founding Fathers from the eighteenth-century French philosopher Montesquieu, has become a trap. The "separate" powers are now *too* separate. Government in Washington all too often resembles a series of bunkers held by mutually suspicious troops, and nothing in the Constitution provides for issuing orders to demobilize.[7]

Governmental fragmentation is complemented by a similar societal phenomenon. Phillips continues:

> Many Americans have loosened their [political party] affiliation, begun to put ideology ahead of party. . . . From time to time, issues like abortion, gun control, the right to work, taxes, busing, feminism and "gay" liberation appear to be superseding parties as the basis of political mobilization. The obvious description: *ideological* Balkanization.[8]

As Mark Peterson and Jack Walker (see Chapter 9) have demonstrated, the interests described by Phillips have indeed developed into organized forces. At the same time, the Congress and the presidency have become increasingly sensitive to the requirements of a Balkanized political environment. In fact, many coalitions arise at the urging, either explicit or implicit, of the principal political actors. Congressional caucuses, such as the Auto Task Force, often serve as the springboard for bringing together diverse automobile industry interests, and the president's Office of Public Liaison is likewise continually working to build issue-based cooperation.

Patterns of Coalition Building

Cooperation among interests, although an increasingly common strategy, is not easily tracked. Many collaborative efforts are informal and unpublicized; others are dominated by a single group. Frequently, groups will join forces to act, but will claim credit separately for outcomes. Several patterns do emerge, however, that tend to highlight the nature of contemporary coalition formation.

First, groupings can be distinguished by the number of issues they coalesce around and the duration of their cooperation (the dimensional perspective). Second, coalitions appear at different points within the policy-making process. Third, the nature of the issue helps to determine the ways in which interests cooperate. Finally, focusing on the coalition builders—brokers such as lawyers, Washington representatives, and consultants—should contribute to an understanding of collaboration among interests. These perspectives are more suggestive than definitive, but they do provide some coherence in examining the role of intergroup cooperation.

A Dimensional Approach

However apt the sentiments expressed in "a rose is a rose is a rose," the same can hardly be said for cooperation among interests. There are coalitions, and then there are coalitions. Consider, for example, the "very funny kind of coalition" that developed in support of 1985 legislation to limit textile imports.[9] The International Ladies Garment Workers Union (ILGWU) joined with the southern-based textile industry to fight for the bill to roll back imports, even though the union and the manufacturers had experienced many vitriolic disagreements in the past. Long-time ILGWU lobbyist Evelyn Dubrow observed that, from the union's point of view, "there's no point in trying to organize an industry if there are no jobs around."[10] Given historic disputes, it is difficult to imagine the union-industry détente continuing for long; this is an ad hoc arrangement, forced upon a pair of hard-pressed, but temporary, partners.

In contrast, the Business Roundtable, an elite group of chief executive officers from the country's largest corporations, was formed to give big business a generally strong voice in national politics. It focuses on a wide range of issues and has lasted, with some ups and downs, since its inception in 1972.[11] Although the Roundtable has weathered internal disputes and fluctuations in influence with the White House, it is an ongoing group that takes positions (often unpublicized) on a range of business-related issues.

Figure 14-1   Coalition Dimensions: Duration and Diversity

Duration

	Short-Term	Extended
Single	AD HOC CAUSE (Union/Textile industry grouping)	CAUSE COALITION (Prolife coalition)
Multiple	AD HOC COMPLEX (1985-1986 Tax reform groups)	COMPLEX COALITION (Business Roundtable; Leadership Conference on Civil Rights)

Number of

In examining cooperation among groups, the two dimensions that appear most significant are *longevity* and *breadth of concern*. The textile coalition represents an ad hoc relationship that coalesced around a specific issue; the Business Roundtable, conversely, has lasted for more than a decade and confronted issues ranging from depreciation schedules to pollution abatement to trade policies. The four possible combinations of duration and range of issues are illustrated in Figure 14-1.

Ad hoc coalitions act differently from groupings that have a history and a future. Short-term cooperation revolves almost totally around the immediate interests of all concerned. This focuses the attention of the group, and the leaders do not have to worry about subsequent coordination. Environmental groups and railroads, historical antagonists, came together in the late 1970s to oppose barge interests, and these strange bedfellows benefited from the absence of any expectations that they would become long-term partners.[12] At the same time, ad hoc coalitions are vulnerable to co-optation by dominant interests. In the 1985-1986 negotiations over tax reform, for example, commercial real estate interests, which have developed sophisticated tax avoidance schemes, were isolated from their partners in opposition to changes in the tax law, as Rep. Dan Rostenkowski, D-Ill., and Sen. Robert Packwood, R-Ore., compromised with various other groups, ranging from state and local governments to Rust Belt industries.

Long-lived coalitions face many of the difficulties that single groups confront in organizing. That is, the coalition leaders must take into account the repercussions of a given action on future cooperative efforts. Thus, certain issues may be avoided, even when a substantial majority of coalition members want to address them. An ad hoc grouping could simply move ahead, with little regard to the possibility of losing the support of a few interests; a long-term coalition has much more at stake and ordinarily takes a more cautious approach. Nevertheless, when such collaboration occurs, organized with energy and intelligence, the results can be imposing. As one well-placed advocate observed of actions carried out by the 160-member Leadership Conference on Civil Rights in 1981-1982, "the coalition is infinitely more effective than any individual group or organization can be." [13]

The experience of the Leadership Conference provides a good example of the challenges that may beset a long-term, broad-based coalition. The organization consists of many diverse groups, ranging from the conventional (the National Association for the Advancement of Colored People, the Urban League, the National Organization for Women, some Hispanic organizations, and various religious groups) to the unexpected (for instance, the Elks, Actors Equity, the Young Men's Christian Association, and the National Funeral Directors and Morticians Association). With more than thirty-five years of experience, the Leadership Conference would appear to be a major force in the politics of civil rights. On occasion, in the 1950s and, especially, in the 1960s, this certainly was the case, although the alliance was never free from internal struggles. Disagreements over antiabortion policies, for example, have weakened 1985-1986 conference efforts to restructure civil rights legislation within higher education, in the wake of the Supreme Court's far-reaching *Grove City College* decision invalidating many basic laws and regulations.

The conference's unified activism in the early 1980s resulted in large part from the issue of voting rights, which appealed to virtually all the coalition members. Even on this issue, labeled "the purest brand of mother-hood" by one congressional aide, coalition members did not concur on all specifics. Nevertheless, internal agreement was reached on a basic set of voting rights provisions. This was crucial because the conference operates on the principle of consensus, not majority rule. Thus, there could be no major dissidents if the coalition was to operate as effectively as possible. During the eighteen-month course of the fight to renew the 1965 Voting Rights Act, the most severe challenges to the coalition's unity were the temptations to compromise during the actual reformulation of the legislation. One NAACP activist noted that maintaining a united front "is difficult now because the opposition is more subtle and sophisticated. . . . [It] doesn't say, 'We are opposed to the Voting Rights Act,' but rather, 'The act needs to be modified in some respects.' " [14]

In the end, the conference prevailed, and the act was extended in accordance with the group's preferences. This success illustrated the great power that truly broad-based coalitions can exert. Part of this power, however, is the relatively infrequent use of full-scale efforts by the coalition, which can only occasionally muster both the consensus and the requisite resources to mount a major campaign. Because such cooperation occurs over time, the group must develop long-term goals and perspectives. David Brody, a B'nai B'rith activist and conference executive committee member, observed:

> You don't do it every day, you don't do it every month. But you build on victory. You win a marathon today, you look ahead to next year's marathon.[15]

From the long-distance runners of the civil rights movement to the single race sprinters of the ILGWU-textile industry grouping, coalitions develop in different ways, according to the time span of their cooperation and the number of issues they confront. Although significant, this view of coalition building provides only one perspective on the growth of collaborative efforts. Equally important is the extent to which cooperation among interests has come to dominate many aspects of the electoral and policy processes.

Coalition Building through the Policy Process

Traditionally, both journalists and scholars have focused their attention on coalition formation in and around the legislative process.[16] This makes sense because the legislature encourages coalition behavior, both among its members and among the interests that seek to obtain influence. Nevertheless, interests cooperate systematically at many other stages of the policy process, including electoral politics, agenda setting, decision making, and implementation and evaluation procedures.

Tilting the Balance: Electoral Politics.   Interests traditionally have coordinated their efforts to elect their favored candidates, but the growth of political action committees (PACs), especially among ideological and business interests, has changed the nature of group involvement in political campaigns (see Chapter 4). Some coordination among PACs is essential, given the complexities of election law, the number of candidates, and the variety of funding sources. In fact, the two major clearinghouses for contributions are prominent PACs and the national political parties.

One conservative activist noted, for example, that "people talk about 2,000 or more PACs, but the truth is that there are only about 45 corporate PACs, 6 conservative PACs, and 15 to 20 trade association PACs that really count . . . a group of less than 75 people." [17] Channeling money from citizens through PACs to candidates is largely a funneling operation and "lead PACs" are crucial to this complex process. Thus, the Business-Industry Political Action Committee (BIPAC) provides information to other PACs on candidate quality, the competitiveness of congressional races, and the candidates who need funds at a given time.

As congressional races become more expensive and more dependent on PAC contributions, coordination among PACs has grown increasingly important, for groups and for candidates alike. Individuals such as BIPAC's Bernadette Budde or the Democratic Congressional Campaign Committee's Rep. Tony Coelho, who can direct funds to "needy" congressional aspirants, can thereby wield influence far beyond their own resources. Moreover, connections developed during fund raising can serve as one foundation for subsequent coalition activities.

Agenda Setting and Policy Formulation.   Although the formulation stage of the policy process is probably characterized more by entrepreneurs than by coalitions,[18] interests have much to gain by aggressively seeking to dictate the terms of the policy debate. Business' Carlton Group, named after its hotel meeting place, won its greatest victory by convincing the Reagan administration to include its accelerated depreciation proposal as one bulwark of the 1981 tax bill.[19] Once this item found its way onto the agenda, business interests could easily follow its progress and protect it from weakening amendments.

Much of the work in formulating policies is neither so clear-cut nor resolved so positively. Coalitions frequently are major actors in framing issues, and even when coalitions do not exist, interests may want to make it appear as if they do. The Natural Gas Supply Association, for example, undertook a major public relations campaign, which operated as the "Alliance for Energy Security," a purposely ambiguous label that implied a cooperative endeavor.[20]

Agenda setting is especially significant in those policy areas in which the public is confused (e.g., decontrol of natural gas prices) or ill informed (e.g., Latin America). The continuing debate over Nicaragua, the Sandinistas, and aid to the contras has been particularly intense. Various conservative groups have joined together to lobby publicly on behalf of increased American intervention, while opponents of such assistance have formed a loose alliance—the Coalition for a New Foreign and Military Policy, a group that one writer labeled "the Sandinista lobby." [21] The coalition has published a "basic information" book on Central America, which presents a relatively benign view of the Nicaraguan regime. Amid the sometimes raucous debate over Latin American policy, such a book is a modest effort. But when the issue fades from public view, the coalition and its opponents remain, fighting a continuing battle to shape the perceptions of both legislators and the public at large.

Decision Making.   However long-term their efforts may be, coalitions attract most attention at the decision-making stage of the policy process. The power of cooperation comes into focus here, especially when the conventional wisdom is upset. In 1977, for example, a well-orchestrated industry effort defeated a prolabor common-site picketing bill that was expected to cruise through the predominantly Democratic House of Representatives.[22]

Impending decisions often prompt cooperation among interests, especially when they feel an imminent threat. The tax reform politics of 1985-1986 activated a variety of coalitions, many of which were newcomers to the arcane world of tax laws. Entering this specialized field at the decision stage placed new entrants at a substantial disadvantage. The Coalition on Women and Taxes or the Coalition on Block Grants and Human Needs were forced to compete with Washington's "veteran tax lobbyists," who "also cultivate relations with key legislators through individual meetings, campaign fund-raisers, and other regular contacts with them and their top staffers." One women's group lobbyist noted, "They are recognized and we're just sort of upstarts." [23]

Ironically, though, even well-established coalitions and their members may have difficulties in wielding influence at the decision-making stage of the policy process. Especially on highly publicized issues, legislators may be less open to influence than during the policy formation stage. Decision making frequently reflects a simple up-or-down vote on a particular proposal. For instance, although the lobbying on a few prominent issues, such as aid to the contras, can be extremely intense, neither members nor coalitions have much room to maneuver once the legislative alternatives have been established.

One final and significant change in cooperative lobbying on policy decisions has been the rapid increase in coalitions' grass-roots activities. Martha Cooper and Sar Levitan cite such work in the business coalition that defeated labor law reform proposals in the late 1970s.[24] Although big business interests dominated the coalition's umbrella group, the National Action Committee for Labor Law Reform, the grass-roots pressure of local small businesses proved decisive in influencing members of Congress. Generally speaking, the most effective grass-roots lobbying comes from interests that have the centralized resources to target these efforts. Coalitions led by the U.S. Chamber of Commerce, for example, potentially can enjoy the advantages of that organization's modern communication facilities and network of local contacts.[25]

Policy Implementation and Evaluation.   Most studies of intergroup collaboration focus on the formulation and decision stages of policy making, but much important work occurs when policies are implemented and evaluated. Once coalitions develop some history of cooperation, as on environmental issues, they become increasingly involved in the assessment of how policies are put into place. Much of the 1985 debate over toxic waste "superfund" legislation and spending levels, for example, revolved around environmentalists' criticisms of the initial implementation of superfund policies by the Environmental Protection Agency (EPA).

In the wake of legislative triumphs (or defeats), coalitions may turn to monitoring policy implementation as one means of staying together. Patterns of information exchange and cooperation become habitual, especially if all the groups see gains from the collaboration. Thus, during the early 1980s defense spending critics met regularly (the "Monday Group") and could quickly mobilize an anti-MX missile group when that issue rose on the agenda.

To summarize, coalitions develop throughout the policy process. Despite the attention placed on the politics of decision making, cooperation among interests may affect policies at least as much during the formulation and implementation of policies. In addition, as coalitions gain more experience, they may well find it advantageous to seek out ways to influence policies across the entire process. At the same time, specific groups retain their distinct identities, and coalitions rarely can act as quickly or decisively as individual interests can.

Issues and Coalitions

I really think that nuclear physics is much easier than tax law. It's rational and always works the same way.[26]

—Jerold Roschwald, education lobbyist

More than anything else, it is the nature of a given issue that affects coalition politics. The private charities' lobby may be activated by a far-reaching tax law proposal, or a major confederation, like the Chamber of Commerce, may not get involved on some trade policies because of the mixed preferences of its members. Sometimes the mere complexity of an issue may dictate cooperation, as with many environmental issues or the tax law revisions noted by Roschwald.

Although issues can determine coalitional behavior in many ways, three major perspectives seem most relevant. First, as Schlozman and Tierney observed, differences among coalitions spring from the nature of the policies they support—in Theodore Lowi's characterization, whether the policies are distributional, regulatory, or redistributive.[27] Second, as noted, cooperation is often necessitated because of issue complexity; only coalitions of interests may be able to understand the Strategic Defense Initiative (Star Wars), to say nothing of lobbying on the subject. Third, coalitions play especially active roles in broadening, or sometimes in restricting, the "scope of the conflict" on a given issue.[28] That is, they seek to control how much, or how little, public attention an issue will receive.

No single issue-based perspective is sufficient to explain coalitional politics. A combination of the three concepts—policy types, complexity, and scope—however, can provide some useful clues, especially as they are applied to a single instance of policy development—in this case, the House of Representatives' reauthorization of superfund legislation in 1984-1985.

Policy Types: No Simple Answers

Borrowing from Lowi's original categorization, Schlozman and Tierney depict *distributive* policies as generating coalitions that are "characteristically stable marriages of noninterference," *regulatory* policies as producing "temporary unions of organizations sharing a joint interest [on] a particular matter," and *redistributive* policies as promoting "almost frozen coalitions" among long-term adversaries.[29] As usual, reality is less tidy than theory.

At first blush, the superfund, administered by EPA, looks to be either a distributive or a regulatory policy. Funds are distributed to clean up hazardous waste dumps, and EPA operates the program in line with highly technical regulatory guidelines. One major component of the issue, however, is redistributive because a continuing question concerns the financing of the $10 billion cost of the fund over five years. Prior to 1986, most financing came from a tax on petroleum products, including feedstocks, but this source was inadequate to sustain the proposed price tag.

Members of the environmental coalition regarded the superfund as first a regulatory matter and second as a distributive issue. That is, they wanted an effective and stringently monitored effort that was well funded. Their view was reflected in the 1984 passage of superfund reauthorization. This legislation died in the Senate, however, where the industry coalition, which included insurance forces as well as chemical/petroleum interests, could convince senators that the House bill was unfairly redistributive and too harsh in its regulatory provisions.

The industry coalition, led by the American Petroleum Institute and major chemical interests, viewed the matter as primarily redistributive and, secondarily, regulatory. As one industry lobbyist put it, "If I had only ten minutes to talk to somebody, I would spend all ten minutes on financing and size." [30] Coalition members were extremely concerned that an enlarged superfund program would result in tax hikes for the industry, especially the producers of petroleum-based feedstocks. The industry group thus wrote provisions that limited the fund to $5 billion, froze the feedstock tax, and stip- ulated a broadly based additional tax to take effect if the $5 billion was inadequate.

In a sharp about-face, the House adopted the industry coalition's point of view in its 1985 passage of superfund legislation. Environmental interests were left on the outside. The previous year their coalition had convinced the House to view the superfund primarily as a regulatory measure that required strict standards. Subsequently, in their 1984 election campaigns, House members could run as strong environmentalists. After that, however, the industry coalition prevailed in redefining the issue, significantly altering the eventual policy outcome in the House.

Complexity, Conflict, Scope, and Cooperation

Policy makers must continually tackle complex policy issues, ranging from nuclear power to tax laws to acid rain. Not only are unlikely coalitions often formed in response to such issues, but the extent of public attention an issue receives frequently depends on the ability of interest groups to make the issues accessible, and important, to the appropriate constituencies. Over the years, environmental groups have done well when they could broaden the scope of the conflict. Indeed, the very existence of superfund legislation reflects successful efforts to bring toxic waste problems to the public's attention.

When legislators and agency personnel focus on the complexities of policies such as toxic waste cleanup or immigration reform, the issues become highly technical, and the scope of the conflict frequently narrows, especially on specific legislative provisions. As of 1986, immigration law changes were still in the formulation stage; thus, despite technicalities, coalitions represent- ing Hispanic organizations or agricultural groups could still hope to publicize the issues, broaden the scope of the conflict, and defeat the entire package. For superfund groups, that possibility did not exist. Everyone agreed that there would be a superfund program, costing between $7 billion and $10 billion. The specifics, however, remained to be hammered out.

The superfund legislation contained any number of significant issues, including, for example, the rights of citizens to know about toxins in their communities and their standing to sue polluting units. The possibilities of coalition building are most evident, however, in an examination of a single, complex policy that key interests sought to *exclude* from superfund coverage. The problem of leaking underground storage tanks (LUST, for short) provides a most instructive illustration. Leaking underground tanks, mostly from gas stations, both operating and defunct, represented "the kind of issue on which lobbyists earn their money: not so large that it is swept along solely by fundamental political currents and not so obscure that Members and their aides check their watches after about a minute of discussing it." [31]

Led initially by the oil companies, a few lobbyists sought to build a coalition by bringing together the many interests affected by tank storage legislation; these included bus companies, rental car operations, airlines, lumberyards, and virtually anyone who maintained a fleet of vehicles. The industry coalition was headed by an oil lobbyist and a lawyer who had specialized in tank storage matters and represented independent gasoline station operators. Although environmentalists participated in the process, they lacked the resources and expertise to mount a consistently strong effort on behalf of tougher standards and liability requirements. In addition, the industry coalition could focus on the single issue of tank storage, while environmentalists were faced with the entire range of superfund considerations.

Although assertions have often been made that "united fronts" are crucial to coalition victory, the industry's LUST grouping did not achieve much tangible success until one of its most visible actors, the American Petroleum Institute, dropped out. Representing the major oil companies, API had less of a stake in the tank storage issue than many of the smaller interests that owned the tanks or the insurance industry, which was faced with very large potential liabilities. For the oil companies, tank storage was one issue among many; for many independent service station operators, tank storage was by far the most salient environmental issue of the 1980s.

In 1984-1985, the industry coalition, cooperating with key staff on the House Energy and Commerce Committee, helped to forge a bill that dealt with the (related) policy and political complexities of the LUST issue. In the end, the expertise of the coalition's key lobbyist, Jeffrey L. Leiter, and its ability to contain the scope of the conflict within the committee's policy orbit led to policies that generally reflected the industry's preferences. Although environmental forces won a few modest changes in liability provisions when the bill moved through the Public Works and Transportation Committee, the key decisions had already been made in the arena where the industry coalition was dominant.

In many ways, the crucial lobbying move came with the initial construction of a strong industry coalition. Well-informed oil interests, operating within the superfund issue network, helped organize a group with adequate technical expertise and political savvy to protect tank owners' interests. As with individual groups, coalitions require organizers, but cooperation dictates that these individuals operate more like brokers than, in Robert Salisbury's term, entrepreneurs.[32]

Coalition Brokers: Bridge Builders in the Balkans

The explosion of interest group advocacy, along with the increasing reach and complexity of policies, has generated a great demand for lobbyists who can bring diverse interests together. A single chapter is no place for any exhaustive examination of this development, but some revealing patterns have developed.

First, and perhaps most important, is that coalitions do not just emerge, somehow. Rather, brokers arrange them in any number of ways. Walter Mondale's former campaign director, Robert Beckel, noted: "I've been putting together alliances since the day I got out of the Peace Corps ... we put together alliances of people and come up with a name of an association or group and we do a campaign." [33] Beckel, like many brokers, often represents specific and narrow interests within a broad coalition, or one that at least is presented as broad.

A continuing struggle over home audio taping reflects this trend. In this legislative battle, the two major opposing forces are the Coalition to Save America's Music and the Audio Recording Rights Coalition. Songwriters, publishers, record companies, and performers make up the former alliance; the latter represents the chief consumer electronics group, other major importers of recording equipment (such as Sears), and an audio tape manufacturer.[34] With many well-connected lawyer-lobbyists on each side, the battle has been fought with grass-roots campaigns and celebrities lobbying on behalf of the America's Music coalition. The consumer electronics alliance, on the other hand, has emphasized the inalienable rights of Americans to tape whatever they want, in the privacy of their own homes. Patriotism and rights aside, however, one of the songwriters' lobbyists viewed the confrontation as "a trade problem.... It's basically a fight between the American music industry and the Japanese manufacturers." [35]

In such a context, brokers become extremely important; this is a long-term fight, and brokers are crucial to maintaining the coalition's visibility and standing. Directed by David Rubenstein, formerly a key Carter administration aide and now an attorney for a Washington law firm with many Japanese electronics industry clients, the audio rights alliance has orchestrated various grass-roots efforts such as running advertisements in *Rolling Stone* to educate the public, or at least one segment, about the potential cost of royalty charges on tapes.

Other examples abound, but the central point is that coalitions, like the groups they represent, require organization. Washington is full of individuals and firms who can provide that service, at a price, regardless of the issue.

This leads directly to the second major trend—that law and public relations firms increasingly act as the brokers for the building of coalitions, whether formally organized or not. This is especially true when groups neither know how to proceed in Washington nor desire much publicity. Although a number of domestic interests fall into this category (for instance, much of the business community), a particularly good example exists in the nascent lobbying efforts of the newly industrialized countries (NICs).

As with the industry coalition on storage tank legislation, NIC lobbying has arisen in response to government action—in this case, the 1979 Trade Agreements Act—and a general public perception that a problem exists. The newly industrialized countries, a grouping that includes South Korea, Singapore, Taiwan, and Brazil, among others, have relied extensively on major Washington brokers to plan strategies and present their cases, although the NICs are rapidly becoming sophisticated actors in their own right. Footwear and textile groupings have each held regular meetings, and the Washington law firm of Patton, Boggs, and Blow, which represented the Retail Industry Trade Action Coalition, often hosted the textile alliance's gatherings.[36]

As Table 14-1 illustrates, law and lobbying firms link interests within and between countries. These are the building blocks for coalitions that can form and re-form on a series of issues. Such flexibility is especially important for NICs, because although their commercial interests frequently coincide, their relationships with the United States on other fronts (e.g., military aid) just as frequently differ. Even on economic matters, Washington representation may paper over many serious differences among NICs. Most cooperation thus remains informal, held together by law firms and lobbying operations.

Table 14-1 Law Firms, Public Relations Firms, and Newly Industrialized Countries' Interests

Law Firms	*Lobbying/PR Firms*
Arnold & Porter	Gray and Co.
Korean Traders Association	Embassy of South Korea
Brazilian Finance Ministry	Hyundai Motor America
Mexican steel companies	Korean Airlines
O'Connor and Hannan	Michael K. Deaver and Associates
Hong Kong knitwear	Government of Singapore
Mexican carbon black producers,	Korean Broadcasting Advertising
cement interests, and toy balloon	Corporation
manufacturer	Government of South Korea

Source: Drawn from information in "Who's Doing the Work for NICs," *National Journal*, Jan. 25, 1986, 203.

Finally, as illustrated in many of the previous examples, coalition brokers do not simply arrange cooperation in Washington at the legislative stage of policy making. Rather, the "full-service" lobbying firms seek to have an impact by building coalitions throughout the electoral and policy processes. Activities range from fund raising to grass-roots campaigns to the coordination of legal maneuvers. Law and lobbying firms undertake such operations on behalf of individual clients, of course, but coalition building also has emerged as a key element in overall strategies of influence. For example, PAC contributions can be "bundled" from a set of related interests, thus overcoming the $5,000 per campaign limitation on such donations.

Overall, lobbyist-brokers are becoming increasingly important in the coalition formation process. Historically, a "lead" interest, such as the Chamber of Commerce or the Sierra Club, has served as the focal point for cooperation. This remains the case much of the time, but brokers offer flexibility, speed, and often access that traditional coalitions may lack. In addition, brokers can organize as broad or as narrow a set of interests as the particular issue requires. In an era of complex policies and convoluted politics (such as tax reform), brokers may provide useful services without the baggage of long-term commitments among interests.

Shifting Coalitions and Tentative Conclusions

Writing in the late 1970s, Anthony King, a keen British observer of American politics, concluded that

> the language of coalition building is no longer the most helpful language in which to describe American politics, indeed that it may be positively misleading. American politicians continue to try to create *majorities;* they have no option. But they are no longer, or at least not very often, in the business of building *coalitions*. The materials out of which coalitions might be built simply do not exist. Building coalitions in the United States today is like trying to build coalitions out of sand. It cannot be done.[37]

What, then, should one make of the extensive cooperative activity among interests in the mid-1980s? First, some of it is certainly, in King's terms, "majority building," frequently based in Washington's lobbying and public relations firms. Words like *alliance* and *coalition* are thrown around largely to mask the fact that no collaboration among established interests is actually taking place.

On the other hand, most signs point to increased coalition building activity. Patterned cooperation in political giving, through PACs, has grown substantially. Washington lawyer-lobbyists earn their keep by forging coalitions, often among diverse partners. Complex issues and fragmented political structures demand that interests collaborate on both technical and political matters.

Patterns in coalition formation remain unclear, although the nature of issues and the roles of intergroup brokers seem increasingly important. In addition, most cooperation derives from contacts within Washington-based issue communities. The interests have settled in the capital, and so have the brokers. Coalition partners may cajole their members and constituents to write their respective representatives and senators, but the tacticians remain firmly ensconced in their K Street bunkers and their Georgetown headquarters.

Notes

1. Arlen J. Large, "Congress Again Tinkers with Daylight Time," *Wall Street Journal,* July 22, 1985, 38.
2. See, among others, Jack Walker, "The Origins and Maintenance of Interest Groups in America," *American Political Science Review* 77 (June 1983): 390-406; Kay Lehman Schlozman and John T. Tierney, *Organized Interests and American Democracy* (New York: Harper & Row, 1986); and Jeffrey Berry, *Lobbying for the People* (Princeton, N.J.: Princeton University Press, 1977).
3. Schlozman and Tierney, *Organized Interests and American Democracy,* 387ff.
4. V. O. Key, *Politics, Parties, and Pressure Groups,* 5th ed. (New York: Crowell, 1964), 159.
5. See Anne N. Costain and W. Douglas Costain, "Interest Groups as Aggregators in the Legislative Process," *Polity* 14 (Winter 1981): 249-272.
6. Kevin P. Phillips, *Post-Conservative America* (New York: Vintage, 1983), chap. 6.
7. Ibid., 82.
8. Ibid., 83.
9. Steven V. Roberts, " 'Funny Kind of Coalition' on Textiles," *New York Times,* Sept. 25, 1985.
10. Quoted in Roberts, " 'Funny Kind of Coalition.' "
11. See Sar A. Levitan and Martha R. Cooper, *Business Lobbies: The Public Good and the Bottom Line* (Baltimore: Johns Hopkins University Press, 1984), 134-140.
12. T. R. Reid, *Congressional Odyssey* (San Francisco: Freeman, 1980).
13. Barton Gellman, "The New Old Movement," *New Republic,* Sept. 6, 1982, 10. The entire discussion of the Leadership Conference relies heavily on this article.
14. Robert Pear, "As House Nears Action on Rights Bill, the Lobbyists Get Busier," *New York Times,* Sept. 27, 1981.
15. Gellman, "The New Old Movement," 10.
16. See, for example, Barbara Hinckley, *Coalitions and Politics* (New York: Harcourt Brace Jovanovich, 1981), especially chap. 11; and Donald Hall, *Cooperative Lobbying: The Power of Pressure* (Tucson: University of Arizona, 1969). For journalists, almost any issue of the *Congressional Quarterly Weekly Report* or the *National Journal* contains a story that considers legislatively oriented coalition formation.
17. Quoted in *PAC Power: Inside the World of Political Action Committees,* by Larry Sabato (New York: W. W. Norton, 1985), 45.
18. See John Kingdon, *Issues, Agendas, and Alternatives* (Boston: Little, Brown, 1984).
19. See Bill Keller, "Coalitions and Associations Transform Strategy, Methods of

Lobbying in Washington," *Congressional Quarterly Weekly Report,* Jan. 23, 1982, 121.

20. Ann Cooper, "Middleman Mail," *National Journal,* Sept. 14, 1985, 2041.
21. Fred Barnes, "The Sandinista Lobby," *New Republic,* Jan. 20, 1986, 12.
22. For details, see the accounts in *Interest Groups, Lobbying and Policymaking,* by Norman J. Ornstein and Shirley Elder (Washington, D.C.: CQ Press, 1978), and Levitan and Cooper, *Business Lobbies,* 119-122.
23. Steven Pressman, "Groups New to Tax Lobbying Seek to Modify Reagan's Plan," *Congressional Quarterly Weekly Report,* Aug. 17, 1985, 1641.
24. Levitan and Cooper, *Business Lobbies,* 131.
25. See Burdett Loomis, "A New Era: Groups and the Grass Roots," in *Interest Group Politics,* 1st ed., ed. Allan J. Cigler and Burdett A. Loomis (Washington, D.C.: CQ Press, 1983), 169-190.
26. Quoted in Pressman, "Groups New to Tax Lobbying," 1641.
27. Schlozman and Tierney, *Organized Interests and American Democracy,* 279-287. The original formulation is that of Theodore Lowi, "American Business, Public Policy, Case Studies, and Political Theory," *World Politics* 16 (1964): 677-715.
28. The idea of the scope of conflict comes from E. E. Schattschneider, *The Semi-Sovereign People* (Hinsdale, Ill.: Dryden, 1975).
29. Schlozman and Tierney, *Organized Interests and American Democracy,* 281.
30. Quoted in "Trench Warfare," by Ronald Brownstein, *National Journal,* Sept. 14, 1985, 2049. Much of the rest of the discussion of the superfund politics relies heavily on this article, as well as on research done by John Leuthold.
31. Brownstein, "Trench Warfare," 2050.
32. See Robert Salisbury, "An Exchange Theory of Interest Groups," *Midwest Journal of Political Science* 13 (February 1969): 1-32.
33. Quoted in "The Power Is Inside, but the Money Is Outside," by Thomas Edsall, *Washington Post National Weekly,* Dec. 2, 1985, 12.
34. Maxwell Glen, "The Latest Chapter in the Home Audio Taping Battle Unfolds in Congress," *National Journal,* Nov. 2, 1985, 2485.
35. Glen, "The Latest Chapter," 2486.
36. Bruce Stokes, "Developing Countries Join the Big Leagues in Washington Trade Lobbying," *National Journal,* Jan. 25, 1986, 206-207.
37. Anthony King, "The American Polity in the Late 1970s: Building Coalitions in the Sand," in *The New American Political System,* ed. Anthony King (Washington, D.C.: American Enterprise Institute, 1978), 371-395.

15. Interest Groups in the Courts: Do Groups Fare Better?

Lee Epstein and C. K. Rowland

When we think of interest group politics, the first things that we are likely to consider are high-powered lobbyists or extravagant political action committee donations. Litigation does not leap to mind as a major interest group strategy. Throughout the twentieth century, however, groups representing the disadvantaged (minorities) and the difficult-to-organize (consumers) have successfully, if unevenly, used the judicial system to win policy victories. At the same time, other interests, representing corporations and other major social institutions, have devised litigation strategies in confronting trade unions or complying with government regulations.

In this chapter Lee Epstein and C. K. Rowland examine whether group sponsorship of litigation makes much difference in obtaining policy victories within the federal judicial system. Although litigation by interest groups, either on behalf of an individual or on its own, has increased substantially since the 1960s, the question of impact remains difficult to answer. Indeed, as the authors note, even addressing the question of group impact requires data that are difficult to collect and analyze. Nevertheless, their initial research efforts lead them to conclude that group intervention does make a difference. To the extent that we have become a society of litigants, the resources and expertise of interest groups can play a major role in shaping the decisions reached and policies imposed by the court system.

Most political commentators and scholars of interest group behavior focus on the lobbying activities of groups in the legislative, executive, and electoral arenas, but organized interests also play an integral role in the judicial process. In courtrooms throughout the United States, attorneys employed by the American Civil Liberties Union (ACLU), the Pacific Legal Foundation, and numerous other organizations try to persuade judges to adopt their policy preferences. Given the rules of adjudication, however, interest group lawyers refrain from approaching decision makers directly. Rather, groups use oral arguments and legal briefs to convince judges of the relative merits of their claims.

In this chapter we explore the use of litigation as an interest group lobbying strategy. Because of the relative "uniqueness" of this tactic, we first present a review of the literature. Based on this review, we conclude that many interest groups view litigation as a viable political strategy. But we also discover that this body of research has not examined systematically the relative "success" of interest groups and other litigants at the trial court level. In the remainder of this chapter, then, we combine these two issues by examining how interest groups (versus nongroups) fare in the federal district courts.

Interest Group Litigation: A Review

Since the 1908 publication of Arthur Bentley's seminal work, *The Process of Government*,[1] scholars have recognized that interest groups use the courts to channel their policy goals into the common law and "actively seek to assure that their view of the legal good is imposed on the society at large."[2] Because of the perceived apolitical nature of the courts, research on lobbying through litigation, at least through the 1950s, was almost nonexistent. Although scholars recognized early that some interest groups might view the courts as influential policy makers, their research emphases implied that groups would most likely achieve important objectives in legislative or executive corridors.

Scholarly interests in groups and the courts changed dramatically in the late 1950s because of the work of political scientist Clement E. Vose.[3] Vose reexamined old assumptions about the judiciary by describing the litigation activities of several diverse organizations, including the National Consumers League (NCL) and the National Association for the Advancement of Colored People (NAACP). Although these organizations had very different political agendas, Vose noted that they shared at least one characteristic—a common belief in the utility of litigation. In documenting the activities of these and other groups, Vose described in minute detail their litigation strategies and their reasons for choosing to use the courts.

The National Consumers League and Labor Law

The National Consumers League took to the courts when employer associations challenged the protective legislation (e.g., maximum hours and minimum wages) for which the league had successfully lobbied in state legislatures. The NCL and its general counsel, Louis Brandeis (who was later to become a distinguished U.S. Supreme Court justice), devised a brilliant strategy, which, Vose argued, enabled the NCL to accomplish what the states alone would have been unable to do: win major victories in the Supreme Court.

The case of *Muller v. Oregon* (1908), for example, tested the constitutionality of the Oregon law for which the NCL had lobbied; the law mandated that women's workdays be limited to ten hours. The employers based their arguments on an earlier Court decision, *Lochner v. New York* (1905), which declared a state maximum-hour law for bakers unconstitutional because it violated the Fourteenth Amendment's due process clause.

Brandeis and the NCL leaders knew they faced a difficult legal challenge. To counter the negative Supreme Court precedent, Brandeis developed two tactics. First, he asked the State Industrial Commission to allow him to represent Oregon in court. Although somewhat unusual, Brandeis's request made a good deal of sense: he wanted sole control of the case at the trial court level so that he could develop a good record for later appeals. Moreover, Brandeis did not want to jeopardize his case by allowing relatively inexperienced state attorneys to handle it.

Second, Brandeis asked NCL workers to gather "facts, published by anyone with expert knowledge of industry in its relations to women's hours of labor such as factory inspectors, physicians, trade unions, economists, and social workers." [4] Brandeis requested this information because he wanted to distinguish *Lochner* by showing the courts that long hours of work, while perhaps safe for male bakers, were detrimental for women. The results of the NCL's fact-finding mission indicated just that: long workdays jeopardized the health of women. This information, which was incorporated into the NCL's legal arguments, later became known as the "Brandeis Brief."

The strategies developed by the NCL paid off. The U.S. Supreme Court distinguished women bakers from their male counterparts and allowed the Oregon law to stand. More important, Brandeis's tactics—control over the case from the trial court level and the use of statistical data—continued to succeed during a judicial era marked by hostility to state regulation of economic activity.

The NAACP and Race Discrimination

Vose's findings on the NAACP, while different from those on the NCL, make an equally compelling case for the utility of interest group litigation. Unlike the NCL, which had successfully lobbied state legislators into passing its favored legislation, the NAACP had no such access. The plight of blacks in the United States in 1909, when the group was founded, was an unpopular cause. To eliminate (or at least chip away at) discrimination, the NAACP was forced into the courts as a plaintiff because the popularly elected branches of government provided no support.

Faced with this situation, the NAACP did not venture haphazardly into the judicial arena. Rather, according to accounts of Vose and others, NAACP leaders, including Thurgood Marshall, its general counsel and current U.S. Supreme Court justice, developed well-planned and well-executed litigation strategies. [5]

The school desegregation cases, involving both higher education and public schools, provide some of the best examples of how the NAACP used litigation as a political weapon. Like the NCL, the NAACP had major legal obstacles to overcome because of the way the courts interpreted the Fourteenth Amendment. Ratified in 1868, the amendment purportedly guaranteed blacks equal protection of the law. But, as is well known now, much of the

South tried to circumvent the amendment by creating separate facilities for the races. When the Supreme Court in 1896 established the doctrine of "separate but equal" *(Plessy v. Ferguson)*, such practices were only reinforced.

When the NAACP was formed, one of its major goals was to eradicate "separate but equal" policies, particularly as they affected education. The organization understood, however, that the courts would resist challenges to the doctrine because only thirteen years had passed since it had been first enunciated. Therefore, instead of trying to eradicate the policy immediately, the NAACP began to whittle away at it through a series of well-planned and carefully executed attacks on separate but decidedly unequal education facilities.

The case of *Sweatt v. Painter* (1950) concerned Homan Sweatt, a black man living in Texas, who wanted to attend law school there, but was denied admission to the all-white University of Texas. The NAACP seized the opportunity to defend Sweatt for two reasons. First, his case violated the separate but equal principle. There was no other "equal" place for him to attend law school. Thus, the NAACP did not have to ask the court to strike down the doctrine. Second, the NAACP leaders thought it was to their advantage to start with discrimination in graduate schools. They believed that the courts would be more willing to eliminate discriminatory practices aimed at older students.

When the case approached trial, the state judge continued it for six months. In the interim, Texas constructed a makeshift black law school, which was to be run by part-time professors from the University of Texas and was to contain less than a quarter of the number of books available in the University of Texas library. When the case reached trial, the judge ignored the NAACP's claim that this black law school was not equal to the University of Texas and ruled in favor of the state. The NAACP appealed, and the case eventually reached the U.S. Supreme Court. The Court, while refusing to review the principle of separate but equal, ruled in favor of Sweatt. The majority fully concurred with the NAACP's argument that the schools simply were not equal and that Sweatt should be admitted to the University of Texas Law School.

After other victories in similar cases, the NAACP decided it was time to shoot for the big victory: eradication of the separate but equal doctrine at all levels of education. It accomplished this goal in the brilliantly conceived and executed case of *Brown v. Board of Education* (1954). The plaintiff in this case was a schoolchild, Linda Brown, who lived down the block from a white public school in Topeka, Kansas, but was forced to go to a black school (of comparable quality) much farther from her home. NAACP leaders were careful to select a case in which the schools would be of comparable quality so that the Court would be forced to rule squarely on the constitutionality of the separate but equal doctrine. Moreover, because the black and white schools in Topeka were not as flagrantly unequal as their counterparts in the South, the precedential value of this case would be clear for future challenges to the

South's segregated schools.

As Vose and others have documented, the NAACP had on its side not only the favorable precedents it helped to build, but also important (and later controversial) data indicating the negative effects of segregation on children.[6] Like the statistical evidence used by Brandeis, these data convinced the justices of the Supreme Court: in a unanimous decision, the Court struck down the doctrine of separate but equal.

The Decline and Resurgence of Studies on Group Litigation

Vose's discussion of the litigation successes of the NCL and NAACP generated a great deal of interest in the subject. Scholars focusing on interest groups began to reexamine past assumptions about the nature of the judiciary and lobbying through litigation. Most concluded that the courts were just as open to political processes as the other branches of government.[7]

Then, although many scholars continued to examine judicial behavior, specific emphasis on interest groups in court came to a grinding halt during the late 1960s with publication of political scientist Nathan Hakman's "folklore" article.[8] Hakman tried to show that group litigation rarely occurred. Ignoring group-sponsored cases (that is, when interest groups provide lawyers for plaintiffs as the NAACP did in *Sweatt*) and focusing exclusively on interest group participation as amicus curiae (groups filing friend of the court or third party briefs), Hakman found that groups filed amicus curiae briefs in only 18.6 percent of all noncommercial cases decided by the Supreme Court from 1928 to 1966. Based on this evidence, Hakman concluded that because interest group participation in cases was mere folklore, scholars should not waste their time studying what was surely an arcane phenomenon.

Academics followed Hakman's advice; for more than a decade, work on interest group litigation was virtually nonexistent. The scholarly community seemed to agree that it was fruitless to study a phenomenon that was almost certainly episodic. The examples of the NAACP and the NCL were treated as anomalies.

Despite the popularity of this view, the subject of interest groups and the courts would not disappear. And, in fact, this field of inquiry recently received a major boost from a 1981 study that replicated and updated Hakman's findings. The authors found that, although interest group participation as amicus curiae during the time Hakman's study was published may have been sporadic, the situation had changed dramatically. Between 1970 and 1980, interest groups had filed amicus curiae briefs in more than half of all the noncommercial cases coming before the Supreme Court.[9]

Since publication of that study, many more scholars have corroborated its results not only for amicus participation, but for group sponsorship as well. For example, Lettie Wenner's study of environmental litigation during the 1970s revealed that environmental groups, such as the Environmental Defense Fund (EDF) and the Natural Resources Defense Council (NRDC), were plaintiffs in 636 cases before federal district courts. The government was a defendant in 575 of these cases, indicating that these groups used the courts to secure implementation of prior successes in the legislative and bureaucratic arenas. Wenner wrote:

> They [environmentalists] were the chief proponents of most of the legisla-
> tion under which these cases were litigated, and they were instrumental in
> inserting provisions for citizen suits into many of the laws. They had a large
> ideological stake in seeing that the laws were used, and [they] were
> committed to the belief that the courts constituted a useful watchdog to prod
> less-than-energetic administrators of the law[s] into realizing the full
> potential of the laws.[10]

The environmental cases by no means exhaust contemporary examples of group litigation. Studies examining cases involving women's rights, abortion, voting rights, religious freedom, handicapped rights, conservative causes, and race discrimination all have found high proportions of cases sponsored by organizations.[11] This is not surprising given that the Center for Public Interest Law, an umbrella organization for litigating groups, now estimates that there are more than 150 groups who use the courts.

In addition to revealing the scope of group litigation, the 1980s work on amicus and sponsorship participation has made explicit the distinctions among forms of participation and encouraged scholars to develop typologies of group participation as a prerequisite to understanding the effects of group litigation on judicial outcomes. Wayne V. McIntosh has distinguished forms of participation at the trial-court level and found that the tendency to focus on amicus activity underestimates group activity here.[12] Susan Olson has offered a typology of roles groups may play in the litigation process. This typology minimizes the problems of distinguishing amicus participation at the appel-late level from other forms of group activity at the trial-court level. Olson distinguishes among interest group-as-lawyer (e.g., the NCL), interest group-as-plaintiff (e.g., the EDF) and cases where both the plaintiff and the lawyer are organized (e.g., an ACLU defense of organizations), noting that, "Each of the official roles ... has rules to channel or constrain group activity in that capacity." [13]

In sum, the 1980s have seen a resurgence of group litigation scholarship that includes case studies and efforts to refine the framework of fundamental research. We know that national organizations can achieve policy goals through concerted, long-term litigation strategies at the U.S. Supreme Court level. Yet, because research has focused primarily on the litigation of groups without controls for nongroups and on the Supreme Court, many questions remain unanswered.

One concerns the effects of group involvement on litigation outcomes. Are interest groups more successful than independent litigators? Are they more successful than other organizations; for example, large law firms, with comparable experience and resources? Do ad hoc local groups and local affiliates of national groups achieve success in trial courts comparable to that achieved at the appellate level by national groups?

Success and Interest Group Litigation

Although the systematic examination of interest group success in litigation is conspicuous by its absence, case studies of their participation in various areas of the law suggest that they perform better than independent litigants. Such an inference emanates from a number of factors. First, interest groups are "repeat players," frequently appearing before the courts to achieve their objectives. Consider the following scenario: two lawyers represent their respective clients before a federal court. One is from the NAACP, has appeared in the same court, making similar claims in dozens of suits, and has the support of the organization's national legal staff. The other lawyer has rarely practiced in this particular court and has no national support staff. The NAACP's advantages, without any further details about the nature of the controversy, are apparent. In fact, in some instances, interest groups are so well known that they take on a status akin to a district attorney or U.S. attorney.

A second advantage of interest groups in court is expertise. Simply stated, many interest groups are known for their ability to select and cultivate outstanding legal talent, such as Alvin Bronstein, director of the ACLU's National Prison Project, a group dedicated to defending prisoners' rights. Before coming to the project, Bronstein served as a consultant to numerous litigating groups, including the Lawyers Constitutional Defense Counsel and the NAACP. One should also keep in mind that two of the legal counsels for organizations that were in the vanguard of litigation became Supreme Court justices! By contrast, our hypothetical adversary is typically an overworked prosecutor or a state attorney engaged in general practice.

A final advantage of interest groups lies at the heart of group litigation itself: groups have long-term policy objectives. Rather than bringing just any case to the court, interest groups try to pick "winners," cases that they cannot only win, but also those that will help them to build favorable precedent. The ability to pick and choose among cases is not a luxury enjoyed by other kinds of lawyers. Typically, lawyers have little choice in deciding whether to take on a client. They must simply do their best to win whatever case they are handling. Interest group lawyers, by contrast, can sift through the various controversies brought to their attention to select those meeting a specified set of criteria.

Given the advantages outlined above, it comes as no surprise that most studies of group litigation at the appellate level are success stories; that is, groups ultimately achieve most of their policy goals. At the local, trial court level, however, group advantages may be mitigated by two countervailing factors. First, local practitioners may be repeat players at home; they may be familiar with local judges' predilections and have advantages in jury selection and in securing the trust or cooperation of witnesses. These advantages are reinforced by the documented "localism" of trial judges[14] and the perception of national litigants as intruders into local disputes.[15] Second, at this level the group litigant may be a local ad hoc organization with few of the advantages associated with national groups. Thus the "resource gap" may be narrowed or closed.

In combination these local conditions may vitiate the advantages of expertise and long-term commitment that national groups enjoy. At a minimum they raise the question: Are group successes at the appellate level replicated by groups in local trial courts? Because the answer to this question is not found in the literature, we address it directly by examining empirically interest group success in the federal district courts.

Group Success in Federal District Courts

We focus our empirical analysis on the federal district courts for three related reasons. First, because the district courts are the final arbiters of most disputes before them, it is important to understand the role of group litigants at this level. Second, as Americans become more litigious and access to the courts expands, groups are encouraged to try to achieve their goals via litigation. This litigiousness is enhanced by the evolution of "fiduciary jurisprudence," a philosophy that views judges as trustees for general, ill-defined rights and duties that subsequently must be specified and applied at trial.[16] Finally, litigation becomes a more attractive avenue for the transformation of group objectives into law as the federal courts become more politicized and receptive to group pressures. Certainly, recent works concerning the Reagan appointment process and the political influences on Carter and Reagan appointees to the lower federal courts suggest that trial court litigation is an increasingly viable vehicle for the pursuit of political goals.[17]

Given the contemporary importance of federal trial courts as forums for group litigation, it is somewhat surprising that relatively few systematic empirical examinations of group effects at this judicial level have been conducted. Several factors may account for this research lacuna. The tendency of public law scholars to focus on the U.S. Supreme Court is well documented.[18] Such a research bent has been reinforced by the case study design of most work on interest groups as litigants. In selecting cases, scholars are attracted to the most visible disputes, those in which questions of national concern are resolved by the nation's highest court.

Moreover, federal trial courts are rather inhospitable research settings. Most of their decisions are not published, which makes data collection time consuming and expensive. Many of these unpublished decisions are routine dispute resolutions; this forces researchers to wade through numerous routine cases of little interest to group litigants to find appropriate group-sponsored or group-litigated cases.

Finally, the diversity of the federal trial courts creates serious problems of comparability among different judges and cases at different times and places. Unlike scholars who focus on a single case or court, those who would systematically compare cases across courts must devise valid categories of analogous cases and controls for inherent factual variation across time and among jurisdictions.

Estimating Groups' Effectiveness

Ultimately, the most accurate way of examining a group's effectiveness and ability to influence a judge's decision is to determine whether a group litigant is more successful than other litigants presenting the same case to the same judge. Because the same judge does not hear identical cases under control for group participation, the question cannot be answered directly. It can, however, be addressed indirectly by comparing the success rates of group litigants and other litigants in cases of analogous fact and law. To do this, one must impose time constraints, develop categories of similar legal disputes, and isolate judges who have resolved these disputes for group and nongroup litigants. Moreover, to obviate the possibility that a judge may be unresponsive to all litigants on either side of these disputes, we must further reduce our focus to those judges who have a balanced record of dispute resolution for the selected category of disputes. We did this by developing a research strategy that focused attention on one category of litigation and on judges who had responded to group and individual claims under the controls proposed above.

To implement this research strategy, we examined cases involving conscientious objection to military service (CO). We first identified judges who had published three or more CO opinions in the *Federal Supplements* between 1968 and 1970 (the time constraints reduced the number of judges and cases; however, they were necessary to enhance the comparability of cases within each category). We then defined group litigation as that involving group-as-plaintiff, group-as-litigator, or group as both plaintiff and litigator. Through correspondence with participating attorneys, we classified each case as individual or group litigation. We then limited our sample to those judges whose published opinions involved group and nongroup cases and whose decisions reflected a balanced record of support and opposition to these First Amendment claims. These controls limited our focus to seven judges, each of whom had heard at least three cases; however, it reinforced our confidence that any observed differences would be the result of group effects rather than surrogates for unacknowledged intervening factors.

Aggregate Group Influence

Table 15-1, which illustrates the success of group versus nongroup cases, indicates that most cases qualifying for our sample involved group litigants. More important, before judges with relatively even propensities to support CO claims, group litigants fared better than independent litigants. The overall success rate before these judges was 59 percent; however, the success rate for groups in this sample was 67 percent, and the success rate for independent litigants dropped to 45 percent. Thus, for this tightly controlled sample of cases, group sponsorship appears to be an advantage.

Several factors may account for these apparent group effects. First, we

Table 15-1 Comparison of Independent and Group Success in
Conscientious Objector Litigation in Selected Federal
District Court Decisions: 1968-1972

	Support CO Claim	Oppose CO Claim
Group (21)	14	7
Independent (11)	5	6
	19	13

Source: Data collected by the authors.

must acknowledge that they may be artifacts of the small sample imposed by
our design constraints. The magnitude of difference, however, suggests that
these group effects reflect group strategies and advantages. That is, their
expertise and information networks and other advantages yielded a substan-
tively significant success rate. Second, closer examination of the cases also
suggests that any "localism" disadvantages may have been neutralized; the
group participants were, with two exceptions, either local groups or local
representatives of national organizations. For example, an Iowan who
resisted the draft on religious grounds was represented by a local group whose
lawyer was a repeat player in the local district court. Likewise, a San
Antonio, Texas, litigant was represented by the ACLU's local affiliate and a
local, repeat player from the ACLU. Thus, whatever disadvantages groups
may have on the local level appear to be offset by localizing group
involvement.

Influence on a Single Judge

Despite the evidence of group success, the possibility remains that
aggregate differences between group and independent litigation may be
accounted for by factors other than group effects. To explore this possibility,
we focused our attention on a single judge who had heard analogous cases
presented by group and independent litigants. The limitations of this
traditional, ideographic analysis are well documented by judicial behaviorists;
nonetheless, it afforded us the opportunity to search for specific corroboration
of the aggregate evidence of group influence on a single judge.

We chose to analyze the opinions of Judge John Reynolds from the
Eastern District of Wisconsin.[19] Reynolds issued six opinions in cases
involving religious objections to draft status. Three involved group litigants,
three did not. Two of his nongroup decisions rejected First Amendment
religious claims, and one supported such a claim. All three of his group-

involved cases supported free-exercise claims against military service. Thus, Reynolds would seem, on the surface, an ideal subject for our textual exploration.

To compare group and nongroup litigation we looked for three things in Reynolds's published opinions: reference to group litigants, different weighing of evidence and precedent between group and independent disputes, and legal argumentation unique to group litigation. Our own analysis was replicated independently by two University of Kansas law professors. Our results do not corroborate the aggregate-level analysis. Neither we nor the professors found evidence of group influence reflected in Reynolds's opinions. This is not to say that the legal reasoning expressed in the opinions did not consciously or unconsciously conceal subtle group influences. Perhaps it did. But analysis of these published opinions reveals no overt group influence. Rather, what appear initially to be group effects, on closer examination, may be interpreted as a traditional adjustment to appellate decisions and changes in controlling precedent.

The possible spuriousness of apparent group effects on Reynolds may be illustrated by comparing his decisions in two cases. In the first, *U.S. v. Shermeister* 286 F. Supp. 1 (1968), no groups were involved, and the judge ruled against a defendant's claim that the local draft board's failure to reconsider his CO petition violated his due process rights. In the second, *U.S. v. Johnson* 310 F. Supp. 624 (1970), CO support groups were involved, and Reynolds ruled that failure to consider a CO petition submitted under analogous circumstances violated the defendant's due process guarantees. Thus, the judge appears to have been influenced by the group litigants. But a more detailed textual analysis suggests a very different interpretation of these differences.

In *Shermeister,* the defendant's motion to reconsider his draft status was filed one day before his induction. This motion was processed by a clerk but not formally considered by the local draft board; Shermeister argued that the board improperly failed to reconsider his classification. Reynolds disagreed. He ruled that the motion for reconsideration revealed no change in the defendant's status that would require reclassification and that the failure to reclassify was, therefore, consistent with federal regulations and due process.

In a 2-1 decision, *Shermeister* was reversed on appeal to the Seventh Circuit. The majority in *U.S. v. Shermeister* (1970) ruled that, despite its last-minute submission, the board's failure to reconsider the petition and its failure to notify the defendant constituted a violation of due process. Moreover, Reynolds's finding that the new petition contained insufficient evidence to merit reconsideration was "surplusage"; in other words, extraneous and beyond the powers of the district court.

In *Johnson,* Reynolds's reasoning was guided explicitly by the Seventh Circuit's *Shermeister* decision. He found that a local draft board violated Johnson's due process guarantees by refusing to consider a CO petition filed after an order to report for induction had been issued. Citing *Shermeister,* Reynolds reasoned that if federal regulations and due process as interpreted in that case require *reopening* claims to CO status after notice, the claim for opening initial claims under analogous circumstances is even more compelling.

Thus, although a judge ruled one way in an "independent" case, then differently in an analogous "group" case, closer examination suggests that the key difference was not group involvement, but the intervening decision by the Seventh Circuit. What are we to make of this?

Conclusion

It seems appropriate to conclude by assessing what we know and do not know about group litigation. We know from the literature that groups often succeed when they use litigation to channel group goals into public policy. We do not know much about group failures because failures are less appealing research topics. We know from our own empirical analysis that group litigants are more successful than are independent litigants in winning a particular kind of dispute, CO status, in the federal district courts. This suggests that, all things being equal, group litigants tend to be more skilled than are independent litigators at this level. However, it does not tell us whether groups as groups influence trial judges. Although individual judges may be responsive to group influences, the apparent responsiveness of our exemplar judge resembled a traditional response to precedent and appellate reversal. Thus, what appears to be group influence may be a surrogate for other skill factors such as case selection or "forum shopping," that attach to large law firms or corporate litigators. In other words, although groups may be inordinately successful adversaries, whether they are more successful than independent litigators of comparable skill, resources, determination, and persistence remains a question for future research.

How can we expand our knowledge about group influence and what leads to group success in the future? The combination of nomothetic and ideographic analysis utilized should be continued and extended to other dispute categories and forums. This replication should be expanded, however, by specifying the nature of group involvement as a control and, more important, by comparing interest groups with other litigants of comparable organizational capacity. Only then can we determine whether groups actually "influence" the courts and whether their success can be differentiated from that of comparable adversaries.

Notes

1. Arthur Bentley, *The Process of Government* (Chicago: University of Chicago Press, 1908).
2. Gregory J. Rathjen, "Lawyers and Appellate Choice: An Analysis of Factors Affecting the Decision to Appeal," *American Politics Quarterly* 6 (1978): 391.

3. Clement E. Vose, "NAACP Strategy in the Restrictive Covenant Cases," *Western Reserve Law Review* 6 (1955): 101-145; Vose, "National Consumers' League and the Brandeis Brief," *Midwest Journal of Political Science* 1 (1957): 178-190; and Vose, *Caucasians Only* (Berkeley: University of California Press, 1959).

4. Vose, "National Consumers' League." See also Karen O'Connor, *Women's Organizations' Use of the Courts* (Lexington, Mass.: Lexington Books, 1980).

5. Vose, "NAACP Strategy"; Vose, *Caucasians Only;* Charles F. Kellogg, *NAACP: A History of the National Association for the Advancement of Colored People* (Baltimore: Johns Hopkins University Press, 1967); Richard Kluger, *Simple Justice: The History of Brown v. Board of Education and Black Americans' Struggle for Equality* (New York: Alfred A. Knopf, 1976).

6. Vose, *Caucasians Only;* and Jack Greenberg, *Judicial Processing and Social Change: Constitutional Litigation* (St. Paul, Minn.: West Publishing, 1977).

7. For an excellent review of this literature, see C. Herman Pritchett, "Public Law and Judicial Behavior," *Journal of Politics* 30 (1968): 480-509.

8. Nathan Hakman, "The Supreme Court's Political Environment: The Processing of Noncommercial Litigation," in *Frontiers of Judicial Research,* ed. Joel B. Grossman and Joseph Tananhaus (New York: John Wiley & Sons, 1969).

9. Karen O'Connor and Lee Epstein, "An Appraisal of Hakman's 'Folklore,' " *Law and Society Review* 16 (1981-1982): 701-711.

10. Lettie M. Wenner, *The Environmental Decade in Court* (Bloomington: Indiana University Press, 1982), 44.

11. O'Connor, *Women's Organizations' Use of the Courts;* Eva R. Rubin, *Abortion, Politics and the Courts: Roe v. Wade and Its Aftermath* (Westport, Conn.: Greenwood Press, 1982); Joseph Stewart and Edward Heck, "Ensuring Access to Justice: The Role of Interest Group Lawyers in the '60s Campaign for Civil Rights," *Judicature* 66 (1982): 84-95; Leo Pfeffer, "Amici in Church-State Litigation," *Law and Contemporary Problems* 44 (1981): 83-110; Susan M. Olson, *Clients and Lawyers—Serving the Rights of Disabled People* (Westport, Conn.: Greenwood Press, 1984); O'Connor and Epstein, "An Appraisal of Hakman's 'Folklore' "; L. Epstein, *Conservatives in Court* (Knoxville: University of Tennessee Press, 1985); and Stephen L. Wasby, "Civil Rights Litigation by Organizations: Constraints and Choices," *Judicature* 68 (1985): 337-352.

12. Wayne V. McIntosh, "And Now for Something Completely Different: Amicus Curiae Activity in Federal District Courts" (Paper delivered at the Annual Meeting of the Northeastern Political Science Association, Boston, Mass., 1984).

13. Susan M. Olson, "Reconceptualizing Interest Group Litigation in Federal Trial Courts" (Paper delivered at the Annual Meeting of the American Political Science Association, New Orleans, La., 1985).

14. Kenneth Vines, "Federal District Judges and Race Relations Cases in the South," *Journal of Politics* 26 (1964): 337-357.

15. Jack W. Peltason, *Fifty-Eight Lonely Men: Southern Federal Judges and School Desegregation* (New York: Harcourt, Brace & World, 1961).

16. Jethro Lieberman, *The Litigious Society* (New York: Basic Books, 1981).

17. Sheldon Goldman, "Reagan's Judicial Appointments at Mid-Term: Shaping the Bench In His Own Image," *Judicature* 66 (1983): 335-347; Robert A. Carp, C. K. Rowland, and Donald Songer, "The Effects of Presidential Appointment, Group Identification, and Fact/Law Ambiguity on Lower-Court Federal Judges' Policy Choices: The Case of Carter and Reagan Appointees on the Lower

Federal Courts" (Paper delivered at the Annual Meeting of the American Political Science Association, New Orleans, La., 1985).

18. Robert A. Carp and C. K. Rowland, *Politics and Policy Making in the Federal District Courts* (Knoxville: University of Tennessee Press, 1983).

19. Judge John Reynolds was born in Green Bay, Wisconsin, in 1921. He received his law degree from the University of Wisconsin and served as Wisconsin attorney general, 1959-1962, and as governor of Wisconsin, 1963-1965. President Lyndon Johnson appointed him to the federal bench in 1965. Reynolds is described as "sympathetic to criminal defendants" and having "a relaxed courtroom style." "1984 Guide to Federal District Judges: Background, Major Rulings and Courtroom Style," *The American Lawyer* (July-August): 65.

16. Groups without Government: The Politics of Mediation

Andrew S. McFarland

What would happen if competing interests attempted to reach policy accords without embracing either the legitimacy, coercive power, or omnipresent reach of the state? Is it possible that long-term antagonists, such as corporations and environmentalists, could agree to mutually acceptable policies if the state allowed them the latitude to negotiate binding agreements? These are not the questions that ordinarily arise when the politics of interest groups is discussed. The government and its agents are involved by definition in *public* policy debates and actions. At the same time, the presence of government officials, who often represent particular interests (e.g., the military, wheat growers, etc.), may not contribute to the timely and effective settlement of policy disputes. Indeed, interests frequently use their government allies to forestall adverse decisions.

In this chapter Andrew McFarland examines an actual case of interest group adversaries trying to reach agreements with minimum governmental involvement. The National Coal Policy Project obtained some general encouragement from the federal government, but received neither advance sanction nor the promise that any agreements would be enacted into law. McFarland chronicles the development of the project, its problems in recruiting representative participants from both industry and the environmental movement, the range of proposals that project negotiators agreed to, and what happened to those proposals. McFarland draws conclusions as to the limits of voluntarism and the need for the authoritative participation of the state in interest-related policy decisions.

After reading about lengthy and bitter conflicts between businesses and citizens' groups over the environment, many people no doubt wonder whether it is possible to bring the opposing groups together to discuss the issues rationally. But, if the adversaries met outside the courtroom, if they avoided bruising legislative struggles, could they not reach compromises? Wouldn't this result in more timely economic decisions, thereby saving the public a good deal of money? Don't the Japanese do this whenever possible and give their economy a competitive advantage over the United States?

The 1977-1978 National Coal Policy Project (NCPP) is the best case to examine for answers to such questions. The NCPP was an elaborate attempt to mediate political conflicts between the coal industry and environmentalists by establishing conferences involving corporate executives and environmental lobbyists. A group of individuals founded the NCPP as an experiment, and they spent $1.4 million trying to make it work.[1] Business donated about 60 percent of this money, with the remainder coming from the federal government and several foundations.[2] In addition, leaders of the project estimated that participants put in fifteen thousand days of work, half of which were paid for by businesses as salaries of executives on released time.[3]

At first, this exercise in group cooperation looked like a big success—the business people and environmentalists reached so many agreements it took eight hundred pages to describe and explain them all.[4] Representatives of groups, acting independently of established political institutions and government, resolved difficult policy issues. But to be truly effective, these groups required legislative action to enact the negotiated settlement into law. Although the executive branch enacted a small part of the NCPP's program in the form of regulations, the government ignored about 90 percent of the agreements. From this perspective, the project must be judged a failure; in the long-run, however, it may encourage more sophisticated efforts in group cooperation.

Groups and the Politics of Negotiation

Several basic characteristics of interest groups help explain the project's failure. Groups within a broad interest sector, such as environmental lobbies or coal companies, do not all feel the same way about compromise with their opposition. In this case, leaders of two environmental lobbies that focus on coal issues—the Environmental Policy Center (EPC) and the Natural Resources Defense Council (NRDC)—believed that the NCPP's negotiations constituted a sellout of environmental values, and these two lobbies declined to participate in the project. Some coal companies had a similar suspicion of the project as a sellout of free enterprise values, and they ignored the NCPP. The participants in the project, while loyal to their respective environmental or free-market ideals, were relative moderates. Even so, considerable mutual suspicion existed between these moderates when the NCPP started its conferences.

Another characteristic of interest groups is the reluctance of group leaders to anger the top representatives of other interests with similar goals. As noted, those actually participating in the project were very successful in negotiating agreements, which were published in the two-volume summary *Where We Agree,*[5] but the moderate representatives could not get their own groups to endorse these agreements. Groups with similar interests often join coalitions to lobby the government[6] (see Chapter 14). Even within coalitions, however, groups seldom agree on top lobbying priorities; consequently, organizations work out deals ("I'll support you in your top goals, if you support me in mine"). Some environmental lobbies generally favored the platform of *Where We Agree,* but did not want to alienate the EPC and NRDC. This cast an informal veto over environmentalist support for the compromise platform. The coal companies did not disagree in public, but a few coal companies seemed to oppose the project. Correspondingly, this discouraged ratification of *Where We Agree* by the National Coal Association (NCA), an organization with members from every part of the industry.

A similar logic holds within an interest group when deciding on a lobbying goal.[7] Leaders strive to avoid splits within their boards of directors and their top staff. Defeated minorities can defect to form rival groups, taking staff and funding sources with them. Moreover, internal conflict depletes staff time and morale. Consequently, if a minority of the board and staff of an interest group strongly opposes a proposed lobbying goal, the majority ordinarily will drop the issue to preserve the group's unity.

The most important characteristic of interest groups working without government is their lack of real authority. Even if opposing groups confer, agree to settle policy conflicts, and implement the compromise, without the full backing of government, the agreements bind only those willing to obey. There is a great incentive for a "rogue" organization to break the contract.[8] If environmentalists agree not to sue to prevent strip mining at a given site, this could tempt a less moderate group to initiate a lawsuit and to get credit for a possible victory. Similarly, if twenty coal companies agree not to strip mine in a specific locale, an outside company might be tempted to start operations there after the cost of leasing lands drops due to the lack of competing bids. As this example illustrates, even exceptional unity among interest groups cannot forge complete compliance with an agreement among private parties. Only the authority of the state can compel obedience from all groups.

History of the National Coal Policy Project

Gerald Decker conceived the NCPP as an outgrowth of his activities as a Dow Chemical Company vice president for energy. From his experience representing Dow on federal and corporate advisory boards, Decker decided in 1973 that the major industrial users of energy should consult with one another on U.S. energy development. He discussed the matter with executives from corporations such as U.S. Steel and Detroit Edison and concluded that the central development problem was dealing with "the environmental uncertainties." In other words, rapid development of coal and nuclear power resources can damage the environment and is almost sure to be hindered by government regulations and environmental lawsuits.

After observing lawsuits over locating electric power plants in Michigan, Decker became convinced that the courtroom's adversary process increased hostility between the contending parties, which made the resolution of disputes more difficult. Decker believed that disputes between environmentalists and industrialists sometimes could be resolved if the parties could come together and work out satisfactory joint solutions in an atmosphere of mutual respect. The National Coal Policy Project grew out of this belief.

In 1976 Decker persuaded an environmentalist friend, Laurence Moss, to help him establish a new institution of conciliation for coal. Larry Moss, a former Sierra Club president, can be seen as the cofounder of the NCPP, and many Washingtonians associate the NCPP with him. The two had met when serving on an advisory board to the Federal Energy Agency, a predecessor of the Department of Energy. Moss had been a leader of the lobbying campaign to pass the Clean Air Act of 1970 and to block federal funds for the construction of a supersonic airliner. By 1975 Moss had the reputation in Washington as a thoughtful, pragmatic leader, who was not afraid to admit that there were two sides to environmental policy issues, that environmental regulation had costs as well as benefits, and so forth.

Decker and Moss joined forces to create an institution to bring business representatives and environmentalists together. Although many of their recruiting efforts were greeted with skepticism, they persuaded a number of executives and environmentalists to participate in a short conference in July 1976 to discuss the possibility of a mediating institution in the coal policy area.

The Decker-Moss idea was sufficiently intriguing to encourage the contribution of financial and personnel resources. Several foundations provided substantial assistance, and ninety corporations contributed money; among these were electric utilities, chemical companies, steel companies, and others particularly concerned about the generation and usage of electricity or about the regulation of air pollution.[9] In addition, four government agencies—the Energy Research and Development Administration (ERDA), the Tennessee Valley Authority (TVA), the Environmental Protection Agency (EPA), and the Department of the Interior—gave financial support. A research institute affiliated with Georgetown University, the Center for Strategic and International Studies (CSIS), provided staff support.

Decker and Moss were successful in recruiting sixty participants for the NCPP, thirty industrialists and thirty environmentalists.[10] The mining industry was represented by several executives, including Harrison Loesch, the leading lobbyist for coal on Capitol Hill, and John Corcoran, former president of Consolidation Coal, the second largest U.S. coal company. Other executives came from electric utilities, chemical, steel, and related industries. None of the participants was a chief executive officer, although many were corporate vice presidents, typically heads of energy and environmental offices.

Some important environmentalists refused to participate. Refusals came from Louise Dunlap, the chief environmental lobbyist on strip-mining issues and head of the Environmental Policy Center, and from Richard Ayres, a leading environmental activist on air pollution issues and a lawyer with the Natural Resources Defense Council. But J. Michael McCloskey, executive director of the Sierra Club, joined. Other participants included several lawyers who had played a prominent role in litigation and in lobbying; namely, Bruce Terris, a Washington law firm head; Grant Thompson, then with the Environmental Law Institute; and Gregory Thomas, then a lobbyist for the Sierra Club.

NCPP organizers claim that consumer representatives were invited to participate, but that they refused. This is not surprising. Consumer lobbyists in Washington have displayed a strong preference for adversary tactics, exemplified by Ralph Nader's activities. The leaders of consumer organizations say that they are woefully understaffed, a reason sufficient in itself for refusing to participate in a venture such as the NCPP. No invitation was extended to the United Mine Workers because at the end of 1976 the UMW was in the throes of a bitterly disputed campaign for control of the union. UMW participants could not have made compromises with coal companies on mine safety issues for fear of being discredited within the union.

The project held its first meeting in January 1977, and the sixty participants formed five major committees: mining, air pollution, transportation, energy pricing, and fuel utilization and conservation. The business "side" within the committees usually appointed an advisory panel of other business people from outside the NCPP. From January 1977 to February 1978, five meetings of twenty-four leading participants were held to review and approve the proposals adopted by the committees.

Father Francis X. Quinn, a priest, labor mediator, and professor, presided over these meetings. Quinn's firm presence was sufficient to keep the sessions within the bounds of "the rule of reason," the principles of decorum and negotiation by which the participants were bound. The principles established rules for discussing disputed issues in a spirit of fairness and concern for establishing the facts.[11] A typical rule was that "data should not be withheld from the other side." The rule of reason apparently succeeded in reducing conflict during meetings, although difficult negotiating sessions occurred.

The committees divided into formal industrialist and environmentalist sides, each with a chairperson and a backup leader. The two chairpersons were considered joint leaders of the committee and represented it to the whole group. Members spent a good deal of time in committee meetings and general sessions during 1977, and by February 1978 the NCPP announced that it had reached a series of agreements, compiled in the two-volume *Where We Agree*. The first volume, running more than 300 pages, contained the reports of four of the five committees; the second, an elaborate 477-page document, was produced by the mining committee. A 70-page summary was issued, a necessity because of the length and technical character of the separate committee reports.[12]

Influential newspapers and magazines received the NCPP report favorably, and the project was the subject of a laudatory cover story in *Fortune.* The *New York Times* gave it front-page coverage and endorsed it in an editorial.[13] Most accounts made reference to Louise Dunlap's denunciation of the project as unrepresentative of groups concerned with coal and as a sellout of environmental legislation. But press accounts that contained such criticism were generally favorable to the NCPP.

National Coal Policy Project Proposals

The proposals of the NCPP can be summarized in three points. First, *Where We Agree* contained details about how coal mining, both surface and underground, could be regulated. Second, the report argued that streamlined, simplified licensing procedures, combined with the financing of research by environmentalists, who would then represent the public at licensing hearings, are in the general interest. Finally, NCPP proposals contained numerous suggestions that public policy reflect the views of market economics—for example, deregulation of transportation.

The Regulation of Mining

The representatives of the coal industry agreed that mining imposes a variety of costs on the environment and the general public, and government regulation was seen as necessary to ensure that mining industry techniques included environmental protection. A wide variety of harmful effects of mining on the environment were detailed in *Where We Agree*. The list included devastation of the surface through strip mining, acid drainage from mines, sedimentation of streams, the disruption of underground water tables, the leaching of minerals from the earth and their deposit in harmful quantities downstream, the collapse of the earth above abandoned mines leading to extensive property losses, uncontrolled fires in unworked mines, the competition for scarce water resources in the West, the pollution of the air by the production of dust, the nerve-racking effects of surface and underground blasting, damage to wildlife and plant species, the destruction of archaeological sites, and the creation of the social pathologies of mining boom towns. *Where We Agree* reminds us of why medieval artists often depicted Hell as a mining operation. Despite this litany of problems, the NCPP by intention did not treat the issues of the health and safety of mine workers.

In return for the industrialists' recognition of the many sins of mining, the environmentalists conceded a need for flexible administration in government regulation of controversial strip-mining practices. Under some circumstances, for example, the environmentalists agreed to permit mountaintop-removal mining in the Appalachian area, if it were done on an experimental basis with controls for acid water runoff. Such an exception might be permitted if there were a need for cheap land to build a subdivision for workers' housing. Activists opposed to strip mining, on the other hand, were angered by the idea of allowing any exception to the ban on mountaintop removal in the Surface Mining Control and Reclamation Act of 1977 (SMCRA). This kind of compromise was one reason the EPC opposed enactment of the proposals articulated in *Where We Agree*.

In addition, the NCPP would permit exceptions to the mandate that strip-mined lands in the Midwest be reclaimed. For example, the NCPP argued that, on occasion, smoothing over the interior "highwalls" of surface mines might actually result in the destruction of some of the remaining top quality farmland. This position contradicted the strip-mining legislation of 1977. Indeed, NCPP environmentalists would permit some exceptions to the ban on mining of alluvial soils (deposited by rivers and streams) in the dry regions of the West. They conceded that it is occasionally possible to strip mine in such areas without destroying scarce farmland and wreaking other environmental havoc. Leaving unreclaimed highwalls and strip mining alluvial valleys run counter to strongly held positions of anti-strip-mining activists. In her press release denouncing the project, Dunlap cited these two exceptions to SMCRA as among its worst features.

Simplified Licensing Procedures

To win approval of a project, such as a power plant or strip mine, a business must demonstrate compliance with each federal, state, and local law regulating such development. If environmentalists contest a project, the permit-granting agency holds hearings at which both sides present their arguments. Business has the money for the background research necessary to develop persuasive testimony, but the environmentalists have an equally effective tool. They are able to block a project by stretching the hearings out over many years. The NCPP proposed that licensing hearings be consolidated, which would prevent delaying tactics. In compensation, the NCPP suggested grants of public money for high-quality research to back the environmental perspective at these consolidated hearings. Officials might then base their decisions more on data and less on the outcome of a protracted series of legal skirmishes.

The trade-off of one-stop licensing and public funding is, in the abstract, an attractive proposal. Electric generating capacity could be increased much more rapidly. Yet the interests of various concerned publics could be represented effectively in the single (albeit elaborate) licensing hearing, because public funding would ensure adequate staff and research for citizens' groups to prepare for the hearing.

The licensing/funding trade-off is a good example of an important NCPP proposal that is difficult to implement. Licensing of power-plant sites is primarily a state government function. Thus, it might be necessary to get the trade-off enacted into law by laborious organizing and campaigning, state by state. Of course, the idea might be said to be successfully implemented, even if it were not adopted by every state. The similar proposal by the mining committee for such a trade-off in mine siting and reclamation suits involves functions that are explicitly recognized under SMCRA as belonging to state government and would thus, presumably, require state-by-state campaigning to achieve passage.

Implementation of proposals that primarily involve state government is difficult. One approach would be to pass trade-off legislation in one or two states judged most friendly to the idea and where the plan would have a fair chance of surviving the administrative process. Moss envisioned a new federal law to enact the trade-off; the act would provide federal funding for the public interest groups and mandate one-stop hearing procedures for federal licenses. In January 1980 the air pollution committee produced a model bill for a "Federal Energy Facility Act" that embodied Moss's idea. A "Model State Utility Siting Statute" also was produced to indicate the type of legislation the federal government would reward with grants.

The problem with the Moss proposal and passage of trade-off legislation at the state level is the business community's overwhelming opposition to public financing of public interest groups. Public financing of citizen intervenors—even in the trade-off situation in which one-stop licensing is mandated—is part of the same family of ideas as Nader's federal consumer agency proposal, which provoked massive business opposition in 1978. Because of these difficulties in implementation, some might argue that the licensing trade-off agreements are not very significant. But these ideas need to be explored further because of their own value and because of the lessons they teach. Trade-offs similar to the NCPP's licensing/funding agreements might be adopted in other types of conflicts.

Concepts from Market Economics

At a meeting in September 1979, Moss addressed the entire group, reminding them of their mutual dedication to the expansion of principles of market economics within the coal sector of the economy. Moss noted that government intervention is justified to get the market to reflect the true social costs of coal production, but that he—and everyone else within the NCPP— was opposed to excessive government intervention in the coal economy. The message presented by the leaders of the NCPP was clear: rational, disinterested, public-spirited discussion can produce agreement between disputants by the application of economic principles and concepts.

Indeed, the NCPP's thirty industrialists and thirty environmentalists frequently were able to reach agreements through the processes symbolized by Moss's sermon and Quinn's call for the reaffirmation of the rule of reason. Of course, one reason for their affability was that some of the environmental participants were recruited by Moss, and his recruits were not offended by the application of economic concepts to environmental issues. Nevertheless, the Quinn/Moss approach would have been productive in other circumstances of mediation. This is because many Americans adhere to values that affirm the importance of individualism, limited government, and coordination of personal activity through the "hidden hand" of the market. These values, as expressed in the concepts of market economics, can compel far-reaching agreement among seemingly disparate people.[14]

The short version of *Where We Agree* states nine principles that summarize the hundreds of NCPP agreements. Five of these nine principles are stated in economic terms: (1) policies that require the beneficiary to pay the full cost of using "public goods" should be encouraged; (2) the government's role in the economic regulation of energy markets should be reduced by placing greater reliance on free-market mechanisms; (3) dollars spent on pollution abatement should achieve the maximum reduction in pollution; (4) public policy should discourage the uneconomical use of energy; and (5) energy policy and social policy should be addressed separately.[15] The last point means that energy usage by the poor or by other groups should not be directly subsidized, although "income transfers . . . might be considered. On the other hand, policies that artificially depress energy prices cause distortions of market and investment decisions, lead to higher rates of inflation, and eventually produce an even greater adverse impact on those of low income." [16]

To find that business representatives value a "free market," minimally constrained by government, is not surprising, nor that industrial leaders find free-market terminology persuasive in justifying NCPP proposals. But many people were surprised to find the environmentalists in the NCPP using free-market terminology. The New Deal liberals of the 1930s through the 1960s usually scorned such terminology, which they associated with arguments against increased federal economic intervention. During the 1970s, partly because of the discrediting of the federal government by Vietnam and Watergate, partly because of shortcomings in the Great Society programs, many politicians and intellectuals of the Center-Left placed less faith in government action and more trust in free-market values. Environmentalists, however, had not contributed visibly to this trend. Indeed, environmentalists still used the vocabulary of natural law, moralism, and populist denunciations of large economic and governmental institutions.[17]

In the 1970s, however, a trend within academic political economy research caught the attention of some environmentalists. During the 1960s and 1970s, economists had been giving increased attention to questions of "market failure" and "public goods," which apply directly to many of the environmentalists' greatest concerns. Market failure refers to situations in which an economic actor imposes "external costs" upon others, but there is no feasible way to charge the actor for these costs without some authoritative intervention. Many cases of pollution have this characteristic; a chimney emitting dirty exhaust is an obvious example. Similarly, a public good is one that is jointly supplied to a group and that cannot be readily appropriated for sale: clean air and water are classic examples. Environmentalists, of course, are often the defenders of public goods, which may be undervalued in the political-economic marketplace.

Economists deal with questions of market failure and of public goods by discussing how the true "social costs" might somehow be measured, and how the "externalities might be internalized" in the cost-benefit calculations of economic actors. Accordingly, some of the more pragmatic environmentalists (such as Larry Moss) realized that the concepts of economics could be used *for* them as well as against them, in arguing that polluters impose costs upon society. Some environmentalists also agreed with economists' arguments that financial incentives to polluters are more effective than governmental *fiat* in attaining clean air and water.

So the stage was set for mutual agreement between some industrialists and environmentalists. Business representatives were naturally pleased that environmentalists in the NCPP spoke their language. In return, the industrialists found it hard to resist the idea of "internalizing the externalities" as it applies to coal mining. When these principles are applied, agreement on another matter, such as governmental deregulation and reduction of subsidies in transportation policy, follows readily. Even in Congress, conservatives favoring business have joined Sen. Edward Kennedy, D-Mass., and some other liberals in pressing for the deregulation of airlines, railroads, and trucking.[18]

Why Implementation Failed

Given the surprising breadth of agreement reached by the National Coal Policy Project, why did the project have so little direct impact upon policy? One reason is that unless the findings of a private mediation effort receive top political priority, such an effort will have little direct impact. Rather, it will be an exercise in setting the policy agenda. An effort like the NCPP must include government participants to ensure that government decision makers will pay serious attention to the results of the mediation effort.

The major flaw of the NCPP was that, although participants could reach agreements when acting as individuals, they could not get their own organizations to endorse these agreements and to lobby for them. Why, then, did lobbies and corporations refuse to endorse the NCPP platform? Or, more precisely, why wouldn't such groups endorse even one or two important planks in the platform?

As stated earlier, most interest groups seek to avoid internal conflicts. Thus, when it became apparent that prominent environmentalists Louise Dunlap and Richard Ayres opposed the project's findings, leaders of other environmental groups lost interest in pushing an endorsement of *Where We Agree* through their organizational governing boards.

Also, as noted, lobbyists ordinarily avoid angering their normal coalition partners. Consequently, on a relatively low-priority issue such as the coal policy project, leaders of environmental lobbies did not endorse *Where We Agree,* because to do so would anger Dunlap's group. As a seasoned Washington lobbyist with a firm grasp of her position, Dunlap made good use of her prestige and understanding of group norms in thwarting the NCPP. She protested to the Sierra Club's executive board the participation of Michael McCloskey, the club's executive director. Dunlap argued that McCloskey was spending too much of his time on the NCPP, that NCPP's goals were suspect, and that McCloskey accordingly was neglecting the Sierra Club's business. Moss tried to refute Dunlap's argument in a confrontation at an executive board meeting, but Dunlap proved more persuasive, and the board ordered McCloskey to cease his NCPP activities. After this, the chances for Sierra Club endorsement became remote, and this, added to the resistance of the other groups, made endorsement by environmental lobbies most unlikely. Without an effective counterattack from the NCPP (which never came), the maneuver by Dunlap was enough to thwart the implementation of *Where We Agree* because Carter administration officials would not look at it unless it had major environmentalist support.

The difficulty in gaining endorsements from environmental lobbies greatly reduced the incentives for obtaining endorsements from trade associations or individual companies. Winning approval from just the corporate side made little sense because the project would then appear as a corporate-sponsored effort to co-opt environmental opinion. In addition, business associations are subject to the same logic of avoiding conflict as any other group. NCPP leaders, for instance, believed that most of the directors of the National Coal Association favored the general position of *Where We Agree*, but that a few companies saw the compromises as standing in the way of deregulating strip mining. In any event, the NCA did not vote on the proposals, and its spokesman refused to discuss the NCA's position, possibly indicating internal divisions on the matter.

Dow Chemical's Gerald Decker was one person who would have risked his job to get a corporate endorsement for the NCPP. Shortly after *Where We Agree* was issued, however, Decker left Dow to work for Kaiser Aluminum, a heavy user of electricity.

The NCPP leadership was surprised by the difficulty in getting government to put *Where We Agree* into practice. There are a number of reasons for the failure. First, the NCPP was a new type of endeavor, and its leaders had no clear idea of what to expect. In fact, the NCPP leaders succeeded more than they had anticipated in getting agreement among the participants. There would have been nothing to implement had there been no agreements. After their initial success, it appeared that little thought had been given to the postagreement stage. The NCPP executive committee turned the implementation phase over to the staff at the Center for Strategic and International Studies; but CSIS personnel, although expert at organizing conferences and seminars, knew little about lobbying tactics. Despite positive media treatment and favorable attention from academic writers on energy policy[19] and the several dozen successful seminars and briefings that were held on the NCPP, little was done in the way of lobbying government.

In the second year after publication of *Where We Agree*, the lobbying failure was recognized, and CSIS hired a former congressional staffer to work for the NCPP platform. Some progress was made, especially when Larry Moss arranged for CSIS to meet with regulation writers from the Federal Energy Regulatory Commission (FERC) and also to comment on proposed Office of Strip Mining (OSM) regulations. And CSIS found a member of Congress, Rep. Don Pease, D-Ohio, who would introduce bills embodying important NCPP measures. Nevertheless, after March 1980, the National Coal Policy Project was shut down, except for report writing.

The leaders of the NCPP had assumed that a detailed and well-reasoned statement of compromise agreements would assume a sort of overwhelming legitimacy with decision makers. The NCPP leadership did not anticipate the refusal of the participants' organizations to endorse the proposals. The expectation apparently was that a grand coalition of groups would come together, which, through political strength and moral prestige, would compel action from government decision makers. The National Coal Policy Project shows, however, that for regulatory negotiations among groups to influence government policy, the state almost certainly must be involved in the negotiation process. Implementing agreements reached by "ambassadors" of contending groups is otherwise too difficult, because group leadership frequently will ignore or disown the work of the ambassadors.

Six years after the NCPP disbanded, it appears that its main impact has been to encourage the development of a still-experimental concept known as "regulatory negotiation." According to its chief advocate, Washington lawyer Philip J. Harter, "Regulatory negotiation is a process by which representatives of the interests that would be substantially affected by a regulation meet together to develop the initial draft of the regulation through direct negotiations." [20] Harter and most proponents of such negotiation now advise that agency representatives assume an active role in this process.

Although this type of negotiation involves group representatives in discussions and compromises much like those carried on by the NCPP, a major difference is that these efforts are tied to specific sets of regulations, often issued by a single governmental agency. Regulatory negotiation is much more specific in its goals than was the NCPP, which aimed to develop a platform to deal with most of the major issues in an entire industrial sector.[21]

Conclusion: The Power Triad

Regulatory negotiation is an example of a "power triad," which may be distinguished from the "iron triangle" or "subgovernment" concepts, discussed in Chapter 11. In an iron triangle, interest groups, executive branch officials, and legislators form a single coalition that breaches the distinction between the public sector and private interest group organization. The power triad, on the other hand, has three participants, but they do not ordinarily form a coalition. The first party is an aggregate of economic producers or related organizations—big corporations, trade or professional associations—with interests in a particular area of government policy. The second participant is one or more interest groups that represent public concerns about the same policy area. The widely shared interest in a healthy environment is one example of this second factor.[22] The state—those government agencies that regulate behavior in the policy area—is the triad's third participant.

The concept of the triad assumes a separation of powers, an adversarial process between economic producers and lobbies representing other widely shared interests. Within the triad, the state has an independent power base, and it has the capacity to initiate policy proposals, perhaps with the intent of satisfying most of the contending groups.[23] One such activity is state-initiated regulatory negotiation; public officials mediate differences between the other two triadic participants for the sake of timely decision making.

For the power triad to exist, environmentalists or other general interests must have organized group representation. For the triad to be whole, the state must participate with its independent and authoritative base of power.

Notes

This paper is based on fifty-one interviews with participants in the National Coal Policy Project, executive branch personnel in coal-related areas, and individuals interested in coal policy issues and in the development of the regulatory negotiation concept. I would like to thank the Ford Foundation and the Russell Sage Foundation for financial assistance. Resources for the Future and the Brookings Institution assisted this research by providing office space.

1. Francis X. Murray, *The National Coal Policy Project: Final Report* (Washington, D.C.: Center for Strategic and International Studies, Georgetown University, 1981), 20-21.
2. These figures are based on my inspection of the records of the NCPP. No company gave more than 3.5 percent of the total NCPP budget.
3. Murray, *Final Report,* 21.
4. See Francis X. Murray, ed., *Where We Agree: Report of the National Coal Policy Project,* 2 vols. (Boulder, Colo.: Westview Press, 1978).
5. Ibid.
6. See James Q. Wilson, *Political Organizations* (New York: Basic Books, 1973), chap. 13; Anne N. Costain, "The Struggle for a National Women's Lobby: Organizing a Diffuse Interest," *Western Political Quarterly* 33 (December 1980): 476-491; Jeffrey Berry, *Lobbying for the People* (Princeton, N.J.: Princeton University Press, 1977), 254-261; Berry, *The Interest Group Society* (Boston: Little, Brown & Co., 1984), 202-205; and Kay Lehman Schlozman and John T. Tierney, *Organized Interests and American Democracy* (New York: Harper & Row, 1985), 278-287.
7. James Q. Wilson, *Political Organizations,* chap. 3; Andrew S. McFarland, *Common Cause* (Chatham, N.J.: Chatham House Publishers, 1984), 95-99; and McFarland, *Public Interest Lobbies: Decision Making on Energy* (Washington, D.C.: American Enterprise Institute, 1976), 83-99.
8. Russell Hardin, *Collective Action* (Baltimore: Johns Hopkins University Press, 1982), especially chaps. 2, 10-14.
9. The Mellon and Ford Foundations were principal backers, and the Rockefeller and Scaife Foundations also contributed.
10. Actually, there were 105 participants in all, largely because business participants sometimes organized backup caucuses of other executives, who were not, however, official participants in NCPP negotiating sessions.
11. Milton R. Wessel, *The Rule of Reason* (Reading, Mass.: Addison-Wesley, 1976).
12. Francis X. Murray, ed., *Where We Agree: Report of the National Coal Policy Project, Summary and Synthesis* (Washington, D.C.: Center for Strategic and International Studies, Georgetown University, 1978).

13. *New York Times,* Feb. 10, 1978, 1.
14. Louis Hartz, *The Liberal Tradition in America* (New York: Harcourt, Brace & World, 1955).
15. *Where We Agree: Summary and Synthesis,* 9-14.
16. Ibid, 12-13.
17. Mary Douglas and Aaron Wildavsky, *Risk and Culture* (Berkeley: University of California Press, 1982).
18. Martha Derthick and Paul J. Quirk, *The Politics of Deregulation* (Washington: The Brookings Institution, 1985), 39-56.
19. See *Energy Future,* 1st ed., ed. Robert Stobaugh and Daniel Yergin (New York: Random House, 1979), 106-107; Sam H. Schurr, *Energy in America's Future* (Baltimore: Johns Hopkins University Press, 1979), 9-11, 540.
20. Philip J. Harter, "Regulatory Negotiation: The Experience So Far," *Resolve* (Winter 1984): 1. (*Resolve* is "a quarterly newsletter on environmental dispute resolution," published by the Conservation Foundation, 1717 Massachusetts Ave., N.W., Washington, D.C. 20036). See also Lawrence Susskind and Gerard McMahon, "The Theory and Practice of Negotiated Rulemaking," *Yale Journal on Regulation* 3 (1985): 133-165.
21. Regulatory negotiation is a current event. As this chapter is being written (February 1986), there is no published discussion of the five experiments in regulatory negotiation conducted by agencies of the federal government during 1982-1985.
22. Andrew S. McFarland, "Public Interest Lobbies Versus Minority Faction," in *Interest Group Politics,* 1st ed., ed. Allan J. Cigler and Burdett A. Loomis, (Washington, D.C.: CQ Press, 1983), 324-353.
23. James Q. Wilson, ed., *The Politics of Regulation* (New York: Basic Books, 1980), chap. 10 and passim.

17. Moving On:
Interests, Power, and Politics in the 1980s

Allan J. Cigler and Burdett A. Loomis

Interest group scholars, after a 15-year hiatus, reawakened in the 1980s to discover both continuity and change in the representation of interests.[1] Political scientists writing in the 1980s, generally confirm what journalists report—there is an explosion in representation, but the real effects of such a trend are extremely difficult to assess. When, ask Kay Lehman Schlozman and John Tierney, does "more of the same" become something qualitatively different?[2] In trying to answer this question, we quickly run into the Madisonian dilemma—our political system encourages the representation of diverse interests, which in turn *can* lead to the systematic granting of preferences to a few favored interests.[3]

More than with most academic subfields, the study of interest groups often has led to overgeneralizations based on scanty evidence. In addition, journalists, opportunistic politicians, and would-be reformers have tended to blame lobbyists and "special interests" for policy outcomes that are produced by the entire political system. Fortunately, a series of major data collection efforts, along with subsequent analyses, have begun to build the foundation for the systematic reexamination of the politics of groups and interests.

In this concluding chapter, we will try to assess some of the emerging developments in the study of interest group politics. The central problem is how to fit major changes, like the growth of PACs, into a broader framework, such as the historic role of money in politics. The rebirth in the 1980s of scholarly work on interest groups is heartening, but if the contributions are to endure, there must be a continuing resonance between our theories and our empirical work. Otherwise, we will fall back to an overreliance on case studies, alarmism, and stereotyping in a field that demands a healthy respect for complexity and for tentative answers to difficult questions.

The work of Mancur Olson and others on the nature of group formation and maintenance illustrates the possibilities for the integration of theory building and empirical work.[4] We know a good deal about why individuals join groups and how the many obstacles to group formation are overcome. Our knowledge is neither as theoretical nor as empirically sound when it comes to assessing the impact of interest group funding of campaigns, the nature of policy networks in the Balkanized state, and changes within

Washington's lobbying and public relations community.

PACs, Parties, and Political Money

Groups, interests, and scholars have had more than a decade to consider the effects of the 1974 legislation that led to the tremendous growth in political action committees (PACs). Aside from basic agreement on the changing scope of PAC activity, no consensus exists on their impact on campaigns or legislative behavior. Rather, we have a good deal of hand wringing about their potentially harmful effects, countered by similar levels of reassurances as to their essentially innocuous nature.

The evidence suggests that the impact of PACs is neither as malignant as reformers suggest nor as benign as supporters proclaim. Money does appear to matter, but its impact varies according to specific circumstances. For example, PAC contributions affect legislative voting more on consensual issues than on conflictual ones, and both party and ideology exert more influence than do financial considerations (see Chapter 6).

The mixed findings on the effects of PACs result in part from assumptions that have equated the amount of money raised (or spent) with groups' political efficiency and unity of purpose. Most PACs are, however, small, based outside of the Washington area, and "remarkably unsophisticated" in their contribution strategies.[5] Many PACs spend the greatest part of their money on maintaining the organization. Nor are most PAC contributions especially large, even among the more affluent corporate groups. A survey of corporate PACs found that the average 1984 donations were $295 for House candidates and $1,103 for Senate aspirants. The mean employee contribution to such PACs was $112 per year, and more than 60 percent were smaller than $100.[6]

This is not to say that relatively small amounts of money cannot have impact, especially when bundled together by the PACs. Rather, money in politics is more than simply PAC activity, and the focus on these committees may obscure as much as it enlightens. Many corporations do not organize PACs. Moreover, a 1986 study found that many PACs are established without any immediate legislative goals. Interviews with PAC managers demonstrated that

> some companies set up PACs as a way to gain a public presence, instead of influencing legislation. Creation of a PAC provides a relatively cheap way to get on the invitation list to public events, prestigious dinners and other publicized gatherings.[7]

As a research strategy, it may make sense to consider PAC activity less as a separate entity and more as one weapon among many in the arsenal of political interests. One corporate government relations manager asserted,

> A PAC simply makes my lobbying job easier; it's a tool, and only as good as my skill in using it. . . . I know of companies with a PAC that are worthless in terms of getting things done in legislatures and those without that know which buttons to push and really get things done.[8]

Scholars also have noted the changing relations between PACs and political parties. During the early years of PAC growth, 1974-1980, PACs and parties often competed hotly for campaign funds. More recently, however, parties have begun to move from "purveyors of the party symbol and conduits to the ballot, to vendors of campaign and organizational service." [9] Political scientist Paul Herrnson has observed that "the institutionalization of the national parties has ... transformed the hostility that surrounded early party-PAC ... relations into a less conflictual and, in many ways, highly cooperative set of relationships." [10]

In the late 1980s parties and PACs are developing mutually beneficial links that reflect a mature stage of growth. Although the Republicans remain far ahead of the Democrats, both national party organizations have formed loose fund-raising alliances with some prominent PACs. The parties have created "booster clubs," financed in part by PACs in exchange for regular briefings and the opportunity to meet with influential legislators. In their emerging role as brokers, the national parties actively assist PACs in directing contributions to particular campaigns. They aid candidates by soliciting funds from potential donor PACs. Managers of the four congressional campaign committees have routine contacts with PACs, as well as providing specialized and timely information to them on key congressional campaigns.

As James Guth and John Green (Chapter 5) point out, PAC contributors are not especially antagonistic to political parties, and the business-labor division among PACs roughly follows the New Deal divisions that continue to differentiate the parties. Even ideological and single-interest PACs have not transformed American politics in any fundamental way. Such groups must still push their issues onto the broad, public agenda, which continues to be dominated by economic concerns. And political parties remain the key mechanism for such agenda setting.

In sum, the political system is attempting to adjust to the PAC phenomenon that took most observers by surprise in the late 1970s. We should remember that even Common Cause, currently the most alarmist of groups, supported the original 1974 legislation. In the end, the "problem" of PACs is a problem of money in politics, and it is difficult to believe that the system of the late 1980s is worse than what led to the "reforms" of the 1970s. In 1972, one individual, W. Clement Stone, gave Richard Nixon's campaign more than $2 million, and Stewart Mott contributed $729,000 to George McGovern. The current PAC limits seem paltry in comparison. Reaching back a bit farther to the golden age of political parties, we find that Republican Mark Hanna could fund William McKinley's presidential campaign through "assessments" on major businesses throughout the nation. PACs and political money do present us with difficult questions, but we should watch how the parties and PACs are adapting, rather than jumping to unfounded, self-righteous conclusions.

Subsystems, Accommodation, and Competition

The expanding presence of the federal government, the proliferation of interests, and the fragmentation of representation (both public and private) have created a paradoxical situation. There are now so many points of view that it is more difficult to set priorities and implement the legislation that does come forth. Like Olson's "free-rider" problem, the intense and effective representation of particular interests can be seen as an obstacle that must be overcome. We thus have "gangs" of top leaders negotiating secret Social Security compromises[11] and Congress opting for the automatic, across-the-board budget cutting requirements of the Gramm-Rudman-Hollings legislation.

One widely held perception about the nation's budget problems is that special interests have captured key parts of the policy process—subcommittees and administrative bodies, for example. As a result, policy makers will not act to hurt these interests in any substantial way. Economist Peter Navarro, a harsh critic of special interest politics, concludes that "the private use of public policy" does more than simply benefit particular groups; there is an additional "net loss to our nation so that the public interest is almost always harmed." [12]

No doubt, interest groups often have such an effect, but we see words such as *capture* or *control* as implying an overly powerful and insidious role for interests—which does not hold up to close scrutiny. This is especially true when we focus on initial policy formulation. There is a good deal of evidence that many outcomes are unintended consequences of policies that interests may have played little part in formulating. Rather, the policies frequently open the door to interest group mobilization in the implementation process.

At the same time, increased representation often leads to heightened levels of competition within a given policy subsystem, particularly as budget demands redefine more and more policies as redistributive. We will briefly examine two developing federal policies—disability "rights" and food stamps—to demonstrate how subsystem politics have evolved and continue to change in the 1980s.

Disability Policy and the Creation of a Subsystem

From small acorns grow mighty oaks, or so the saying goes. A policy forest sprouted from one sentence in the Rehabilitation Act of 1973. Section 504 states, in its entirety, "No otherwise handicapped individual in the United States, as defined in Section 7, shall, solely by reason of his handicap, be excluded from participation in, denied the benefits of, or be subjected to discrimination under any program or activity receiving Federal financial assistance."

Section 504 was a routine, noncontroversial statement that implied no immediate, major changes. No legislative meetings were held to explain it; it produced no discussion on the floor of either chamber, aroused no public debate, and caused no concern over the costs of implementation. In fact, Section 504 was an afterthought, "the result of a spontaneous impulse by a group of Senate aides who had little experience or knowledge about the problem of discrimination against disabled people." [13] As this acorn of policy grew apace it entailed the expenditure of billions of dollars, both public and private, to modify architectural designs and transportation systems, as well as affecting employment in any federally funded program.

The Department of Health, Education, and Welfare (HEW) assumed the task of interpreting the 1973 legislation. Within HEW, Section 504 was assigned to the Office of Civil Rights (OCR), rather than to the Rehabilitation Services Administration (RSA). This decision benefited the handicapped because OCR attorneys tended to emphasize rights and procedures, rather than voluntary compliance, the policy RSA preferred. The OCR staff wrote the Section 504 regulations without the assistance of organized groups and without any regard for the costs of implementation because "rights" were at stake.

It was not until 1975, at the urging of OCR professionals, that various disability-based organizations came together to influence policy results. As an outgrowth of a meeting of the President's Committee on Employment of the Handicapped, nineteen groups formed the American Coalition of Citizens with Disabilities. *Funding for the coalition came from HEW.* As might be expected, a tightly knit subgovernment quickly developed, and it became difficult to draw clear distinctions between the public and private sectors. Some government officials moved to consulting positions with handicapped rights groups, and lobbyist/advocates for the disabled joined the staffs of congressional committees and government agencies. By the late 1970s the triangular bonds among the legislative and administrative branches and the interests were thus cemented, and no effective opposition was mobilized. [14] In policy sectors where unopposed minorities operate, special interests tend to dominate, and issue networks frequently are unified and autonomous.

While valuable in depicting how groups (with some assistance) can "capture" a policy area during implementation, this brief handicapped rights example does not typify most Washington-based policy making in the 1980s. Although the notions of autonomous subgovernments and iron triangles can be highly useful as pedagogical devices, they are more accurately applied to distributive policies, where benefits are concentrated and costs diffused (e.g., veterans' benefits, maritime subsidies, defense procurements). In searching for tight triangles of influence, political scientist Hugh Heclo observed that "we tend to miss the fairly open networks of people that increasingly impinge upon government." [15]

Whatever we label these permeable policy subsystems—issue networks or policy communities—the fact remains that openness and complexity are their hallmarks. This has real consequences for interests and groups as the subsystems become more competitive and as countervailing power develops into more of a reality and less a promise of pluralist theory.

Food Stamps and the Growth of a Competitive Policy Community

As with handicapped rights policies, unelected government officials played the major role in initiating the food stamp program. John Kennedy touched upon the idea in the 1960 presidential campaign, but it took several years before food stamps became a reality, as developed by U.S. Agriculture Department (USDA) officials.

From an initial pilot effort, food stamps grew into a multibillion-dollar program that produces continuing controversy among the "hunger lobby," a set of agricultural groups, the USDA, and the relevant congressional committees and subcommittees. In the view of political scientist Jeffrey Berry,

> The food stamp issue network is relatively open rather than tightly knit ...
> [without] the unity of purpose associated with iron triangles. A common
> outlook and cooperative working relationship among the committee, USDA,
> and lobbyists has been the exception and not the rule. ... Sometimes two
> sides of the triangle have worked against a third. ... "Is the food stamp
> network a mutual self-help arrangement?" It hardly appears so. Instead, it
> is composed of shifting coalitions and principled infighters.[16]

Despite its controversial nature, from a democratic theory perspective the food stamp program appears to work fairly well. Major policy decisions can be affected by executive leadership, by the outcomes of congressional elections, and even by public opinion preferences. In addition, both conservatives and liberals are included within the loose network, and congressional oversight of the program is reasonably effective.[17] Issue network politics resists strong generalizations, but, for highly contentious policies, open and changing subsystems may be the rule.

The New Subsystem Politics

We see the recent proliferation of groups and well-represented interests as changing not only the number of participants in the policy process, but also leading to a qualitative difference in the scope and competitiveness of the pressure system. Several developments seem notable. First, many distributive policy areas have been politically redefined as redistributive; in a related vein, the policy agenda is no longer tightly controlled by a narrow group of interests. The classic example may be the agriculture sector (see Chapter 10), which has moved from a relatively closed set of subgovernments to a loose issue network with participants ranging from traditional farm groups to environmentalists to churches. The 1985 farm bill was both highly visible and complex; large numbers of interests and governmental actors took part in its formulation and enactment.

Second, the period between the Kennedy and Reagan administrations can be regarded as a "regulatory and redistributive revolution in American public policy." [18] Regulatory and redistributive politics are not characterized by compromise, accommodation, and secrecy; rather they involve confrontation, a wider scope of conflict, and the potential for enhanced public scrutiny.

Unlike iron triangle politics, where the final arbiter is a key bureau or subcommittee, the politics of regulatory and redistributive issues is typified by involvement of the full Congress, the executive branch, and even the president.

As more interests take part in the policy process, fewer unopposed minorities can hold sway. For example, those subgovernment partners, the elderly and Social Security officials, have begun to face organized opposition from younger taxpayers and others who question the long-term vitality of the Social Security system. Even the imposing and powerful National Rifle Association faces opposition from gun control groups and a threat from an emerging animal rights movement.[19]

In short, more areas of policy are becoming competitive. Even in handicapped rights policy, affected interests, such as universities and public transportation systems, which found compliance with the law very costly, have fought back to modify standards and requirements. Moreover, Reagan appointees in relevant agencies may have disturbed the "cozy" relations between government officials and special interests (see Chapters 9 and 11). Understanding the contemporary politics of interests and groups is less a matter of dealing with autonomous and impervious subgovernments and more a question of grasping the complexity and fluidity of issue networks in highly controversial, and often technical, policy areas. This development can lead to a new set of difficulties for scholars and policy makers alike. Scholars find issue networks sloppy and unpredictable, and elected officials may not have the time, expertise, or desire to expend the political capital essential to win control of network policy making. The politics of access and influence have thus changed, and dramatically so, during the 1980s.

Two Tiers of Access

Historically, political scientists and lobbyists alike have emphasized the importance of access for interest group success. An interest group could not take part in the policy debate without knowing the key players, although access alone was not enough to guarantee success. Robert K. Gray, chairman of one of Washington's top lobbying and public relations firms, expresses the conventional wisdom here:

> Access is an earned, essential raw material for the lobbying process but vastly overrated as a finished product all by itself. No dam was ever built . . . solely on the basis of access. . . .
> Today, many public officials are moving to private practice. . . . [For those who] put in the time and effort to develop expertise and credibility . . . the raw material of instant recognition can be refined into a lifetime of access. For the rest, access will evaporate without doing them or their clients any good.[20]

Professional Washington representatives, like other political actors, rely heavily on establishing long-term, trusting relationships, but they must also be capable of adapting to changing political circumstances.

To the extent that policy communities have become less tightly structured and more permeable, lobbying practices also have been affected. Although the job of a rank-and-file Washington representative may have changed relatively little since the 1960s, the tremendous growth in the number of lobbyists (Senate registrations rose to 20,400 from 5,662 between 1981 to 1985) has created a setting in which *top-level* access is extremely important, or is at least perceived as such.[21] In a fragmented system of policy making, the ability to reach the president, his key aides, and top congressional leaders becomes an increasingly valuable, and expensive, resource.

Such high-level access-mongering reflects a central irony of contemporary policy making. Fragmentation requires that legions of lobbyists and allied group members work diligently to influence dozens of members of Congress, midlevel agency officials, and their staffs. The politics of complex policies and expansive issue networks demands this kind of detailed, labor-intensive effort. The 1985-1986 efforts to revise the tax code represent a good case in point. Literally hundreds of lobbyists from hundreds of interests monitored the proceedings as the revisions moved from the president to the House to the Senate. These efforts exemplify the lower-tier type of lobbying. Small points and narrow interests, relatively speaking, are considered in the context of an extended discussion among policy experts.

At the same time, top-echelon "government relations professionals," such as Gray, Charls Walker, or ex-Reagan aide Michael Deaver, often seek to rise above the fragmentation by communicating directly with the highest ranking decision makers. Much, though not all, of this upper-tier access is obtained through the efforts of individuals who have spent time within the administration that they are attempting to influence. To demonstrate their influence,

> many former Reagan officials emphasize their ability to reach back into the White House, and even place ground-to-air telephone calls to Air Force One, but few have been involved in the nitty-gritty of lobbying. With [one] exception, they were in scant evidence through the debate on the tax bill, which brought hundreds of lobbyists to Capitol Hill.[22]

The lobbying activities of "in and outers" have long been questioned, and some modest rules govern the ability of ex-government officials to make contact with their past agency on behalf of a client. With many more lobbyists roaming the halls of Congress and populating the K Street and Georgetown office buildings, the "more of the same" question, posed at the beginning of this chapter, begs to be addressed.

Although there are no simple answers here, we see much of the lower-tier lobbying as an extension of those practices that have evolved in the politics of the modern, post-FDR period. Two key differences seem apparent. First, the sheer number of interests and lobbyists tends to redefine many policies from distributive (e.g., more guns *and* farm subsidies) to redistributive (e.g., more guns *or* continued farm subsidies). To the extent that policy decisions are defined in redistributive, zero-sum terms, lobbyists and policy makers may be less inclined toward flexibility and compromise, which traditionally have dominated the American policy process.

Second, when the "more of the same" of interest representation comes packaged in a new way, it may turn into something qualitatively different. Particularly important is the development of "full-service" lobbying/public relations/campaign organizations, such as the Kamber Group, Pat Caddell's Cambridge Survey Research, and the overlapping firms of Black, Manafort, Stone and Atwater/Kelly (Atwater works only for the campaign firm, Kelly only for the lobbying firm; the other partners work for both). The range of services offered by such organizations permits them to undertake coordinated broad-gauged attempts to influence policy outcomes. This is especially significant for interests that are both wealthy and untutored in national politics—foreign nations and a good many corporations come immediately to mind. More qualitative differences have taken place in the upper-tier business of providing access. Top lobbyists ply their trade more openly than ever, represent many foreign clients, and deal with decisions that have extraordinary financial implications.

Openness

Lobbyists traditionally have shunned mass publicity, although the best ones have always been sensitive to maintaining a reputation for power. By the 1980s, however, as veteran Washington journalist Meg Greenfield observed,

> individuals known to be close to the president enjoyed enormous, sudden business success in [Washington]. . . .
> But is it new? I would say yes—or at least it is recent. Some people have been cutting deals, trading on their government jobs and the rest since anyone can remember. But I would argue that there is a near *universality and openness* to the hustle now that didn't use to exist. There is something undignified, almost shameless in certain cases. All the lines—political, personal, professional—are crossed.[23]

This notion, that all lines have been crossed, is important because social contacts are as crucial for many top lobbyists as are key policy links. Often, in fact, they are presented as one and the same thing. A U.S. senator noted, disparagingly, "[Lobbyist Robert] Gray is so overrated it's unbelievable. He makes a big splash at parties, but his clients are not getting much for their money." [24] Regardless of their ultimate impact, many upper-tier lobbyists thrive on publicity, whether in the news pages of the *Washington Post* or in its widely read Style section. And politicians seem resigned to, if not totally comfortable with, the new role of high-profile lobbyists.

Foreign Representation

According to Sen. Paul Laxalt, R-Nev., "Everybody needs a Washington representative to protect their hindsides, even foreign governments. So the constituency for [lobbyists] is the entire free-world economy." [25] No aspect of the politics of access has witnessed greater change or more controversy than the representation of foreign interests. The international impact of American tax and trade laws, as well as the billions available in economic and military aid, has created a tremendous demand for the services of Washington representatives. Foreign interests are almost perfect clients for the top lobbying/public relations firms, which can cater to their customers' relative ignorance of the American political process. The international clients are convinced that they are doing everything they can to protect themselves within the arcane worlds of the U.S. Congress and the bureaucracy. Often all they can get is an expensive reassurance. After receiving $950,000 to advise Ferdinand Marcos on media relations, Paul Manafort admitted that if Reagan repudiated Marcos, "I don't know if we will continue to be helpful." [26]

Any number of ethical questions arise with the representation of foreign governments and corporations, especially when American interests are at stake. Nevertheless, such representation seems here to stay, largely because the American policy arena is so important to increasing numbers of foreign interests (see Chapters 13 and 14).

High Stakes and High Fees

In 1977 Charls Walker, then coming into his own as a powerful Washington lobbyist, noted that his income, after a few years on the job, should rise to more than $100,000 per year. [27] Less than a decade later, lobbyists Robert Beckel and David Aylward, less formidable advocates than Walker, estimated that they would each be earning $400,000 by the third year of their firm's existence. [28] The fees commanded by many Washington representatives derive in part from the tremendous stakes involved in policy decisions. A million-dollar "investment" is of little consequence when $100-million-plus corporate tax advantages are under consideration. Not only are top fees very high for upper-tier lobbyists, but interests also provide adequate support for the rapidly growing number of Washington-based lobbyists, lawyers, and public relations consultants.

Assessing the impact of higher stakes and rising fees is difficult. Independent observers often see interests as getting little for their expenditures. To the extent that stakes and fees remain high, however, we can expect the community of Washington lobbyists/lawyers/public relations experts to prosper and become increasingly institutionalized. This makes sense because public relations firms promote themselves as well as their clients. The telling question will be whether the Washington representatives can continue to claim credit as their interests gain more experience and political sophistication.

Conclusion

Political scientist Michael Malbin reminds us of the contingent nature of most political change.

Interest groups, far from being independent actors in the national policy-making process, change their objectives, shift their institutional focus, and modify their lobbying strategies in response to forces beyond their control [which were] produced by the state of the economy ... by a skilled president's ability to control the policy agenda, and ... through the self-consciously adopted changes in Congress and other governmental institutions.[29]

Certainly some parts of the interest group universe have changed substantially in the past fifteen years. In 1976, for example, there was no American Agriculture Movement, and Sun Oil had just won the right to canvass its employees in establishing a PAC. The numerical explosion of group and interest representation in Washington has been nothing short of phenomenal in the private sector, among institutions (e.g., universities, cities, and local governmental units), and within the diverse "public interest" community, where "2,500 ... organizations represent almost every conceivable political viewpoint." [30]

At the same time, the essence of interest representation, like the heart of the legislative process, remains much as it was envisioned by the Framers or witnessed by the cautious revolutionaries who recast American politics in the 1930s. With the evolution of the political system have come related transformations in interest group activities and approaches. Veteran lobbyist Leonard Garment observed, the Constitution would not

actually be a live enterprise without lobbies because that's the way one petitions for the redress of grievances.

This is a country that is so large that the federal notion of representative government saturates our life, and that's very much the case with lobbying.[31]

We thus come full circle, returning to the central question of representation. Political action committees, expanding issue networks, and Washington-based "full-service" lobbying firms all derive from interests' desires for responsiveness within a political system that often is slow and indifferent. In such circumstances, we are likely to find lobbyists offering expensive reassurances to increasing numbers of clients, campaign expenditures continuing to rise, and more interests taking part in the complex politics of issue networks. As our political context changes, so too will interest group politics. Our system may lack responsiveness, but no one can accurately accuse interests and groups of the same shortcoming.

Notes

1. See, among others, Jack L. Walker, "The Origins and Maintenance of Interest Groups in America," *American Political Science Review* 77 (June 1983): 390-406; Kay Lehman Schlozman and John T. Tierney, *Organized Interests and American Democracy* (New York: Harper & Row, 1986); Jeffrey Berry, *The Interest Group Society* (Boston: Little, Brown & Co., 1984); John E. Chubb,

Interest Groups and the Bureaucracy (Stanford, Calif.: Stanford University Press, 1983); and Terry M. Moe, *The Organization of Interests* (Chicago: University of Chicago Press, 1980).

2. Schlozman and Tierney *Organized Interests*, 388ff.
3. Berry, *The Interest Group Society*, 212-213.
4. Mancur Olson, Jr., *The Logic of Collective Action* (New York: Schocken Books, 1968); and Robert H. Salisbury, "An Exchange Theory of Interest Groups," *Midwest Journal of Political Science* 13 (February 1969): 1-32.
5. Theodore J. Eismeier and Philip H. Pollock, "Political Action Committees: Varieties of Organization and Strategy," in *Money and Politics in the United States,* ed. Michael J. Malbin (Chatham, N.J.: Chatham House Publishers, 1984), 122-141.
6. "Putting PACs in Perspective," Editorial, *Nation's Business* 74, May 1986, 96.
7. Thomas B. Edsall and Sandra Evans, "Buying Attention, but Not Votes," *Washington Post National Weekly Edition,* April 14, 1986, 33.
8. As quoted in "Business Involvement in Campaign Finance: Factors Influencing the Decision to Form a Corporate PAC," by Gary J. Andres, *PS* 18 (Spring 1985): 219. By the 1980 election only 52 percent of the companies in the Fortune 500 had formed PACs. Even major companies like Gulf Oil and American Airlines, in highly regulated areas, chose not to form a PAC. See ibid., 215.
9. Stephen E. Frantzich, "Republicanizing the Parties: The Rise of the Service-Vendor Party" (Paper delivered at the Annual Meeting of the Midwest Political Science Association, Chicago, Ill., April 10-12, 1985), 4.
10. Paul S. Herrnson, "National Party Organizations and Congressional Campaigning: National Parties as Brokers" (Paper delivered at the Annual Meeting of the Midwest Political Science Association, Chicago, Ill., April 10-12, 1985), 7.
11. Paul Light, *Artful Work* (New York: Random House, 1985).
12. Peter Navarro, *The Policy Game: How Special Interests and Ideologues Are Stealing America* (New York: John Wiley & Sons, 1984), ix.
13. Richard Scotch, *From Good Will to Civil Rights: Transforming Federal Disability Policy* (Philadelphia: Temple University Press, 1985), 139.
14. Ibid., 82-120, 154-156.
15. Hugh Heclo, "Issue Networks and the Executive Establishment," in *The New American Political System,* ed. Anthony King (Washington, D.C.: American Enterprise Institute, 1978), 88.
16. Jeffrey Berry, *Feeding Hungry People: Rulemaking in the Food Stamp Program* (New Brunswick, N.J.: Rutgers University Press, 1984), 135.
17. Ibid., 133-140.
18. Thomas L. Gais, Mark A. Peterson, and Jack L. Walker, "Interest Groups, Iron Triangles, and Representative Institutions in American National Government," *British Journal of Political Science* 14 (1984): 165.
19. Robert Kasowski, "Showdown on the Hunting Ground," *Outdoor America,* Winter 1986, 8-11, 33-34.
20. Robert K. Gray, "In Defense of Lobbyists," *New York Times,* April 25, 1986.
21. Figures cited in "Ex-Reagan Aides' Lobbying Leads to Call for New Rules," by Martin Tolchin, *New York Times,* April 17, 1986, 15.
22. Ibid.
23. Meg Greenfield, "The Washington Hustlers," *Newsweek,* April 21, 1986, 92.
24. Quoted in "Peddling Influence," by Evan Thomas, *Time,* March 3, 1986, 36.
25. Ibid., 27.

26. Quoted in *Newsweek*, March 3, 1986, 24.
27. Elizabeth Drew, "Charlie," *New Yorker*, Jan. 8, 1978.
28. Thomas B. Edsall, "The Power Is Inside, But the Money Is Outside," *Washington Post National Weekly Edition*, Dec. 2, 1985, 12.
29. Michael J. Malbin, "Comments: Governability, Iron Triangles, and Scarcity," in *The Reagan Presidency and the Governing of America*, ed. Lester M. Salamon and Michael S. Lund (Washington, D.C.: Urban Institute Press, 1984), 330.
30. Haynes Johnson, "Turning Government Jobs into Gold," *Washington Post National Weekly Edition*, May 12, 1986, 7.
31. Ibid.

Contributors

William P. Browne is a professor of political science at Central Michigan University. Most of his research has been in agricultural policy or interest groups, including work with the Economic Research Service of the United States Department of Agriculture.

Allan J. Cigler is an associate professor of political science at the University of Kansas. His research and teaching interests include political parties, participation, psychology and politics, and interest groups.

M. Margaret Conway is a professor of government and politics at the University of Maryland. Her research interests include political participation and electoral behavior, especially the role of political parties and interest groups in developed democracies.

Lee Epstein is an assistant professor of political science at Southern Methodist University. Her research interests include the judicial process and interest group politics.

Diana M. Evans is an assistant professor of political science at Trinity College. In addition to research on political action committees, she writes on the relationship between members of Congress and their constituents, especially through casework and mass mailings.

John C. Green is an assistant professor of political science at Furman University. His research and writing concern American campaign finance: contributors, contributions, and reform.

James L. Guth is a professor of political science at Furman University, where he teaches courses in American politics. His research and writing have focused on interest groups and social movements, agricultural policy, and business-government relations.

Michael T. Hayes is an assistant professor of political science at Colgate University. He specializes in American government and public policy, with an emphasis on interest groups and theories of the policy process.

Marjorie Randon Hershey is a professor of political science at Indiana University. Her research centers on political psychology, parties, and campaigns.

Charles H. Levine is a senior specialist in American national government and public administration at the Congressional Research Service of the Library of Congress. He has written extensively on urban politics, intergovernmental relations, and public organization and management.

Burdett A. Loomis is an associate professor of political science at the University of Kansas. His writing and research deal with political careers, legislatures, and interest groups.

Andrew S. McFarland is an associate professor of political science at the University of Illinois at Chicago. He has written extensively on public interest lobbies, including a recent study of Common Cause.

Mark A. Peterson is an assistant professor of government at Harvard University. His research interests include domestic policy making by the president and Congress, as well as the relationship between interest groups and American national institutions.

C. K. Rowland is an associate professor of political science at the University of Kansas. He is coauthor (with Robert Carp) of *Policy Making and Politics in the Federal District Courts*. His work on the lower federal courts has appeared in the *American Journal of Political Science,* the *Journal of Politics,* and other academic journals.

Robert H. Salisbury is Souers Professor of American Government at Washington University in St. Louis, where he has taught since 1955. He is best known for his work on interest groups and interest group theory.

James A. Thurber is the director of the Center for Congressional and Presidential Studies and an associate professor of government at the American University. His research and writing have focused on congressional budgeting, interest groups, and public policy making.

Eric M. Uslaner is a professor of government and politics at the University of Maryland — College Park. He has written on legislative politics in the United States and Israel and on energy policy. In 1981-1982 he was Visiting Fulbright Professor of American Studies and Political Science at the Hebrew University of Jerusalem.

Jack L. Walker is a professor of political science and public policy at the University of Michigan. His research deals with processes through which emerging social problems are recognized and defined, the avenues through which citizens are mobilized for political action, and the major factors stimulating policy change and social learning in American politics.

Graham Wilson is a professor of political science at the University of Wisconsin—Madison. He is the author of several books on interest groups and public policy in the United States and Europe.